Estimating
Equilibrium
Exchange Rates

JOHN WILLIAMSON
Editor

Estimating
Equilibrium
Exchange Rates

Institute for International Economics
Washington, DC
September 1994

John Williamson, *Senior Fellow*, was economics professor at Pontifíca Universidade Católica do Rio de Janeiro (1978–81), University of Warwick (1970–77), Massachusetts Institute of Technology (1967, 1980), University of York (1963–68), and Princeton University (1962–63); Adviser to the International Monetary Fund (1972–74); and Economic Consultant to the UK Treasury (1968–70). He has published numerous studies on international monetary and Third World debt issues, including *The Political Economy of Policy Reform* (1993), *Economic Consequences of Soviet Disintegration* (1993), *Trade and Payments After Soviet Disintegration* (1992), *From Soviet disUnion to Eastern Economic Community?* with Oleh Havrylyshyn (1991), *Currency Convertibility in Eastern Europe* (1991), *Latin American Adjustment: How Much Has Happened?* (1990), and *Targets and Indicators: A Blueprint for the International Coordination of Economic Policy* with Marcus Miller (1987).

INSTITUTE FOR INTERNATIONAL ECONOMICS
11 Dupont Circle, NW
Washington, DC 20036–1207
(202) 328-9000 FAX: (202) 328-5432

C. Fred Bergsten, *Director*
Christine F. Lowry, *Director of Publications*

Cover design by Michelle M. Fleitz
Typesetting by BG Composition
Printing by Automated Graphic Systems

Printed in the United States of America
97 96 95 94   5 4 3 2 1

Library of Congress Cataloging-in-Publication Data

Estimating equilibrium exchange rates /
    John Williamson [editor].
        p. cm.
    "September 1994."
    Includes bibliographical references and index.

    1. Foreign exchange rates—Mathematical models. 2. Equilibrium (Economics)—Mathematical models.
    I. Williamson, John, 1937–
HG3823.E88   1994
332.4'5—dc20   94-27350
                                                CIP

ISBN 0-88132-076-5

Marketed and Distributed outside the USA and Canada by Longman Group UK Limited, London

The views expressed in this publication are those of the authors. This publication is part of the overall program of the Institute, as endorsed by its Board of Directors, but does not necessarily reflect the views of individual members of the Board or the Advisory Committee.

Contents

v

Preface

Throughout its existence, the Institute for International Economics has attached the highest priority to exchange rates and the exchange rate system. John Williamson, the editor of this volume, has published a number of seminal Institute studies on the issue. He and I first developed the proposal for target zones in "Exchange Rates and Trade Policy" (published in *Trade Policy in the 1980s*, 1983). He elaborated that proposal in *The Exchange Rate System* (1983, revised 1985) and embedded it within a comprehensive system for international policy coordination in *Targets and Indicators: A Blueprint for the International Coordination of Economic Policy* (with Marcus H. Miller, 1987). Dr. Williamson has also analyzed specific exchange rate problems in Canada (in his appendix to Paul Wonnacott's *The United States and Canada: The Quest for Free Trade*, 1987) and the newly industrialized economies of East Asia (in *Adjusting to Success: Balance of Payments Policy in the East Asian NICs* with Bela Balassa, 1987, revised 1990).

Reform of the international exchange rate system remains very much on the global agenda, particularly in this 50th anniversary year since the Bretton Woods conference. The Institute is in fact simultaneously releasing a new volume on *Managing the World Economy: Fifty Years After Bretton Woods* (edited by Peter B. Kenen) that includes a chapter on "The Monetary System" by Dr. Williamson and C. Randall Henning and another on "Managing the World Economy of the Future" by me, both calling for reform of the exchange rate regime.

One of the central issues in the international monetary debate is the feasibility of calculating the "fundamental equilibrium exchange rates" on which a new regime would rest. This topic was treated by Dr. Williamson in *The Exchange Rate System* (second edition, 1985), but we recently decided that it was time to review the state of the art. We were pleased to discover that a number of scholars had been turning their attention to the topic, and in this volume we present the work of several of them. The book also includes an introductory overview by Dr. Williamson and a concluding assessment by Professor Stanley Black of the University of North Carolina, Chapel Hill. Our hope is that these essays will stimulate additional work that will further narrow the range of uncertainty in estimating equilibrium exchange rates.

The Institute for International Economics is a private nonprofit institution for the study and discussion of international economic policy. Its purpose is to analyze important issues in that area and to develop and communicate practical new approaches for dealing with them. The Institute is completely nonpartisan.

The Institute is funded largely by philanthropic foundations. Major institutional grants are now being received from the German Marshall Fund of the United States, which created the Institute with a generous commitment of funds in 1981, and from the Ford Foundation, the William and Flora Hewlett Foundation, the William M. Keck, Jr. Foundation, the Andrew Mellon Foundation, the C. V. Starr Foundation, and the United States–Japan Foundation. A number of other foundations and private corporations also contribute to the highly diversified financial resources of the Institute. About 12 percent of the Institute's resources in our latest fiscal year were provided by contributors outside the United States, including about 5 percent from Japan.

The Board of Directors bears overall responsibility for the Institute and gives general guidance and approval to its research program—including identification of topics that are likely to become important to international economic policymakers over the medium run (generally, one to three years), and which thus should be addressed by the Institute. The Director, working closely with the staff and outside Advisory Committee, is responsible for the development of particular projects and makes the final decision to publish an individual study.

The Institute hopes that its studies and other activities will contribute to building a stronger foundation for international economic policy around the world. We invite readers of these publications to let us know how they think we can best accomplish this objective.

C. FRED BERGSTEN
Director
August 1994

Introduction

JOHN WILLIAMSON

Fritz Machlup's many enunciations on questions of economic semantics included the charge that attempts to identify positions of economic equilibrium were instances of "misplaced concreteness or disguised politics" (Machlup 1958). Despite being a former student of Machlup, I have long made free use of the concepts of currency overvaluation and undervaluation, which imply a willingness to make judgments about where an equilibrium exchange rate lies. I have indeed gone beyond this in some of my writings, notably Williamson (1985), to attempt to calculate one reasonably well-specified concept of the equilibrium exchange rate, which I called the "fundamental equilibrium exchange rate" (FEER). I returned to that quest in a project known as the FEERs Update, which was launched at the Institute for International Economics in 1987 but never reached fruition.

The next section of this chapter describes the difficulties that I encountered, which prevented publication in the form that I had originally hoped, containing a bottom line consisting of estimates with which I was reasonably comfortable of the FEERs of the currencies of all the Group of Seven major industrialized countries (the G-7). Since I nevertheless believed that much of the analysis was worthwhile—an assessment that seemed corroborated by the frequency with which my unpublished 1990 manuscript or results therefrom were cited in both academic works and the press—I sought a way to publish without a bottom line. The development by other economists of a substantive body of work addressed to much the same problem suggested the value of assembling a series of papers that would summarize the present state of the art and perhaps give an impetus to further work on estimating equilibrium exchange rates.

The papers in this volume were collected with those aims in mind. To give some intellectual coherence to the enterprise, it seemed natural to limit the contributors to those with compatible intellectual views. Two views are of critical importance in this context.

First is rejection of the still-common assumption in international monetary economics that markets have well-defined views of the equilibrium exchange rate determined by the fundamentals, even though economists are totally unable to make worthwhile estimates of where those equilibria might lie. I, and I think all of the other economists who have contributed papers aiming to estimate equilibrium rates to this volume, find both halves of that view unconvincing. In the first place, we do not believe that the market typically has a well-defined, rational expectations view of what is implied by the fundamentals. Sometimes the market may develop a very well-defined view that a rate being defended by the authorities is *inconsistent* with the fundamentals, which leads to the famous one-way bet, but that is very different from claiming that the market always has a well-defined view of what the equilibrium rate *is*. It seems that there is typically a wide range within which the market does not know or care what the equilibrium rate is; what it cares about is where the rate may go in the next few minutes.

Furthermore, the contributors to this volume all believe that equilibrium rates can be calculated, within some margin of error, by an appropriate use of econometric techniques, and therefore that it is sensible to devote intellectual effort to doing so. This does not mean that we believe we can predict exchange rate movements over any time horizon that would interest a foreign-exchange trader, although I imagine we would be upset if it turned out that we could not outpredict the market over horizons of two or three years.

Our second point of agreement consists in rejecting the view that the best possible estimates of equilibrium exchange rates are provided by the criterion of purchasing power parity (PPP).[1] We all believe that equilibrium real exchange rates can change over time, by enough to matter, as a result of changes in productivity (Bela Balassa's "productivity bias"), the terms of trade, foreign asset positions, and underlying capital flows.[2] Most of the papers in this volume elaborate on this point.

---

1. The absolute version of PPP holds that the equilibrium exchange rate between two currencies will be such as to equate purchasing power in the two countries involved. The relative version of PPP holds that the equilibrium exchange rate must change so as to offset differential inflation between the two countries and thus leave the real exchange rate unchanged. See chapter 7 for amplification.

2. The papers by Edwards and Elbadawi also include tariffs, and the level and composition—in terms of traded versus nontraded goods—of government expenditure, among the fundamentals.

I invited several economists whom I knew to be trying to estimate equilibrium exchange rates by approaches other than PPP comparisons to join me in a volume that would present our several approaches to this problem. The response was gratifying. Sebastian Edwards, Ibrahim Elbadawi, Jerome Stein, and a team from the International Monetary Fund (IMF) consisting of Tamim Bayoumi, Peter Clark, Steve Symansky, and Mark Taylor all agreed to provide samples of their work for inclusion in this volume, along with the bulk of my 1990 paper. All of the above, plus Paul Armington, Philip Bagnoli, Stanley Black, Fred Bergsten, Ralph Bryant, Hali Edison, William Helkie, Peter Hooper, Warwick McKibbin, Jacques Polak, and Reza Siregar, attended a study group at the Institute for International Economics in April 1993 to discuss the relationships among the various approaches and how we might present our work to make a coherent collection.

The volume contains two other papers. One is a survey of the evidence on PPP by Janice Boucher Breuer, which we decided to commission because there have begun to appear in the journals a growing number of papers using cointegration analysis (as do several of the papers in this volume) and claiming to find evidence favoring PPP. Since cointegration is an econometric technique ideally suited to discovering whether the concept of equilibrium is just an abstract analytical construct à la Machlup, or whether it is something that can be identified empirically, I concluded it was important to have this literature examined critically. The key question is of course whether the claim to have found empirical confirmation of PPP contradicts the conclusion of the studies in this volume, which claim to have identified changes in the equilibrium real exchange rate.

Janice Breuer was recommended to us by Stanley Black (whose role in the study is further discussed below) as someone technically well placed to do such a study. Her paper reports that even the recent empirical results on PPP continue to be distinctly mixed. A number of the claims to have confirmed PPP are based on no more than a finding that domestic prices, foreign prices, and the exchange rate are cointegrated, without imposing what Breuer terms the proportionality and symmetry constraints. This means that they are not even claiming to have found that the real exchange rate is stationary, let alone that it is a constant (as the relative version of PPP claimed), and certainly not that it is a constant equal to unity (as the absolute version claimed). This is a major weakening as compared with the traditional concept of PPP.

However, Breuer also finds that a number of the recent studies have provided some degree of empirical support for PPP in its traditional interpretation. This tendency is more pronounced the longer the time period considered and the narrower the price index used. The latter finding is unsurprising: a narrow price index tends to contain a large proportion of highly tradable, homogeneous primary commodities whose prices will be equated by arbitrage whether or not there is enough similarity in the internal price structure to produce PPP in an economically meaningful sense. The more interesting finding is that studies over very long time periods do show some evidence of a tendency to return to PPP even using a broad price index.

I had conjectured that the reported empirical confirmation of PPP might arise because the noise that drives rates away from the equilibrium real rate results in deviations from equilibrium that are large relative to changes in that equilibrium real rate. Breuer offers a different reconciliation: that changes in the equilibrium real exchange rate may themselves tend to vary around a constant value (''PPP'') in the very long run. (That constant value does not, however, necessarily equal one; i.e., it is relative rather than absolute PPP that finds some support.) This seems plausible on a priori grounds where the countries are at a similar stage of development throughout, so that the Balassa productivity bias effect does not come into play, since the other principal factors that theory predicts will cause changes in the equilibrium real exchange rate are likely either to be trendless (the terms of trade and fiscal deficits[3]) or to change in parallel for countries at a similar stage of development (underlying capital flows). Both explanations leave intact the presumption underlying the papers in this volume, namely, that the equilibrium real exchange rates relevant for policy purposes can change over time.

Stanley Black agreed to write a concluding chapter that would compare the alternative approaches and assess how much we had accomplished. We invited him to do this in part because, although he did not have a prior commitment in favor of the enterprise of estimating equilibrium exchange rates, we thought that he would be sympathetic provided the work merited support. But it was also important that he was someone whom we would not expect to be willing to jeopardize his professional reputation by declining to call a spade a spade should he conclude that we were engaged in a misconceived exercise.

After describing the evolution of my own work and outlining how much of it is presented in chapter 6, I proceed in the next part of this chapter to give a brief introduction to the work of the remainder of my fellow authors. I then offer my own comparison of our approaches. I both document the analytical points that we have in common and offer a taxonomy of two issues that to some extent divide us: what we classify as a ''fundamental,'' and the concept of the equilibrium exchange rate that we use. The chapter concludes by citing some examples of why the task addressed in this volume is important.

---

3. If the latter is judged to be a relevant fundamental; see the subsequent discussion of this point.

The History of the FEERs Update Project

I decided early on that I wanted to adopt an ex ante approach to estimating FEERs, rather than the ex post plus update approach in Williamson (1985).[4] I therefore approached the proprietors of the principal multi-country macroeconometric models for cooperation in running simulations as described in chapter 6. Most of the proprietors were extremely cooperative and went out of their way to help. (I even got the impression that in some cases they were rather pleased to find someone who wanted to ask a serious question of the model into which they had poured so much labor, in place of the usual inane requests to forecast quarterly inflation three years out to two decimal places.)

Despite the cordial reception, however, complications soon emerged. The model at the Japanese Economic Planning Agency (EPA) was undergoing reestimation and therefore unavailable at the time. Some of the other proprietors of officially sponsored models felt unable to accede to my request to run simulations for fear that the results would be misinterpreted as carrying some sort of official endorsement. They were, however, helpful in providing alternative ways of using their models: in the case of the IMF by redirecting me from that organization's Multimod to the closely related Intermod, which a research assistant ran here at the Institute, and in the case of the Organization for Economic Cooperation and Development (OECD) by having me visit the agency's offices in Paris and take direct responsibility for the simulations on the Interlink model. Hence I ended up with results from six models: William R. Cline's EAG (developed at the Institute for International Economics), steady-state GEM (National Institute for Economic and Social Research, London), Interlink, Intermod, Mimosa (a collaborative project of two French economic research institutes), and MSG; see the section below titled "Comparisons of the Alternative Approaches" and appendix 1 of chapter 6 for details).

The simulations sought trajectories for the macroeconomies, and more specifically the exchange rates, of the major industrial countries that would achieve and maintain simultaneous internal and external balance, as those concepts are quantified in chapter 6. The results showed a substantial degree of variation across models, so it was necessary to combine the results in one way or another. I argued in favor of choosing the results of one of the models rather than weighting the results of the different models together, with one criterion being that the model chosen should be one whose results were representative of the group of models as a whole. The model chosen by the criteria that I selected was steady-state GEM.

---

4. See chapter 6 for an elaboration of the distinction.

A draft study with results from steady-state GEM referring to the first quarter of 1990, with the target for achieving macroeconomic equilibrium being 1995, was completed in October 1990 and presented to a study group of experts (with a substantial overlap with those who later attended the April 1993 meeting mentioned above). My main reservation about the study was that my intuition told me that the estimated equilibrium rate for the deutsche mark ($1 = DM1.41) was wrong, implying the need for an unrealistically large appreciation of the German currency; my instinct would have placed the mark-dollar rate in the 1.5 to 1.6 range. This result also had the effect of exaggerating the misalignment within the European Exchange Rate Mechanism (ERM) and calling for an implausibly low (DM2.24 = £1) rate for sterling to enter the ERM.

The study group was critical of my analysis on a different ground, however. Participants argued that it was a mistake to conclude by relying exclusively on a single model. It would be better, they suggested, to calculate multipliers from each of the models, average these, and then use the average multiplier to calculate the changes in policy that would be needed to reach the desired targets (a procedure similar to that employed in the comparative static portion of the paper by the IMF team in chapter 2 of this volume). This assumed that it would be possible to find a convincing base case with sufficient detail to allow one to apply the multipliers to find the desired path.

Philip Bagnoli came to the Institute in the spring of 1991 to implement this program. He calculated and averaged multipliers, but we were unable to complete the suggested research program because we could not establish a suitable baseline path. It seems that official organizations regard baselines as even more confidential than simulation results.

I then reverted to the idea of basing my results on GEM. Unfortunately, by then the previous set of results was already rather dated, so I requested the National Institute for Economic and Social Research to run a new set of simulations. However, GEM was in for repairs, renovation, and reestimation in order to fit it for a world with one Germany instead of two. By the time it came back on line Simon Wren-Lewis had left the National Institute, and I never got results from the reestimated GEM from his successor.

The work reprinted as chapter 6 contains most of what I first wrote in the spring of 1990 and then revised in the fall. The first four sections are unchanged except for the occasional clarification or correction, or the addition of the odd footnote intended to update. (I could not, for example, resist the temptation to point out how much better someone taking a three-year position on the yen-dollar rate would have done by looking at my FEERs than by acting on the basis of the reported—PPP-based—consensus forecasts of the time.) The core of my old sections 5 (describing the models used) and 6 (giving simulation results) have been combined in the section of chapter 6 titled "The Simulations," while details of both the models and the simulations have been relegated to two appendixes.

The original paper concluded with a section on policy implications, most of which has been omitted from chapter 6 as it has (unsurprisingly) been overtaken by events. It may, however, be of interest to summarize what I argued at that time. I first discussed the implications for G-3 (Germany, Japan, and the United States) policy, pointing out that the dollar appeared to be again mildly *overvalued*, rather than chronically *undervalued* as the PPP-based exchange rate forecasting industry was proclaiming. The yen was again seriously undervalued (contrary to the PPP view), which of course contributed to the reemergence of the big Japanese current account surplus that has caused so much tension since. German unification meant that there was at last a chance that Germany would take the highly expansionary fiscal actions that were the necessary complement to a strong mark in adjusting down the German surplus.

I next discussed the implications for the ERM. Here I was somewhat uncomfortable because of my sense that the model had estimated an unrealistically strong FEER for the mark. Certainly I would not have called on the ERM to have realigned the rates between the mark and the French franc or the lira to anything like those implied by the FEER estimates in the absence of German unification. But I indicated my skepticism with the then-prevalent belief in Europe that Germany was going to be able to redirect the real resources going into its external surplus to the task of eastern German reconstruction without the help of an ERM realignment, labeling such an "immaculate transfer" wishful thinking. I reasoned that the attempt to avoid such a realignment posed "a danger, indeed likelihood, that the putative German boom will end up by having the paradoxical effect of creating a recession in the rest of the [European Monetary System]." I did not foresee that this refusal to realign currencies would end up destroying the narrow-band ERM, and only much later (in the fall of 1992) did I realize that the appropriate policy response was a temporarily wide band for the mark rather than a once-for-all appreciation.

The third topic I addressed was the rate at which sterling should enter the ERM. The tense in which this was written had to be changed at the last minute, since just before my draft was finalized the pound was inserted at a rate that my FEER estimates, like those of Wren-Lewis et al. (1990), showed to significantly overvalue the British currency. Black Wednesday—withdrawal from the ERM by Britain in September 1992—was the logical consequence of our advice being ignored.

The last topic I considered was the implications of the results for the feasibility of the Williamson-Miller "blueprint" proposals (Williamson and Miller 1987). I tried to assess whether the deviations between the new FEER estimates and my previous estimates discredited the idea of using the exchange rate as an intermediate target. This material is included at the end of the section on "The Simulations" in chapter 6.

The IMF Paper

If there was a particular moment at which I conceived the idea of publishing a collection of papers on equilibrium exchange rates, I suspect that it was when I learned that Peter Clark and a group of his colleagues at the IMF had embarked on a project to develop a methodology for making estimates of what he cautiously termed a "FEER-like concept." This has now emerged as a "DEER," or "desirable equilibrium exchange rate," to emphasize the normative content of the concept (a point also made in my own paper even though not acknowledged by my term; see chapter 6).

I had for years lamented the withdrawal of the IMF from its Smithsonian-era use of a multilateral exchange rate model (MERM) to estimate equilibrium exchange rates among the major industrial countries. I could not see how the Fund could expect to play a central role in the international monetary system without the analytical capacity to judge whether existing exchange rates were consistent with satisfactory and sustainable macroeconomic outcomes. Hence I very much welcomed the news of the Clark team's initiative, and of their willingness to contribute a paper to a collection that I might edit.

We of course recognized that such a study would have to be undertaken with an arbitrary set of current account targets, rather than targets that carried some sort of implicit international endorsement. It was nonetheless something of a disappointment to learn that the study that materialized was focused on a period of time over 20 years in the past, and hence cannot help inform the current policy debate on, for example, the appropriate yen-dollar rate. The study presents results for 1971, the year of the Smithsonian Agreement, a time when there was acute interest in how much the dollar needed to be devalued.

The main focus of the paper by Tamim Bayoumi, Peter Clark, Steve Symansky, and Mark Taylor is not so much on whether the dollar devaluation agreed at the Smithsonian was inadequate, but rather on the methodological issues involved in calculating DEERs. They compare calculations using a simple static partial-equilibrium trade system with those yielded by the IMF staff's dynamic macroeconometric model, Multimod. The two methods yield broadly similar estimates of equilibrium real exchange rates. However, the authors demonstrate that, while the exchange rate results are similar, the manner in which the exchange rate target is reached can, according to the model, have important implications for other macroeconomic variables. They also show that changes in the assumed objectives for internal and external balance and plausible variations in some of the underlying parameters produce quite large differences in calculated equilibrium rates, in the range of 10 percent to as much as 30 percent for any one country. This wide range is consistent with the plus or minus 10 percent that I had previously guessed would be necessary for an officially adopted target zone for currencies to accommodate uncertainty about where the equilibrium rate may lie. The paper also contains a discussion of the magnitude of the dynamic complications that arise when the exchange rate is away from its equilibrium value. Finally, the paper provides reassurance that, subject to the margin of uncertainty, the IMF has the analytical capacity to develop estimates of appropriate target zones, if and when it should be decided that such an exchange rate system is desirable.

Edwards and Elbadawi

The work of the IMF team, like my own, has used large macroeconometric models[5] in order to estimate the equilibrium real exchange rates of large industrial countries, using a definition of the real exchange rate couched in terms of the relative price of domestically produced and foreign-made goods. Both Sebastian Edwards and Ibrahim Elbadawi come at a somewhat different problem from a somewhat different direction: they use small, purpose-built models to estimate the equilibrium real exchange rates of nonindustrial countries, and they employ a definition of the real exchange rate that treats it as the price of tradables in terms of nontradables.

These differences are not unimportant, but they are in a very real sense superficial. It is just as crucial for nonindustrial countries to prevent their exchange rates becoming misaligned as it is for industrial countries, so the fact that some economists have directed their effort to one group of countries and some to another is all to the good. The type of model that one employs presumably reflects, in part at least, what is there: since off-the-shelf models were available for the industrial countries but less so for the others, it is unsurprising that purpose-built models were used for the latter but not always for the former.[6] And, of course, a multicountry model is unnecessary for a small country whose impact on the world economy is negligible. Finally, as argued below, both groups have probably picked the most relevant concept of the real exchange rate for the countries with which they were dealing.

---

5. Although the IMF team also use multipliers from Multimod to make partial-equilibrium estimates.

6. As noted below, Stein uses a purpose-built model to estimate the equilibrium exchange rate of the dollar.

An even more superficial difference concerns nomenclature. Where I refer to FEERs and the IMF team to DEERs, Edwards and Elbadawi write of ERERs ("equilibrium real exchange rates"). We all mean the same thing but have not attempted to force a standardization of terminology. Another semantic difference is that Edwards refers to a real devaluation of the domestic currency as an increase in the real exchange rate, whereas the others (if they use such ambiguous terms at all) would call this a decrease in the real exchange rate.

The similarities between the approaches are far more interesting. All the authors conceive the equilibrium of the real exchange rate to be characterized by simultaneous internal and external balance. All recognize that this equilibrium value varies, rather than being a natural constant as the PPP theory supposes. All agree that the equilibrium value of the domestic currency will be increased by a larger ("permanent") inflow of capital or an improvement in the terms of trade, and that there may be trend changes due to productivity bias or foreign asset accumulation. Edwards and Elbadawi also allow a possible role for the level and composition of government expenditure.

The paper of Sebastian Edwards (chapter 3) is an article first published in the *Journal of Development Economics* in 1988. It lays out "a model of real exchange rate determination that allows for both real and nominal factors to play a role in the short run . . . [although] only real factors—the 'fundamentals'—influence the *equilibrium real exchange rate*" (emphasis in original). This equation is estimated for 12 developing countries, less with a view to deriving estimates of the equilibrium real exchange rate than with the objective of testing the legitimacy of his decomposition of the factors that influence the real exchange rate into those determining its equilibrium value and those that influence its deviation from, and return to, equilibrium. Nonetheless, it is clear that the analysis could be adapted for the purpose of estimating equilibrium rates.

The paper of Ibrahim Elbadawi (chapter 4) shows what is possible using the approach pioneered by Edwards. He uses cointegration analysis to estimate equilibrium rates for Chile, Ghana, and India over the period 1965–90 (1965–88 in the case of India). His results confirm Edwards's finding that the ERER is not constant over time as supposed by PPP. However, it is important to appreciate two limitations of his results.

The first is that the analysis still requires a normalization to calibrate the ERER. In this it resembles the relative version of PPP, which requires that one pick a particular year (the "base year") as having been in equilibrium. This means that, when one observes that (for example) Elbadawi's estimate of the Indian ERER shows it close to, and depreciating in parallel with, the actual exchange rate for the rupee for most of the period 1967–81, one cannot conclude that India had no problem of an overvalued rupee during that period. What it may mean is that the actual depreciation was just enough to offset the reduction in protection, leaving a margin of overvaluation that was roughly constant but not necessarily near zero.

The second limitation can be perceived by observing that the Ghanaian ERER is shown as having undergone a substantial appreciation over the period 1974–82, when the currency itself appreciated even more, followed by a depreciation back to (or slightly beyond) the original level of the ERER in 1982–87 as the actual real value of the cedi fell back. Of course, the analysis still shows that a massive overvaluation emerged from the mid-1970s to the early 1980s, but that does not dispose of the question as to why the equilibrium value of the currency should have risen during that period. It was not a terms-of-trade effect; rather, it seems that it resulted from the large and unsustainable fiscal expansion of the period.

This recalls an argument that Fred Bergsten and I had with then-chairman of the Council of Economic Advisers Martin Feldstein a decade ago (see Williamson 1985, 32–33). What we dubbed the "Feldstein doctrine" held that in calculating the dollar's equilibrium exchange rate one should take the fiscal deficit to be exogenous—an argument that led to the conclusion that the dollar's appreciation (at least until mid-1984) was largely an equilibrium phenomenon that had the beneficial effect of limiting the crowding out of investment that would otherwise have resulted from Ronald Reagan's fiscal profligacy. Bergsten and I counterargued that the fiscal deficit and its consequences were unsustainable, and that it was paradoxical to define an equilibrium exchange rate as that produced by unsustainable policies; instead, what one should do was calculate what the exchange rate would have been with a sustainable fiscal policy. Similarly, what Elbadawi has done is to calculate what would have been the equilibrium exchange rate of the cedi had Ghana's actual fiscal policy been sustainable (due, for example, to vast "permanent" receipts of foreign aid). To find what the equilibrium exchange rate would have been had Ghana been pursuing a sustainable fiscal policy, one would have to insert some estimate of what fiscal policy would have been sustainable into his equation.

Stein

Jerome Stein's work has been directed to building what he describes as the NATREX (*natural real exchange* rate) model and using it to see to what extent it can explain the behavior of the real exchange rate of the US dollar (that is, the real effective rate vis-à-vis the currencies of the other members of the G-10) since the mid-1970s. Work with several of his peers and students involves using the same type of model to try to explain the behavior of other currencies.

Stein defines the NATREX as the real exchange rate that would prevail if speculative and cyclical factors were removed. It is a moving equilibrium rate, responding both to exogenous real disturbances and to the gradual endogenous changes in capital stocks and net foreign debt induced by real disturbances.[7]

When I first saw Stein's results, I was puzzled to see that the dollar's NATREX appreciated along with its actual exchange rate for most of Reagan's first term, merely omitting the final speculative bubble of 1984–85 but tracking some two-thirds of the total appreciation. This is the sort of result yielded by models that take interest rates as a part of the fundamentals, whereas Stein emphasizes that the NATREX is the exchange rate that would prevail if one could remove cyclical factors, one of which I usually think of as interest rates. In fact, what the NATREX does is to treat an increase in the interest rate that results from a permanent increase in consumption[8] as a "fundamental" and other interest rate increases as transitory. Since most of the high interest rates in the early 1980s resulted from the loose fiscal policy of the Reagan period, this translates into an appreciation of the NATREX.

Comparisons of the Alternative Approaches

Stanley Black has made some comparisons among the various approaches in his concluding chapter, but it seemed to me that it might be useful if I also offered some thoughts on the relationships between the different papers.

As noted above, all the authors offering estimates of equilibrium exchange rates in this volume share a conviction that it is possible and useful to develop empirical measures of the equilibrium exchange rate. We also share the view that PPP does not provide a correct measure of the equilibrium exchange rate. *Ceteris paribus*, of course, restoration of the original real outcome following a change in the price level either at home or abroad will require an equivalent change in the nominal exchange rate (in which case the real exchange rate will return to its original level): that is the element of truth in PPP. But restoration of equilibrium following a real change will in general require a change in the real exchange rate.

---

7. Stanley Black argues in chapter 8 that Stein offers a neoclassical concept of the equilibrium exchange rate, inasmuch as he assumes that output is at full employment on average over his 12-quarter averaging period. It seems to me that if the averaging period were equal to the length of a business cycle, Stein's procedure would remove cyclical factors in a suitably Keynesian way, so that the charge of failure to adjust for deviations from internal balance is valid only to the extent that business cycles generally last more than three years.

8. This increases his "social time preference index," $(C + G)/GNP$.

The article on PPP in *The New Palgrave* by Dornbusch (1987) suggests that few academic economists subscribed to PPP at that time, prior to the recent spate of work reviewed by Janice Breuer in chapter 7. But *The Economist* has for years appealed to PPP to make judgments about whether currencies are overvalued or undervalued, even inventing a Big Mac index to aid it in this misconceived endeavor,[9] and even at the same time as it used market exchange rates rather than Kravis-style PPP estimates to convert GNPs to a common currency. Now that the magazine has followed the IMF in recognizing that GNPs need to be converted at PPP rates, one may hope that it will also recognize that (absolute) purchasing power is virtually irrelevant to identifying where exchange rates ought to be. Then there will only be the exchange rate forecasters to convert.

Our approaches share one other vitally important feature. We all interpret "equilibrium" in macroeconomic terms, most of us quite explicitly in the Keynes-Meade-Mundell sense of simultaneous internal and external balance. (Stein does it slightly differently, combining what I think of as a conventional internal balance specification with a portfolio equilibrium condition; but since the latter implies a capital flow outcome that the current account must match in equilibrium, the end result is similar.) None of us interprets "external balance" as implying current account balance, that is, as excluding capital flows. The precise way in which we derive our internal and external balance conditions does, unsurprisingly, differ.

One other point of agreement is that how one goes about identifying equilibrium exchange rates is not dependent in an essential way on whether a country is developed or developing. Whereas the IMF team and I use large, multicountry models of a type that is not available for developing countries, Stein uses a small, purpose-built model to estimate the NATREX for the United States. (And some of his students have used the same approach to estimate NATREXs for developing countries.)

We seem to differ in two important dimensions. One concerns what we treat as fundamentals. We all agree that the relevant fundamentals include the terms of trade, tariffs and trade restrictions (or a surrogate in the form of a measure of openness), and exogenous capital flows. Edwards and Elbadawi include also the composition and level of gov-

---

9. Their index compares observed prices of Big Mac hamburgers at McDonald's restaurants in different countries to arrive at an exchange rate that equalizes the currencies' purchasing power over a consumption basket consisting of Big Macs. (A colleague of mine observed recently that Burger King Whoppers were priced in Lugano, Switzerland, at SF6.00, versus $1.89 in Baltimore, MD—a better than 3:1 ratio; the market exchange rate meanwhile was about SF1.35 = $1.00! My colleague did not test whether the discrepancy was due to nonhomogeneity of the two goods.)

ernment consumption. I have always doubted the empirical significance of the former, and the evidence for including it still looks weak. The level of government expenditure is another matter, which raises the question of principle, discussed above in the context of Reagan and Ghana, about whether one should describe a potentially unsustainable position as an equilibrium. Productivity growth (because of the Balassa effect) and asset accumulation (especially of foreign assets) are other variables that everyone agrees to be relevant in principle, but whose importance has sometimes been queried. The IMF paper contains a valuable quantification of the significance of asset accumulation, which one could summarize as concluding that it matters, but not enormously much.

Most economists would classify interest rates as a "fundamental" when it comes to modeling exchange rates. For example, when Dominguez and Frankel (1993, 43–44) discuss whether a speculative bubble rather than "the fundamentals" drove the dollar up in 1984–85, they clearly treat the high interest rates induced by Reaganomics as a part of the fundamentals. Most of the authors in this volume, in contrast, do not. My own approach, for example, is to treat interest rates as a policy instrument that the authorities can use, inter alia, to prevent the exchange rate from deviating too far from its FEER (i.e., from moving outside its target zone). Of course, this difference in classification reflects our different objectives rather than any conflict in analysis. As noted earlier, Stein is something of an exception to the other contributors in the volume, insofar as he distinguishes between interest rate increases that result from an increase in social time preference, which are a part of his fundamentals, and those that result from, say, a cyclical upswing, which are transitory and thus not a part of the fundamentals that help determine the NATREX.

The other significant difference between the various modelers concerns the concept of the real exchange rate that we utilize. I was brought up in the tradition that says, since the nominal exchange rate is the relative price of two national monies, the real exchange rate must be the relative price of two national outputs. This idea seemed to make good sense in terms of the economies of the industrial countries, toward which my work on exchange rates has been primarily directed, since the differentiated manufactured products that dominate their trade can and do vary in price (as formalized by Armington 1969). In contrast, Edwards uses the 1970s-vintage Chicago definition of the real exchange rate as the price of traded goods in terms of the price of nontraded goods,[10] and Elbadawi uses its inverse. This definition seems natural to

---

10. I agree with Stanley Black that the importance of this relative price was first recognized by the Australian school, but the practice of labeling it the real exchange rate surely originated in Chicago.

those who have worked primarily with nonindustrial countries whose exports are predominantly primary products subject to the law of one price, and whose export volume is determined by the supply offered on the world market at a parametric world price rather than by the demand forthcoming at a quoted price. In such an economy the relative price of nontraded goods determines the incentive to produce exports.

What is the relationship between these two concepts of the real exchange rate? Contrary to what I have asserted in the past,[11] there is no simple, one-to-one correspondence between them, even in the fantasy world of homogeneous products. However, Polly Reynolds Allen (1994), in an introductory chapter to work on the NATREX project, has developed a general formula for the case of a three-good world (country 1's exportable, good 1; its importable, good 2; and a nontraded good n) where there is perfect arbitrage in the two traded goods. Her formula for the real exchange rate r is (in logarithms):

$$r = \alpha \, (p_n - p_1) - \alpha' \, (p_n' - p_2') + (1 - \beta - \beta') \, (p_1 - p_2),$$

where α and α' are the weights of nontradables in GDP at home and abroad, respectively, and β and β' are the weights of importables in GDP at home and abroad, respectively.

This formula reduces to the two familiar ones in the two special cases. Where each country produces only one commodity, so that $p_n = p_1$, $p_n' = p_2'$, and $\beta = \beta' = 0$, r collapses to the terms of trade, $p_1 - p_2$. Where the country is small in the world market for tradable goods, so that the terms of trade as well as $p_n' - p_2'$ are parametric, the real exchange rate varies only with the relative price of nontradables at home, $p_n - p_1$.

In general, however, the correct formula is the price level at home relative to that abroad using a wide price index, preferably the GDP deflator. This is not to question the legitimacy of using the Chicago concept in the sorts of countries where it is applied by Edwards and Elbadawi, but it is to ask those who use it to accept that it is a simplification that is useful in certain situations rather than an insight that makes use of the more general concept illegitimate.

One other difference between authors is surely *not* important. Edwards, Elbadawi, and Stein model the real exchange rate as determined by dynamic adjustment toward the ERER, and provide for short- to medium-run macroeconomic and exchange rate policy to shift the real exchange rate relative to the ERER. My analysis, and that of the IMF team, simply did not address those issues; had I tried to do so, I would surely have approached them on very much the same lines.

---

11. In note 12, p. 218, of Williamson and Milner (1991). My error was to write $p_m = ep^*$ in place of $p_m = ep_m^*$, where p_m is the price of tradables and an asterisk denotes a foreign variable.

The Importance of the Topic

Some economists, generally of a monetarist persuasion, will regard the enterprise reported in this volume as thoroughly misconceived. They hold that there are only two logical exchange rate systems, completely fixed and freely floating exchange rates, neither of which has any need for estimates of an equilibrium exchange rate defined as one consistent with a satisfactory macroeconomic outcome.

But it is also possible to hold the view that domination of the debate on exchange rate policy by the two classic alternatives of complete fixity and free floating has served to stultify debate, since it results in bypassing most of the important, policy-relevant issues. Almost any intermediate regime demands some sort of estimate of where the equilibrium exchange rate may lie.[12] Such estimates are, for example, critical to the sort of episodic exchange rate management that the G-7 has periodically engaged in since the Plaza Agreement of 1985, including the half-hearted attempt to operate a system of reference ranges after the Louvre Accord in 1987. Without estimates of equilibrium exchange rates, initiatives such as the bear squeeze that halted the dollar's free fall at the beginning of 1988, or the joint intervention that prevented the yen going above 100 to the dollar in August 1993, would have been pure gambles. Because they were well informed, both initiatives proved successful.

Estimates of equilibrium exchange rates are obviously even more central to the sorts of proposals for policy coordination among the major industrial countries that we have developed at the Institute for International Economics, namely, the target zone proposal (Bergsten and Williamson 1983, Williamson 1985) and the more ambitious "blueprint for policy coordination" (Williamson and Miller 1987). Recognition of their importance in this context was indeed the motivation for launching my own work on estimating equilibrium exchange rates and for deciding to put together the present collection of papers.

Such estimates are also critical for regional or national exchange rate policies. As pointed out earlier, ignoring the available estimates of sterling's equilibrium exchange rate at the time of its entry to the ERM led directly to Black Wednesday. Ignoring the evidence of the lira's overvaluation in the summer of 1992 led to the first of the crises that ultimately paralyzed the ERM. Ignoring the evidence of the current overvaluation of the Argentinian and Mexican pesos risks destroying the stabilizations that those countries have so painfully achieved. Con-

---

12. The only forms of exchange rate management that do not demand an estimate of a target or equilibrium rate are: intervention confined to smoothing disorderly markets; leaning against the wind, meaning a symmetrical willingness to buy reserves when the currency is rising and sell them when it is falling; and unqualified commitment to the nominal anchor strategy.

versely, the willingness to make and act on such estimates has been a critical ingredient of the East Asian miracle and more recently of Chile's economic success. In short, being able to make sensible estimates of equilibrium exchange rates is of key importance to rational, outward-oriented macroeconomic management of the sort that has been increasingly widely adopted in recent years.

Since this volume does not contain up-to-date estimates of equilibrium exchange rates for the main industrial countries that could be used as a basis for offering macroeconomic policy advice, it leaves important unfinished business.

References

Allen, Polly Reynolds. 1994. "The Economic and Policy Implications of the NATREX Approach." In J. L. Stein, P. R. Allen, L. Crouhy-Veyrac, M. Saint Marc, M. Connolly, and J. Devereux, eds., *Fundamental Determinants of Exchange Rates*, chapter 1. Oxford: Oxford University Press.

Armington, Paul. 1969. "A Theory of Demand for Products Distinguished by Place of Production." International Monetary Fund *Staff Papers* (March).

Bergsten, C. Fred, and John Williamson. 1983. "Exchange Rates and Trade Policy." In W. R. Cline, ed., *Trade Policy for the 1980s*. Washington: Institute for International Economics.

Dominguez, Kathryn M., and Jeffrey A. Frankel. 1993. *Does Foreign Exchange Intervention Work?* Washington: Institute for International Economics.

Dornbusch, Rudiger. 1987. "Purchasing Power Parity." In P. Newman, M. Milgate, and J. Eatwell, eds., *The New Palgrave*. London: Macmillan.

Machlup, Fritz. 1958. "Equilibrium and Disequilibrium: Misplaced Concreteness and Disguised Politics." *Economic Journal* (March).

Williamson, John. 1985. "The Exchange Rate System." POLICY ANALYSES IN INTERNATIONAL ECONOMICS 5 (rev. ed.). Washington: Institute for International Economics.

Williamson, John, and Marcus H. Miller. 1987. "Targets and Indicators: A Blueprint for the International Coordination of Economic Policy." POLICY ANALYSES IN INTERNATIONAL ECONOMICS 22 Washington: Institute for International Economics.

Williamson, John, and Chris Milner. 1991. *The World Economy: A Textbook in International Economics*. Hemel Hempstead: Harvester Wheatsheaf.

Wren-Lewis, Simon, Peter Westaway, Soterios Soteri, and Ray Barrell. 1990. *Choosing the Rate: An Analysis of the Optimum Level of Entry for Sterling into the ERM*. NIESR Discussion Papers. London: National Institute for Economic and Social Research (February).

2

The Robustness of Equilibrium Exchange Rate Calculations to Alternative Assumptions and Methodologies

TAMIM BAYOUMI, PETER CLARK, STEVE SYMANSKY, AND MARK TAYLOR

The turmoil in foreign-exchange markets in Europe in the fall of 1992 and the summer of 1993 focused attention on the causes of exchange market tensions and the extent to which exchange rates are in line with economic fundamentals. In these episodes, tensions were concentrated in the currencies that were pegged as part of the European Monetary System (EMS), but the issue of appraising the level of exchange rates arises also in connection with currencies that are floating. In this connection it is useful to look at trends over time in indicators of a country's external competitiveness and at developments in its balance of payments to see whether its real exchange rate is likely to be consistent with a sustainable external account. An analysis based on differential movements in international competitiveness—that is, an approach based on the concept of purchasing power parity (PPP)—may be helpful in making such an appraisal. However, it is incomplete because it involves examining changes in relevant variables from some base period and therefore does not address the issue of whether the exchange rate was at an equilibrium level originally. Moreover, a PPP-based approach fails to take into account major changes in economic policies or in economic structure, such as significant movements in a country's terms of trade.

Tamim Bayoumi, Peter Clark, and Steve Symansky are economists at the International Monetary Fund (IMF), as was Mark Taylor when this paper was written; he is now at the University of Liverpool. The views expressed here are those of the authors and do not necessarily reflect those of the staff or the Board of the IMF. They gratefully acknowledge the helpful comments of Charles Adams, Jacques Artus, Leonardo Bartolini, Ulrich Baumgartner, Sterie Beza, Jack Boorman, Bankim Chadha, Hamid Faruqee, and Morris Goldstein, without in any way implicating them in any of the views expressed in this paper.

To overcome the deficiencies of an approach based mainly on indicators, it is necessary to relate the discussion and analysis of exchange rates more directly to the notion of a sustainable or equilibrium exchange rate. The concept of the equilibrium exchange rate is not unique. As Frenkel and Goldstein (1986) have noted, there are at least three approaches to determining the equilibrium exchange rate: those based on structural exchange rate models such as the monetary model or the portfolio balance model of exchange rate determination, the PPP approach, and the "underlying balance" approach.[1] In this last approach, the equilibrium exchange rate is defined as the real effective exchange rate that is consistent with medium-term internal and external macroeconomic balance. This definition is discussed further below.

The underlying balance approach to the equilibrium exchange rate was developed by International Monetary Fund (IMF) staff during the 1970s (see Artus 1977 and IMF 1984).[2] More recently, the equilibrium rate associated with underlying balance has been labeled the "fundamental equilibrium exchange rate" (FEER) by Williamson (1985). The concept of "fundamental" equilibrium would be more applicable, however, to a *long-term* situation where all underlying economic forces had worked themselves out, in particular where actual asset stocks are at their desired levels. Moreover, we wish to stress that the concept of the equilibrium real exchange rate consistent with underlying macroeconomic balance is based upon a set of desired macroeconomic objectives. In this paper, therefore, we shall use the term "desired equilibrium exchange rate" (DEER) to refer to this concept. This terminology is not meant to imply that the calculated equilibrium exchange rate is desired in and of itself, but rather that it is consistent with, and necessary for, achieving "desired" positions of internal and external balance. Thus the DEER should not be viewed as an ultimate target itself, but rather as facilitating the achievement of macroeconomic objectives.

The DEER has been used as an analytical device by a number of authors to assess exchange rate misalignment (e.g., by Williamson 1985 and 1990, Barrell and Wren-Lewis 1989, and Church 1992) as well as in the context of discussions of "blueprints" for international policy coordination (e.g., by Williamson and Miller 1987, Frenkel and Goldstein 1986, and Currie and Wren-Lewis 1989), and in discussions of the "appropriate level" at which to join a pegged exchange rate system such as the EMS (Williamson 1991 and Wren-Lewis et al. 1991).

In this paper we explore a number of methodological considerations that relate to DEER calculations. Our objective is not to obtain precise and up-to-date estimates of DEERs for individual countries, but rather to

---

1. See Taylor (1994) for a recent survey relating to the first two of these approaches. Frenkel and Goldstein (1986) discuss the relative merits of the three approaches.

2. See also Nurkse (1945) and IMF (1970) for precursors of this approach.

lay out a number of issues involved in the calculation of DEERs that need to be addressed before applying them in the appraisal of exchange rates. We begin with a comparative static analysis. We then examine the dynamic interaction between the current account and the stock of net foreign assets by taking account of certain hysteresis effects on the DEER. Finally, we present some illustrative general-equilibrium calculations of DEERs using Multimod, the international macroeconometric model developed by the IMF. The objective of the analysis is to show the extent to which calculated DEERs depend not only on the choice of assumptions regarding positions of internal and external balance, for example, but also on whether a comparative static or a dynamic macroeconomic analysis is employed to generate the estimate.

As noted by Wren-Lewis (1992), the DEER is often treated as a comparative static calculation. Given values of the full-employment level of output and of the current account, the DEER is defined as the level of the real effective exchange rate consistent with achieving these goals in the medium term. Three elasticities are needed to make this comparative static, partial-equilibrium approach operational: the sensitivity of the current account to domestic activity, to foreign activity, and to the real exchange rate, all of which can be derived from estimated trade equations. We use the elasticities from Multimod as our base case. In the next section of this paper, calculations using this approach are reported for the seven largest industrial countries at the time of an actual historical episode, namely, the breakup of the Bretton Woods exchange rate system in the early 1970s. Alternative estimates of DEERs are obtained using different assumptions about underlying elasticities, the historical period used as the base period, the level of potential output, and the external balance position. Attention is focused on the sensitivity of the DEERs to these and other alternative values of key parameters and variables; it is shown that plausible estimates of DEERs vary over quite a wide range.

In this paper we generally refer to a sustainable level of a real effective exchange rate. However, as long as inflation rates differ among countries, the sustainable level of a country's nominal exchange rate will vary over time. Moreover, to the extent that the underlying economic conditions affecting a country's DEER are themselves changing, the calculated DEER will not be a fixed number but will also vary over time. It is only for purposes of simplification that the concept and calculation of the DEER are discussed in terms of a level rather than a path.

The subsequent section, on "A Dynamic DEER," discusses the interaction between the path to equilibrium and the DEER itself in more detail. Although not entirely overlooked in the literature (see Wren-Lewis 1992), the issue of how the DEER shifts for any given path toward it has received relatively little attention. Given that deviations from the DEER involve movements in the current account and hence in the amount of equilibrium debt service, it is clear that the level of the real exchange rate consistent with medium-term external balance will be shifting as long as the actual real exchange rate is away from the DEER. Moreover, movements in the DEER arising from changes in the current account will tend to increase the degree of misalignment since, for example, an overvaluation of a currency will entail a decline in its DEER value. Thus, the final DEER arrived at will not be independent of the path chosen toward it. The notion that different equilibrium values may not be independent of the dynamic adjustment paths toward them is generally termed "hysteresis." We derive the dynamic solution for the exchange rate and assess the importance of hysteresis effects for a given path of adjustment and set of initial conditions.

In the penultimate section of the paper we use Multimod to provide illustrative calculations of the DEER. As Multimod is a fully specified, dynamic macroeconomic model, all major simultaneous effects are taken into account, including, for example, the hysteresis effects described above as well as the impact of changes in the external balance on the domestic economy. It is important to realize that, as the exchange rate is determined endogenously in the model, it is necessary to use a "forcing" or exogenous variable to change the exchange rate by the amount needed to achieve the desired change in the external balance. Moreover, the particular manner in which the exchange rate change is achieved will have an effect on the entire macroeconomic system and will therefore influence the level of the real effective exchange rate that is consistent with desired positions of internal and external balance. First, we assume that currency preferences shift in such a way as to generate the same trade balance positions as in the base case. Second, we examine the effect on the DEERs of changes in fiscal policy that would be needed to achieve these same positions. We then calculate estimates of DEERs for the major industrial countries in the early 1970s on the assumption that they were at full-employment levels of output and attained the same external balance positions. Finally, we examine what difference it makes if the external balance objective is specified in terms of the current account rather than the trade balance. The results of these illustrative calculations show that the desired current account position is consistent in some cases with rather different changes in macroeconomic variables. For example, in those countries where an improved external position is brought about by a shift in currency preferences, there is a rise in real interest rates and a decline in potential output, and internal and external balance is restored through a fall in actual output. On the other hand, if the same external position is achieved through a cut in government spending, both potential and actual output rise.

As already noted, the objective of this paper is to examine methodological issues arising in connection with the calculation of exchange rates consistent with internal and external balance. There is a whole set of analytical and policy issues related to the question of the appropriate course of action in the event that actual exchange rates are out of line with calculated DEERs. These issues are important and relevant, and are in fact the logical next step in the analysis. However, as they deserve a full, systematic treatment, they are beyond the scope of this paper.

The final section of the paper provides some concluding comments and observations.

DEER Calculations Using a Comparative Static, Partial-Equilibrium Approach

The Concept of the DEER

The DEER is defined as the real effective exchange rate at which an economy is in both internal and external macroeconomic balance in the medium term. The medium term in this context means the period needed for output to return to potential and for changes in competitiveness to be reflected in trade volumes, which would appear to be in the range of four to six years. As explained above, external equilibrium is defined in terms of a sustainable value of the current account balance. Internal balance is usually defined as potential full-employment output; in most computations (e.g., those of Williamson 1985 and 1990) this is computed independently and thus not dependent on the real exchange rate itself; we follow that tradition in this section dealing with comparative static analysis. On this assumption the DEER associated with internal and external balance is illustrated in figure 1, where full-employment income Y^* is drawn as a vertical line in real exchange rate (R) and real income (Y) space. The current account (CA) schedule is drawn for a given level of the current account balance and, for well-known (net import propensity) reasons, slopes downward from left to right; as real income increases, (net) imports tend to rise, requiring a devaluation of the real exchange rate to maintain an unchanged current account position. The solutions for R^* and Y^* give the DEER and the internal balance position. As income (GNP) is generally close to output (GDP), the full-employment level of income, Y^*, will be approximately the same as the full-employment level of output.

One important issue that will not be dealt with in detail in this paper is how to define the sustainable level of the current account. One approach, which Williamson uses (chapter 6), is to calculate it from the difference between desired levels of saving and investment. Williamson notes that, as the current account is a flow variable, representing the rate of international lending or borrowing of an economy, one needs to examine whether a given current account position is likely to lead to an unsustainable debt buildup in the medium term. This suggests that the desired level of the current account could be approached by considering

Figure 1 Internal and external balance

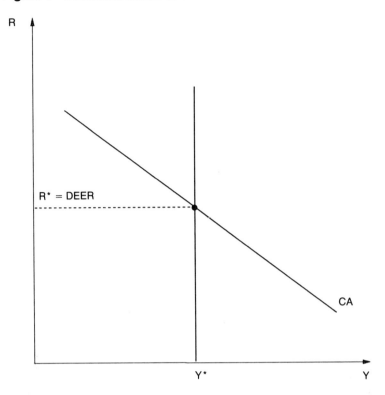

the underlying stock equilibrium for international assets. Once this equilibrium has been identified, the desired path for the current account would depend both upon the underlying equilibrium level of net foreign assets for the economy in question and upon the adjustment path toward this equilibrium. This desired path for the current account could then be used to identify the appropriate DEER trajectory.

Although Williamson has generally used large macroeconomic models to calculate DEERs, it is basically a comparative static, partial-equilibrium calculation, as noted by Wren-Lewis (1992). Given values of the desired levels of output and the current account, the DEER is the level of the real effective exchange rate consistent with achieving these goals in the medium term. If we denote with asterisks the levels of domestic income (Y), foreign income (FY), and the current account (CA) that correspond to internal and external balance, the DEER is then R^*, the value of the real exchange rate R derived from equation (1):

$$CA^* = CA(Y^*, FY^*, R^*). \tag{1}$$

The easiest method of calculating the DEER is to start from the values of Y, FY, CA, and R in the current (i.e., base) period and then compute the change in R implied in moving Y to Y^*, FY to FY^*, and CA to CA^* using the following function:

$$CA = CA(Y, FY, R). \tag{1'}$$

Although there appear to be three targets and only one instrument, it is assumed that Y and FY move to Y^* and FY^*, respectively, through the natural operation of economic forces, so that there is in effect one instrument, R, to achieve CA^*.

The three elasticities required to make equation (1) operational are the sensitivities of the current account to domestic activity, foreign activity, and the real exchange rate, which can be derived from estimated trade equations. In the calculations below the elasticities from the Multimod equations for nonfactor trade are used.[3] These are given in tables 1 and 2; other inputs used in the calculations described in this section are given in table 3. As estimated elasticities are subject to a degree of uncertainty, we explore below the sensitivity of calculated DEERs to a range of estimates.

One feature of the exercise outlined above is that fiscal policy has no explicit role in the calculation. This may appear surprising at first sight, but there can be reasons for taking the view that fiscal policy has little *independent* effect on the DEER for given levels of Y^*, FY^*, and CA^*. Of course, fiscal policy affects the current account in the short run through two main channels—changes in the exchange rate and movements in output relative to potential—and both of these channels are taken into account in the calculation of the DEER. But this is not to say that fiscal policy cannot have an independent impact on the DEER. Fiscal policy can have a direct impact on the current account (and hence the DEER) over and above its indirect effects through aggregate demand. For example, if government consumption has a different import multiplier from other domestic spending, or if changes in fiscal policy affect the level of potential output, then it would be appropriate to include a separate effect of fiscal policy on the DEER.[4]

The comparative static, partial-equilibrium approach has certain advantages and disadvantages. On the positive side, the calculations are simple and transparent—features that also make it easy to test the sensitivity of the calculations to alternative assumptions. On the other hand,

---

3. For a description of the Multimod macroeconomic model see Masson, Symansky, and Meredith (1990).

4. Fiscal policy also provides a potential policy tool for moving the current exchange rate to its equilibrium level, rather than as a major independent factor in the DEER calculation. The use of fiscal policy in this manner is described in the penultimate section of this paper.

Table 1   Multimod absorption and output elasticities

Country	Absorption elasticities		Implied output elasticities[a]	
	Exports	Imports	Exports	Imports
Canada	2.00	2.05	2.81	3.25
France	2.00	2.21	2.76	3.34
Germany	2.00	1.44	2.93	2.01
Italy	2.00	2.27	2.62	3.26
Japan	2.00	1.66	2.21	1.86
United Kingdom	2.00	1.38	3.09	1.85
United States	2.00	1.51	2.28	1.65

a. Taking into account the effect on net exports.

Source: Masson, Symansky, and Meredith (1990).

Table 2   Multimod real exchange rate elasticities

Country	Real exchange rate elasticities		Adjustment due to effect on absorption		Total effect
	Exports	Imports	Exports	Imports	
Canada	0.71	0.45	0.13	0.06	1.35
France	0.71	0.72	0.11	0.10	1.63
Germany	0.71	0.90	0.14	0.14	1.89
Italy	0.71	0.40	0.10	0.05	1.25
Japan	0.71	0.77	0.05	0.04	1.55
United Kingdom	0.71	0.37	0.13	0.07	1.27
United States	0.71	1.10	0.04	0.07	1.91

Source: Masson, Symansky, and Meredith (1990).

Table 3   Actual current account and trade balances and output gaps, 1971 and 1972 (percentages of GDP)

Country	Current account[a]		Trade balance[a]		Output gap[b]	
	1971	1972	1971	1972	1971	1972
Canada	0.38	−0.26	2.54	1.80	−1.42	−0.96
France	0.08	−0.18	0.54	0.54	4.22	2.77
Germany	0.45	0.47	3.12	3.29	1.29	2.09
Italy	1.72	1.49	0.49	0.0	0.04	−1.50
Japan	2.51	2.17	3.38	2.94	−0.72	0.79
United Kingdom	1.89	0.30	0.33	−1.15	−1.66	−0.71
United States	−0.13	−0.48	−0.21	−0.53	−1.80	0.53

a. A negative number indicates a deficit.
b. A negative number indicates output below potential.

Source: IMF Research Department.

certain dynamic factors are inevitably ignored. As noted above, this approach assumes that the current account in the base period has fully adjusted to past changes in output and the real exchange rate. In addition, it ignores the impact on the DEER of the path to equilibrium. For example, continuing current account imbalances may imply a significant change in the level of net external assets, which in turn feeds back onto the net flows of interest, dividends, and profits. Moreover, policies that affect the level of investment will change the level of potential output and hence the medium-term level of activity. This can be seen very clearly in the penultimate section of this paper, where the choice of the policy or "forcing" variable that is altered to achieve a current account target has very different effects on real interest rates, potential output, and the real exchange rate. Finally, the comparative static, partial-equilibrium approach abstracts from considerations relating to asset market equilibrium and thus implicitly assumes that, over the medium term, interest rates (nominal and real) have settled down at their equilibrium levels. These dynamic and asset market effects are taken into account and analyzed in the sections below.

Some Illustrative DEER Calculations

To illustrate the DEER approach, this section reports some calculations based on an actual historical episode, namely, the breakup of the Bretton Woods exchange rate system in the early 1970s. The Bretton Woods system, which involved fixed but adjustable exchange rates, was set up immediately after World War II. The system worked as a dollar standard backed by gold, with the US dollar having a fixed parity against gold and the other members of the system having fixed parities against the dollar.[5] The heyday of the system, involving full convertibility of all major currencies, lasted from 1959 to 1968. In 1968 financial market tensions forced the separation of the private and official markets for gold, effectively ending the private convertibility of the dollar into gold at a fixed price.

The system continued as a dollar standard with fixed parities until 1971. In May of that year the deutsche mark and the Dutch guilder were floated, and in August the United States suspended the gold convertibility of the dollar even for official borrowers. At that point most major currencies began to float against the dollar while negotiations on a new set of exchange rate parities were initiated with the objective of returning to a fixed exchange rate system. New parities were agreed at a ministerial conference of the Group of 10 at the Smithsonian Institution in Washington on 18 and 19 December. These involved a devaluation of the dollar in terms of gold from $35 to $38 per ounce, a general revaluation of other Group of Ten currencies against the dollar that resulted in an effective devaluation of the dollar of 9.1 percent, and a widening of the intervention limits from ± 1 percent to $\pm 2\frac{1}{4}$ percent. With the exception of the pound sterling, these parities held until February 1973, when

---

5. See McKinnon (1993) for a fuller description of this system.

the dollar was devalued a further 10 percent just prior to the general collapse of the system in March.[6]

This section illustrates how the DEER approach can be used to analyze the collapse of the Bretton Woods exchange rate system. There are many issues involved in that episode, including divergent monetary policies, the asymmetrical position of the dollar, the level of liquidity in the system, and the ability to adjust parities. This section will abstract from these issues and focus on the appropriateness of the underlying parities. Two issues are examined. First, to what degree were the exchange rate parities of 1970, just prior to the initial collapse of the system, out of line with estimated DEERs? Second, to what extent did the Smithsonian parity adjustments move exchange rates between the major industrial countries toward their estimated DEERs?

Tables 4 and 5 show a number of alternative calculations of DEERs for the major industrial countries; the calculations highlight the importance of different assumptions in these calculations using the comparative static, partial-equilibrium approach. Conceptually, the DEER calculations can be thought of as being carried out in three steps, although in practice these steps are performed simultaneously. First, the impact of moving output to potential in all countries is calculated by taking the implied movements in (trade-weighted) foreign output and in domestic output for each country and multiplying these changes by the short-run elasticities of exports and imports with respect to real output, respectively, and by the ratio of exports and imports to GDP.[7] Next, the change in the real multilateral exchange rate required to move this adjusted current account to its desired level is calculated for each country. These calculations use the aggregate real exchange rate elasticities reported in the last column of table 2.[8] Finally, trade weights are used to derive the

---

6. A number of descriptions of the collapse of the Bretton Woods system have been published by academics (Williamson 1977, Garber 1993), institutional historians (de Vries 1976), and policymakers (Solomon 1982, Volcker and Gyohten 1992).

7. The elasticities are shown in table 1. The first two columns show the estimated absorption elasticities used in Multimod (Multimod uses absorption as the activity variable in the export and import equations). The output elasticities shown in the next two columns, which are the numbers actually used in the calculation, take account of the relationship between absorption, output, and net exports. Since changes in net exports feed directly into absorption but not into output, the output elasticities are somewhat higher than the absorption elasticities.

8. The aggregate effect is made up of the real exchange rate elasticities for exports and for imports plus an adjustment for the multiplier effects of these movements in exports and imports on absorption. These adjustments tend to increase the overall real exchange rate elasticity. For example, an appreciation in the real exchange rate lowers exports and raises imports. This in turn lowers net exports, which, for a given level of domestic output, raises domestic absorption and hence raises the demand for imports.

Table 4 Bretton Woods parities, base case DEERs, and Smithsonian parities

	Bilateral exchange rates[a]			Real effective exchange rates[b]		
	1970 Bretton Woods parities	Base case DEER	Smithsonian parities[c]	1970 parities	Base case DEER	Smithsonian parities[c]
Country						
Canada	1.044[d]	1.037	1.089[d]	100	94.7[d]	90.7
France	5.55	4.64	4.95	100	106.0	99.6
Germany	3.66	3.22	3.13	100	99.6	105.8
Italy	625	515	564	100	107.6	98.3
Japan	360	277	305	100	125.1	113.3
United Kingdom	0.417	0.365	0.358	100	101.7	105.2
United States	1	1	1	100	87.7	90.9

a. In units of local currency per US dollar.
b. 1970 parity = 100.
c. Nominal parities adjusted for differences in inflation between 1970 and 1972.
d. Actual market rate (the Canadian dollar was floating during this period).

Table 5 Alternative calculations of DEERs (1970 parity = 100)

		Alternative assumption				
Country	Base case	No adjustment for cyclical factors[a]	Trade balance equal to 1 percent of GDP[b]	1972 data[c]	Export price elasticities = 1	Import price elasticities = 0.75
Canada	94.7	94.3	114.0	87.0	97.3	97.3
France	106.0	95.3	108.5	103.2	104.0	105.7
Germany	99.6	98.6	108.0	101.9	99.8	99.4
Italy	107.6	110.9	87.9	101.0	102.9	102.5
Japan	125.1	124.6	138.9	127.5	116.2	125.8
United Kingdom	101.7	108.6	86.0	92.5	100.5	100.4
United States	87.7	89.0	87.0	91.0	90.8	79.5

a. Calculations take no account of deviations of output from potential.
b. The trade balance rather than the current account balance is taken as the target.
c. The lag between exchange rate changes and their impact on the trade balance is assumed to be two years rather than one.

changes in the real bilateral rates against the US dollar from the change in the real effective exchange rate.[9]

---

9. The methodology used here is similar in some respects to that described in Artus and Rhomberg (1973). Their approach, which is also one of comparative statics, involves the use of a highly disaggregated model of traded and nontraded goods. There are supply and demand equations for a number of traded goods and demand equations for nontraded goods. Where this approach differs from that used in this section is that the response of trade flows reflects both supply and demand responses to exchange rate changes. Both approaches are partial-equilibrium approaches in that they do not include induced effects on domestic output arising from exchange rate changes or the interaction between trade flows, net foreign assets, and net interest payments. These macroeconomic effects are taken into account in the Multimod simulation results reported in later in this paper.

Table 3 shows the current account, the trade balance, and the gap between output and potential output as ratios to GDP for 1971 and 1972. The United States had the weakest current account of all of the major industrial countries in both years, followed by France and Canada. At the other end of the spectrum, Japan had the largest surplus, followed by Italy. Britain is notable for the size of the deterioration in its external position between 1971 and 1972. Trade balances show a similar picture for the United States and Japan, but in this case Germany and Canada also exhibit strong balances and Britain and Italy weak ones. The estimated output gaps indicate that in 1971 the United States, Britain, Canada, and, to a lesser extent, Japan were below potential output. All three showed some recovery in 1972, the largest change occurring in the United States. In continental Europe, France and, to a lesser extent, Germany were significantly above potential in 1971. By and large these changes in output gaps are reflected in opposite movements in the current account; however, significant perverse responses are found for France and Italy.

"Base case" values for the DEERs of the major industrial countries in 1970 are reported in table 4.[10] They were generated on the assumption that the targeted current account surplus for each country was equal to 1 percent of GDP in 1971. This has been adopted as a relatively neutral assumption that is useful for illustrating how the DEER approach can be used. A 1 percent surplus was chosen both because it is close to the actual surplus of the major industrial countries as a group in 1971 and because it was the approximate stated objective of the US administration during the Smithsonian discussions.[11] The reason for using 1971 current accounts with 1970 exchange rates is that exchange rates affect the current account with a lag. Although there is some uncertainty as to the length of these lags, one year appears to be a reasonable estimate. Results from using a two-year lag (i.e., using 1972 current account positions with 1970 exchange rates) are also reported as one of the variations on the base case.

The DEERs reported in table 4 are measured both on a real bilateral basis against the dollar (using 1970 prices) and as real effective exchange

---

10. No attempt is made to reproduce the calculations of appropriate exchange rates made at the time of the Smithsonian Agreement by the IMF and the Organization for Economic Cooperation and Development, which used a set of desired adjustments in the current account that were different from the uniform 1 percent surplus assumed here. Rather, as noted above, the objective here is to illustrate the potential use of DEER calculations.

11. In 1971 the United States ran a current account deficit of just over 0.1 percent of GDP. The goal of the United States was a turnaround of some $13 billion (about 1.2 percent of GDP) in the current account, which implies a target surplus of about 1 percent of GDP. It should be noted that the IMF staff does not regularly compute the type of desired current account positions that are referred to in this paper; the current account positions here are used for illustrative purposes only.

rates (1970 parities = 100). Compared with the 1970 Bretton Woods parities, the DEER calculations imply that a significant real appreciation against the dollar was necessary for the five major currencies participating in the Bretton Woods fixed exchange rate system; this finding reflects the weakness of the balance of payments in the United States at that time. The magnitude of the implied changes in bilateral rates is relatively large: between 13 and 22 percent for the four European currencies and 30 percent for the yen. The one currency that was floating over this period, the Canadian dollar, was almost exactly at its calculated bilateral DEER against the US dollar. Given the relatively stylized nature of these calculations, these calculated values should not be viewed as precise estimates of the actual underlying equilibrium exchange rate values. As will be shown below, they are sensitive to many of the underlying assumptions in the model.

The real effective exchange rate DEER calculations highlight some interesting implications for the real bilateral rates. For the US dollar, achieving a current account surplus equal to 1 percent of GDP is estimated to require a devaluation in real effective terms on the order of 12 percent.[12] Despite their large calculated bilateral misalignments against the dollar, the deutsche mark and the pound sterling were relatively close to their calculated DEERs on a real effective exchange rate basis, and for the French franc and the lira an effective real appreciation of only 6 to 8 percent was needed. This reflects both the fact that intra-European real bilateral exchange rates were quite close to their estimated DEERs and the importance of these intra-European exchange rates for the real effective exchange rate calculations. In contrast, the importance of the United States in Japanese trade can be seen in the 25 percent real effective appreciation required to move the yen to its calculated DEER. In effective terms, therefore, these DEER calculations suggest that the misalignments in 1970 mainly involved the United States and Japan. These contrasts between the bilateral and multilateral measures of real exchange rates illustrate the potential importance of third-country effects in the exchange rate calculations, and underline the importance of making the computations on a multilateral basis.

These base case calculations can be compared with the parities agreed to at the Smithsonian meeting in December 1971 and maintained through February 1973 (except for the pound sterling, which was floated in mid-1972), which are also reported in table 4.[13] To convert these 1972 nominal bilateral parities into their real 1970 equivalents, the parities

---

12. The importance of Canada in US trade can be seen from the fact that the bilateral misalignments against all currencies except the Canadian dollar were greater than 17 percent.

13. Since the Canadian dollar was floating throughout this period, the average market rate was used as the "parity" in both 1970 and 1972.

reported in table 4 have been adjusted for differences in inflation between 1970 and 1972.[14]

Compared with the 1970 parities, the Smithsonian parities generally moved the bilateral real exchange rates against the dollar toward their estimated bilateral DEERs. Between half and two-thirds of the gap between the 1970 parities and calculated bilateral exchange rates was closed in the case of the franc, the lira, and the yen. For the deutsche mark and the pound sterling the new parities actually overshot the estimated real bilateral DEERs. The Canadian dollar, which as noted above was floating, moved away from its estimated real bilateral DEER over the period. The implied adjustments in effective exchange rates are also shown. In effective exchange rate terms, both the US dollar and the yen moved between half and three-quarters of the way toward their estimated 1970 DEERs. In contrast, the appreciation of the deutsche mark and the pound sterling resulting from the Smithsonian Agreement moved their real effective rates significantly further from their estimated DEERs. Hence, on these calculations, the overall impact of the Smithsonian parities was to move the US dollar, the yen, the French franc, and the lira toward their estimated DEERs, but to move the deutsche mark and the lira away from theirs.

Thus far the analysis has focused upon the set of assumptions in the base case. Table 5 shows the DEERs resulting from alternative assumptions about the targeted external balance position, trade elasticities, and deviations from potential output, to provide a sense of the range of plausible results involved in such calculations. The first set of alternative results shows the impact of the economic cycle on the calculations; it reports the estimated DEERs when no account is taken of deviations of output from potential. The impact of this change on the estimated DEERs is generally modest. However, in the case of the French franc, the calculated DEER is roughly 11 percent lower than the DEER in the base case (a 5 percent depreciation instead of a 6 percent appreciation), whereas that for the pound sterling rises by over 7 percent relative to the base case. These examples illustrate that a country's cyclical position can have a substantial impact on its calculated DEER.

The next set of results shows the impact of targeting an alternative measure of the external position, namely, the merchandise trade balance rather than the current account. The DEERs calculated using the trade balance as the targeted external position differ significantly in several

---

14. The nominal parities against the dollar agreed at the Smithsonian meeting were ¥308, DM3.22, 5.12 French francs, 582 lira, and £0.384. Inflation was higher in Europe and Japan than in the United States over this period; hence the reported bilateral exchange rates for the yen and the European currencies are lower than the actual Smithsonian parities (the opposite is true for the Canadian dollar). The largest adjustment is for Britain, whose GDP deflator rose by 7 percent more than that in the United States over the period.

cases from those using the current account. On an effective exchange rate basis the estimated DEER rises by 11 percent for the yen, 20 percent for the Canadian dollar, and 8 percent for the deutsche mark relative to the base case, while falling by over 15 percent for the lira and the pound sterling, reflecting the large trade surpluses in Japan, Germany, and Canada and the relatively weak trade positions of Italy and Britain. These results also change the interpretation of the Smithsonian parities somewhat, particularly as regards the European countries. On these calculations the Smithsonian parities implied a large overvaluation of the pound sterling and the lira compared with their DEERs, while putting the deutsche mark about in line with its estimated DEER.

The next column shows the impact of changing the lag between the exchange rate change and its current account impact from one year to two years; this involves calculating the DEERs implied by using 1972 current accounts and deviations from potential output, rather than 1971 values.[15] The DEERs calculated using the 1972 data are generally similar to those in the base case, the largest change being depreciations of over 8 percent for the DEERs of the pound sterling and the Canadian dollar, which reflect a deterioration in the current account of Britain and Canada from 1971 to 1972. More modest depreciations in the estimated DEERs occur for the lira and the French franc, counterbalanced by appreciations of the US dollar, the yen, and the deutsche mark compared with the base case.

The next two columns illustrate the impact on the estimated DEERs of changing the assumed values of the price elasticities for imports and exports. Raising the export price elasticities from 0.71 to unity (these elasticities are constrained to be equal across all countries in Multimod) produces an across-the-board reduction in the size of the implied exchange rate changes required to reach the assumed current account positions. This reflects the fact that increasing the real exchange rate elasticities in the import equations makes the current account more sensitive to changes in the exchange rate, and hence smaller exchange rate changes are required to achieve a specific current account value. These results are somewhat closer to those implied by the Smithsonian parities, particularly for the US dollar and the yen. Hence, one possible interpretation of the Smithsonian parities is that they reflected a relatively optimistic set of assumptions about the underlying price elasticities of trade.

The second experiment involves making all of the import price elasticities (whose estimated values can vary across countries in Multimod) equal to 0.75, the approximate mean of the estimated values. This signif-

---

15. The aggregate external position of the major industrial countries deteriorated by around half a percent of GDP between 1971 and 1972. Accordingly, the current account target was lowered from 1 percent of GDP to $1/2$ percent for each country in the calculations.

icantly increases the exchange rate adjustment required to move to the DEER for the US dollar, where the estimated import price elasticity is relatively large, and lowers the adjustment in Italy, Britain, and Canada, where the import elasticities are relatively small. Clearly, the estimated trade elasticities have a significant impact on the estimated DEERs.

The results from table 5 indicate that changes in the underlying assumptions can have a significant impact on estimated DEERs, with the range between the highest and lowest estimates of the DEER in effective terms lying between 10 and 30 percent. This wide range underlines the need for caution in identifying any given set of exchange rates as ''the'' appropriate set of values. Nevertheless, all of the calculations imply that the US dollar was overvalued and the yen undervalued at their 1970 parities, and the effective exchange rate for the dollar implied by the Smithsonian parities was within the estimated range of DEERs, while that for the yen lay slightly below the lowest estimate of the DEER. The calculations also generally indicate that the effective appreciation of the deutsche mark and the pound sterling implied by the Smithsonian parities moved these currencies away from their DEERs. However, this reflects the underlying assumption in these calculations that an appropriate objective for all the major industrial countries would be to run the same current account (or trade balance) as a ratio to GDP.

A Dynamic DEER: Taking Account of the Path Toward Equilibrium[16]

Hysteresis in the DEER

As discussed in the previous section, the comparative static approach does not incorporate adjustments in the DEER that may be needed to take account of changes in the country's stock of international debt, and therefore in debt service, as long as the current account is not at the desired level. To take this dynamic behavior into account, the DEER needs to be computed as a trajectory, as the equilibrium exchange rate will not be independent of the path of the exchange rate toward its ultimate sustainable value.[17]

It is easy to see from figure 1 how hysteresis in the DEER can arise. Suppose that the actual exchange rate happens to correspond initially to its DEER value and that internal balance is at the desired level—in other words, that there is no problem of the starting point or transition period.

---

16. This section draws on a more extensive treatment of this issue given in Artis and Taylor (1993).

17. The need to take account of the path of the exchange rate toward its equilibrium value has been emphasized by Wren-Lewis (1992). See also Branson (1979).

In terms of the figure, we are at (Y^*, R^*). Now suppose that in the next period there is a misalignment, so that the actual real exchange rate departs from its DEER value—specifically, that the currency appreciates—while output remains at Y^*. The appreciation causes the current account to deteriorate relative to the initial equilibrium position, which in this section is assumed to be zero, and as a consequence the DEER calculation must be performed afresh because net foreign indebtedness rises as a result of the deficit and creates an obligation to service the higher debt. Even if we disregard any desire to eliminate the increase in indebtedness, the obligation to service more debt causes the CA schedule to move to the left; the real exchange rate that would have been consistent with the current account target in the absence of the increased debt service will now produce a deficit due to the increased debt service obligation. More precisely, the *trade* account target has changed to provide a surplus sufficient to cover the increased debt service obligation. The current account target remains the same, as it includes debt service, but its composition has changed, forcing CA to shift downward and to the left.

The departure of the actual exchange rate from its DEER value (trajectory) thus forces a revision of the DEER. A "hysteresis loop" (Cross 1992) would ensue if the previous DEER were to be reestablished. The currency would need to "overdepreciate" in order to reinstate the previous schedule. As shown in figure 2, a displacement of the actual real rate of exchange from its DEER value—say, to point A—involves a real appreciation and a current account deficit relative to the current account balance underlying CA. This requires a shift of the CA schedule to CA', and a devaluation of the DEER from R^* to $R^{*'}$. Alternatively, if it were desired to reduce the stock of debt to the original level and for the DEER to be reestablished at R^*, an overdepreciation would be needed, resulting in the "hysteresis loop" shown.

How large a revision of the DEER is required as a result of a misalignment? To derive an answer to this question, imagine again that, starting from a position where the current real exchange rate is at its DEER value and internal balance is realized, the current exchange rate departs from its DEER value by x percent. For concreteness, suppose that this is an appreciation. Then a deficit in the current account will appear of $x(\mu + \tau)X$, where μ and τ are the import and export elasticities, respectively, and X is the volume of exports (and imports—we suppose the two to be approximately equal). If this is a one-off deviation of one year's duration, then the DEER will have to be devalued to the extent necessary to service the additional debt incurred. It is convenient to assume that the DEER adjustment depends on the same elasticities.[18]

---

18. It might be objected that the short-run elasticities differ from the medium-run elasticities used in constructing the DEER. A further adjustment could be made for any such differences.

Figure 2 Hysteresis effects

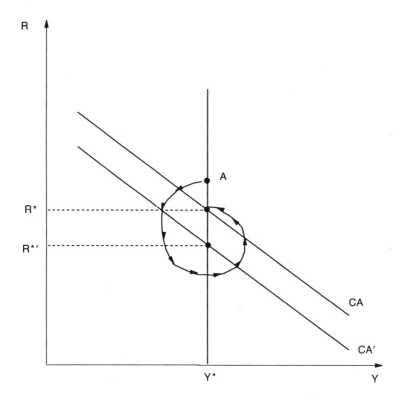

While the adjustment needs only to be large enough to service the interest cost of the extra debt incurred, it is easy to see that, if the interest rate is r, the adjustment required is $\delta = rx$. The change in the DEER δ must yield $rx(\mu + \tau)X$ to cover the debt service, or $\delta(\mu + \tau)X = rx(\mu + \tau)X$. If the deviation is sustained for two years, the total adjustment required will be twice as large. Thus, each initial x percent deviation of the actual from the desired equilibrium exchange rate will require a DEER adjustment of rx percent in the opposite direction if DEERs are adjusted annually.

This adjustment makes no allowance for the need to reverse the increment in debt acquired through the initial assumed appreciation of the current exchange rate over its DEER value. The reason for this is that the DEER external balance criterion is typically given in terms of a flow equilibrium involving a change in net foreign assets rather than a particular stock of net foreign assets scaled, for example, by GDP. However, from a longer-term wealth accumulation perspective, the stock of net foreign assets may well be the appropriate target in terms of private-sector behavior. In this case, a shock that causes a departure from the initial desired stock equilibrium condition might be expected to lead to a response calculated to offset it. In this case every x percent appreciation of the currency over its DEER value would require a subsequent depreciation large enough to pay back the debt over a defined period of time. The size of hysteresis effects will clearly be potentially much larger if the DEER adjustment needs to be of sufficient magnitude to repay the debt incurred, rather than simply to service the additional interest obligation. In what follows, however, we calculate DEER adjustments sufficient to cover only the cost of the additional interest payments arising from misalignment. This case is clearly the more conservative one to take and sets a natural lower bound to the size of the hysteresis problem. This simplifies the analysis, and we thereby avoid having to specify—quite arbitrarily—the speed with which debt repayments would occur. Finally, like that in the preceding section, this is a partial-equilibrium analysis and abstracts from the issue of the source of the exchange rate change. Therefore, real output and interest rates are assumed to be independent of the exchange rate change. However, as shown in the penultimate section, the source of the exchange rate change can influence these variables and might alter the hysteresis calculations.

We now proceed to derive a formula for the DEER adjustment process that expresses formally the hysteresis effect—the dependence of the DEER on the path of the actual exchange rate. Suppose that initially, in year 0, the actual real exchange rate is at its DEER value, which has a flat (stationary) trajectory at that point in time. Internal balance is assumed to be maintained at its given level throughout. Then any deviation of the actual rate from the DEER value implies a deviation from the current account balance and requires a recomputation of the DEER on the lines indicated above.

Approximately, then:

$$R_n^* = R_{n-1}^* - r(R_{n-1} - R_{n-1}^*) \tag{3}$$

or

$$R_n^* = (1 + r)R_{n-1}^* - rR_{n-1}, \tag{4}$$

where R_n^* is the logarithmic value of the DEER in year n, R_n is the logarithm of the actual real exchange rate in year n, and r is the rate of interest.[19]

Equation (4) implies that:

---

19. Note that the trade price elasticities do not enter this equation, since it is assumed for convenience that these elasticities are the same at all points in time.

$$R_{n-1}^* = (1 + r)R_{n-2}^* - rR_{n-2} \tag{5}$$

$$R_{n-2}^* = (1 + r)R_{n-3}^* - rR_{n-3}. \tag{6}$$

Recursive substitution—of equations (6) and (5) into equation (4), and so forth—yields:

$$R_n^* = (1 + r)^n R_0^* - r\sum_{i=1}^{n}(1 + r)^{i-1}R_{n-i}. \tag{7}$$

Equation (7) shows how the initial stationary trajectory for R^*, R_0^*, will require updating in light of the evolution of the actual real exchange rate. Thus the DEER is not independent of the history of exchange rate movements. In particular, if the authorities wished to move the current exchange rate to the DEER by the end of n periods, they would need to choose a path for the real exchange rate $(R_1, R_2, \ldots, R_n)$ such that $R_n = R_n^*$, with R_n^* as defined in equation (7). Thus, given a deviation of the actual rate from the DEER and a desire ultimately to equate the two, the DEER arrived at when the actual rate again coincides with it will not be independent of the path taken by the exchange rate toward this goal. Indeed, as equation (3) makes clear, if R deviates from R^*, R^* will actually move *away* from R at speed r per period. Intuitively, therefore, we should expect that the eventual convergence of R^* and R would require a movement of R toward R^* at a speed greater than r in the following period. As demonstrated formally in Artis and Taylor (1993), this intuition turns out to be correct.

Converging on the DEER: Rules of Thumb

In light of the hysteresis effects involved in calculating the DEER, the following question naturally arises: Given an initial misalignment of the exchange rate and a desire to correct it over a certain finite period, by how much does the required movement in the exchange rate differ from the initial misalignment? For example, suppose that the currency is undervalued relative to the DEER and that it is desired to correct this over a period of, say, five years. Assuming that the desired adjustment is uniform (e.g., annual appreciation by a constant percentage), then, by our arguments, the DEER at the end of the fifth year, when the misalignment is zero, will be higher than the initial calculated DEER. Thus, the total required movement in the exchange rate will be greater than the initial difference between the exchange rate and the DEER. The additional movement in the exchange rate over the five-year period (over the initial misalignment measure) is thus, in some sense, a measure of the importance of hysteresis effects arising during misalignment.

If the rate of capacity utilization is held constant at 100 percent, then the overall movement in the DEER will be equal to the cumulative misalignment each period multiplied by the interest rate. Table 6 gives some illustrative examples of movements in the DEER, assuming an interest rate of 5 percent, initial undervaluation or overvaluation of 10 or 20 percent, and a constant annual percentage change in the exchange rate over a five-year convergence period. These trajectories are essentially found by fine-tuning the annual percentage change in the exchange rate to find $R_5 = R_5^*$ with R_n^* as given in equation (7), for given R_0^* and R_0.[20]

The results in table 6 show that the effect of a changing net asset stock due to currency misalignment is to increase the total required exchange rate adjustment by some 1.5 percentage points for an initial 10 percent misalignment, and by 3 percentage points for an initial 20 percent misalignment. Note that the revision due to debt accumulation or disaccumulation is greater in the case of undervaluation, since the initial exchange rate on which the percentage is calculated is at a depressed level.

As a very rough rule of thumb, therefore, for economies operating near full capacity utilization, the results of this section suggest that the initial measure of misalignment should be increased by about 1.5 percentage points for each 10 percent misalignment if the desired period of convergence is five years. Thus, an initial misalignment of 10 percent would suggest a required exchange rate movement of about 11½ percent over five years.

Dynamic Macroeconomic Calculations of DEERs using Multimod

In this section we use Multimod to calculate the change in the real effective exchange rate needed to achieve the desired change in the external position of the major industrial countries. The first objective is to obtain results that are as closely comparable as possible to those derived above using a simple comparative static approach. The aim is to see what difference it makes to the calculated change in the real effective exchange rate using a full-model simulation, as well as to obtain an estimate of the likely domestic economic effects of the change in the external balance. It is demonstrated that the manner in which the exchange rate is changed affects the whole macroeconomic system, including real output and the real exchange rate. In particular, the two types of shocks considered here (changes in currency preferences and fiscal policy) have different implications for medium-term real output

20. In fact, the precise calculations were slightly different because we used percentage differences rather than logarithmic differences. A spreadsheet program was used to perform the calculations.

Table 6   Five-year convergence trajectories between actual exchange rate and DEER in presence of hysteresis effects[a]

	Year					
	0	1	2	3	4	5
Initial 10 percent overvaluation						
Actual exchange rate	100.00	97.61	95.27	92.99	90.70	88.60
DEER	90.00	89.55	89.18	88.90	88.70	88.60
Misalignment (%)	+10.00	+8.26	+6.40	+4.41	+2.28	+0.00

Annual exchange rate movement = −2.39 percent
Overall movement in the DEER = −1.56 percent
Overall movement in the exchange rate = −11.40 percent
Difference between initial misalignment and overall exchange rate movement = 1.4 percentage points

	0	1	2	3	4	5
Initial 10 percent undervaluation						
Actual exchange rate	100.00	102.24	104.52	106.86	109.25	111.70
DEER	110.00	110.55	111.00	111.34	111.58	111.70
Misalignment (%)	−10.00	−8.13	−6.20	−4.19	−2.13	0.00

Annual exchange rate movement = +2.24 percent
Overall movement in the DEER = +1.54 percent
Overall movement in the exchange rate = +11.70 percent
Difference between initial misalignment and overall exchange rate movement = 1.7 percentage points

	0	1	2	3	4	5
Initial 20 percent overvaluation						
Actual exchange rate	100.00	95.03	90.30	85.81	81.55	77.49
DEER	80.00	79.20	78.54	78.03	77.67	77.49
Misalignment (%)	+20.00	+16.66	+13.03	+9.07	+4.75	0.00

Annual exchange rate movement = −4.97 percent
Overall movement in the DEER = −3.14 percent
Overall movement in the exchange rate = −22.51 percent
Difference between initial misalignment and overall exchange rate movement = 2.51 percentage points

	0	1	2	3	4	5
Initial 20 percent undervaluation						
Actual exchange rate	100.00	104.34	108.87	113.60	118.54	123.68
DEER	120.00	121.20	122.18	122.93	123.43	123.68
Misalignment (%)	−20.00	−16.16	−12.22	−8.21	−4.13	0.00

Annual exchange rate movement = +4.34 percent
Overall movement in the DEER = +3.07 percent
Overall movement in the exchange rate = +23.68 percent
Difference between initial misalignment and overall exchange rate movement = 3.68 percentage points

a. Calculations assume a constant, 100 percent rate of capacity utilization and an annual interest rate of 5 percent per year.

and interest rates and ultimately the DEER. The same ''base case'' regarding the external position is used as before; namely, it is assumed that the desired level of the current account surplus is 1 percent of GDP in all countries. However, to make the results from the two methods as comparable as possible, no allowance is made initially for moving the economies to potential output in the Multimod simulations. Thus, the comparable calculation of the DEER in table 5 is that identified as "No adjustment for cyclical factors."

It should be pointed out that the simulations using Multimod involved shocking the model away from its baseline values in order to achieve the change in the real effective exchange rate consistent with attaining the desired current account position. As the historical baseline values of GDP used in the Multimod simulations do not involve a return of real output to its potential level, the deviations of the variables from the baseline reported below do not capture the effects of the movement of actual output to potential. To estimate these effects on the DEER, it is necessary to undertake a specific simulation in which potential output is raised relative to actual output in those countries where there is an output gap. The results of this simulation are reported at the end of this section.

As noted above, the base case involves achieving current account surpluses equal to 1 percent of GDP. However, the calculations using Multimod involved changing the trade balance by the same magnitude as the current account in the base case considered above using comparative statics. The reason for this modification is that, in the simplified approach used in that section, only changes in trade flows were taken into account, as no allowance was made for the impact of changes in interest rates and in the net foreign asset position on net debt service flows, and therefore what was reported in the analyses using comparative statics as a change in the current account is in fact restricted to trade flows only. This modification has been implemented in the simulations using Multimod by aiming at a change in the trade balance–GDP ratio equal to the difference between the current account–GDP ratio in 1971 (reported in table 3) and 1 percent.

DEERs Resulting from a Change in Currency Preferences

The exchange rate changes required to achieve the set of trade balance objectives just described were first implemented by introducing changes in currency preferences into the equations determining exchange rates in Multimod. Thus, for the countries that had a current account deficit or a surplus less than 1 percent of GDP in 1971, asset preferences are assumed to shift away from the currencies of these countries and in favor of the currencies of the countries that had surpluses larger than 1 percent. Such shifts in currency preference can be viewed as a market response to the external imbalances that have been identified as illustrative examples. These currency preference shifts are designed to correct the imbalances and are exogenously imposed on the model—that is, they are not policy instruments. More specifically, these changes in currency preferences are implemented in the uncovered interest parity equations that are the proximate determinants of bilateral exchange rates in Multimod. Such a modified equation in general form is the following:

$$E_i = E_{i,t+1} + r_i - r_{us} + CP_i - CP_{us} \tag{8}$$

where:

E_i = US dollars per unit of currency i (the nominal exchange rate)
r_i = the short-term interest rate in currency i
r_{us} = the US short-term interest rate
CP_i = currency preference shift variable in favor of currency i
CP_{us} = currency preference shift variable in favor of the US dollar.

In terms of equation (8), the exchange rate needed to realize a particular external balance objective is achieved by varying the currency preference shift variables. For example, in the case of Japan and the United States, the reduction in the Japanese surplus and in the US deficit is achieved in part by adjusting the shift variables in favor of the Japanese yen and against the US dollar by an amount sufficient to attain the needed changes in the bilateral exchange rate of the dollar against the yen. Comparable adjustments are made in the equations for the other bilateral dollar exchange rates for the other major industrial countries. In all these simulations, nominal monetary targets remain unchanged and all exchange rates are fully flexible. Given the considerable number of dynamic interactions in Multimod, considerable experimentation is needed to find the set of currency preference shifts required to achieve bilateral and real effective exchange rate changes that will be consistent with the targeted or desired external balance positions. The currency shift parameters are introduced in 1971 and then varied somewhat over time to reach the desired change in the trade balance. The specific adjustment of currency preferences is somewhat arbitrary. In general, the average preference shift is 150 basis points for every 1–percentage-point deviation in the trade balance as a percentage of GDP from its desired target, and it cumulates over time as long as the deviation persists.

As noted above, a major difference between the comparative static approach and that described in this section is that here the domestic economic effects of exchange rate changes are taken into account in calculating the changes needed to attain any given external balance objective. Moreover, the lags in the effect of exchange rate changes on the external sector, and through this sector on the domestic economy, are incorporated in the Multimod simulations. To allow for these lags, the results reported in table 7 are for the values of the indicated variables

Table 7   Calculation of DEERs using Multimod: targeted trade balances with changes in currency preferences[a]

Variables and calculated DEERs	Canada	France	Germany	Italy	Japan	United Kingdom	United States
Trade balance as a ratio to GDP	0.5	0.8	0.6	-1.1	-1.7	-1.1	1.0
Current account as a ratio to GDP	-0.3	1.0	1.2	-2.9	-2.5	-1.6	1.4
GDP	-0.3	-0.5	-0.4	1.1	1.8	0.5	-0.8
Domestic absorption	-0.7	-1.7	-1.3	3.6	4.6	2.8	-2.5
Foreign absorption	-1.7	0.3	0.2	-0.5	-1.2	-0.4	0.2
Real long-term interest rate[b]	0.5	0.6	0.5	-0.6	-1.7	-1.0	0.7
PX/PFM[c]	-3.9	-2.8	-1.3	9.8	16.6	6.9	-12.3
PGDP/PM[d]	-0.4	-4.3	-2.1	14.5	28.0	9.1	-13.5
Nominal effective exchange rate	-2.0	-6.1	-3.4	17.4	36.0	10.9	-17.5
DEER calculations (1970 parity = 100)							
From table 5, column 2	94.3	95.3	98.6	110.9	124.6	108.6	89.0
Average of changes in PX/PFM and PGDP/PM	97.8	96.5	98.3	112.2	122.3	108.0	87.1

a. Results are expressed as percentage deviations from baseline in 1975, unless otherwise indicated.
b. In percentage points.
c. Export price divided by competitors' prices in foreign markets.
d. GDP deflator divided by the import deflator.

in 1975. For most countries it takes roughly five years for the lags to work themselves out. This makes these results comparable to those obtained using the comparative static approach where long-run elasticities were used. Moreover, a five-year adjustment period is consistent with the medium-term notion of a DEER.[21] However, because the dynamic adjustment path is also of interest, the simulation results for one country—the United States—are also included for each year from 1971 to 1977. These are shown in table 8.

In looking at the results in table 7, it is important first to take account of the domestic economic effects of the shifts in currency preferences that are assumed to bring about the exchange rate changes. In particular, equation (8) shows that shifts in currency preferences will have an impact not only on exchange rates but also on short-term interest rates in order for the uncovered interest parity condition to hold; thus, a depreciation is generally reflected in a rise in the real interest rate, and an appreciation in a fall, as shown in the sixth line of table 7. Therefore, for those countries in which a positive change in the trade balance is needed, the real interest rate rises, whereas in those countries—Japan, Italy, and Britain—where a reduction in the trade balance is targeted, there is a decline in the real interest rate. The positive interest rate changes work in the same direction as changes in the real exchange rate since they reduce domestic absorption and thus improve the trade balance. Of course, this effect can be offset by similar changes in domestic absorption in the country's trading partners.

The simulated changes in the trade balance in 1975, expressed as a percentage of baseline GDP in the first line of table 7, are not exactly the same in all cases as the targeted changes, which are equal to the difference between the actual current account–GDP ratio in 1971 (shown in table 3) and 1 percent.[22] The reason for these discrepancies is that, given the lags in the trade and other variables in a macroeconomic model, it is difficult to hit simultaneously the targeted trade balances for all the industrial countries in any given year with a shift in currency preferences. For example, in Italy the trade balance as a percentage of GDP in 1975 declined relative to baseline by 1.1 percent of GDP, compared with the targeted fall of 0.7 percent. This overshooting in the adjustment in the trade balance disappears in the long run: after 20 years the fall in the

---

21. Although, as noted, the dynamics of trade equations indicate an adjustment period on the order of five years, it takes significantly longer for Multimod to converge to a steady state. In some cases the figures reported below represent an overshooting of the target, while for other countries the external balance targets have not yet been achieved after five years.

22. These targeted changes in the trade balances in percentages of GDP are as follows: United States, 1.13; Japan, −1.49; Germany, 0.55; Britain, −0.89; France, 0.92; Italy, −0.72; and Canada, 0.62.

Table 8 Calculation of DEER for the US dollar using Multimod: targeted trade balances with changes in currency preferences[a]

Variable	1971	1972	1973	1974	1975	1976	1977
Trade balance as a ratio to GDP	0.0	0.7	1.0	1.1	1.0	1.0	1.0
Current account as a ratio to GDP	0.0	0.8	1.2	1.4	1.4	1.4	1.4
GDP	0.1	0.0	−0.4	−0.8	−0.8	−0.8	−0.6
Domestic absorption	−0.6	−1.4	−2.0	−2.4	−2.5	−2.5	−2.5
Foreign absorption	0.0	0.2	0.4	0.5	0.2	0.3	0.2
Real long-term interest rate[b]	1.0	1.2	1.2	0.9	0.7	0.5	0.4
PX/PFM[c]	−11.7	−11.3	−11.5	−11.9	−12.3	−12.5	−12.4
PGDP/PM[d]	−13.2	−12.6	−12.6	−13.0	−13.5	−13.9	−13.8
Nominal effective exchange rate	−16.8	−16.6	−16.8	−17.2	−17.5	−17.5	−17.2

a. Results are expressed as percentage deviations from baseline, unless otherwise indicated.
b. In percentage points.
c. Export price divided by competitors' prices in foreign markets.
d. GDP deflator divided by the import deflator.

trade balance is 0.7 percent. Again, the United States achieved a 1.0 percent increase in the trade balance instead of the targeted 1.1 percent in 1975. Table 8 shows that there was a considerable lag—four years—before the targeted change was achieved.

Turning now to the DEERs calculated using Multimod, table 7 reports two different measures of the real effective exchange rate: the price of a country's exports relative to the prices of competing goods in foreign markets (*PX/PFM*), which is used in Multimod's export behavioral equation, and the price of domestic output relative to the price of imports (*PGDP/PM*), which is used in the import behavioral equation.[23] These figures can be compared with the DEERs reported in the relevant column in table 5 ("No adjustment for cyclical factors"), where only one real exchange rate measure is used. In the case of Germany, France, and Britain the differences are quite small. In the case of Japan the two

23. In general, the change in the former is less than the change in the latter. This reflects the fact that the export prices for one country are influenced by the export prices of competing countries in the short to medium run, whereas import and GDP deflators are less closely connected. Thus in Multimod Japanese export prices are estimated to be much more closely tied to competitors' prices than US export prices, and therefore the real effective exchange rate change using relative export prices is much smaller than using *PGDP/PM* in Japan, as compared with the United States.

DEERs from Multimod bracket those calculated using comparative static analysis. The same is true for Italy, but the simulated change in the trade balance—a reduction equal to 1.1 percent of GDP—is considerably larger than the targeted change of -0.72 percent, which is the basis for the calculated DEER using the comparative static approach. If one were to make a crude adjustment for this difference by scaling down the calculated real effective exchange rate changes for Italy reported in table 7, these changes (6.4 percent and 9.3 percent, respectively) are less than the 10.9 percent appreciation calculated using the comparative static approach. These lower figures appear to reflect the fact that the rise in GDP in Italy, which occurs in the Multimod simulation but is absent from the comparative static estimate, means that a smaller exchange rate change is needed to achieve a given change in the trade balance.[24]

The case of the United States is interesting in that Multimod DEERs are somewhat larger than the partial-equilibrium estimate. One factor that could account for this difference is that much of US trade is with developing countries, and the external financing constraint of developing countries that is a feature of Multimod implies that there is little scope for their trade balance to change at the margin. Moreover, the high US interest rate reduces inflows into these countries and raises their debt servicing costs, thereby reducing their imports. Therefore the United States needs a larger change in its real effective exchange rate against other industrial countries to achieve a given trade balance objective.

In contrast, it is somewhat puzzling that in the case of Canada the calculated changes in the DEER are smaller than the comparative static estimate of a real effective depreciation of 5.3 percent. As foreign absorption declines by 1.7 percent and thereby adversely affects Canada's exports, one would have expected that the Multimod calculations would have yielded a larger estimate of the depreciation of the Canadian dollar needed to achieve a given improvement in the trade balance. Two technical measurement factors appear to account for this anomaly. First, Multimod allows for the fact that the shares of imports and exports in GDP increased over the period 1971 to 1975, whereas the comparative static estimates are based on shares at the beginning of the period; as a consequence the necessary exchange rate change is lower in Multimod. Second, the comparative static estimates do not distinguish between import and export price elasticities. In contrast, the Multimod calculations take account of differences in these elasticities and differences in export and import shares, and this again results in a lower required exchange rate change.

---

24. It should be noted that although the comparative static analysis does take some account of the effect of changes in absorption on trade flows by assuming that a change in net trade directly alters absorption, it does not include any induced changes in real output.

DEERs Resulting from a Change in Fiscal Policy

Table 9 is comparable to table 7 in that the trade balance target is the same, but here it is achieved by means of changes in an alternative exogenous variable—specifically, changes in government spending—rather than changes in currency preferences.[25] However, there are some differences between the first line in table 9 and that in table 7 because of the difficulties in achieving exactly the same trade balance in the two different experiments for each country. Bilateral exchange rates are still assumed to be fully flexible and determined by equation (8), but now the currency preference shift variables are set equal to zero. The changes in real government spending by 1975 needed to achieve the trade balance targets range from a decline of 6.2 percentage points of GDP in the United States to an increase of 6.4 percentage points in Britain.[26] The effect on the domestic economy is quite different from that arising from currency preference shifts. The cut in government spending in those countries assumed to aim at an improved trade balance position (United States, Germany, France, and Canada) results in lower real interest rates and releases the resources needed for the improvement in the external position. Moreover, part of these resources are used to raise investment spending. Consequently, in these countries output rises in table 9, whereas in table 7 output falls. Partly as a result of this higher output, domestic absorption either does not fall as much relative to baseline as in table 7, or, in the case of Canada, it actually increases. However, the rise in output occurs only in the medium term as the fiscal consolidation crowds in domestic investment. Table 10 shows that, in the case of the United States, the decline in real government spending reduces output below its baseline path in 1971 and 1972; only in 1973 does it rise above baseline. Although the different levels of output in these scenarios may appear inconsistent with internal balance, the change in GDP reflects the change in potential output resulting from differences in real interest rates.

For these four countries the required real exchange rate change brought about by fiscal policy is somewhat higher than in the case considered above where currency preferences shifted. This would appear to

---

25. Although there are several other exogenous variables that could have been used to attain the current account targets, two likely candidates, one a policy variable and the other a structural shift, were infeasible. Monetary policy could not be used since it is neutral in Multimod after several years. Surprisingly, productivity changes could not be used to attain a current account target. An increase in potential output raises real income and lowers prices, and these have opposite effects on the trade balance. The net effect, which depends on several underlying parameters, was very small, and therefore productivity shocks could not be used to achieve a given level of the current account.

26. These calculations are, again, purely illustrative and in no way reflect policy recommendations. It is quite unlikely that a fiscal expansion of 6.4 percent of GDP for Britain would have been politically feasible or an optimal policy stance.

Table 9 Calculation of DEERs using Multimod: targeted trade balances with changes in fiscal policy instead of currency preferences[a]

Variables and calculated DEERs	Canada	France	Germany	Italy	Japan	United Kingdom	United States
Trade balance as a ratio to GDP	0.6	0.8	0.5	−0.6	−1.4	−1.0	1.0
Current account as a ratio to GDP	2.4	0.8	1.0	−1.4	−2.1	−2.6	0.8
GDP	1.8	1.5	0.9	0.8	0.2	−1.2	1.8
Domestic absorption	1.3	−0.3	−0.1	3.4	2.9	2.4	−0.1
Foreign absorption	0.2	1.1	1.0	0.5	0.4	0.6	1.1
Real long-term interest rate[b]	−2.4	−2.1	−1.6	−1.0	−1.4	0.8	−2.2
PX/PFM[c]	−5.2	−6.0	−2.5	12.5	18.7	15.0	−14.3
PGDP/PM[d]	−1.1	−8.6	−3.1	19.5	32.4	20.6	−14.9
Nominal effective exchange rate	−1.4	−7.2	−3.0	17.6	31.2	11.9	−15.3
DEER calculations (1970 parity = 100)							
From table 5, column 2	94.3	95.3	98.6	110.9	124.6	108.6	89.0
Average of changes in PX/PFM and PGDP/PM	96.8	92.7	97.2	116.0	125.6	117.8	85.4
Memorandum item:							
Change in real government spending as percentage of GDP	−3.3	−4.8	−3.4	2.7	4.3	6.4	−6.2

a. Results are expressed as percentage deviations from baseline in 1975, unless otherwise indicated.
b. In percentage points.
c. Export price divided by competitors' prices in foreign markets.
d. GDP deflator divided by the import deflator.

Table 10 Calculation of DEER for the US dollar using Multimod: targeted trade balances with changes in fiscal policy instead of currency preferences[a]

Variable	1971	1972	1973	1974	1975	1976	1977
Trade balance as a ratio to GDP	0.2	0.8	1.0	1.1	1.0	1.0	1.0
Current account as a ratio to GDP	0.2	0.7	0.9	0.9	0.8	0.8	0.9
GDP	−2.4	−0.9	0.6	1.4	1.8	1.6	1.5
Domestic absorption	−3.4	−2.6	−1.3	−0.5	−0.1	−0.3	−0.4
Foreign absorption	−0.5	0.2	0.9	1.2	1.1	1.1	1.0
Real long-term interest rate[b]	−1.2	−2.0	−2.3	−2.4	−2.2	−1.9	−1.6
PX/PFM[c]	−13.2	−14.3	−15.0	−15.0	−14.3	−13.3	−12.7
PGDP/PM[d]	−15.0	−15.7	−16.0	−15.7	−14.9	−14.2	−13.7
Nominal effective exchange rate	−17.0	−17.1	−16.8	−16.3	−15.3	−14.4	−13.9

a. Results are expressed as percentage deviations from baseline, unless otherwise indicated.
b. In percentage points.
c. Export price divided by competitors' prices in foreign markets.
d. GDP deflator divided by the import deflator.

reflect the fact that the increase in output induced by the fiscal policy change results in a smaller decline in domestic absorption than in table 7 without any offset in foreign absorption, thereby necessitating a larger depreciation to achieve the same trade balance objective. The same argument applies, but in the opposite direction, to those countries (Japan, Britain, and Italy) that are assumed to alter fiscal policy to reduce their trade surpluses. The assumed increase in government spending in these countries lowers output by 1975 relative to the simulation described in table 7, thereby moderating the rise in absorption and increasing the magnitude of the appreciation needed to reduce the trade balance by the amount shown in the first line of the table. In comparing the results of tables 7 and 9 it is also interesting that the impact on the current account is quite different in a number of cases depending on whether a country is a net creditor or a net debtor. These differences arise in part because, in the scenario in table 9, interest rates on dollar-denominated instruments are considerably lower (roughly 3 percentage points) than in the results reported in table 7. As a result, the United States—a net creditor in those years—experiences a much smaller improvement in its current account, whereas Canada—a net debtor—experiences a substantially greater improvement in its current account in table 9 compared with table 7.

DEERs Associated with a Move to Potential Output

As noted at the beginning of this section, the calculations of DEERs described above using Multimod do not take account of departures of actual output from potential in 1971. Output was estimated to be below potential in all the major industrial countries except Germany and France, where output was estimated to be above potential, and Italy, where output was equal to potential. We now take account of this discrepancy between actual and potential output in the calculation of the DEERs. In order to calculate the effect of moving to potential, we exogenously shifted productivity beginning in 1971 to open the gap between actual and potential output that was estimated to exist in that year.[27] Between 1971 and 1975 the natural economic forces operating in the model are sufficient to close this gap by the end of the five-year period. For example, for countries below potential there is downward pressure on prices, interest rates, and the exchange rate that induces a rise in total spending that brings output back to potential. These endogenous effects are incorporated in the simulation results reported in table 11. In addition, currency preference shift variables are introduced in the same manner as in table 7 to achieve the same trade balance objectives as in the second line of that table. Thus, the figures in table 11 reflect the effects of a compound experiment that involves both moving the major industrial countries to potential output by 1975 and achieving trade surpluses equal to 1 percent of GDP in 1975.

The effect of moving to potential output can be seen by comparing the results in table 11 with those in table 7. For those countries that had output gaps in 1971—the United States, Japan, Britain, and Canada—the comparison shows that, as one would expect, the deviation of output and domestic absorption from baseline is either positive or less negative as a result of moving to potential output. As a consequence, a larger real effective exchange rate depreciation is needed to achieve a given improvement in the trade balance in the case of the United States. In the case of Canada, the improvement in the trade balance can be achieved with roughly the same real depreciation, because a move by the United States to potential output significantly increases the demand for Canadian exports and offsets the effect of higher output in Canada on its demand for imports. The appreciation of the yen is the same in both cases, as the higher output and absorption, which would tend to reduce the needed appreciation, are counterbalanced by a smaller reduction in foreign absorption that would tend to result in higher demand for Japanese exports. In the case of Britain, the higher output and domestic

---

27. An alternative method would have been to lower the baseline level of output by the amount of the gap. As Multimod is fairly linear in the neighborhood of potential output, this alternative calculation would have yielded results similar to those reported.

Table 11 Calculation of DEERs using Multimod: targeted trade balances and achieving potential output with changes in currency preferences[a]

Variables and calculated DEERs	Canada	France	Germany	Italy	Japan	United Kingdom	United States
Trade balance as a ratio to GDP	0.6	0.6	0.6	-1.0	-1.7	-1.2	1.0
Current account as a ratio to GDP	0.0	0.8	1.3	-2.9	-2.5	1.9	1.3
GDP	1.0	-4.3	-1.5	0.8	2.5	2.2	0.8
Domestic absorption	0.5	-4.1	-2.1	3.2	5.2	3.4	-1.1
Foreign absorption	-0.6	0.3	0.1	-0.9	-0.6	-0.5	0.6
Real long-term interest rate[b]	0.3	0.8	0.6	-0.6	-1.7	-1.2	0.5
PX/PFM[c]	-4.3	4.1	0.2	9.8	16.5	1.2	-14.2
PGDP/PM[d]	-0.3	5.4	-0.5	13.9	28.3	1.1	-15.1
Nominal effective exchange rate	-2.0	0.7	-3.0	16.7	35.6	4.6	-18.9
DEER calculations (1970 parity = 100)							
From table 5, column 1	94.7	106.0	99.6	107.8	125.0	101.7	87.7
Average of changes in PX/PFM and PGDP/PM	97.7	104.8	99.7	111.8	122.4	101.1	85.4

a. Results are expressed as percentage deviations from baseline in 1975, unless otherwise indicated.
b. In percentage points.
c. Export price divided by competitors' prices in foreign markets.
d. GDP deflator divided by the import deflator.

absorption, combined with little difference in the change in foreign absorption between the two scenarios, mean that the appreciation required to reduce the trade surplus by a given magnitude is reduced.

Looking now at France and Germany—the two countries whose output was above potential in 1971—the effect of moving output down to potential (i.e., removing the cyclical excess demand) is to put upward pressure on the exchange rate. In the case of France, this causes a switch in the sign of the exchange rate change from a depreciation to an appreciation. This happens because the decline in output and absorption is so large that an appreciation is needed to offset what would otherwise be an excessively sharp drop in import demand.[28] The case of Germany is similar, but the magnitude of the shift is much less sharp.

The Multimod simulations of the effects of moving to potential output reported in tables 11 and 12 can be compared with the results in the base case in table 5 obtained using the comparative static approach. After scaling the exchange rate changes in table 11 by the ratio of the targeted change in the trade balance–GDP ratio to the actual trade balance–GDP ratio shown in table 11, the calculated exchange rate changes are quite close for four countries (Germany, France, Italy, and Britain). The Multimod calculations show a somewhat larger depreciation in the case of the United States, and a smaller depreciation in the case of Canada; the reasons for these differences from the results of the comparative static analysis would appear to be those already discussed above in connection with table 7. In the case of Japan, the calculated appreciation of the yen is smaller in the Multimod simulation on account of the large increase in GDP, which means that a smaller appreciation is needed to achieve a given change in the trade balance compared with the comparative static approach, where output is exogenous. It is also noteworthy that the estimated impact on the real exchange rate of moving to potential output is quite similar whichever of the two methods is used, as can be seen by comparing tables 11 and 7 for Multimod and the base case with the results under "No adjustment for cyclical factors" in table 5 for the comparative static method.

Current Account versus Trade Balance Targets

Up to this point the analysis has focused on achieving a given change in the trade balance relative to GDP. This was done for two reasons: first, so that the results could be compared directly with the earlier comparative static calculations, and second, to avoid complications from interactions between the trade account and net interest payments arising

---

28. The estimated excess of actual output over potential output in 1971 in France may well be too high. Nonetheless, this simulation result illustrates the importance of taking account of cyclical developments in calculating DEERs.

Table 12   Calculation of DEER for the US dollar using Multimod: targeted trade balances and achieving potential output with changes in currency preferences[a]

Variable	1971	1972	1973	1974	1975	1976	1977
Trade balance as a ratio to GDP	−0.1	0.7	1.0	1.1	1.0	1.0	1.0
Current account as a ratio to GDP	−0.1	0.8	1.1	1.4	1.3	1.3	1.4
GDP	0.5	0.9	0.9	0.8	0.8	0.9	1.0
Domestic absorption	−0.4	−0.6	−0.9	−1.0	−1.1	−1.1	−1.0
Foreign absorption	0.0	0.4	0.6	0.8	0.6	0.6	0.6
Real long-term interest rate[b]	0.8	0.8	0.8	0.6	0.5	0.4	0.4
PX/PFM[c]	−13.7	−13.6	−13.8	−14.0	−14.2	−14.2	−14.0
PGDP/PM[d]	−15.1	−14.7	−14.6	−14.9	−15.1	−15.3	−15.2
Nominal effective exchange rate	−19.4	−19.0	−18.9	−19.0	−18.9	−18.7	−18.3

a. Results are expressed as percentage deviations from baseline, unless otherwise indicated.
b. In percentage points.
c. Export price divided by competitors' prices in foreign markets.
d. GDP deflator divided by the import deflator.

directly as well as indirectly from valuation effects due to exchange rate changes. However, it is important to take these interactions into account, as was emphasized in the preceding section. Consequently a Multimod simulation was run in which the objective was to achieve a change in the current account–GDP ratio as close as possible to that achieved for the trade balance–GDP ratio in table 7.

The results of this simulation are reported in table 13, where again the required exchange rate movements were brought about by changes in currency preferences. Because the impact of changes in the net foreign asset position on the current account is taken into account, and the effects on net interest payments go in the same direction as the trade balance, the required change in the real effective exchange rate is typically smaller than if the trade balance is targeted. A comparison of the results for exchange rate changes in table 13 with those in table 7 shows that this is indeed the case for all countries except Canada, which is discussed below. Moreover, a comparison of tables 14 and 8 shows that the magnitude of the real effective exchange rate change in the US dollar to achieve a given improvement in the US current account declines over time (relative to the change needed for the same improvement in the trade balance) on account of the change in net foreign assets.

The interaction between the net foreign asset position and the current account was discussed in detail in the previous section. However, the

Table 13 Calculation of DEERs using Multimod: targeted current account balances with changes in currency preferences[a]

Variables and calculated DEERs	Canada	France	Germany	Italy	Japan	United Kingdom	United States
Trade balance as a ratio to GDP	1.0	0.5	0.3	-0.5	-1.4	-0.9	0.7
Current account as a ratio to GDP	0.4	0.7	0.6	-1.1	-1.5	-0.9	1.0
GDP	-0.6	-0.3	-0.3	0.6	1.6	0.4	-0.6
Domestic absorption	-1.7	-1.1	-0.6	1.7	3.6	2.1	-1.8
Foreign absorption	-1.2	0.1	-0.1	-0.4	-0.9	0.1	-0.1
Real long-term interest rate[b]	1.6	0.6	0.5	-0.5	-1.8	-1.2	0.7
PX/PFM[c]	-4.4	-1.6	-0.3	4.4	12.1	4.9	-8.4
PGDP/PM[d]	-2.4	-2.4	-0.7	6.3	19.5	6.2	-9.1
Nominal effective exchange rate	-5.5	-3.8	-1.7	8.0	26.3	8.5	-12.1

a. Results are expressed as percentage deviations from baseline in 1975, unless otherwise indicated.
b. In percentage points.
c. Export price divided by competitors' prices in foreign markets.
d. GDP deflator divided by the import deflator.

Table 14   Calculation of DEER for the US dollar using Multimod: targeted current account balances with changes in currency preferences[a]

Variable	1971	1972	1973	1974	1975	1976	1977
Trade balance as a ratio to GDP	0.0	0.5	0.7	0.8	0.7	0.6	0.7
Current account as a ratio to GDP	0.0	0.6	0.9	1.0	1.0	0.9	1.0
GDP	0.1	0.0	−0.3	−0.6	−0.6	−0.6	−0.5
Domestic absorption	−0.5	−1.1	−1.5	−1.8	−1.8	−1.8	−1.7
Foreign absorption	−0.1	0.0	0.1	0.1	−0.1	−0.1	−0.1
Real long-term interest rate[b]	0.8	1.0	1.0	0.9	0.7	0.6	0.5
PX/PFM[c]	−0.9	−8.8	−8.6	−8.5	−8.4	−8.2	−7.8
PGDP/PM[d]	−10.5	−9.8	−9.3	−9.2	−9.1	−9.1	−8.8
Nominal effective exchange rate	−13.4	−13.0	−12.5	−12.3	−12.1	−11.8	−11.3

a. Results are expressed as percentage deviations from baseline, unless otherwise indicated.
b. In percentage points.
c. Export price divided by competitors' prices in foreign markets.
d. GDP deflator divided by the import deflator.

analysis there considered the case where the initial real effective exchange rate differed from the initial estimate of the DEER, leading to a final adjustment of the DEER *larger* than the initial misalignment. Thus, that analysis dealt with an adjustment to the DEER to account for an initial misalignment. In contrast, the comparison of tables 13 and 7 does not involve a misalignment; rather, the required change in the real effective exchange rate needed to achieve a change in the current account is *smaller* than that required to realize a change in the trade balance of the same magnitude, because of the effects on debt service, which have an impact on the current account but not on the trade balance.

However, the simulation results for Canada run counter to this general tendency; the Canadian dollar depreciates by a larger amount even though the change in the current account is only 0.4 percent, which is less than the 0.5 percent change in the trade balance actually achieved in table 7 and less than the targeted change of 0.6 percent. The reason for this difference is that, because Canada is a large net debtor, there are two factors operating to counteract the positive effect of the trade balance on the current account. First, interest rates on US dollar–denominated claims rise, and as it is assumed that the net foreign assets of all major industrial countries are denominated in US dollars, this increases Canadian net interest payments in US dollars. Second, as the targeted current account is measured in local currency, and as the Canadian dollar depreciates slightly against the US dollar, there is a negative valuation effect that also adversely affects the flow of net interest payments. As a result of these two factors, a larger exchange rate change is needed to achieve the fairly substantial change in the trade balance required for the assumed improvement in the current account.

Concluding Remarks

As noted at the beginning of this paper, the focus of the analysis has been on methods for calculating exchange rates consistent with a desired position of internal and external balance. The basic approach taken here is that making an assessment of a country's exchange rate not only involves looking at recent developments in a country's international competitive position and external accounts, but also requires taking a broader perspective by examining the extent to which a country's real effective exchange rate is consistent with sustainable positions of internal balance. This broader approach has aimed at estimating what have been referred to in the literature as "equilibrium" or "fundamental equilibrium" exchange rates in a multilateral context in which all major industrial countries are at their desired positions of macroeconomic balance.

Attention has concentrated on illustrating the use of two different methods to compute such rates: a comparative static, partial-equilibrium approach based on elasticities and multipliers, and a dynamic macroeconomic approach using the International Monetary Fund's Multimod macroeconomic model. In addition, we demonstrated how dynamic complications (hysteresis effects) may arise while the actual real exchange rate is away from the desired equilibrium exchange rate. It should be realized, first of all, that the use of these approaches to derive estimates of DEERs is itself at a preliminary stage; the methods employed in each approach need to be developed further and refinements made in the analysis in order to develop confidence in the robustness of the results. Second, it should be clear from the application of both approaches that the estimated DEERs depend very much on the assumptions made about desirable positions for an economy both domestically and internationally. In particular, the section on comparative static analyses pointed out that the calculated DEER is very sensitive to the assumption regarding external balance. Therefore it needs to be stressed that the objective of achieving trade and current account balances equal to 1 percent of GDP was assumed for illustrative purposes only and is not meant to have any normative significance.

It is perhaps surprising that in many cases the estimates obtained using the two approaches are fairly similar, differing by no more than 10 percent for any country. Where differences are significant, the reason often seems to lie in the fact that the general-equilibrium approach takes account of the country's net international investment position and net investment income as well as the domestic and foreign macroeconomic effects of the exchange rate.[29] Although the results for the exchange rate are often similar, the simulated effects on other macroeconomic variables, such as real interest rates and output, can be quite different, depending on the manner in which the exchange rate change is achieved. For example, these results show that a country requiring a reduction in its external deficit will experience a significantly better economic performance if the exchange rate change is brought about through appropriate fiscal action rather than through changes in currency preferences.[30] From this perspective, the general-equilibrium approach would appear to have a clear advantage over the simpler comparative static method. However, the latter has the advantage of being easy to implement, so that the implications of alternative assumptions can be obtained quickly. Moreover, this method can easily be extended to other countries without the need to estimate an entire model. Thus, although Multimod is a more appropriate vehicle for estimating DEERs because it takes account of macroeconomic interactions, the partial-equilibrium approach has certain clear advantages that lend themselves to practical applications.

An important conclusion is that a range of estimates of DEERs can be obtained using alternative but plausible assumptions regarding underlying parameters and variables, with the range between the highest and lowest estimates of the DEER for any country lying between 10 and 30 percent in the illustrative calculations presented in the section using a comparative static approach. The width of this range underlines the need for caution in identifying any given set of exchange rates as "the" appropriate equilibrium values. Nevertheless, the analysis presented here provides a useful framework that can be used to generate a plausible set of estimates of the DEER as a benchmark for judging whether exchange rates are in line with economic fundamentals.

References

Artis, Michael J., and M. P. Taylor. 1993. "DEER Hunting: Misalignment, Debt Accumulation, and Desired Equilibrium Exchange Rates." Working Paper No. WP/93/48. Washington: International Monetary Fund (June).

---

29. In some cases, however, the Multimod results appear to reflect specific assumptions, such as the assumption that all foreign assets are denominated in US dollars.

30. In this connection it should be noted that the IMF staff in its work on exchange rates tries to encourage countries to pursue appropriate underlying economic policies and would take account of the implications of the different adjustment paths described here.

Artus, Jacques. 1977. "Methods of Assessing the Long-Run Equilibrium Value of an Exchange Rate." Working Paper No. DM/77/124. Washington: International Monetary Fund (December).

Artus, Jacques, and Rudolph R. Rhomberg. 1973. "A Multilateral Exchange Rate Model." *Staff Papers* 20: 591–611. Washington: International Monetary Fund.

Barrell, R., and S. Wren-Lewis. 1989. "Equilibrium Exchange Rates for the G7." Discussion Paper No. 323. London: Centre for Economic Policy Research.

Branson, William. 1979. "Exchange Rate Dynamics and Monetary Policy." In Assar Lindbeck, ed., *Inflation and Employment in Open Economies*. Amsterdam: North-Holland.

Church, Keith B. 1992. "Properties of Fundamental Equilibrium Exchange Rate Models of the UK Economy." *National Institute Economic Review* (August): 62–70.

Cross, R. 1992. "On the Foundations of Hysteresis in Economic Systems." Discussion Paper No. 4. Strathclyde, Scotland: International Centre for Macroeconomic Modelling, University of Strathclyde.

Currie, D., and S. Wren-Lewis. 1989. "Evaluating Blueprints for the Conduct of International Macropolicy." *American Economic Review* 79: 264–69.

de Vries, Margaret Garritsen. 1976. *The International Monetary Fund, 1966–71: Volume 1, Narrative*. Washington: International Monetary Fund.

Frenkel, J. A., and M. Goldstein. 1986. "A Guide to Target Zones." *Staff Papers* 33: 633–73. Washington: International Monetary Fund.

Garber, Peter M. 1993. "The Collapse of the Bretton Woods Fixed Exchange Rate System." In Michael D. Bordo and Barry Eichengreen, eds., *A Retrospective on the Bretton Woods System*. Chicago: University of Chicago Press.

International Monetary Fund. 1970. "The Role of Exchange Rates in the Adjustment of International Payments: A Report by the Executive Directors." Washington: International Monetary Fund.

International Monetary Fund. 1984. "Issues in the Assessment of the Exchange Rates of Industrial Countries." Occasional Paper No. 29. Washington: International Monetary Fund.

Masson, P., S. Symansky, and G. Meredith. 1990. "MULTIMOD Mark II: A Revised and Extended Model." Occasional Paper No. 71. Washington: International Monetary Fund.

McKinnon, Ronald I. 1993. "The Rules of the Game: Money in Historical Perspective." *Journal of Economic Literature* 31: 1–44.

Nurkse, R. 1945. "Conditions of International Monetary Equilibrium." Essays in International Finance 4. Princeton, NJ: Princeton University Press.

Solomon, Robert. 1982. *The International Monetary System, 1945–81*. New York: Harper and Row.

Taylor, M. P. 1994. "Exchange Rate Behavior Under Alternative Exchange Rate Regimes." In P. Kenen, ed., *Understanding Interdependence: The Macroeconomics of the Open Economy*. Princeton, NJ: Princeton University Press.

Volcker, Paul A., and Toyoo Gyohten. 1992. *Changing Fortunes: The World's Money and the Threat to American Leadership*. New York: Times Books.

Williamson, John. 1977. *The Failure of World Monetary Reform, 1971–74*. New York: New York University Press.

Williamson, John. 1985. "The Exchange Rate System." POLICY ANALYSES IN INTERNATIONAL ECONOMICS 5. Washington: Institute for International Economics.

Williamson, John. 1991. "FEERs and the ERM." *National Institute Economic Review* (August).

Williamson, John, and Marcus H. Miller. 1987. "Targets and Indicators: A Blueprint for the International Coordination of Economic Policy." POLICY ANALYSES IN INTERNATIONAL ECONOMICS 22. Washington: Institute for International Economics.

Wren-Lewis, Simon. 1992. "On the Analytical Foundations of the Fundamental Equilibrium Exchange Rate." In C. P. Hargreaves, ed., *Macroeconomic Modeling of the Long Run*, pp. 323–38. Aldershot, England: Edward Elgar.

Wren-Lewis, Simon, P. Westaway, S. Soteri, and R. Barrell. 1991. "Evaluating the United Kingdom's Choice of Entry Rate Into the ERM." *Manchester School* 59 (Supplement): 1–22.

3

Real and Monetary Determinants of Real Exchange Rate Behavior: Theory and Evidence from Developing Countries

SEBASTIAN EDWARDS

Recent discussions on macroeconomic policy in the developing and developed countries have emphasized the crucial role played by the real exchange rate (RER) in the adjustment process. There is growing agreement that sustained real exchange rate misalignment will usually generate severe macroeconomic disequilibria, and that the correction of external imbalances (i.e., current account deficits) will generally require both demand management policies *and* a real exchange rate devaluation. Also, in recent policy evaluations of the performance of the less developed countries it has been argued that more "successful" developing countries owe much of their success to having been able to maintain the real exchange rate at its "appropriate" level.[1] It is not an overstatement

This is a revised version of a paper presented at the first InterAmerican Seminar on Economics (IASE), Mexico City, 17-19 March 1988. Parts of this paper were written while the author was a visiting scholar in the Research Department of the IMF. Conversations with Peter Montiel and Mohsin Khan have been very helpful. The author is grateful to Ignacio Trigueros, Nisso Bucay, Herminio Blanco, and Albert Fishlow for very helpful comments. The author has also benefited from comments by the participants of the National Bureau of Economic Research Mini-Conference on "International Trade and Finance with Limited Global Integration," Cambridge, MA, 20 February 1988. The author thanks Miguel Savastano and David Gould for efficient research assistance. Financial support from the National Science Foundation and from the Academic Senate of the University of California, Los Angeles is gratefully acknowledged.

1. On the role of real exchange rate misalignment see, for example, Dornbusch (1982) and Williamson (1985). On real exchange rates and economic performance see Harberger (1986) and Dervis and Petri (1987).

to say that real exchange rate behavior now occupies a central role in policy evaluation and design.

In spite of the importance that real exchange rates have attained in recent policy discussions, there have basically been no attempts to analyze empirically the forces behind real exchange rate behavior in the developing countries.[2] In many ways the issue of real exchange rate determination in the developing countries has remained murky, with most of the discussion being carried on at an informal level. Moreover, in reviewing the literature on the subject it is surprising to find virtually no studies that formally attempt to explain the distinction between equilibrium and disequilibrium (i.e., misaligned) real exchange rates. The purpose of this paper is to develop a theory of real exchange rate behavior and empirically test its main implications using data for a group of developing countries. In particular this research seeks to analyze the relative importance of monetary and real variables in the process of real exchange rate determination in both the short and the long run.

The paper is organized as follows: in the next section a dynamic model of real exchange rate determination for a small, open economy with a dual nominal exchange rate system is developed. Subsequent sections provide preliminary data analysis on real exchange rate behavior for a group of 12 developing countries, and test empirically the main implications of the model using data for the same 12 countries. The final section presents the conclusions.

The Model

This section develops a model of real exchange rate determination that allows for both real and nominal factors to play a role in the short run. In the long run, however, only real factors—the "fundamentals"—influence the *equilibrium real exchange rate*. The model attempts to capture in a simple way some of the most salient macroeconomic features of the developing economies, including the existence of exchange controls, trade barriers, and a freely determined parallel exchange rate for financial transactions.

The model considers a three-good—exportables, importables, and nontradables—small, open economy. There is a dual nominal exchange rate system and a government sector. It is assumed that this country produces the exportable (X) and nontradable (N) goods and consumes the importable (M) and the nontradable goods. Nationals of this country hold both domestic money (M) and foreign money (F). Initially it is

---

2. The situation is not really better when it comes to the developed countries. Here most recent empirical work has dealt with whether real exchange rates have a unit root, without significant efforts being devoted to analyzing the way in which RERs have responded to fundamentals. In the case of developing nations the study by Khan (1986) is an exception.

assumed that there are effective capital controls, so that there is no international capital mobility. However, it is assumed that the private sector has inherited a given stock of foreign money F. The government consumes importables and nontradables and uses both nondistortionary taxes and domestic credit creation to finance its expenditures. It is assumed that the government, as well as the private sector, cannot borrow from abroad. Also, it is assumed that there is no domestic public debt. Later, the assumption of no capital mobility is relaxed; it is assumed that the government is not subject to capital controls, and that there are some capital flows in and out of the country.

The dual nominal exchange rate system is characterized by a fixed nominal exchange rate (E) for commercial transactions and a freely floating nominal exchange rate (δ) for financial transactions. This latter rate takes whatever level is required to achieve asset market equilibrium. This assumption of a dual exchange rate system is made as a way of capturing the fact that in most developing countries there is a parallel market (many times a "gray" or "black" market) for financial transactions. It is assumed that there is a tariff on imports (τ) and that, in the tradition of international trade theory, its proceeds are handed back to the public in a nondistortionary way. It is assumed that the price of exportables in terms of foreign currency is fixed and equal to unity ($P_X^* = 1$). Finally, it is assumed that there is perfect foresight.

The model is given by equations (1) through (16) below:

Portfolio decisions

$$A = M + \delta F$$

$$a = m + \rho F \tag{1}$$

where:
$$a = A/E, \quad m = M/E, \quad \rho = \delta/E \tag{2}$$

$$m = \sigma(\dot\delta/\delta)\rho F, \quad \sigma' < 0; \tag{3}$$

$$\dot F = 0. \tag{4}$$

Demand side

$$P_M = EP_M^* + \tau, \quad e_X = E/P_N, \quad e_M = P_M/P_N, \quad e_M^* = (P_M^* E)/P_N; \tag{5}$$

$$C_M = C_M(e_M, a), \quad \frac{\partial C_M}{\partial e_M} < 0, \quad \frac{\partial C_M}{\partial a} > 0; \tag{6}$$

$$C_N = C_N(e_M, a), \quad \frac{\partial C_N}{\partial e_M} > 0, \quad \frac{\partial C_N}{\partial a} < 0. \tag{7}$$

Supply side

$$Q_X = Q_X(e_X), \quad \frac{\partial Q_X}{\partial e_X} > 0; \tag{8}$$

$$Q_N = Q_N(e_X), \quad \frac{\partial Q_N}{\partial e_X} < 0. \tag{9}$$

Government sector

$$G = P_N G_N + E P_M^* G_M; \tag{10}$$

$$\frac{E P_M^* G_M}{G} = \lambda; \tag{11}$$

$$G = t + \dot{D}. \tag{12}$$

External sector

$$CA = Q_X(e_X) - P_M^* C_M(e_M, a) - P_M^* G_M; \tag{13}$$

$$\dot{R} = CA; \tag{14}$$

$$\dot{M} = \dot{D} + E\dot{R}; \tag{15}$$

$$e = \alpha e_M^* + (1 - \alpha)e_X = \frac{E[\alpha P_M^* + (1 - \alpha)P_X^*]}{P_N}. \tag{16}$$

Equation (1) defines total assets (A) in domestic currency as the sum of domestic money (M) plus foreign money (F) times the free market nominal exchange rate. Equation (2) defines *real* assets in terms of the exportable good, where E is the (fixed) commercial rate and $\rho = \delta/E$ is the spread between the free (δ) and the commercial (E) nominal exchange rate. Equation (3) is the portfolio composition equation and establishes that the desired ratio of real domestic money to real foreign money is a negative function of the expected rate of depreciation of the free rate δ. Since perfect foresight is assumed, in equation (3) expected depreciation has been replaced by the actual rate of depreciation. Equation (4) establishes that there is no capital mobility and that no commercial transactions are subject to the financial rate δ. It is assumed, however, that this economy has inherited a positive stock of foreign money, so that $F_0 > 0$.

Equations (5) through (9) summarize the demand and supply sides. Variables e_M and e_X are the (domestic) relative prices of importables and exportables with respect to nontradables. Notice that e_M includes the tariff on imports. Variable e_M^*, on the other hand, is defined as the relative price of importables to nontradables that excludes the tariff. Naturally, e_M is the relevant price for consumption and production decisions. Demand for nontradable and importable goods depends on the relative price of importables and on the level of real assets; supply functions, on the other hand, depend on the price of exportables relative to nontradables. Equations (10) and (11) summarize the government sector, where G_M and G_N are consumption of M and N, respectively. It is convenient to express real government consumption in terms of exportables as

$$g = g_M + g_N,$$ (10')

where $g = G/E$, and $g_N = G_N P_N/E$. Equation (11) defines the ratio of government consumption on importable goods as λ. Equation (12) is the government budget constraint and says that government consumption has to be financed via nondistortionary taxes (t) and domestic credit creation $\dot{D}$. Notice, however, that under fixed nominal commercial rates a positive rate of growth of domestic credit ($\dot{D} > 0$) is not sustainable. Stationary equilibrium, then, is achieved when $G = t$ and $\dot{D} = 0$. If, however, a crawling peg is assumed for the commercial rate [i.e., $(\dot{E}/E) > 0$], it is possible to have a positive $\dot{D}$ consistent with the rate of the crawl.

Equations (13) through (16) summarize the external sector. Equation (13) defines the current account in foreign currency as the difference between output of exportables Q_X and total (private plus public sector) consumption of importables. Equation (14) establishes that in this model, with no capital mobility and a freely determined financial rate, the balance of payments ($\dot{R}$) is identical to the current account, where R is the stock of international reserves held by the central bank, expressed in foreign currency. It is assumed that initially there is a positive stock of international reserves (R_0). Equation (15) provides the link between changes in international reserves, changes in domestic credit, and changes in the domestic stock of money. Finally, the model is closed with equation (16), which is the definition of the real exchange rate as the relative price of tradables to nontradables. Notice that this definition of the RER excludes the tariff on imports. This is done because most empirical measures of RER exclude import tariffs or taxes. Naturally, for the theoretical discussion it would be trivial to compute all the results for an alternative definition of RER that included τ.[3]

Long-run sustainable equilibrium is attained when the nontradable goods market and the external sector (current account and balance of payments) are simultaneously in equilibrium. Because of the assumption of tight exchange controls, long-run sustainable equilibrium in the external sector implies that the current account CA is in equilibrium in *every* period. In the short and even the medium run, however, there can be departures from $CA = 0$. This, of course, will result in the accumulation or disaccumulation of international reserves. A steady state is

---

3. In Edwards (1989) I discuss in detail the issues related to alternative definitions of the real exchange rate; see also Edwards (1988a).

attained when the following four conditions hold simultaneously: the nontradables market clears; the external sector is in equilibrium: $\dot{R} = 0 = CA = \dot{m}$; fiscal policy is sustainable: $G = t$; and portfolio equilibrium holds. The real exchange rate prevailing under these steady-state conditions is the *long-run equilibrium real exchange rate* ($\bar{e}_{LR}$).

The nontradable goods market clears when

$$C_N(e_M, a) + G_N = Q_N(e_X). \tag{17}$$

Notice that $G_N = e_X g_N$, where g_N is *real* government consumption of N in terms of exportable goods. From equation (17) it is possible to express the *equilibrium* price of nontradables as a function of a, g_N, P_M^*, and τ:

$$P_N = v(a, g_N, P_M^*, \tau) \quad \text{where} \quad \frac{\partial v}{\partial a} > 0, \frac{\partial v}{\partial g_N} > 0, \frac{\partial v}{\partial P_M^*} > 0, \frac{\partial v}{\partial \tau} > 0. \tag{18}$$

Notice that since the real value of total assets (a) is an endogenous variable we have to investigate how changes in g_N, P_M^*, and τ affect real wealth (a) before solving for P_N.

Since the nominal exchange rate for commercial transactions is fixed, ($\dot{\delta}/\delta$) in the portfolio equilibrium condition in equation (3) can be substituted by the rate of change of the spread ($\dot{\rho}/\rho$). Thus, we can write $m/\rho F = \sigma(\dot{\rho}/\rho)$. Inverting this equation and solving for $\dot{\rho}$, we obtain

$$\dot{\rho} = \rho L\left(\frac{m}{\rho F}\right), \quad L'(\cdot) < 0. \tag{19}$$

In figure 1 the $\dot{\rho} = 0$ schedule has been drawn; it is positively sloped because in order for the public to hold larger amounts of m we need a higher ρ. The greater the spread, the lower the expectations of further increases in the free rate, and thus the greater the amount of (real) domestic money the public is willing to hold.

From equations (10), (12), (13), (14), and (15), the following expression for $\dot{m}$ can be derived:

$$\dot{m} = Q_X(e_X) - C_M(e_M, a) + g_N - t/E. \tag{20}$$

Equilibrium of the external sector requires that $\dot{m} = 0$ (see figure 1). Under the steady-state requirement that government expenditures are fully financed with taxes, the $\dot{R} = 0$ schedule will coincide with the $\dot{m} = 0$ schedule. The intuition for the negative slope of $\dot{m} = 0$ is related to the effects of wealth changes on the current account and on relative prices. An increase in m results in a higher a and in a current account deficit; in order to regain equilibrium, real assets (a) should go down via a decline in ρ.

Figure 1 Equilibrium real balances and parallel market premium

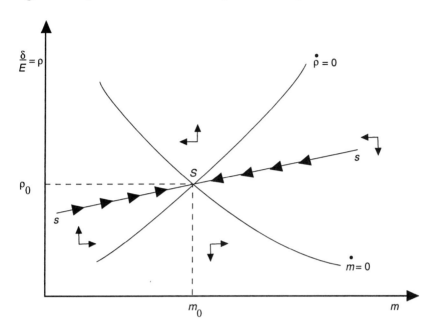

In figure 1 the intersection of the $\dot{\rho} = 0$ and the $\dot{m} = \dot{R} = 0$ schedules determines the steady-state level of real balances m_0 and the steady-state parallel market premium ρ_0. It is easy to show that this system is characterized by saddle path equilibrium. ss is the saddle path, and the arrows denote the dynamic forces at work in this system.[4]

After the steady-state values of ρ and m are determined, equation (18) can be used to find, for the corresponding (exogenous) values of g_N, P^*_M, and τ, the long-run equilibrium price of nontradables. Equation (16) can then be used to find the long-run equilibrium real exchange rate:

$$\tilde{e}_{LR} = v(m_0 + \rho_0 F_0, g_{N_0}, \tau_0, P^*_{M_0}). \tag{21}$$

As can be seen from equation (21), the long-run equilibrium real exchange rate is a function of real variables only—the so-called *fundamentals*. Whenever there are changes in these variables, there will be changes in the *equilibrium* RER. In the short run, however, changes in monetary variables, such as D, $\dot{D}$, and E, will also affect the RER. In the

---

4. The relevant expressions for determining the saddle path stability are:

$$\frac{\partial \dot{m}}{\partial m} = -\left\{ \left[\left(\frac{\partial Q_X}{\partial e^X} \right) \frac{E}{P_N^2} - \left(\frac{P^*_M}{P_N} \right) \left(\frac{\partial C_M}{\partial e_M} \right) \left(\frac{P_M}{P_N} \right) \right] \frac{\partial v}{\partial a} + P^*_M \left(\frac{\partial C_M}{\partial a} \right) \right\} < 0,$$

and $\partial \dot{\rho}/\partial \rho = (L(\cdot) - L'\sigma) > 0$.

rest of this section we analyze how changes in fundamentals affect the long-run equilibrium RER, and how monetary disturbances affect the short-run RER.

Real Disturbances and the Equilibrium Real Exchange Rate
A Tariff Increase

Consider an (unanticipated) increase in import tariffs. In this case the $\dot{\rho} = 0$ schedule will not be affected; the $\dot{m} = 0$ schedule, however, will shift. The parallel movement of this schedule is given by

$$dm|_{\dot{m}=0} = -\frac{\left\{B\left(\dfrac{\partial v}{\partial \tau}\right) + \dfrac{P_M^*}{P_N}\left(\dfrac{\partial C_M}{\partial e_M}\right)\right\}d\tau}{B\dfrac{\partial v}{\partial a} + P_M^*\left(\dfrac{\partial C_M}{\partial a}\right)} \lessgtr 0, \tag{22}$$

where

$$B = \left\{\left(\frac{\partial Q_X}{\partial e_X}\right)\frac{E}{P_N^2} - \frac{P_M^*}{P_N}\left(\frac{\partial C_M}{\partial e_M}\right)\frac{P_M}{P_N}\right\} > 0.$$

The sign of equation (22) is undetermined because $(\partial v/\partial \tau) > 0$ and $(\partial C_M/\partial e_M) < 0$. This implies that as a consequence of the (unanticipated) tariff increase the equilibrium real exchange rate can either appreciate or depreciate. This result is consistent with previous static analysis by Edwards and Van Wijnbergen (1987). The most plausible outcome, however, corresponds to the situation where the direct effect of e_M on demand is stronger than the effect of the tariff on P_N. In what follows it will be assumed that the numerator in equation (22) is positive. In this case the $\dot{m} = 0$ schedule will shift to the right, and the new steady-state equilibrium will be characterized by higher ρ and m (figure 2), and a higher equilibrium price of nontradables. This is both because in this case a higher τ results in substitution in demand away from importables and into nontradables, and because the increases in m and ρ generate a higher value of real assets (a) and thus an additional increase in the demand for N. The dynamics of the adjustment process are also depicted in figure 2; on impact the system jumps to R and then proceeds on the new saddle path to the new steady state T. During the adjustment there is a current account surplus and international reserves are accumulated.

The effect of a hike in import tariffs on the long-run equilibrium real exchange rate e_{LR} is given by

$$d\bar{e}_{LR} = -\left(\frac{e}{P_N}\right)\left\{\left(\frac{\partial v}{\partial a}\right)\left[\frac{\partial m}{\partial \tau} + \frac{\partial \rho}{\partial \tau}\right] + \frac{\partial v}{\partial \tau}\right\}d\tau < 0. \tag{23}$$

Figure 2 The dynamics of adjustment to a tariff increase

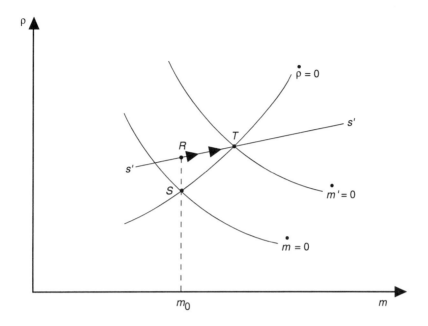

Under the assumption that schedule $\dot{m} = 0$ shifts to the right $(\partial m/\partial \tau) > 0$ and $(\partial \rho/\partial \tau) > 0$, and higher import tariffs will result in a long-term equilibrium real appreciation. The dynamic path followed by e can be easily traced from figure 2.

A Terms-of-Trade Disturbance

Consider now the effects of a worsening in the international terms of trade generated by an increase in the international price of importables P_M^*. As before, the $\dot{\rho} = 0$ schedule is not affected; the $\dot{m} = 0$ schedule, however, will shift. Its parallel movement will be given by

$$
dm\big|_{\dot{m}=0} = -\frac{\left\{ B\dfrac{\partial v}{\partial P_M^*} + \eta + 1 \right\}}{B\dfrac{\partial v}{\partial a} + P_M^*\left(\dfrac{\partial C_M}{\partial a}\right)}\, dP_M^*,
\tag{24}
$$

where $\eta = \{(e_M/C_M)(\partial C_M/\partial e_M)\}$ is the price elasticity of the demand for importables, and B is the same as in equation (22). Again it is not possible to know a priori whether $\dot{m} = 0$ shifts upward or downward. If the demand for importables is sufficiently elastic, and the numerator in equation (24) is positive, the $\dot{m} = 0$ schedule will shift up, and the effects of this disturbance on the system—including on the equilibrium real exchange rate—will be qualitatively the same as in the tariffs case discussed above.

The effects of changes in government consumption on the long-run equilibrium real exchange rate can be analyzed in a similar way. It is easy to show, for example, that an increase in the ratio of government consumption of nontradables will result in an equilibrium long-run real exchange rate appreciation.

Capital Flows

The model presented above assumes that capital controls fully isolate the country from capital movements. Although most developing countries have some kind of capital controls, the assumption of a complete absence of capital flows is not totally satisfactory. In fact, after the debt crisis a number of poor countries had to transfer significant amounts of capital to the international banks. These payments, of course, represent a reversal from the situation in the 1970s, when most developing nations experienced large capital inflows.

The simplest way to incorporate capital flows into the model is by assuming that they are restricted to the government, and by treating them as exogenous. This means equations (12) and (14) have to be modified. In the government budget constraint represented by equation (12) the domestic currency value of these (exogenous) capital flows has to be added to the sources of funds; the foreign-currency value of these capital flows should also be added to the right-hand side of equation (14). Now the current account is no longer equal to the balance of payments. The model is closed by adding an intertemporal budget constraint that establishes that the present value of net capital flows has to be equal to zero, or to the initial stock of foreign debt. Denoting the exogenous capital flows by H and the discount factor (the world interest rate) by r^*, this intertemporal budget constraint is written as follows:

$$\int_0^\infty H e^{-r^* t} dt = 0.$$

In this case changes in the intertemporal distribution of H will have important effects on the dynamics of the real exchange rate. For instance, an (unanticipated) decrease in H, generated by the payment of foreign debt, will result in an equilibrium real depreciation on impact. This real depreciation will last for as long as the country makes the transfer to the rest of the world. Once this is completed a real appreciation will ensue.

Macroeconomic Policies, Real Exchange Rate Misalignment, and Devaluations

We have seen how changes in fundamentals affect the long-run equilibrium RER. We now turn to the effect of nominal disturbances on the actual RER and, thus, on the differential between actual and equilibrium real exchange rates. This will allow us to discuss misalignment issues.

Consider first a once-and-for-all *unanticipated* increase in the stock of domestic credit (D). On impact, this means that there will be a jump in the real stock of money, since $m = M/E = R + D/E$. This is illustrated in figure 3 by the new real stock of domestic money m_1. Assuming that the initial stock of international reserves is "sufficiently" large, the system moves from S to Q on the stationary saddle path, with a higher stock of money m_1 and spread ρ_1 (see below for the case with low reserves). From equation (18) it is easy to see that at Q the *actual* real exchange rate has appreciated relative to its long-run equilibrium value:

$$de = -\frac{e}{P_N}\left\{\left(\frac{\partial v}{\partial a}\right)dm + \left(\frac{\partial v}{\partial a}\right)F\,d\rho\right\} < 0. \tag{25}$$

The reason for this lower short-run real exchange rate is that the demand for nontradables is a function of real assets and of e. At Q the higher m and the higher ρ imply a higher $a(= m + \rho F)$ and, consequently, an incipient excess demand for N, which requires a lower e to reestablish nontradable equilibrium.

Notice that at Q there is also a higher δ. In order to induce the public to (temporarily) hold the higher m relative to F, it is required for them to expect an appreciation of δ [i.e., $(\dot{\delta}/\delta) < 0$]. This is exactly what will happen during the transition period.

The difference between the actual short-run real exchange rate e and its long-run equilibrium level is defined as *real exchange rate overvaluation*. In this case, however, the overvaluation will be short lived, since there will be forces moving the system back toward equilibrium. After the initial once-and-for-all increase in D the economy will adjust along the saddle path ss, moving from Q to S, with reductions of m and ρ. Throughout the transition two things will happen: the stock of international reserves will decline as the public gets rid of the excess domestic money; and the real exchange rate will continuously depreciate via reductions in P_N, moving back toward its long-run sustainable level. However, throughout the adjustment the actual real exchange rate will still be overvalued (i.e., throughout the transition actual e will be below e_{LR}). Only after S is achieved has real exchange rate equilibrium been reestablished.

In the final equilibrium, m, ρ, and e are the same as before the increase in D: monetary disturbances do not affect the long-run equilibrium real

Figure 3 Unanticipated increase in stock of domestic credit

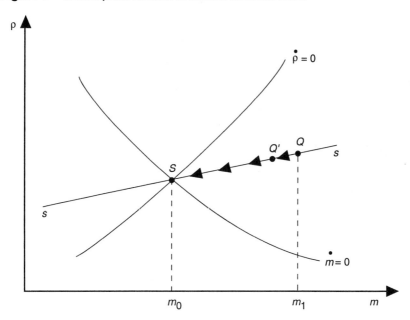

exchange rate. There is, however, a new composition of domestic money with a higher level of D and a lower level of R.

The time taken to move back from Q to S in figure 3 will depend on a number of variables including the magnitude of the original shock and the different elasticities involved. One possible way to accelerate the adjustment is by implementing an unanticipated discrete nominal devaluation of the commercial rate (E). As a result of the higher E the real stock of money (M/E) will jump down. Notice, however, that an important characteristic of discrete nominal devaluations is that, if undertaken from a situation of equilibrium, they will only have short-run effects. If, on the other hand, they are engineered when the economy is out of equilibrium—such as at point Q' in figure 3—they can help speed up the adjustment process. For example, in our case an unanticipated nominal devaluation of the "right amount" in terms of the commercial rate, implemented when the economy is at Q' in figure 3, will result in a jump from Q' to S. The adjustment is much faster than if the system had been left to work its way back to S on its own. Moreover, with the discrete devaluation the total loss of reserves would have been reduced.

For the move from Q to S in figure 3 to be a feasible adjustment path we have to assume that the initial stock of reserves is sufficiently high to cover the loss of reserves that takes place during the transition. If, however, initial reserves are not high enough, the public will anticipate a balance of payments crisis that will include a discrete devaluation in terms of the commercial rate.[5] In this case the adjustment is as depicted in figure 4. Now, at the time of the actual increase in D the public anticipates a future devaluation of E, and as a result there is a further jump in the free rate δ and thus in the spread ρ. On impact then, the system moves to point C in figure 4. As before, at this point the real exchange rate suffers an appreciation relative to its long-run equilibrium level (i.e., it becomes overvalued). The system then moves along the divergent path CG.

Throughout this adjustment path reserves are being lost, and the actual real exchange rate is still overvalued—that is, it is below its long-run sustainable level. The actual depreciation of the fixed rate E takes place when the central bank "runs out" of reserves—or more precisely when reserves reach a predetermined lower threshold. In figure 4 it is assumed that this happens when the system reaches point G. Exactly at this time E is devalued and the system jumps to point H; from there onward the adjustment continues on the saddle path ss. At the time of the devaluation the real stock of money is abruptly reduced, since $m = M/E$. The nominal free rate δ, however, does not jump.[6] The spread $\rho = \delta/E$, on the other hand, does jump down. In terms of the diagram, the fact that δ does not jump when the anticipated devaluation of E actually takes place is captured by point H on the saddle path being along a ray from the origin that goes through G. In figure 4 the magnitude of the devaluation of E is such that the new after-devaluation real stock of money m_2 is below the steady-state level. This means that the final part of the adjustment will take place along the saddle path from H to S, with some of the reserves previously lost being replenished. Notice that at H the real exchange rate has depreciated by more than is required to achieve RER equilibrium.[7]

The initial level of international reserves plays an important role in determining the exact dynamic path followed by this economy. In terms

---

5. On balance of payments crises and speculative attacks see, for example, Krugman (1979), Obstfeld (1984), Flood and Garber (1984), and Calvo (1987). These papers, however, do not consider the case of a dual nominal exchange rate system.

6. If the free rate were to jump there would be an "infinite" return to speculation. This is ruled out by the perfect foresight assumption. Economies with dual exchange rates are investigated by Dornbusch (1986a, 1986b), Lizondo (1987a), Kiguel and Lizondo (1987), and Aizenman (1985).

7. Instead of assuming an unanticipated increase in D, an alternative exercise would consist of a fully expected increase of D. In this case ρ will jump when the public anticipates the future increase of D. Then the system will move toward the northwest on a divergent path; the spread will continue to increase, and reserves will begin to go down even before the shock. At the time when D actually goes up we will observe the jump in m. The free rate δ and the spread, however, will not jump at that time. The system will at that time move to the saddle path, and the more conventional adjustment will take place.

Figure 4 Adjustment with low level of initial reserves

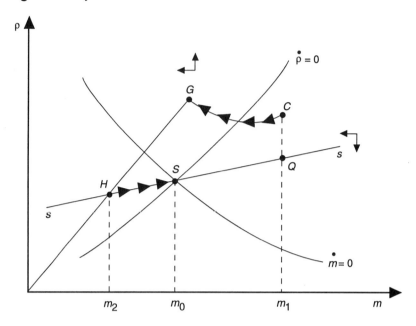

of figure 4, the initial level of reserves will determine the location of point G.

Up to now we have considered once-and-for-all increases in domestic credit D. It is easy, however, to analyze the case of a temporary increase in D. Again in this case we find out that expansive domestic credit policies result in a real exchange rate appreciation (i.e., overvaluation) and, if the central bank does not hold "sufficient" reserves, in a speculative attack and a devaluation crisis (see Edwards 1989).

To summarize, the model developed in this section provides a unified dynamic framework for analyzing the behavior of the real exchange rate and the parallel market spread. Monetary and real factors will affect the real exchange rate in the short run. In the long run, however, real factors only—the so-called fundamentals—will affect the sustainable equilibrium real exchange rate. Under the most plausible conditions higher import tariffs will result in an equilibrium real appreciation. This will also be the case for increases in the consumption of nontradables by the government. An improvement in the terms of trade can result in either an equilibrium real depreciation or a real appreciation. An increase in (exogenous) capital inflows will result in an equilibrium real appreciation. The model predicts that expansive (i.e., nonsustainable) macroeconomic policies will generally be associated with: a loss in international reserves; a current account deficit; an increase in the spread between the free and the fixed nominal rates during the initial period;

and a real exchange rate overvaluation. The form in which the disequilibria are resolved will depend on the nature of the disturbances, the nominal exchange rate policy pursued, and the existing initial stock of international reserves. Although the assumption of perfect foresight introduces some limitations, the model is still able to capture some of the more important stylized facts related to macroeconomic policies in small, open economies.

Real Exchange Rate Behavior in Selected Developing Countries: The Data

The construction of empirical measures of real exchange rates has for some time posed a nontrivial problem to applied researchers. In particular, it is not easy to find exact empirical counterparts to P_N or P_T^*. The numerous discussions on how to appropriately measure the real exchange rate have, in fact, generated little agreement among practitioners. In this paper we follow a number of researchers and use the following proxy for the (bilateral) real exchange rate:[8]

$$\text{RER} = e = \frac{E \cdot WPI^{US}}{CPI}, \tag{26}$$

where E is the nominal exchange rate between the domestic currency and the US dollar, WPI^{US} is the wholesale price index in the United States and is a proxy for the foreign price of tradables P_T^*, and CPI is the domestic consumer price index and is considered as a proxy of the domestic price of nontradables.[9] As in the previous section an increase (decrease) in the RER reflects a real depreciation (appreciation).

Table 1 contains summary statistics of RERs for 12 developing countries used in the regression analysis reported in the next section. The period included covers, for most cases, 1960–85. The index of the RER was set equal to 100 for 1980. Figure 5 depicts the behavior of the real exchange rate index for these countries. As before, an increase in this index reflects a real depreciation while a reduction refers to a real appreciation. These figures portray a number of interesting properties of real exchange rates in these countries. First, in every country the RER has experienced significant movements in the 25–year period. Second, in some of these countries—Sri Lanka being the best example—there is an apparent structural break that, one can hypothesize, may have been

---

8. See, for example, Harberger (1986) and Díaz-Alejandro (1986).

9. An important limitation of this index is that it refers to a *bilateral* real exchange rate. On the attributes of this and other empirical measures of real exchange rates see Edwards (1988a).

Table 1 Summary statistics on real exchange rates for the 12 countries in the sample, 1965–85 (1980 = 100)

Country	Mean	Standard deviation	Minimum	Maximum
Brazil	84.0	17.5	67.4	132.8
Colombia	102.2	12.2	76.0	126.4
El Salvador	107.8	11.6	77.6	129.3
Greece	108.4	6.7	95.0	128.6
India	87.1	12.6	63.2	109.8
Israel	93.4	12.2	71.8	112.5
Malaysia	96.2	5.2	85.7	105.3
Philippines	98.6	14.4	55.7	121.6
South Africa	107.5	5.5	99.2	119.7
Sri Lanka	54.4	31.7	28.8	107.7
Thailand	103.4	2.5	99.2	108.8
Yugoslavia	105.1	26.9	52.9	164.3

Source: These are bilateral real exchange rate indexes constructed from data obtained from International Monetary Fund, *International Financial Statistics*, various years.

generated by a structural change in one of the RER fundamentals. Third, it is difficult to establish a real exchange rate appreciation trend, as some observers have suggested (Wood 1987). Fourth, with a few exceptions— El Salvador being the most notable—in the last two years of the sample the majority of these countries experienced a significant RER depreciation. This was basically the consequence of deliberate nominal exchange rate policies pursued after the unleashing of the debt crisis in 1982 (see, e.g., Cline 1983 and Edwards 1988b). Notice, however, that although the RER index has been fairly variable in all countries, the extent of variability has differed quite significantly across them.

An important and difficult issue is whether these series are stationary.[10] If the series are nonstationary, standard regressions that try to explain the logarithm of the RER would be meaningless; the standard errors of the parameters would be incorrect. Moreover, if the logarithm of the RER is a random walk, the variance of forecasts into the future would be infinite; in a way, the system would not be anchored. In this paper the stationarity question is analyzed using two procedures. First, the quarterly detrended time series are analyzed using the Box-Jenkins technique. In most cases the pattern of autocorrelation and partial autocorrelation functions suggests for most countries an ARMA(1,1).

---

10. Some recent papers on the more advanced economies have been concerned with whether the time series of RER indexes have a unit root. In many ways these discussions have been inserted in a new statistically oriented literature that inquires (once again) whether purchasing power parity holds (Kaminsky 1987, Huizinga 1986). In the case of our data set it is clear from a simple inspection of the diagrams that the simple version of PPP is a grossly inadequate representation of RER behavior. In fact, formal tests on the time series properties of these indexes—Box-Pierce *Q* tests—strongly reject the null hypothesis that the strong (or absolute) version of PPP holds.

Figure 5   Real exchange rates for the 12 countries in the sample, 1964–85
(1980 = 100)

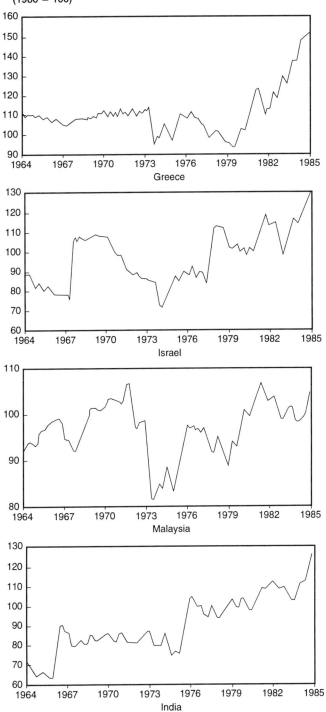

Figure 5 (continued)

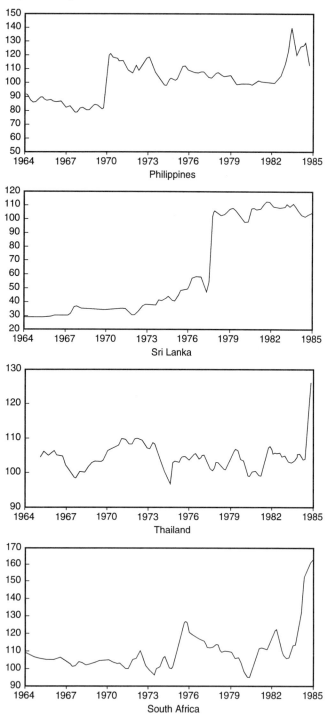

Philippines

Sri Lanka

Thailand

South Africa

Figure 5 (continued)

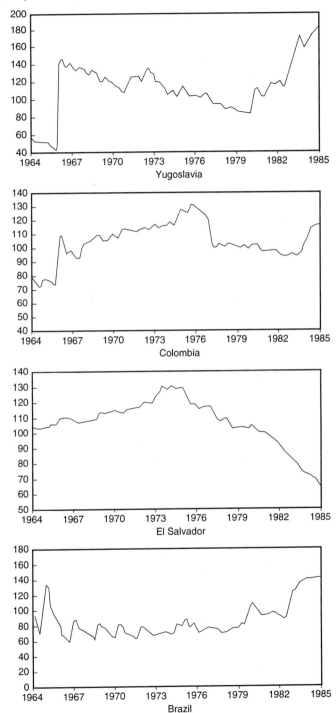

Yugoslavia

Colombia

El Salvador

Brazil

Second, the augmented Dickey-Fuller test for the presence of unit roots is also computed.

Table 2 contains the estimated coefficient of the ARMA(1,1) processes for the (detrended) logarithm of the RER index. These computations were performed on quarterly data and exclude Brazil because of the lack of a long enough time series. As can be seen, in all cases the AR term was quite high and always significant. For most countries the MA term was negative and also significant. However, what is more important is that in 9 of the 11 cases—the exceptions being El Salvador and Malaysia—it is not possible to reject the hypothesis that these series indeed follow a stationary and invertible ARMA(1,1) process. Table 3, on the other hand, presents two computations for the augmented Dickey-Fuller τ-statistic. The first computations were performed using 3 lags for the differences of the logarithm of the RER, whereas the second used 13 lags. These figures provide a somewhat different picture from that in table 2. In fact, according to the augmented Dickey-Fuller test, with the exception of India and Sri Lanka, it is not possible to reject the null hypothesis of a unit root. The evidence, then, is inconclusive regarding the stationarity of these series. This is, of course, usually the case when the AR term is very near the unit circle. What is clear, however, is that the first differences of the logarithm of RER are stationary.

Real and Monetary Determinants of Real Exchange Rates: The Empirical Evidence

In this section we use data for our 12 developing countries to test the most important implications of the model. These implications were as follows: First, in the short run, real exchange rate movements will respond to both real and monetary disturbances. Second, in long-run equilibrium real exchange rate movements will depend on real variables only. Third, inconsistently expansive macroeconomic policies will generate, in the short run, a situation of real exchange rate misalignment (i.e., an overvaluation). Fourth, nominal devaluations will only have a lasting effect on the equilibrium real exchange rate if they are undertaken from a situation of real exchange rate misalignment and if they are accompanied by ''appropriate'' macroeconomic policies. The model also predicts that there will be a negative relation between the parallel market spread and the actual (as opposed to the equilibrium) real exchange rate. These two variables, of course, are endogenous. In addition, the model provides a list of (some of) the relevant real ''fundamentals'' that determine the behavior of the equilibrium RER (i.e., import tariffs, terms of trade, composition of government consumption, capital flows).

Table 2 Estimates of ARMA(1, 1) for log RER: quarterly data, 1965–83[a]

Country	AR	MA	Q(15)
Brazil	n.a.	n.a.	n.a.
Colombia	0.980	−0.476	21.6
	(0.021)	(0.100)	
El Salvador	0.997	−0.428	38.7
	(0.104)	(0.104)	
Greece	0.871	0.338	21.7
	(0.075)	(0.142)	
India	0.737	−0.458	10.8
	(0.090)	(0.114)	
Israel	0.834	−0.115	11.3
	(0.073)	(0.131)	
Malaysia	0.946	−0.387	29.2
	(0.112)	(0.112)	
Philippines	0.874	−0.202	16.2
	(0.122)	(0.122)	
South Africa	0.894	−0.287	17.2
	(0.116)	(0.116)	
Sri Lanka	0.958	−0.557	8.7
	(0.040)	(0.096)	
Thailand	0.904	−0.238	17.0
	(0.054)	(0.134)	
Yugoslavia	0.332	−0.096	4.2
	(0.130)	(0.099)	

n.a. = not available.
a. Numbers in parentheses are approximate standard errors. Q(15) is the Box-Pierce statistic for autocorrelation check of the residuals. It is distributed as χ^2 with 15 degrees of freedom. The critical value of the χ^2 distribution at the 95 percent level of significance and 15 degrees of freedom is 25. Brazil was excluded due to the lack of long enough quarterly time series.

An Equation for the Dynamics of RERs

The following equation for the dynamics of RER behavior captures the basic points made by our theoretical analysis:

$$\Delta \log e_t = \theta\{\log e_t^* - \log e_{t-1}\} - \lambda\{Z_t - Z_t^*\}$$
$$+ \phi\{\log E_t - \log E_{t-1}\} - \psi[PMPR_t - PMPR_{t-1}], \tag{27}$$

where e is the actual real exchange rate; e^* is the equilibrium real exchange rate, in turn a function of the fundamentals; Z_t is an index of macroeconomic policies (i.e., the rate of growth of domestic credit); Z_{t-1}^* is the sustainable level of macroeconomic policies (i.e., the rate of increase of demand for domestic money); E_t is the nominal exchange rate; $PMPR$ is the spread in the parallel market for foreign exchange; and θ, λ, ψ, and ϕ are positive parameters that capture the most important dynamic aspects of the adjustment process.

Equation (27) establishes that the actual dynamics of real exchange rates respond to the four forces identified in the description of the

Table 3   Augmented Dickey-Fuller tests for stationarity: log RER levels, quarterly data, 1965–84[a]

$$X_t = \alpha + \text{time} + \rho X_{t-1} + \sum_{i=1}^{K} \beta_i \sum (X_{t-i} - X_{t-i-1}) + \epsilon_t$$

Country	$\tau(\rho)$ $K = 3$	$\tau(\rho)$ $K = 13$
Brazil	n.a.	n.a.
Colombia	−2.910	−2.034
El Salvador	−2.699	−1.710
Greece	−1.087	−1.068
India	−6.006	−4.458
Israel	−2.928	−2.207
Malaysia	−1.041	−1.148
Philippines	−2.833	−2.689
South Africa	−1.835	−0.320
Sri Lanka	−2.238	−3.627
Thailand	−1.220	−0.987
Yugoslavia	−1.167	−1.271

a. X_t denotes the logarithm of the bilateral real exchange rate. The critical value at the 90 percent level is −3.15 for 100 observations. Brazil was excluded due to the lack of long enough quarterly time series.

model. First, there will be an autonomous tendency for the actual real exchange rate to correct existing misalignments, given by the partial adjustment term $\theta\{\log e_t^* - \log e_{t-1}\}$. With all other things given, this self-correcting process tends to take place, under pegged nominal rates, through reductions in prices of nontradable goods or increases in "the" world price of tradables P_T^*. The speed at which this self-adjustment takes place is captured in equation (27) by parameter θ. The smaller is θ (i.e., the closer it is to zero), the slower will be the speed at which real exchange rate misalignments will be corrected. Theoretically, the value of θ will depend on the value of the different parameters in the model. In addition, a number of institutional factors, including the existence of wage indexation rules, will influence its level.

The second determinant of real exchange rate movements is related to macropolicies and is given by $-\lambda\{Z_t - Z_t^*\}$. This term states that if macroeconomic policies are unsustainable in the medium to longer run and are inconsistent with a pegged rate (i.e., $Z_t > Z_t^*$), there will be pressures toward a real appreciation: that is, if $(Z_t - Z_t^*) > 0$, with other things given, $\Delta \log e < 0$. Notice that if macroeconomic disequilibrium and/or λ are large enough, these forces can easily dominate the self-correcting term, generating an increasing degree of overvaluation through time.

The third determinant of RER movements is related to changes in the nominal exchange rate (i.e., to nominal devaluations) and is given by the term $\phi\{\log E_t - \log E_{t-1}\}$. This term closely captures the implications from our model. A nominal devaluation will have a positive effect on the real exchange rate on impact, generating a short-run depreciation; the actual magnitude of this real depreciation will depend on parameter ϕ.

The fourth element refers to the effect of changes in the parallel market premium on the real exchange rate. As shown above, increases in the parallel market spread will be related to a real exchange rate appreciation. Naturally, both e and $PMPR$ are endogenous variables.

An important property of equation (27) is that, as in the model, although nominal devaluations will have an effect on the real exchange rate *in the short run*, this effect will not necessarily last through time. In fact, as in the model, whether the nominal devaluation will have any impact over the medium to longer run will depend on the other two terms of equation (27), or, more precisely, on the initial conditions captured by (log e^* − log e) and on the accompanying macropolicies, captured by $[Z_t - Z_t^*]$.

The Equilibrium Real Exchange Rate

According to the model developed above, the most important "fundamentals" in determining the behavior of equilibrium RERs are: the external terms of trade, the level and composition of government consumption, import tariffs, and capital flows. However, given the relative simplicity of that model some other possible real determinants of the equilibrium RER that were not explicitly derived from the model were also included in some of the equations estimated. For example, a variable representing technological progress was included in order to capture the possible role of the so-called Ricardo-Balassa effect on the equilibrium real exchange rate. According to this hypothesis, countries experiencing a faster rate of technological progress will experience an equilibrium RER appreciation (Balassa 1964).

For the purpose of estimating equation (27) the equilibrium real exchange rate was written in the following form:

$$\log e_t^* = \beta_0 + \beta_1 \log(TOT)_t + \beta_2 \log(NGCGDP)_t$$
$$+ \beta_3 \log(TARIFFS)_t + \beta_4 \log(TECHPRO)_t + \beta_5(KAPFLO)_t \qquad (28)$$
$$+ \beta_6 \log(OTHER)_t + u_t,$$

where the following notation has been used:

e^* = the equilibrium real exchange rate;
TOT = the external terms of trade, defined as (P_X^*/P_M^*);
NGCGDP = the ratio of government consumption on nontradables to GDP;
TARIFFS = a proxy for the level of import tariffs;
TECHPRO = a measure of technological progress;
KAPFLO = capital inflows (a negative value denotes capital outflows);

OTHER = other fundamentals, such as the investment-GDP ratio;
   u = error term.

A problem in the implementation of this analysis is the unavailability of time series for some of the real exchange rate fundamentals in equation (28). In fact, the only fundamentals for which we have reliable data are the external terms of trade (TOT) and capital flows (KAPFLO). This means that in the estimation of the RER equation either the other fundamentals have to be excluded, or proxies for them have to be found. In this investigation both approaches were followed, estimating real exchange rate equations under alternative specifications that either omitted variables or used proxies for those for which data were not available. The following proxies were used. Technological progress was proxied by the rate of growth of real GDP. This type of proxy has been used in a number of empirical investigations dealing with the Ricardo-Balassa effect. With respect to import tariffs, implicit tariffs were computed as the ratio of tariff revenues to imports. This proxy, however, has some limitations, since it is only available for a few years for each country, and it ignores the role of nontariff barriers. The ratio of government consumption on nontradables to GDP was replaced by the ratio of the government consumption to GDP (GCGDP). This is an admittedly limited proxy, since it is possible for GCGDP to increase even when the share of nontradables in government expenditure is going down. This means that the actual sign of GCGDP can be either positive or negative.

Macroeconomic Policies

In the RER dynamics equation (27) the term $-\lambda\{Z_t - Z_t^*\}$ measures the role of macroeconomic policies in real exchange rate behavior. According to the model, with other things given, if macroeconomic policies are "inconsistent" the RER will become overvalued. In the estimation the following components of $\{Z_t - Z_t^*\}$ were used:

- Excess supply of domestic credit (EXCRE) was measured as the rate of growth of domestic credit minus the lagged rate of growth of real GDP:

$$\text{EXCRE}_t = \{d \log \textit{Domestic Credit}_t - d \log \text{GDP}_{t-1}\};$$

   this assumes that the demand for domestic credit has a unitary elasticity with respect to real income.

- Also, the ratio of the fiscal deficit to lagged high-powered money (DEH) was incorporated as a measure of fiscal policies.

- Alternatively, instead of our measure for the excess supply of domestic credit, in a number of equations the rate of growth of domestic credit was included (DPDC).

Estimation

After replacing the equation for log e_t^* and the expressions for $\{Z_t - Z_{t-1}^*\}$ into equation (27) we obtain an equation that could, in principle, be estimated using conventional methods. For example, when EXCRE is the only element of the macroeconomic policies vector $\{Z_t - Z_t^*\}$, the equation to be estimated is

$$\Delta \log e_t = \gamma_1 \log(TOT)_t + \gamma_2 \log(GCGDP)_t$$
$$\gamma_3 \log(TARIFFS)_t + \gamma_5(KAPFLO)_t + \gamma_6 \log(TECHPRO)_t \qquad (29)$$
$$-\theta \log e_{t-1} - \gamma EXCRE_t + \phi NOMDEV_t$$
$$-\psi(PMPR_t - PMPR_{t-1}) + u_t,$$

where NOMDEV stands for nominal devaluation, and where the γ's are combinations of the β's and θ.

In our case the estimation of equation (29), or of its variants, is a task not completely free of problems. First, there are measurement errors. Starting with the dependent variable, many of the variables involved are only proxies of the ideal, correctly measured, variables. Second, for any particular country, the time series available for some of these variables are extremely short, making the country-by-country estimation of equation (29) all but impossible. For this reason pooled data procedures were used. Third, a number of these variables—most notably the parallel market premium—are endogenous, making results obtained from ordinary least squares estimates suspicious. This last problem is compounded by the fact that since log e_{t-1} appears on the right-hand side, the use of lagged endogenous variables as instruments is not completely appropriate. In evaluating the results reported above, these problems should be kept in mind.

Results

Several versions of equation (29) were estimated using pooled data for the group of 12 countries. These countries were chosen because of data availability. They were the only ones with long enough time series for all the relevant variables (except the proxies for import tariffs). Also, throughout the period all of these countries had predetermined nominal exchange rate regimes—either pegged or crawling. Moreover, all of them except El Salvador experienced substantial nominal devaluations during the period under analysis. In some of the regressions the change in the parallel market spread ($APMPR_t$) was omitted since it is highly colinear with the other right-hand side variables.[11]

The estimation was performed using instrumental variables on a fixed-effect procedure, with country-specific dummy variables included in each

---

11. Moreover, as discussed below, the black market premium may very well be picking up the effects of exchange controls and capital market impediments.

regression.[12] Table 4 contains a summary of the results obtained from the estimation of a number of variants of equation (29). The results are quite satisfactory and provide support for the view that short-run movements in real exchange rates respond to both real and nominal variables.

In most of the regressions the coefficients on the measures of macroeconomic policy—the excess supply of domestic credit (EXCRE), the fiscal deficit ratio (DEH), and the rate of growth of domestic credit (DPDC)—are significantly negative. This indicates that, in accordance with the implications obtained from the model, as these policies become increasingly expansive—higher deficits or increased excess supply for credit—the real exchange rate will *appreciate*. Naturally, if we start from RER equilibrium and other things including the fundamentals remain constant, this appreciation will reflect a mounting disequilibrium. For the excess supply for credit (EXCRE) the estimated coefficients ranged from −0.147 to −0.075. Although these coefficients appear somewhat small, they do imply that inconsistent domestic credit policies maintained for periods of three to four years can generate very substantial disequilibria. Consider, for example, the case of equation (29.2) with a coefficient for EXCRE of −0.147; if domestic credit grows at a rate of 25 percent per year and real income at 5 percent, after three years there will be an accumulated real appreciation of 9.1 percent. In this sense, the estimates for the macroeconomic variables coefficients strongly support the view that inconsistent policies will result in growing pressures that will generate real exchange rate overvaluations.

The results in table 4 show that real variables (the "fundamentals") have also influenced RER behavior in these countries. In all regressions the coefficient of the (logarithm of the) terms of trade is negative, and significant at conventional levels in a number of them. Remember that according to our model the sign of the TOT coefficient was theoretically ambiguous. The results, however, give support to the popular view that suggests that improvements in the terms of trade—an increase in log (TOT)—will result in an equilibrium real appreciation (Edwards and Van Wijnbergen 1987). The value of the coefficient is rather small; the reason is that this is the short-run coefficient. The long-run coefficient, of course, is much larger.

---

12. All the data except the black market premiums and the tariff proxies were obtained from International Monetary Fund (IMF), *International Financial Statistics,* various years. Parallel market data come from *Pick's Currency Yearbook,* various years; and tariff proceeds from IMF, *Government Finance Statistics,* various years. The following instruments were used: fiscal deficit; contemporaneous, lagged, and twice lagged GDCDPP; NOMDEV; lagged NOMDEV; contemporaneous, lagged, twice and three times lagged log of nominal exchange rate; lagged e; terms of trade and lagged terms of trade; EXCRE and lagged EXCRE; contemporaneous and up to three lags unexpected money; contemporaneous and up to three lags unexpected credit growth; DPDC, lagged and twice lagged DPDC; and country-specific dummies.

Table 4 Real exchange rate equations (instrumental variables)[a]

Variable	Equation								
	(29.1)	(29.2)	(29.3)	(29.4)	(29.5)	(29.6)	(29.7)	(29.8)	(29.9)
$EXCRE_t$						−0.099 (−1.985)			−0.134 (−3.680)
$DPDC_t$	−0.132 (−3.462)	−0.147 (−4.075)		−0.075 (−1.439)	−0.075 (−3.404)		−0.116 (−2.987)		
DEH_t			−0.052 (−0.898)		−0.019 (−2.016)		−0.016 (−2.148)	−0.175 (−5.660)	−0.015 (−1.759)
ΔNOM_t	0.665 (13.213)	0.689 (13.340)	0.431 (4.226)	0.467 (10.451)	0.634 (11.130)	0.516 (7.443)	0.678 (13.400)	0.561 (14.973)	0.702 (13.604)
$\Delta PMPR_t$			−0.525 (−3.056)	−0.486 (−2.940)		−0.392 (−3.074)			
$LTOT_t$	−0.052 (−2.100)	−0.056 (−2.234)	−0.042 (−1.247)	−0.044 (−1.378)	−0.003 (−0.840)	−0.018 (−0.503)	−0.057 (−2.276)	−0.019 (−0.873)	−0.062 (−2.310)
$TARIFF_t$				−0.345 (−0.750)	−0.396 (−0.682)	−0.335 (−0.749)			
$KAPFLO_{t-1}$								−0.163 (−1.376)	−0.040 (−0.820)
$LGCGDP_t$	0.021 (0.774)	0.027 (0.995)	0.006 (0.153)	0.009 (0.263)	−0.016 (−0.589)	−0.015 (−0.497)	0.025 (0.908)	−0.047 (−2.422)	0.029 (1.086)
$GROWTH_t$	0.146 (4.762)	0.150 (4.968)	0.633 (1.282)	0.702 (1.483)	0.090 (3.220)	0.085 (0.219)	0.146 (4.796)		0.148 (4.844)
$Log\ e_{t-1}$	−0.072 (−2.390)	−0.072 (−2.387)	−0.088 (−2.147)	−0.084 (−2.147)	−0.123 (−2.184)	−0.203 (−2.899)	−0.059 (−4.568)	−0.041 (−1.970)	−0.058 (−1.750)
N	225	225	225	120	120	120	225	225	225
r^2	0.524	0.529	0.396	0.422	0.678	0.663	0.532	0.591	0.540
χ^2	50.9	58.9	61.6	65.3	29.8	38.5	55.2	49.8	51.3

a. Numbers in parentheses are t-statistics. N is number of observations; χ^2 is the test for testing that all nonmonetary variables are jointly zero.

Because of the lack of data on the composition of government consumption, the ratio of government expenditures to GDP (log GCGDP) is the only real variable related to government behavior incorporated in the analysis. In most cases this coefficient was not significant, and in a number of equations it was positive. Notice that the coefficient of real growth turned out to be positive in all regressions and significant in a number of them. To the extent that growth is considered to be a measure of technological progress, this result seems to contradict the Ricardo-Balassa hypothesis. The estimated coefficient of the proxy for tariffs was negative, as suggested by the theory, although not significantly different from zero.

In all equations where it was included, the coefficient of the change in the parallel market spread was negative, as suggested by the theory. It should be noticed that this variable may be capturing the effect of broadly defined exchange (i.e., trade and capital) controls. It is well known that as countries impose additional external restrictions the parallel market coverage and rate rapidly increase. Also, the coefficient of the capital flows variable had the negative sign predicted by the theoretical model when it was included as an explanatory variable. It turned out, however, that those coefficients were not significant at the conventional levels.

The estimated coefficients of nominal devaluation (NOMDEV) and lagged RERs provide the last two elements of analysis for the dynamics of RERs. The coefficient of NOMDEV is always significantly positive, ranging from 0.467 to 0.698. This indicates that, even with all other things given, a nominal devaluation will be converted into a less than one-to-one real devaluation in the first year. The size of this coefficient is, however, quite large and provides evidence supporting the view that nominal devaluations can indeed be a quite powerful device to *reestablish real exchange rate equilibrium*. If, for instance, as in our prior example, the real exchange rate becomes overvalued by 9 percent, a nominal devaluation of approximately 15 percent will help regain equilibrium. Naturally, for the nominal devaluation to have a lasting effect, it is necessary that the sources of the original disequilibrium—the positive EXCRE and DEH—be eliminated. If this is not the case, soon after the devaluation the RER will again become overvalued.

The coefficients of lagged RER are quite low in all regressions, but significantly different from zero. This is not surprising in light of the analysis of the time series properties of RERs discussed earlier. From an economic perspective these low values for the coefficients imply that, in the absence of other intervention, actual real exchange rates converge very slowly toward their long-run equilibrium level. This, indeed, supports the view that when there is a real exchange rate misalignment, nominal devaluations, if properly implemented, can be a very powerful tool to help reestablish equilibrium.

The χ^2 tests reported at the bottom of table 4 test the null hypothesis that all nonmonetary variables are jointly zero. The critical value of the χ^2 distribution at the 95 percent level of significance is 7.38 for two degrees of freedom, 9.35 for three degrees of freedom, and 11.1 for four degrees of freedom. As can be seen, all the χ^2 statistics are well above these critical values, indicating that the real factors as a group have indeed played an important role in determining RER behavior in these countries.

Summary, Conclusions, and Extensions

The purpose of this paper has been to analyze RER behavior in developing countries. For this purpose the paper started with the presentation of a dynamic model of a small, open economy with a dual exchange rate system. The model, although highly stylized, provided a number of important testable implications. The aim of the empirical part of the paper was to analyze whether, as the theoretical model suggests, real exchange rate movements have historically responded to both real and nominal disturbances. In order to carry out the analysis, an equation for real exchange rate dynamics was postulated. This equation captures in a simple and yet powerful way the most important features of the theoretical analysis: discrepancies between actual and equilibrium real exchange rates will tend to disappear slowly if left on their own; nominal devaluations are neutral in the long run, but can be potentially helpful to speed up the restoration of real exchange rate equilibrium; macroeconomic disequilibria affect the real exchange rate in the short run; the long-run equilibrium real exchange rate responds to changes in the fundamentals. In addition, the model provided us with a list of such fundamentals and the way in which they affect the equilibrium real exchange rate.

This dynamic equation was estimated using pooled data for a group of 12 countries. The estimation was done using a fixed-effect procedure with country-specific fixed terms. The results obtained provide broad support for the model. In these countries short-run real exchange rate movements have responded to both nominal and real disturbances. In particular, expansive and inconsistent macroeconomic policies have inevitably generated forces toward real overvaluation.

The estimation also indicates that the autonomous forces that move the RER back to equilibrium operate fairly slowly, keeping the country out of equilibrium for a long period of time. These results, in fact, indicate that if a country is indeed in disequilibrium, nominal devaluations can greatly help to speed up the real exchange rate realignment.

This analysis can be extended in several ways. One of the most interesting directions is related to estimating indexes of real exchange rate misalignment and, in turn, to using those indexes to investigate whether real exchange rate disequilibrium has indeed been associated with poorer economic performance. One possible—and rather simple—way of doing this is the following. First, from the estimation of equation (29) the coefficients of the long-run equilibrium real exchange rate equation can be obtained. Second, using estimated equilibrium "sustainable" values of the fundamentals, estimated equilibrium RERs can be generated for each country. Third, RER misalignment can then be defined as the difference between these estimated equilibrium RERs and actual RERs. Fourth, average indexes of RER misalignment can then be calculated for each country. Finally, these average indexes of misalignment can be used to estimate whether it has been the case that countries exhibiting larger misalignments have performed worse, with other things given, than those countries with the smaller degree of RER misalignment. This last step can be performed using cross-country regression analysis. (For a preliminary analysis along these lines see Edwards 1988a.)

References

Aizenman, J. 1985. "Adjustment to Monetary Policy and Devaluation under Two-Tier and Fixed Exchange Rate Regimes." *Journal of Development Economics* 18, no. 1: 153–69.

Balassa, B. 1964. "The Purchasing Power Parity Doctrine: A Reappraisal." *Journal of Political Economy* 72: 584–96.

Calvo, G. 1987. "Balance of Payments Crises in a Cash in Advance Economy." *Journal of Money, Credit and Banking* 19 (February): 19–32.

Cline, W. 1983. *The International Debt Problem.* Cambridge, MA: MIT Press.

Dervis, K., and P. Petri. 1987. *The Macroeconomics of Successful Development.* Cambridge, MA: NBER Macroeconomics Annual.

Diaz-Alejandro, C. 1986. "Comment on Harberger." in S. Edwards and L. Ahamed, eds., *Economic Adjustment and Exchange Rates in Developing Countries.* Chicago: University of Chicago Press.

Dornbusch, R. 1982. "Equilibrium and Disequilibrium Exchange Rates." *Zeitschrift für Wirtschafts und Sozialwissenschaften* 102 (December).

Dornbusch, R. 1986a. "Special Exchange Rates for Capital Account Transactions." *World Bank Economic Review* 1 (September): 3–33.

Dornbusch, R. 1986b. "Special Exchange Rates for Commercial Transactions." In S. Edwards and L. Ahamed, eds., *Economic Adjustment and Exchange Rates in Developing Countries.* Chicago: University of Chicago Press.

Edwards, S. 1988a. *Exchange Rate Misalignment in Developing Countries.* Baltimore: Johns Hopkins University Press.

Edwards, S. 1988b. "Structural Adjustment in Highly Indebted Countries." In J. Sachs, ed., *The Developing Countries' Debt Crisis.* Chicago: University of Chicago Press.

Edwards, S. 1989. *Real Exchange Rates, Devaluation and Adjustment.* Cambridge, MA: MIT Press.

Edwards, S., and S. Van Wijnbergen. 1987. "Tariffs, the Real Exchange Rate and the Terms of Trade." *Oxford Economic Papers* 39: 458–564.

Flood, R., and P. Garber. 1984. "Collapsing Exchange Rate Regimes: Some Linear Examples." *Journal of International Economics* 17 (August): 1–16.

Harberger, A. 1986. "Economic Adjustment and the Real Exchange Rate." In S. Edwards and L. Ahamed, eds., *Economic Adjustment and Exchange Rates in Developing Countries.* Chicago: University of Chicago Press.

Huizinga, J. 1986. "An Empirical Investigation of the Long Run Behavior of Real Exchange Rates." Paper prepared for the Carnegie-Rochester Conference on Public Policy (November).

Kaminsky, G. 1987. "The Real Exchange Rate in the Short Run and in the Long Run." San Diego: University of California, San Diego (mimeographed).

Khan, M. 1986. "Developing Country Exchange Rate Policy Responses to Exogenous Shocks." *American Economic Review* 76 (May): 84–87.

Khan, M., and J. S. Lizondo. 1987. "Devaluation, Fiscal Deficits and the Real Exchange Rate." *World Bank Economic Review* (January): 357–74.

Kiguel, M., and J. S. Lizondo. 1987. "Theoretical and Policy Aspects of Dual Exchange Rate Systems." World Bank Discussion Paper No. DRD201. Washington: World Bank.

Krugman, P. 1979. "A Model of Balance of Payments Crises." *Journal of Money, Credit and Banking* 11 (August): 311–25.

Lizondo, J. S. 1987a. "Exchange Rate Differential and Balance of Payments under Dual Exchange Markets." *Journal of Development Economics* 26: 37–53.

Lizondo, J. S. 1987b. "Unification of Dual Exchange Markets." *Journal of International Economics* 22: 57–77.

Obstfeld, M. 1984. "Balance-of-Payments Crises and Devaluation." *Journal of Money, Credit and Banking* 16 (May): 208–17.

Van Wijnbergen, S. 1985. "Taxation of International Capital Flows." *Oxford Economic Papers* 37 (September): 382–90.

Williamson, J. 1985. "The Exchange Rate System." POLICY ANALYSES IN INTERNATIONAL ECONOMICS 5. Washington: Institute for International Economics.

Wood, A. 1987. "Global Trends in Real Exchange Rates: 1960–1984." Brighton, England: University of Sussex (mimeographed).

4

Estimating Long-Run Equilibrium Real Exchange Rates

IBRAHIM A. ELBADAWI

The concept of the real exchange rate (RER) has assumed a central position in past and current debates in the literature on economic development and growth strategies and in the more recent literature on structural adjustment and macroeconomic stabilization. The RER, generically defined as the relative price of nontradables to tradables (or tradables to nontradables),[1] is taken to be the most important relative price signaling intersectoral growth in the long run. The relevance of the RER to export promotion and generation of optimal output and employment paths can be shown in rigorous behavioral models of utility and expenditure function.[2] Díaz-Alejandro (1984) drew from the experience of Latin America to argue that RER misalignment and especially RER overvaluation (with

Ibrahim Elbadawi is Research Coordinator, African Economic Research Consortium (AERC) in Nairobi. He is currently on leave from the World Bank. The views expressed here are not necessarily those of the World Bank or affiliated organizations. This paper benefited from previous collaborative work with Stephen O'Connell and Larry Hinkle. The author is grateful to Stephen Younger, John Williamson, and participants in an Institute for International Economics workshop (April 1993) on "Updating Fundamental Equilibrium Exchange Rates." Helpful comments by John Muellbauer and other participants at the Weekly Seminar at Nuffield College of the University of Oxford (October 1993) are gratefully acknowledged. Any remaining errors or omissions are the sole responsibility of the author. The author would also like to acknowledge excellent research assistance by Raimundo Soto and word processing support by Anna Marañon.

1. The most frequently used empirical measure of the RER is the multilateral index, defined as the ratio of the consumer price index to the nominal effective exchange rate index multiplied by the wholesale price indexes of the trading partners. This is the measure of the RER adopted in this paper, where a rise in the RER is consistent with an appreciation and a decline implies a depreciation.

2. Examples include Edwards (1986a, 1986c), Edwards and van Wijnbergen (1986, 1987), Mussa (1974, 1978), and Pinto (1988), to mention a few.

respect to the equilibrium RER) can be detrimental to an export-oriented development strategy, and Caballero and Corbo (1989) emphasized the importance of RER stability for export promotion, while Serven and Solimano (1991) found RER stability to have a significant positive effect on private investment.

Measuring the degree of misalignment is difficult, since it requires measuring an unobserved variable, the "equilibrium" real exchange rate. A common approach is based on the purchasing power parity (PPP) doctrine: a base period is chosen in which the economy is thought to have been in equilibrium, and then the real exchange rate for this year is dubbed the equilibrium for the remainder of the sample period. A fundamental problem with this approach, however, is that economic theory tells us that the real exchange rate moves over time in an economy in equilibrium. The PPP approach therefore runs the risk of identifying as a misalignment what may in fact be an equilibrium movement in the real exchange rate.[3]

We follow Edwards in defining the "equilibrium real exchange rate" (ERER) as "the relative price of nontradables to tradables[4] which, for given sustainable values of other relevant variables such as taxes, international terms of trade, commercial policy, capital and aid flows and technology, results in the simultaneous attainment of *internal* and *external* equilibrium" (Edwards 1989, 16). Internal equilibrium is achieved when the market for nontradable goods clears in the present and is expected to clear in the future; external equilibrium holds when present and future current account balances are compatible with long-run sustainable capital flows.

As pointed out by Edwards, this definition of the ERER differs from the traditional PPP definition in treating the ERER as a function of other real variables (the "fundamentals") rather than as a fixed number. Furthermore, since the above notion of equilibrium is necessarily intertemporal in nature, the path of the ERER will be affected not only by the current values of the fundamentals, but also by expectations regarding the future evolution of these variables.[5]

The ERER therefore moves in response to exogenous and policy-induced shifts in its real fundamentals. In addition, however, the observed RER is influenced in the short to medium run by macroeconomic and exchange rate policies that are not part of the fundamentals. RER misalignments can occur (as in the standard PPP theory) when those policies are inconsistent with the fundamentals. In a system of

---

3. For an interesting discussion of the PPP approach, see chapter 6 of this volume.

4. In fact, Edwards defines the RER as the relative price of tradables to nontradables.

5. Edwards (1986b; 1989, chapter 2) formalizes this concept of the ERER in the context of an intertemporal optimizing model; see also Lizondo (1989).

pegged nominal exchange rates, expansionary fiscal and monetary policy can be a cause of persistent real overvaluation; Edwards (1989) and Elbadawi (1992a) provide strong empirical evidence of this. The remainder of this section is devoted to formulating a simple and parsimonious model of the real exchange rate. As indicated above, a successful modeling strategy should have at least three elements:

- it should specify the ERER as a forward-looking function of the fundamentals

- it should allow for flexible dynamic adjustment of the RER toward the ERER, and

- it should allow for the influence of short- to medium-run macroeconomic and exchange rate policy on the RER.

The following section states the basic traded-nontraded model of Dornbusch (1973), which gives the ERER that solves the equilibrium condition in the home goods market under static expectations and assuming a given level of capital flows.[6] In the subsequent section we extend this model by linking domestic absorption to anticipated future RER depreciation. The extended model solves the ERER as a forward-looking function of its fundamentals (the first element listed above), and the assumption of stochastic stationarity[7] and cointegration[8] allows the

---

6. We actually start off from the version of the Dornbusch model developed by Rodriguez (1989), which disaggregates tradables into exportables and importables (see also Sjastad 1980 and Edwards 1989).

7. Formally, let $y_t = TD_t + Z_t$ be an economic series composed of a deterministic trend TD_t and a stochastic component. For simplicity assume that Z_t can be described by an autoregressive moving-average process $A(L)Z_t = B(L)e_t$, where $A(L)$ and $B(L)$ are polynomials in the lag operator L, and e_t is a sequence of i.i.d. (independent and identically distributed) innovations. The noise function Z_t is assumed to have a mean of zero; the moving-average polynomial is also assumed to have roots strictly outside the unit circle. Then Z_t has a unit root if $A(L)$ has one unit root and all other roots lie strictly outside the unit circle. In this case $(1 - L)Z_t = \Delta Z_t$ is a stationary process and $(1 - L)y_t = \Delta y_t$ is stationary around a fixed mean. If, on the other hand, $A(L)$ has all its roots outside the unit circle, then Z_t is a stationary process and y_t is stationary around a trend.

8. The basic idea of cointegration is that even though individual series may have a unit root, there may exist various linear combinations of variables that are stationary. Stated more formally in the context of the definition of note 7, let the n-vector y_t be composed of $(y_{1t}, \ldots, y_{nt})$, where y_{it} is defined as in note 7. Then y_t is said to be cointegrated if there exists at least one n-element vector β such that $\beta'y_t$ is trend stationary. This is a milder definition of cointegration (Campbell and Perron 1991), which is more suited to analysis of economic data since it permits the inclusion of deterministic components (such as trends and structural break dummies) in the cointegration model along with other nonstationary stochastic variables.

model solution to satisfy the second and third elements above.[9] It is also pointed out that a very convenient feature of the model is that it shows that the basic simple model remains adequate for the implications of Edwards's definition, given the assumptions of stochastic nonstationarity and cointegration.

Williamson (1993) recommends an ex ante approach for "estimating the set of real effective exchange rate (paths) needed to achieve simultaneous internal and external balance by some date in the medium-run future and to maintain balance thereafter." Calculating the so-called "fundamental equilibrium exchange rate" (FEER) therefore calls for specifying (or assuming) behavioral specifications for the fundamentals and using the real exchange rate equations in the context of a bigger model to derive paths for the equilibrium real exchange rate, given the assumed paths for the fundamentals. The derived ERER index for Chile in the simulation model described later in this paper is consistent with this concept. The ERER indexes derived in this paper for Chile, Ghana, and India are equivalent to the ex post version of the FEER concept, where the ERER paths are based on the "permanent" historical time series components of the fundamentals. The model is applied to the cases of Chile, India, and Ghana to test for and estimate long-run cointegration specifications for the ERER as well as the corresponding short-run error correction specification. Also, the estimated long-run relationships are used to derive indexes of ERER and RER misalignment relative to the estimated ERER index. Also described are some simulation exercises for Chile to assess the appropriateness of that country's recent nominal revaluation policy, from the viewpoint of maintaining competitiveness and averting future RER overvaluation.

A Basic Model of the ERER

The model starts off with an identity for nominal domestic absorption, A:

$$A = EXP_G + EXP_P,\tag{1}$$

where EXP_P is private domestic expenditure and EXP_G is government (public) expenditure, which is assumed to be a policy variable and is given as a fixed ratio to GDP:

---

9. Engle and Granger (1987) show that cointegration implies that an error correction specification is adequate for the underlying data-generating process (and vice versa). Also, in addition to transitory movements in the long-run fundamentals, the error correction specification may be influenced by other stationary, short-run, "nonfundamental" factors such as nominal devaluations and indicators of expansive macroeconomic policy (e.g., Domowitz and Elbadawi 1987).

$$EXP_G = g \cdot Y. \tag{2}$$

Furthermore, government expenditure on nontradables, EXP_{GN}, is given as a fixed ratio to total government expenditure, EXP_G:

$$EXP_{GN} = g_N \cdot EXP_G = g_N \cdot g \cdot Y. \tag{3}$$

On the other hand, the ratio of private-sector expenditure on nontradables relative to total private-sector expenditure, EXP_{PN}/EXP_P, is endogenously determined as a function of the domestic prices of exports (P_x), imports (P_m), and nontradables (P_N):

$$EXP_{PN} = d_{P_N}(P_x, P_m, P_N) \cdot E_P = d_{P_N}(P_x, P_m, P_N) \cdot [A - g \cdot Y]. \tag{4}$$

Now equations (3) and (4) allow stating the demand for nontraded goods as follows:

$$EXP_N = EXP_{PN} + EXP_{GN} = d_{PN}(P_x, P_m, P_N) \cdot [A - g \cdot Y] + g_N \cdot g \cdot Y. \tag{5}$$

The supply of nontraded goods relative to GDP is also specified as a function of the three aggregate prices:

$$S_N = s_N(P_x, P_m, P_N) \cdot Y, \tag{6}$$

and equation (7) sets the equilibrium condition in the nontraded goods market ($S_N = EXP_N$):

$$s_N(P_x, P_m, P_N) = d_{PN}(P_x, P_m, P_N) \cdot \left[\frac{A}{Y} - g \right] + g_N \cdot g. \tag{7}$$

Let the (dollar-denominated) international prices of exportables and importables be given by P^*_x and P^*_m, respectively. By invoking the small-country assumption, P^*_x and P^*_m can be considered as exogenous variables. Therefore, for a given set of exchange rate and commercial policies, the corresponding domestic prices P_x and P_m are determined by P^*_x and P^*_m, respectively. Let E be the nominal exchange rate in units of domestic currency per US dollar. Also let t_x and t_m be, respectively, the net export and import tax rates. The domestic price of exports and imports can then be defined as follows:

$$P_x = E(1 - t_x)P^*_x \tag{8}$$

$$P_m = E(1 + t_m)P^*_m. \tag{9}$$

Now define the real exchange rate e as:

$$e = P_N/E \cdot P^{*\alpha}_x \cdot P^{*1-\alpha}_m. \tag{10}$$

Equations (1) through (10) can be solved for the level of the RER that ensures instantaneous equilibrium in the nontraded goods market for given levels of some exogenous and policy fundamentals:[10]

$$e = e\left(\frac{A}{Y}, TOT, t_x, t_m, \frac{EXP_{GN}}{EXP_G}, \frac{EXP_G}{Y}\right). \tag{11}$$
$$(+) \quad (?) \quad (+)(+) \quad (+) \quad\quad (?)$$

The above solution suggests that higher and "sustainable" levels of the domestic absorption ratio, foreign trade taxes, and public expenditure on nontradables (indicated by the plus signs under the variables) are consistent with equilibrium RER appreciation; on the other hand, the effects due to changes in the terms of trade and the total government expenditure ratio could not be signed a priori. However, consistent empirical regularity shows that improved terms of trade and higher government expenditure tend to lead to RER appreciation, because the income effect of a terms-of-trade improvement usually dominates its substitution effect, and governments tend to have a higher propensity to spend on nontraded goods than does the private sector.

A Forward-Looking ERER Model

As noted in the introduction, the above ERER solution does not satisfy the identification conditions set by Edwards's definition since it ensures only nontraded goods equilibrium at a given point in time and does not account for the effect due to the anticipated evolution of the fundamentals, nor does it offer any guidance as to how to internalize the concept of "sustainability" of the fundamentals, or the dynamic behavior of the actual RER around its equilibrium. This section provides an extension of the above model along these directions. But before doing that I will state the following linearized empirical version of equation (11)—which will be the one used for further analysis:

$$\begin{aligned}
\log e = \alpha_0 &+ \alpha_1 \log (TOT) - \alpha_2 \log (OPEN) \\
&+ \alpha_3 \log\left(\frac{A}{GDP}\right) \\
&+ \alpha_4 \log\left(\frac{G \cdot EXP}{GDP}\right) \\
&+ \alpha_5 \log\left(\frac{CURR \cdot G \cdot EXP}{G \cdot EXP}\right),
\end{aligned} \tag{12}$$

where OPEN = (EXPORT + IMPORT)/GDP.

---

10. Other relevant determinants such as technological or productivity change (proxied by $[(\text{Inv.}/Y)/(\Delta Y/Y)] = (\text{Inv.}/\Delta Y)$ or simply a time trend) may be introduced to the above equation through s_n (.).

The motivation for using OPEN as a proxy for commercial policy (t_x, t_m) is twofold: first, it is difficult to obtain good time series data on t_x and t_m; and second, the OPEN proxy may account not only for explicit commercial policy but also for implicit, although very important, factors such as quotas and exchange controls. Note also that empirical regularity regarding the terms of trade and $(G \cdot EXP/GDP)$ effects is assumed.[11]

Equation (12) is assumed to hold at present and in the future for sustainable values of its arguments. The equation by itself is not adequate for RER determination, however, since A is endogenous (as, potentially, are Y and G_N as well). To complete the model, we endogenize A by specifying an equation linking private absorption to the sustainable level of net capital inflows NKI (i.e., to the sustainable current account deficit) and to the real consumption rate of interest:

$$\frac{A}{GDP} = a\left(\underset{(+)}{\frac{NKI}{GDP}}, \underset{(-)}{r^* - \sigma \cdot [_t \log(e_{t+1}) - \log(e_t)]}\right), \tag{13}$$

where NKI is a measure of "sustainable" net capital inflows, r^* is the world interest rate, σ is the share of nontraded goods in consumption, and the notation $_tX_{t+j}$ means the expectation of X_{t+j} at time t. A rise in sustainable capital inflows allows a higher sustainable level of absorption; a rise in the real interest rate, either through a rise in r^* or through a rise in the expected rate of real depreciation relative to the current (i.e., $_t \log e_{t+1} - \log e_t < 0$), increases the demand for saving and thus reduces absorption relative to income.

Abstracting from r^*[12] we rewrite equation (13) in the following linearized form:

$$\log\left(\frac{A}{Y}\right)_t = \beta_0 + \beta_1\left(\frac{NKI}{Y}\right)_t - \beta_2(_t \log e_{t+1} - \log e_t). \tag{14}$$

Solving equations (12) and (14) together yields the following reduced-form dynamic equation for the real exchange rate:

$$\log e_t - \lambda_t \log e_{t+1} = \delta_0 + \delta_1 \log(TOT)_t - \delta_2 \log(OPEN)_t + \delta_3\left(\frac{NKI}{GDP}\right)_t$$
$$+ \delta_4 \log\left(\frac{G \cdot EXP}{GDP}\right)_t + \delta_5 \log\left(\frac{Curr \cdot G \cdot EXP}{G \cdot EXP}\right)_t, \tag{15}$$

---

11. The above equation appears in many guises in the empirical tradition of this literature: see, e.g., Edwards (1989, 1986b), Elbadawi (1992a, 1992b), Mundlak et al. (1987), and Valdés (1985).

12. Eliminating the international interest rate from the equation is motivated by empirical convenience, since it is not clear what is the most relevant rate for any given country.

where $\lambda = \alpha_3 \beta_2/(1 + \alpha_3 \beta_2) < 1$, and where the δ's are corresponding coefficients on the right-hand side.

The equilibrium real exchange rate, $\bar{e}$, is that value of the RER that satisfies equation (15) for sustainable values of the right-hand side variable. Equation (15) can be solved forward for log $(\bar{e}_t)$ by recursive substitution. By defining the parameter vector $\delta = (\delta_0, \delta_1, -\delta_2, \delta_3, \delta_4, \delta_5)'$ and the vector of fundamentals,

$$F = \left[1, \log(TOT), \log(OPEN), \frac{NKI}{GDP}, \log \frac{G \cdot EXP}{GDP}, \log \frac{Curr \cdot G \cdot EXP}{G \cdot EXP} \right]',$$

we get the following forward-looking expression $\bar{e}$ for given sustainable values of the fundamentals vector (we denote sustainable values of F by $\tilde{F}$):

$$\log \bar{e}_t = \sum_{j=0}^{\infty} \lambda^j \delta_t' \tilde{F}_{t+j}.^{13} \tag{16}$$

It can be shown that if $\tilde{F}$ are stationary in first differences [i.e., I(1)],[14] then the following cointegration relationship exists (see, e.g., Kaminsky 1988):

$$\log \bar{e}_t = \frac{1}{1 - \lambda} \delta' \tilde{F}_t + \eta_t, \tag{17}$$

where $1/(1 - \lambda)\delta$ is the cointegration vector and η is a stationary disturbance term.

Abstracting from the "sustainability" issue, equation (17) is identical to the basic ERER solution given by the basic model. This is a fundamental advantage of the I(1) and cointegration assumption, since it allows the derivation of a simple empirical framework from a much more complicated theoretical model. A practical approach to introducing the concept of "sustainability" on the part of the fundamentals is still needed. Here again stochastic nonstationarity proved to be a useful property.

The permanent (or sustainable) components of the fundamentals are obtained by using the time series technique introduced by Beveridge and Nelson (1981) and further elaborated upon by Nelson and Plosser (1982), Cuddington and Winters (1987), and Cuddington and Urzúa

---

13. Notice that the ERER solution in equation (16) is not unique, since it is a function of policy fundamentals as well as external fundamentals. In a more original sense, even for a given set of fundamentals, solutions of rational expectations martingales such as equation (15) are not unique (see, e.g., Pesaran 1988). This characteristic of the ERER solution will figure very prominently in the computation of the ERER index below.

14. F is stationary of order k [$I(k)$] if $\Delta^j F$ is stationary for $j \geq k$, but not for $j < k$, where Δ is the difference operator.

(1989). Beveridge and Nelson show that any variable x_t with an integrated process (i.e., a unit root) can be decomposed into a random walk with drift and stationary components, that is,

$$x_t = x_{t-1} + \mu_t + C(L) \epsilon_t. \tag{18}$$

This technique is desirable for the problem at hand because, unlike the trend stationary model-based decomposition, it allows the steady-state growth path of the time series to shift upward or downward over time. Fluctuations around the (shifting) permanent path reflect cyclical effects. The stochastic and growing nature of the permanent fundamentals predicted by this procedure is indeed a minimal identification condition for the derived ERER to be consistent with the concept of RER equilibrium as outlined above.

An Error Correction Equation for the RER

If the cointegration relationship in equation (17) is valid, then that equation not only can be interpreted as a long-run equilibrium but is also consistent with a dynamic error correction specification (Engle and Granger 1987). The error correction equation consistent with the (assumed) cointegration equation is:

$$\Delta\log e_{t+1} = b_0\left(\frac{1}{1-\lambda}\delta'F_t - \log e_t\right)$$
$$+ b_1'\Delta F_{t+1} - b_2\,\Delta\log E_{t+1}$$
$$+ b_3\,\Delta\log\,(\text{Dom. Cred./Real GDP})_{t+1} \tag{19}$$
$$+ \epsilon_{t+1}$$

where E, as previously defined, is the exchange rate in terms of domestic currency per unit of the foreign currency, and where the disturbance ϵ_{t+1} is a stationary random variable composed of the one-step-ahead forecast error in the RER (i.e., $\Delta\log e_{t+1} - t\Delta\log e_{t+1}$).

The error correction term $[1/(1 - \lambda)\delta'F_t - \log e_t]$ in equation (19) clearly incorporates the forward-looking sources of RER dynamics. Suppose, for example, that we start from an initial condition of real overvaluation (i.e., the error correction term is negative); now the self-correcting mechanism that calls for future depreciation in the actual RER will be set in motion. This effect is captured by the negative error correction term and its positive coefficient in the $\Delta\log e_{t+1}$ specification. The speed with which this automatic adjustment operates depends on the parameter b_0, which falls in the interval $(0, 1)$. A value of b_0 equal to one signifies prompt adjustment over just one period; smaller values signify slower rates of adjustment.

In addition to the equilibrium long-run impact of the fundamentals, which is captured by the cointegration vector $1/(1 - \lambda)\delta$, temporary changes in the fundamentals may also have short-run effects, which are captured by the vector b_1. Short-run effects due to expansive macroeconomic policy are given by the coefficient of $\Delta\log$ (Dom. Cred./Real GDP). Finally, the short-run impact of nominal depreciation is given by the coefficient $(-b_2)$. As pointed out by Edwards (1989), a nominal devaluation will help the adjustment process only to the extent that the initial situation is one of overvaluation, and only if the nominal exchange rate adjustment is accompanied by supporting macroeconomic policy; in other words, in terms of our equation, the error correction term is negative and the rate of domestic credit expansion net of real GDP growth is not positive.

An Application to Chile, Ghana, and India

In this section the above model is applied to three countries: Chile, Ghana, and India. The first two countries are examples of a very proactive style of macroeconomic and exchange rate management. Both experienced episodes (1965–73 for Chile, 1973–82 for Ghana) of expansive and unsustainable macroeconomic policies that produced massive real appreciation and deteriorating economic performance. Also, both were able to reverse the economic decline and achieve sustained and significant growth when they undertook (1974–81 and 1982–90 for Chile, 1983–90 for Ghana) deep macroeconomic reforms in which the real exchange rate played a key role (see figures 1 and 2 and tables 1 and 2).[15]

India, on the other hand, belongs to a different breed of countries, where elaborate controls were maintained but macroeconomic policy has been rather conservative. It exhibits none of the extremes of external shocks and policy changes—including massive real appreciation or depreciation—or of outcomes such as accelerated growth or lasting major recessions accompanied by large increases in unemployment or inflation and debt servicing problems (Joshi and Little 1989; see also figure 3 and table 3).

Chile not only was able to reverse its economic decline decisively and restore economic growth, but in fact further consolidated its gains on the macroeconomic front by effecting major microeconomic and sectoral reforms over the second half of the 1980s (Valdés 1992). Ghana was also able effectively to eliminate its sizable parallel market for foreign exchange and achieve exchange rate unification, and appears to be on the verge

---

15. For more on Chile's economic reform see Corbo and Solimano (1991), Serven and Solimano (1991), Corbo (1985a), and Harberger (1982), to mention a few. For Ghana see Islam and Wetzel (1991), Chhibber and Leechor (1992), Younger (1992), Youngblood (1992), and Jebuni et al. (1991), among others.

Figure 1 Chile: real exchange rate, real GDP, and terms-of-trade index, 1965–89

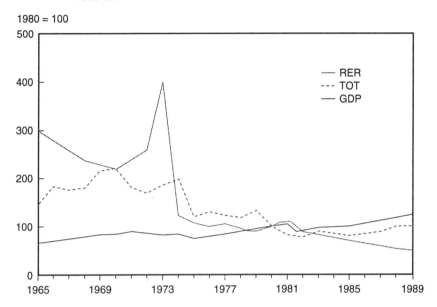

1980 = 100

Source: World Bank data base.

of winning the battle against inflation (Chhibber and Leechor 1992). Thanks to its sustained macroeconomic reforms and the considerable real depreciation it effected, Ghana was also able to improve its growth performance and to reestablish its previous international market share in the cocoa market, the mainstay of the economy (Coleman et al. 1992). The challenge Ghana faces now is to undertake further microeconomic and sectoral reforms, to pursue an aggressive export diversification drive, and to invest in sources of long-term growth such as human capital (Chhibber and Leechor 1992). On the other hand, economic performance and policy stance in India continued to be steady with no major changes. More recently,[16] however, there is evidence of slowly rising inflation, as monetary growth has started to increase as a result of accelerated borrowing from the reserve bank and the commercial banking system.

The Econometric Results

In this section equations (12) and (19) above are estimated for each of the three countries, using annual data from 1967 to 1990 for Chile and

---

16. This development occurred after 1988 and hence is not captured by table 3. However, government expenditure between the periods 1974–81 and 1982–88 increased by more than 3 percentage points of GDP.

Figure 2   Ghana: real exchange rate, real GDP, and terms-of-trade index, 1965–88

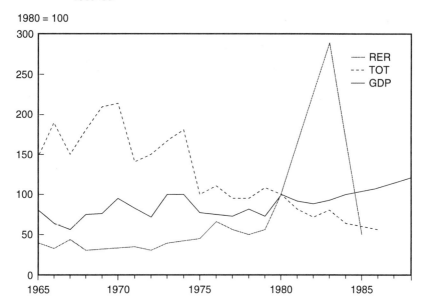

1980 = 100

Source: World Bank data base.

Ghana and from 1967 to 1988 for India. The basic data for all three countries are provided in appendix tables A1 to A3. As mentioned above, for the interpretation of equation (12) as describing the long-run RER equilibrium to be justified, and for the error correction of the second equation to be considered adequate for the data-generating process of the observed RER, the individual variables that enter into the equation must be cointegrated.

The Long-Run Equilibrium

Appendix table A4 provides the formal unit root tests for the individual variables of equation (12). As can be seen from the table, all the variables are shown to have unit roots. The remaining condition to satisfy the above interpretations is cointegration. The results of the tests are provided by the Dickey-Fuller statistics of table 4. In all three cases the tests provide strong support for cointegration, thus permitting an equilibrium interpretation of the estimates of table 4[17] as well as providing a justification for the error correction specification estimates of table 5.

17. Strictly speaking, consistency with the theoretical model requires testing the null of cointegration (Fischer and Park 1991), rather than testing the null of no cointegration, in table A4.

Table 1 Chile: real exchange rate and its fundamentals, 1965–90

	Period 1 1965–73	Period 2 1974–81	Period 3 1982–90
Real effective exchange rate (1980 = 100)	269.8	104.9	73.2
Average annual real appreciation (percentage)	5.4	−9.0	−8.6
Average annual real GDP growth (percentage)	2.2	2.0	4.9
Terms-of-trade index (1980 = 100)	186.4	121.6	90.3
Government expenditure (percentage of GDP)	26.4	20.8	26.3
Government current expenditure (percentage of total government expenditure)	98.7	97.9	90.9
Resource balance (percentage of GDP)	−0.1	−2.4	2.7
Average annual real export growth (percentage)	4.9	7.6	12.4
Openness of the economy (percentage of GDP)[a]	28.1	46.1	56.4
Excess money supply[b] (percentage)	24.8	157.2	57.1
Average annual domestic inflation (percentage)	121.4	102.1	21.8
Average annual nominal devaluation (percentage)	220.2	80.5	21.8

a. Exports plus imports divided by GDP.
b. Defined as (change in domestic credit)/$M_2(t − 1)$ − world inflation − nominal devaluation − real GDP growth rate.

Source: World Bank data base.

Table 2 Ghana: real exchange rate and its fundamentals, 1965–90

	Period 1 1965–72	Period 2 1973–82	Period 3 1983–90
Real effective exchange rate (1985 = 100)	61.1	191.2	109.2
Average annual real depreciation (percentage)	−2.4	34.7	−23.8
Average annual real GDP growth (percentage)	4.2	0.6	4.1
Terms-of-trade index (1980 = 100)	186.3	127.8	83.9
Government consumption (percentage of GDP)	14.0	10.9	9.1
Investment (percentage of GDP)	12.4	7.8	10.1
Capital flows (percentage of GDP)[a]	−1.1	−1.4	3.1
Average annual real export growth (percentage)	8.5	−14.5	30.5
Openness of the economy[b] (percentage)	41.6	26.5	22.1
Excess money supply[c] (percentage)	6.0	28.6	−38.1
Average annual domestic inflation (percentage)	7.3	62.8	44.8
Average annual nominal devaluation (percentage)	37.0	28.8	124.6

a. Negative numbers represent capital outflows.
b. Exports plus imports divided by GDP.
c. Defined as (change in domestic credit)/$M_2(t − 1)$ − world inflation − nominal devaluation − real GDP growth rate.

Source: World Bank data base.

Starting with the long-run regressions of table 4, the estimates strongly corroborate the prediction of the theoretical model: all effects have the expected signs and are statistically significant at conventional levels. The terms of trade have a positive effect, indicating that worsening terms of trade call for equilibrium RER depreciation. Even though

Figure 3   India: real exchange rate, real GDP, and terms-of-trade index, 1965–88

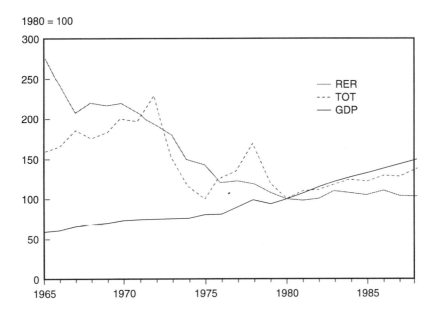

1980 = 100

Source: World Bank data base.

theoretically the influence on ERER of the terms of trade could not be signed a priori, this result confirms an empirical regularity in economics, namely, that the income effect tends to dominate the substitution effect. Both Chile and Ghana experienced sustained worsening in their terms of trade after the second half of the 1960s, which at least partially explains the corresponding substantial RER depreciation in the two countries. On the other hand, both the RER and the terms of trade in India changed very little after the mid-1970s (figures 1 to 3 and tables 1 to 3).

Also, the results indicate that a declining rate of capital inflows, and more liberalized and open trade regimes, require a more depreciated ERER. The implication of the finding on the effect of openness is that trade liberalization is not sustainable without commensurate RER depreciation or, put differently, that open economies require a more depreciated ERER than do controlled ones. The finding on the capital flows' effect on the ERER is particularly consistent with RER behavior in the case of Chile, which experienced significant real depreciation between 1974 and 1981, and again between 1982 and 1990, and net capital outflow in the later period, reversing the net inflow of the previous period (table 1).

On the other hand, in Ghana the 1983–90 economic reform was supported by massive foreign aid and concessional lending, yet the country

Table 3   India: real exchange rate and its fundamentals, 1965–88

	Period 1 1965–73	Period 2 1974–81	Period 3 1982–88
Real effective exchange rate (1980 = 100)	218.2	119.9	106.0
Average annual real depreciation (percentage)	−5.0	−6.9	0.7
Average annual real GDP growth (percentage)	3.3	4.8	6.0
Terms-of-trade index (1980 = 100)	183.7	122.1	121.4
Government consumption (percentage of GDP)	10.3	12.8	16.1
Government current expenditure (percentage of total government expenditure)	90.6	74.9	69.8
Resource balance (percentage of GDP)	−1.2	−1.3	−2.0
Average annual real export growth (percentage)	6.0	9.6	6.4
Openness of the economy[a] (percentage)	10.0	14.8	14.4
Excess money supply[b] (percentage)	12.7	35.0	8.8
Average annual domestic inflation (percentage)	9.7	5.9	9.2
Average annual nominal devaluation (percentage)	2.9	2.1	6.7

a. Exports plus imports divided by GDP.
b. Defined as (change in domestic credit)/$M_2(t - 1)$ − world inflation − nominal devaluation − real GDP growth rate.

Source: World Bank data base.

still achieved real depreciation despite experiencing a net capital inflow compared with a net outflow in the previous period. Therefore the significant real depreciation of the RER in this period clearly reflects the effects of other fundamentals (table 2). Finally, India has always been less open, and the country continued to experience net capital inflows throughout the entire period, but like the RER the ratio of the inflows to GDP did not change much after the second half of the 1970s (table 3).

The ratio of aggregate government expenditure to GDP has positive and significant elasticities for the cases of Chile and India; surprisingly, however, the corresponding effect for Ghana was not significant. The implication of this result is that governments in these two countries—as in many others (see, e.g., Edwards 1989)—tend to devote more of their expenditure to nontraded goods than do their private sectors. Excessive and unsustainable government expenditure, therefore, leads to RER appreciation and overvaluation. The composition of government expenditure is not found to be significant, however, and is subsequently dropped from the specification.[18] Finally, for the case of Chile a time trend reflecting productivity growth is found to be significant and to

18. In general, however, the composition of government expenditure matters. It has been argued that government development or capital goods expenditure tends to be traded goods-intensive, and hence the brunt of the cuts should be borne by current expenditure in order to avoid RER appreciation (Matin 1992).

Table 4   Cointegrating regression[a]

	Chile	Ghana	India
Constant	4.92	1.07	−3.99
	(7.34)[b]	(2.49)	(−3.65)
TREND	−0.05	..[c]	..
	(−5.97)		
Log TOT	0.29	0.30	1.93
	(2.36)	(4.13)	(12.0)
FLOW[d]	1.87	2.53	3.32
	(2.61)	(2.86)	(3.28)
Log OPEN[e]	−0.41	−1.52	−0.79
	(−1.85)	(−18.9)	(−11.8)
Log (G.EXP/GDP)	0.85	..	0.54
	(4.00)	..	(4.16)
Range	1965–90	1965–90	1965–88
r^2	0.972	0.953	0.975
Adjusted r^2	0.966	0.947	0.970
ADF(0)	−4.34	−5.45	−3.14
MacKinnon critical values			
1%	−3.73	−3.73	−3.73
5%	−2.99	−2.99	−2.99
10%	−2.63	−2.63	−2.63

TOT = terms of trade; G.EXP = government expenditures; ADF = augmented Dickey-Fuller statistic.
a. The dependent variable is log RER (real exchange rate).
b. Numbers in parentheses are t-statistics.
c. The variable was not included in the regression.
d. FLOW = imports minus exports divided by GDP; for Ghana this measure is given by the negative of the trade balance minus the change in reserve assets converted to cedi and then scaled by nominal GDP (see Youngblood 1992).
e. OPEN = imports plus exports divided by GDP.

have a negative effect on the ERER. To the extent that productivity growth in the nontraded goods sector in Chile has been higher than that of the traded goods sector,[19] the estimated negative coefficient will be consistent with prior expectations (see, e.g., Edwards 1989); otherwise the trend may be reflecting other generalized influences that may or may not correspond to productivity growth.

The Short-Run Error Correction Estimation

The error correction estimation gives the short-run dynamic specification of the RER determination. For the cases of Chile and India, the results (table 5) strongly support the error correction model, with the coefficients of the error correction term $[1/(1 − \lambda)\delta'F_t − \log e_t]$ all positive, less than one, and highly significant. The corresponding estimate for Ghana is also positive and less than one but is only moderately significant. The elasticities are estimated at 0.78, 0.71, and 0.67 for Chile,

---

19. Given the spectacular export growth rates achieved in Chile after its reforms (table 1), such a possibility is unlikely, however.

Table 5   Error correction regressions[a]

	Chile	Ghana	India
Log RÊR(−1) − log RER(−1)[b]	0.78	0.71	0.67
	(3.78)[c]	(1.75)	(3.42)
Δlog TOT	0.32	0.26	2.51
	(1.91)	(2.31)	(4.63)
ΔFLOW	1.59	3.08	1.08
	(2.49)	(2.99)	(0.88)
Δlog OPEN	−0.45	−1.37	−0.49
	(−2.22)	(−5.67)	(−3.48)
Δlog (G.EXP/GDP)	0.63	..[d]	..
	(2.94)		
Δlog (Dom. cred./real GDP)	0.04	..	−0.22
	(1.08)		(−2.87)
Nominal devaluation	0.12	..	0.32
	(1.97)		(1.69)
Nominal devaluation (−1)	−0.21	..	..
	(−3.16)		
Dummy (1966–67, 1972–73, 1979–80)[e]	..	..	0.066
			(2.31)
Dummy 1984[f]	..	−0.48	..
		(−2.00)	
Range	1967–90	1967–90	1967–88
r^2	0.91	0.87	0.72
Adjusted r^2	0.88	0.85	0.59
DW	1.68	2.29	1.68

Dom. cred. = domestic credit; DW = Durbin-Watson statistic; see table 4 for definitions of other variables.
a. The dependent variable is $\Delta \log RER_t$.
b. The notation "(−1)" denotes a variable lagged one year.
c. Numbers in parentheses are t-statistics.
d. The variable was not included in the regression.
e. These were years of drought or major declines in food production.
f. 1984 witnessed the beginning of a major change in policy in Ghana.

Ghana, and India, respectively. This coefficient reflects the dynamic self-correcting mechanism of the error correction model. If the fundamentals in the previous period call for a lower RER than that observed [i.e., $1/(1 − \lambda)\delta'F_t − \log e_t < 0$], then since the coefficient is positive, the RER will depreciate in the following period. The above individual estimates of automatic adjustment for these three countries are much larger than the 0.19 obtained by Edwards (1989) for a group of developing countries using a partial adjustment model.

The error correction coefficients can be manipulated, in the context of the error correction specification, to derive the corresponding adjustment speed in terms of the number of years needed to eliminate a given percentage of an exogenous shock (table 6). According to the calculation in table 6, it takes 0.46 year to eliminate 50 percent of the effects of an exogenous shock in Chile, 0.56 year in Ghana, and 0.60 year for India. To clear 99.9 percent of the shock the corresponding periods are 4.6, 5.6, and 6.2 years, respectively.

Table 6   Speed of automatic adjustment to an exogenous shock

Country	Coefficient of the error correction term[a]	Years to eliminate effects of exogenous shock[b]	
		50 percent	99.9 percent
Chile	0.78	0.46	4.6
Ghana	0.71	0.56	5.6
India	0.67	0.60	6.2

a. These are the coefficients of [log $\hat{RER}(-1)$ − log RER(-1)] in the error correction regressions of table 5.
b. The number of years to clear 100 percent of an exogenous shock through "automatic adjustment" alone can be computed from the formula $(1 - \alpha) = (1 - \hat{\beta})T$, where $\hat{\beta}$ is the estimated coefficient of the error correction term and T is the required number of years.

The short-run effects due to expansive macroeconomic policy and the nominal exchange rate devaluations, however, were not found to be as uniformly significant as in the case of the automatic adjustment effect. The first effect is positive in the case of Chile, as expected, but only marginally significant. Surprisingly, the indicator of macroeconomic policy is significant for India but with the wrong sign. To the extent that the chain of causality goes from the real exchange rate to domestic credit policy in India (i.e., that the authorities adjust domestic credit to RER changes), this result could be explainable. The effect due to nominal devaluation is only marginally statistically significant in the case of India; however, it is highly significant for Chile—with a total negative effect (contemporaneous plus lagged). The results for India and Chile validate the view that when starting from an initial condition of real overvaluation, other things held fixed, a nominal devaluation could accelerate the process of convergence toward the RER equilibrium. Surprisingly, the effects of nominal devaluation and macroeconomic policy were found to be consistently insignificant in the case of Ghana. Hence both variables were subsequently dropped from the equation.

In the short run the RER is also influenced by the transitory movements of the fundamentals (terms of trade, capital flows, the degree of openness, and government expenditure). Both openness and the terms of trade have statistically significant short-run effects across the three countries, while capital flows have had significant effects in Chile and Ghana only. In all cases the short-run effects are consistent with the corresponding long-run influences, indicating that, in both the long and the short run, more openness, worsening terms of trade, and reduced capital flows lead to real depreciation. The short-run influence of government expenditure (estimated only for Chile) is significant at conventional levels and positive, indicating that unsustainable government expenditure leads to RER overvaluation. Finally, the beginning of the reform programs in Ghana in 1984 was shown to have had a negative impact (i.e., a depreciation) on the RER, and a dummy representing droughts or major declines of food production in India was found to have had a significant and positive influence on the RER in the short run.[20]

The ERER Indexes for Chile, Ghana, and India

Now we proceed to compute the indexes for the ERER using the long-run estimates of table 4 for given "sustainable" or "permanent" values of the fundamentals. As mentioned above, time series techniques can be deployed to decompose the data on the fundamentals into permanent and transitory components. Appendix table A5 provides a brief description of the decomposition process. The table also contains the results of ARIMA model estimation required for the decomposition, where decomposition is given for those series for which time series processes more complicated than a random walk exist. These are log TOT and FLOW for Ghana, and log TOT, log(OPEN), and log(G · EXP/GDP) for Chile. For all other fundamentals in these two countries, in addition to all the variables for India, only a random walk process exists.[21] For these variables permanent components were proxied by five-year moving averages. The choice of a five-year period is not arbitrary, however, since it reflects the median of the number of years needed to eliminate an exogenous shock (table 6). Furthermore, it should be noted that the computed ERER index does not represent a unique equilibrium in terms of the intercept—the position of the ERER in a given year.[22] The ERER index has to be normalized according to some rule. To emphasize the importance of the external balance for this analysis, I have chosen the resource balance criterion. Hence, the ERER index was scaled so that its average is equal to the average of the actual RER over the years in which the resource balance is "close" to the equilibrium level (that is, either positive or, if negative, by not more than 5 percent of GDP).

---

20. The Indian economy is basically a closed monsoon economy (Joshi and Little 1989), where the natural shocks to agriculture, especially the food sector, have important macroeconomic implications. More recently, Delgado (1992), reflecting similar concerns in the context of West Africa, argues that the aggregate food price should enter as a determinant of the ERER.

21. A simple random walk process may be adequate for some variables such as the terms of trade. On the other hand, the number of annual observations available to us may be too small to allow us to find a more complex structure.

22. This is because the rational expectations solution for the ERER is not unique (note 13). In addition, if we assume the unknown ERER function to be given by $g^*(x)$ and the corresponding rational expectations solution to be given by a general Taylor approximation $g(x/\theta)$—which is assumed to approximate $g^*(x)$ fairly closely—then using the regression (on the observed RER) $y = g(x/\theta) + \epsilon$ to estimate $g(x/\theta)$ by $\hat{g}(x/\theta) = g(x/\hat{\theta})$ does not guarantee that $g(x/\hat{\theta})$ and $g(x/\theta)$ are equal for each point x in the space of the fundamentals (White 1980; see also Elbadawi 1983 on the validity of the Taylor series interpretation of the regression estimator).

Figure 4 Chile: actual and equilibrium exchange rates, 1965–90

1980 = 100

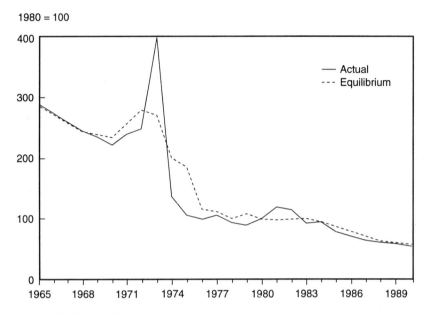

Source: World Bank data base.

The derived ERER series are shown in figures 4 and 5, 6 and 7, and 8 and 9, for Chile, Ghana, and India, respectively. The figures also show the corresponding RER misalignment, computed as [(RER − ERER)/ ERER]*100 percent. Our derived indexes agree with those of Edwards in that the ERERs show some variability. It follows that at least part of the observed RER variability is related to equilibrium behavior, and that analyses of RER misalignment based on historical comparisons of observed RER levels (i.e., the PPP approach) may lead to erroneous conclusions. The figures show a remarkable success on the part of the computed indexes in reproducing the well-known overvaluation (and undervaluation) episodes of the recent macroeconomic history of Chile and Ghana. In addition, figures 8 and 9 confirm the absence of any dramatic swings in India's macroeconomic story.

For example, the economic and political crisis in Chile that preceded the 1974 coup was reflected in a more than 50 percent real overvaluation, followed by considerable undervaluation (31, 40, and 14 percent) in each of the following three years (table 7). The undervaluation was brought about by the strong fiscal and monetary stabilization imposed by the military regime as reflected by the decelerating inflation (table 1). The other major episode reproduced by our estimates is the much-discussed RER appreciation around 1981, blamed on the interest rate

Figure 5   Chile: exchange rate misalignment,[a] 1968–90

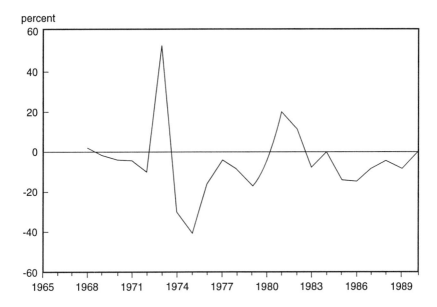

percent

a. Deviation of the actual rate from the estimated equilibrium rate.
Source: World Bank data base.

policy at the time, which precipitated massive capital flows into Chile (Corbo 1985). According to our estimates there were overvaluations of 22 percent and 11 percent in 1981 and 1982, respectively. The currency then became undervalued in real terms for most of the remainder of the 1980s, before converging to equilibrium by 1990.

The evolution of the real exchange rate in Ghana is also consistent with major shifts in policy regimes and with the terms-of-trade shocks (mainly in the price of cocoa) experienced over the period. For example, the period up to 1976 was characterized by a real undervaluation, which reached a peak of 20 percent in 1972 (table 8). Then a major reversal took place in 1977, as the currency became overvalued in real terms by about 58 percent; the overvaluation fell to 21 percent in 1978. The following two years represent a period of unsustainable reforms, but also a period of improved terms of trade, thus leading to an average annual real undervaluation of about 25 percent. Then, however, the 1981–83 period, during which cocoa prices collapsed and the earlier policy reforms were reversed, witnessed the most significant overvaluation episodes, which started at 48 percent in 1981 and peaked at a staggering 73 percent in 1982 before coming down to the still high rate of about 26 percent the following year. Thereafter the Ghanaian currency experienced sustained

Figure 6 Ghana: actual and equilibrium exchange rates, 1965–90

1985 = 100

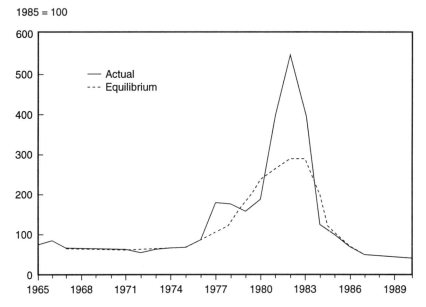

Source: World Bank data base.

double-digit undervaluation for the 1984–87 period, followed by a slight overvaluation (about 5 percent) in 1988, virtual equilibrium in 1989, and a slight undervaluation of about 7 percent in 1990. During this period Ghana undertook an aggressive fiscal and monetary stabilization supported by massive nominal devaluations and external finance (see table 2).

The above analysis suggests that exchange rate policy in Ghana may have constituted a sort of overkill from the RER perspective, because the main objective of the policy was to achieve unification of the official and parallel market exchange rates. The rather low credibility attached to government policy at the beginning of the reform and the possible negative budgetary implications of the loss of the implicit tax (on exporters) as the premium was reduced (Pinto 1987, 1988a, 1988b) could have dictated a much deeper fiscal and monetary retrenchment and supporting exchange rate policy than would be required in the absence of a parallel market. In any case this undervaluation is consistent with the still high inflation (above 40 percent) that persisted until 1990 and has only recently been reduced.

The foregoing analysis, however, is subject to some criticism in that it does not account for the severe droughts of 1977 and 1983, which resulted in drastic food price inflation. Therefore, the overvaluation estimated for those two years (table 8) may in fact be consistent with the

Figure 7 Ghana: exchange rate misalignment,[a] 1967–90

percent

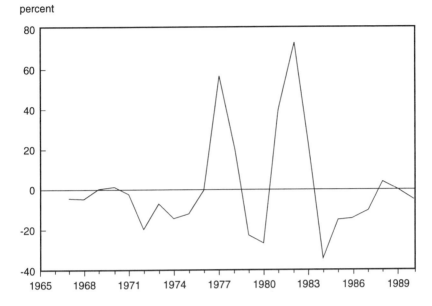

a. Deviation of the actual rate from the estimated equilibrium rate.
Source: World Bank data base.

regime shifts that were caused by the drought. The failure to account for the drought effect may have been the factor that resulted in the estimated overvaluation in the first place. Furthermore, since the implemented trade liberalization lagged behind envisaged reforms in this area for some time in Ghana, it may be that the measured proxy for a "sustainable" trade regime understated the permanent degree of trade openness that was ultimately achieved in Ghana. In addition, it is not likely that nominal devaluations have had adverse fiscal consequences. On the contrary, rapid devaluation helped the government's fiscal position, both because Ghana is a net exporter (inclusive of foreign aid) and because it taxes imports at the official exchange rate.[23] Taking both arguments into consideration and noting that since 1988 RER misalignment has in fact been small, it appears that, at least since 1988, the RER in Ghana has been kept close to its equilibrium level.

Finally, the case of India, as mentioned above, is devoid of any spectacular episodes. Except for 1965 and 1986, which witnessed episodes of overvaluation of 16.3 and 10.6 percent, respectively, the period is characterized by single-digit RER misalignments, most of which are actually

---

23. I am grateful to Stephen Younger for pointing out these counterarguments to me.

Figure 8 India: actual and equilibrium exchange rates, 1965–88

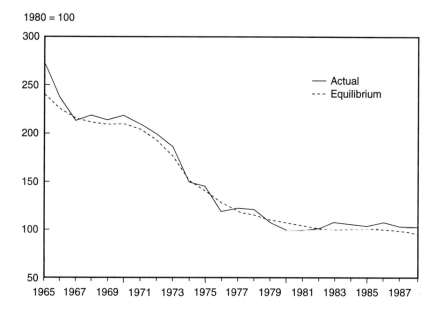

1980 = 100

Source: World Bank data base.

quite small (table 9). This finding supports the view that India, while maintaining an elaborate ensemble of economic controls, has nonetheless adopted a rather conservative macroeconomic policy. Therefore the country was able to avoid massive overvaluation, even though perhaps at the expense of achieving only modest growth. This growth performance has been attributed by some to India's lesser degree of openness (and hence its relatively low ERER)—see, for example, Valdés (1985), Edwards (1992), and Matin (1992). The above finding also points to the need to distinguish between a low ERER due to less openness (as in India) and RER overvaluation caused by unsustainable macroeconomic policy (as in Chile and Ghana before their reforms). In a recent paper Helleiner (1992) emphasizes this distinction and argues that the latter is harmful, whereas the former amounts to a choice of a development strategy or a practical necessity (for example, foreign trade taxes in sub-Saharan Africa).

Some Simulations for Chile

Recently a nominal *revaluation* has been considered in Chile as a means of stemming excessive capital inflows and serving as a nominal anchor against inflationary expectations. To test the consistency of such a policy

Figure 9 India: exchange rate misalignment,[a] 1965–88

percent

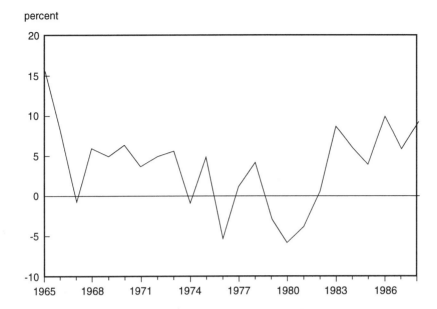

a. Deviation of the actual rate from the estimated equilibrium rate.
Source: World Bank data base.

with external competitiveness—reflected by the level of the RER relative to its equilibrium—we ran a simple simulation model centered around equations 12 and 19 above. The model is fully outlined in the appendix. A brief description follows.

The model assumes the real GDP growth path for 1991–95 forecast by the Central Bank of Chile. The ratio of copper exports to GDP is adjusted from the 1990 base period by the ratio of the price of copper in the simulation year to that in the base year, the ratio of government expenditure to GDP is assumed to remain at its average for 1989–92, the terms-of-trade forecasts were obtained from the World Bank projections, and noncopper exports and demand for imports were predicted by behavioral equations. When combined with the Chile equation of table 4, the above system allows the simulation of the ERER. To compute the simulations for the actual RER, the ratio of domestic credit to GDP was assumed to remain at the average for 1991, and the rate of nominal devaluation was assumed to remain at the annualized average for January to December 1991. Adding the Chile error correction equation of table 5 to the above completes the ingredients needed for simulating the actual RER.

According to the simulations, the results of which are reported in table 10, the Chilean peso should depreciate in real terms by 1.4 percent

Table 7   Chile: actual real exchange rates and misalignment from equilibrium rate[a]

Year	Real exchange rate (actual 1980 = 100) Actual	Real exchange rate (actual 1980 = 100) Equilibrium	Misalignment (percentages)
1965	294.3	..	..
1966	275.4	..	..
1967	261.7	..	..
1968	244.0	238.8	2.2
1969	234.1	239.0	−2.1
1970	223.2	236.4	−5.6
1971	242.7	261.1	−7.0
1972	254.2	285.7	−11.0
1973	398.2	259.4	53.5
1974	136.1	196.8	−30.8
1975	103.7	172.7	−39.9
1976	99.0	115.7	−14.4
1977	106.4	109.7	−3.0
1978	88.1	100.3	−12.2
1979	87.4	105.9	−17.4
1980	100.0	104.5	−4.3
1981	118.1	96.5	22.3
1982	109.5	98.5	11.2
1983	87.7	96.9	−9.5
1984	87.0	87.0	0.0
1985	70.4	81.7	−13.9
1986	63.3	73.0	−13.3
1987	60.2	65.4	−8.0
1988	54.7	56.8	−3.6
1989	52.8	57.5	−8.2
1990	51.4	51.6	−0.3

a. The base period for rescaling the equilibrium exchange rate was determined as the unweighted average of the observations in those years in which the resource balance was either zero or positive.

Source: World Bank data base.

in 1991 relative to 1990, but a different story emerges thereafter. To avoid RER overvaluation in the first half of 1990, the currency must be depreciated in real terms by 3.3 percent in 1992 relative to its 1991 level, and by a further 5.4 percent in 1993 relative to the 1992 level, by 1995 the required RER depreciation from the previous year will be 5.6 percent. These numbers[24] suggest that even if a nominal currency revaluation in Chile could be justified from the viewpoint of other macroeconomic objectives, it is nevertheless likely to compromise the external competitiveness of the economy, especially if the change in policy is not a one-shot devaluation. The above simulations may need to be qualified, however, by the recent evidence that attributes the recent RER appreciation (i.e.,

24. These derived rates of required RER depreciation are in fact conservative, since a nominal revaluation was not assumed in the simulation period.

Table 8   Ghana: actual real exchange rates and misalignment from equilibrium rate[a]

| Year | Real exchange rate (actual 1980 = 100) | | Misalignment (percentages) |
	Actual	Equilibrium	
1965	72.8	..	..
1966	79.9	..	..
1967	60.4	65.8	−8.2
1968	56.8	62.1	−8.5
1969	59.2	59.1	0.1
1970	57.8	57.4	0.7
1971	57.6	60.1	−4.1
1972	44.4	55.5	−20.0
1973	50.8	55.6	−8.7
1974	51.3	60.2	−14.8
1975	58.9	68.3	−13.8
1976	90.7	91.6	−1.0
1977	177.2	112.4	57.6
1978	167.9	138.3	21.5
1979	144.7	186.2	−22.3
1980	189.3	261.4	−27.6
1981	432.3	292.7	47.7
1982	549.0	316.4	73.5
1983	388.8	308.7	25.9
1984	134.6	202.0	−33.4
1985	100.1	117.1	−14.5
1986	67.4	78.5	−14.2
1987	49.3	55.4	−10.9
1988	45.6	13.6	4.7
1989	44.2	44.4	−0.4
1990	44.0	47.1	−6.6

a. The base period for rescaling the equilibrium exchange rate was determined as the unweighted average of the observations in those years in which the resource balance was either zero or positive.

since January 1991) in Chile and other Latin American countries to exogenous capital inflows, caused by the US recession and lower dollar interest rates (Calvo et al. 1992). To the extent that these inflows are not temporary, the ensuing RER appreciation is consistent with equilibrium. On the other hand, if the capital inflows are perceived to be temporary, these authors recommend taxes or direct capital controls to stem their flow rather than a nominal revaluation.

Conclusions

This paper follows Edwards in defining the "equilibrium real exchange rate" (ERER) as "the relative price of tradables to nontradables which, for given sustainable values of other relevant variables such as taxes, international terms of trade, commercial policy, capital and aid flows and technology, results in the simultaneous attainment of *internal* and

Table 9 India: actual real exchange rates and misalignment from equilibrium rate[a]

| Year | Real exchange rate (actual 1980 = 100) | | Misalignment (percentages) |
	Actual	Equilibrium	
1965	275.5	236.9	16.3
1966	239.6	222.7	7.6
1967	212.8	215.8	−1.4
1968	218.8	206.3	6.1
1969	215.0	205.5	4.6
1970	218.2	205.8	6.0
1971	206.7	200.5	3.1
1972	197.0	187.8	4.9
1973	180.0	170.9	5.3
1974	149.6	152.5	−1.9
1975	143.2	136.7	4.7
1976	119.5	127.0	−5.9
1977	121.2	119.1	1.7
1978	118.9	113.7	4.6
1979	106.8	110.2	−3.1
1980	100.0	106.7	−6.3
1981	99.6	103.2	−3.5
1982	101.1	100.7	0.4
1983	109.5	100.8	8.6
1984	107.9	101.8	6.0
1985	105.4	101.6	3.8
1986	110.2	99.6	10.6
1987	104.5	98.4	6.2
1988	103.6	94.7	9.4

a. The base period for rescaling the equilibrium exchange rate is 1974–79.

external equilibrium'' (Edwards 1989, 16). This paper has argued that, given the above concept of equilibrium, a successful modeling strategy should have at least three elements: it should specify the ERER as a forward-looking function of the fundamentals; it should allow for flexible dynamic adjustment of the RER toward the ERER; and it should allow for the influence of short- to medium-run macroeconomic and exchange rate policy on the RER.

This paper has developed a model that accounts for the above features and extends the basic model (i.e., that of Dornbusch 1974, Edwards 1989, and Rodriguez 1989) by linking capital flows to expected real depreciation in the context of a linear rational expectations model. A desirable property of the model is that, in the presence of stochastic nonstationarity and cointegration, the forward-looking solution of the long-run ERER path collapses to the simple equation predicted by the basic model. Furthermore, stochastic nonstationarity suggests a natural methodology for generating the "sustainable" components of the fundamentals, by using the Beveridge-Nelson type of decomposition.

Given the generally accepted empirical regularity regarding the prevalence of unit root nonstationarity in macroeconomic time series, this

Table 10 Chile: simulation of the real exchange rate, 1991-95[a]

	ERER model		RER model[b]		Required RER depreciation[c]
Year	$\frac{X-M}{GDP}$	ERER	$\frac{X-M}{GDP}$	RER	
1989	3.6	52.0	3.6	52.8	..
1990	2.9	48.7	2.9	51.4	..
1991	3.4	50.0	1.4	49.3	−1.4
1992	2.6	48.3	0.5	49.8	3.3
1993	1.2	46.1	−0.6	48.6	5.4
1994	1.3	44.3	−0.9	46.7	5.3
1995	1.3	42.5	−1.4	44.8	5.6

a. The simulation is based on the model described in the appendix. The first two rows are historical data reported for purpose of comparison.
b. The RER model is simulated on the assumption that macroeconomic policy over 1991–95 will be on average the same as in 1988–90, and nominal exchange rate policy the same as in 1991.
c. Given by $\frac{RER - ERER}{RER} \times 100$.

modeling strategy permits tractable empirical estimation of the ERER in a manner that is also consistent with theory. This was demonstrated by applying the model to three countries: Chile, Ghana, and India. The first two countries are examples of a very proactive style of macro-economic and exchange rate management. Both countries experienced episodes of expansive and unsustainable macroeconomic policies that produced massive real currency appreciation and deteriorating economic performance. Yet both were able to reverse their economic decline and achieve sustained and significant growth when they undertook profound macroeconomic reforms in which management of the real exchange rate played a key role.

In India, on the other hand, elaborate controls were maintained but macroeconomic policy has been rather conservative. India exhibits none of the extreme external shocks or policy changes experienced in Chile and Ghana—including massive real appreciation or depreciation—and none of the extreme outcomes such as accelerated growth or lasting major recessions accompanied by large increases in unemployment or inflation and debt servicing problems. More recently, however, there is evidence of slowly rising inflation, as monetary growth has started to increase as a result of accelerated borrowing from the reserve bank and the commercial banking system.

The estimation of the long-run cointegration equation of the ERER and the corresponding dynamic error correction specification strongly corroborates the model and produced fairly consistent results across the three countries. Using proxies for "sustainable" fundamentals and subject to a "sensible" normalization rule, the estimated long-run equations were used to derive indexes of the ERER. Furthermore, for the case of Chile a simple simulation model, centered around the two RER equations, was used to assess the potential implications for external competitiveness of the envisaged nominal exchange rate revaluation policy. The estimated ERERs and the corresponding rates of RER misalignment confirm that the ERER is not a fixed, immutable number (Edwards)—a finding that implies that simple PPP modeling of the RER could be a misleading simplification. Also, the above-derived indicators were fairly successful in reproducing the salient episodes and characteristics of the three countries.

References

Beveridge, S., and C. Nelson. 1981. "A New Approach to Decompositions of Economic Time Series into Permanent and Transitory Components with Particular Attention to Measurement of the Business Cycle." *Journal of Monetary Economics* 7: 151–74.

Caballero, R., and V. Corbo. 1989. "How Does Uncertainty About the Real Exchange Rate Affect Exports?" Policy Research Working Paper Series No. 221. Washington: World Bank (June).

Calvo, G., L. Leiderman, and C. Reinhart. 1992. "Real Exchange Rate Appreciation in Latin America." Washington: International Monetary Fund (unpublished memorandum).

Campbell, J., and P. Perron. 1991. "Pitfalls and Opportunities: What Macroeconomists Should Know about Unit Roots." Paper presented at the Sixth Annual Conference on Macroeconomics, sponsored by the National Bureau of Economic Research, Cambridge, MA (March).

Chhibber, A., and C. Leechor. 1992. "From Adjustment to Growth in Sub-Saharan Africa: The Lesson of East Asian Experience." Paper presented at the International Conference on African Economic Issues, Abidjan (October).

Coleman, J. R., T. Akiyama, and P. N. Varangis. 1992. "Impact of Recent Policy Changes in Major Sub-Saharan Cocoa Producing Countries." Washington: World Bank (unpublished).

Corbo, V. 1985. "Reforms and Macroeconomic Adjustment in Chile During 1974–84." *World Development* 13, no. 8:893–916.

Corbo, V., and A. Solimano. 1991. "Chile's Experience with Stabilization Revisited." In M. Bruno et al., eds., *Lessons of Economic Stabilization and Its Aftermath*. Cambridge, MA: MIT Press.

Cuddington, J., and C. Urzúa. 1989. "Trends and Cycles in Colombia's Real GDP and Fiscal Deficit." *Journal of Development Economics* 30: 325–43.

Cuddington, J., and L. Alan Winters. 1987. "The Beveridge-Nelson Decomposition of Economic Time Series: A Quick Computational Method." *Journal of Monetary Economics* 19: 125–27.

Delgado, C. 1992. "Determinants of Growth and Comparative Advantage in Semi-Open West African Agriculture." *Journal of African Economies* 1, no. 3 (November): 446–71.

Díaz-Alejandro, C. F. 1984. "Exchange Rates and Terms of Trade in the Argentine Republic: 1913–76." In M. Syrquin and S. Teitel, eds., *Trade, Stability, Technology and Equity in Latin America*. New York: Academic Press.

Domowitz, Ian, and Ibrahim Elbadawi. 1987. "An Error-Correction Approach to Money Demand: The Case of the Sudan." *Journal of Economic Development*. 26: 257–75.

Dornbusch, R. 1973. "Tariffs and Non-Traded Goods." *Journal of International Economics* 4: 177–85.

Edwards, S. 1986a. "The Order of Liberalization of the Current and Capital Accounts of the Balance of Payments." In A. Cleoksi and D. Papageorgio, eds., *Economic Liberalization in Developing Countries*. Oxford: Blackwell.

Edwards, S. 1986b. "Commodity Export Prices and the Real Exchange Rate in Developing Countries: Coffee in Colombia." In S. Edwards and L. Ahamed, eds., *Economic Adjustment and Exchange Rates in Developing Countries*. Chicago: University of Chicago Press.

Edwards, S. 1986c. "Tariffs, Terms of Trade and Real Exchange Rates in an Intertemporal Model of the Current Account." NBER Working Paper No. 2175. Cambridge, MA: National Bureau of Economic Research.

Edwards, S. 1989. *Real Exchange Rates, Devaluation and Adjustment: Exchange Rate Policy in Developing Countries*. Cambridge, MA: MIT Press.

Edwards, S. 1992. "Trade Orientation, Distortions and Growth in Developing Countries." *Journal of Development Economics* 39: 31–57.

Edwards, S., and S. van Wijnbergen. 1986a. "The Welfare Effects of Trade and Capital Market Liberalization." *International Economic Review* 27, no. 1 (February): 141–48.

Edwards, S., and S. van Wijnbergen. 1987. "Tariffs, Real Exchange Rates and the Terms of Trade: On Two Popular Propositions in International Economics." *Oxford Economic Papers* 39 (September): 458–64.

Elbadawi, Ibrahim. 1983. "Semi-Nonparametric Analysis of Consumer Demand Systems." Unpublished Ph.D. dissertation, North Carolina State University, Raleigh, NC.

Elbadawi, Ibrahim. 1992a. "Terms of Trade, Commercial Policy and the Parallel Market for Foreign Exchange: An Empirical Model of Real Exchange Rate Determination." *Journal of African Finance and Economic Development* 1, no. 2: 1–26.

Elbadawi, Ibrahim. 1992b. "Real Overvaluation, Terms of Trade Shocks, and the Cost to Agriculture in SSA: The Case of the Sudan." *Journal of African Economies* 1, no. 1 (March).

Engle, R., and C. Granger. 1987. "Co-Integration and Error-Correction: Representation, Estimation, and Testing." *Econometrica* 35: 251–76.

Fischer, E., and J. Y. Park. 1991. "Testing Purchasing Power Parity under the Null Hypothesis of Co-integration." *Economic Journal* (November): 1476–84.

Harberger, A. C. 1982. "The Chilean Economy in the 1970s: Crisis, Stabilization, Liberalization, Reform." In K. Brunner and A. M. Meltzer, eds., *Economic Policy in a World of Change*. Carnegie-Rochester Conference Series on Public Policy Vol. 17.

Helleiner, G. 1992. "Trade Policy, Exchange Rates, and Relative Prices in Sub-Saharan Africa: Interpreting the 1980s." Paper presented at the Gothenburg Conference, Sweden (6–8 September).

Islam, R., and D. Wetzel. 1991. "The Macroeconomics of Public Sector Deficits: The Case of Ghana." Policy Research Working Paper Series No. 672. Washington: World Bank.

Jebuni, C. D., N. K. Sowa, and K. A. Tutu. 1991. "Exchange Rate Policy and Macroeconomic Performance in Ghana." Research Paper No. 6. Nairobi: African Economic Research Consortium (AERC).

Joshi, V., and I. M. D. Little. 1989. "Indian Macroeconomic Policies." In G. Calvo, R. Findlay, P. Kouri, and J. Macedo, eds., *Debt, Stabilization and Development: Essays in Memory of Carlos Díaz-Alejandro*. Helsinki: World Institute for Development Economics Research (WIDER).

Kaminsky, G. 1988. "The Real Exchange Rate Since Floating: Market Fundamentals or Bubbles." San Diego: University of California, San Diego (mimeographed).

Lizondo, J. Saul. 1989. "Overvalued and Undervalued Exchange Rates in an Equilibrium Optimizing Model." Policy Research Working Paper Series No. 223. Washington: World Bank (August).

Matin, K. 1992. "Openness and Economic Performance in Sub-Saharan Africa." Washington: World Bank (mimeographed).

Mundlak, Yair, D. Cavallo, and R. Domench. 1987. "Effects of Trade and Macroeconomic Policies on Agriculture and Economic Growth: Argentina 1913-1984." Paper presented at a Workshop on Trade and Macroeconomic Policy's Impact on Agriculture, sponsored by the International Food Policy Research Institute, Annapolis, MD (27-29 May).

Mussa, M. L. 1974. "Tariffs and the Distribution of Income: The Importance of Factor Specificity Substitutability and Intensity in the Short and Long Run." *Journal of Political Economy* 82, no. 6: 1191-1203.

Mussa, M. L. 1978. "Dynamic Adjustment in the Heckscher-Ohlin-Samuelson Model." *Journal of Political Economy* 86, no. 5: 775-91.

Nelson, C., and C. Plosser. 1982. "Trends and Random Walks in Macroeconomic Time Series: Some Evidence and Implications." *Journal of Monetary Economics* 10: 139-62.

Perron, P. 1989. "The Great Crash, the Oil Price Shocks and the Unit Root Hypothesis." *Econometrica* 57: 1361-1401.

Pesaran, M. Hasem. 1987. *The Limits to Rational Expectations*. Oxford: Blackwell.

Pinto, B. 1987. "Exchange Rate Unification and Budgetary Policy in Sub-Saharan Africa." Washington: World Bank (mimeographed).

Pinto, B. 1988a. "Black Markets for Foreign Exchange, Real Exchange Rates and Inflation: Overnight vs. Gradual Reform in Sub-Saharan Africa." Washington: World Bank (mimeographed, revised, May).

Pinto, B. 1988b. "Black Market Premia, Exchange Rate Unification, and Inflation in Sub-Saharan Africa." Washington: World Bank (mimeographed).

Rodriguez, Carlos A. 1989. "Macroeconomic Policies for Structural Adjustment." Policy Research Working Paper Series No. 247. Washington: World Bank.

Serven, L., and A. Solimano. 1991. "An Empirical Macroeconomic Model for Policy Design: The Case of Chile." Policy Research Working Paper Series No. 709. Washington: World Bank (June).

Sjastad, Larry A. 1980. "Commercial Policy, True Tariffs, and Relative Prices." In John Black and Brian Hindley, eds., *Current Issues in Commercial Policy and Diplomacy*. New York: St. Martin's Press.

Valdés, A. 1985. "Exchange Rates and Trade Policy: Help or Hindrance to Agricultural Growth." Proceedings of the 19th International Conference of Agriculture Economists, Malaga, Spain (September).

Valdés, A. 1992. "Gaining Momentum: Economy Wide and Agricultural Reform in Latin America." Washington: World Bank (mimeographed).

White, H. 1980. "Using Least Squares to Approximate Unknown Regression Functions." *International Economic Review* 21: 149-70.

Youngblood, C. 1992. "Determinants of the Real Exchange Rate in Ghana: Implications for Export Promotion." Raleigh, NC: Sigma One Corporation (mimeographed).

Younger, S. 1992. "Aid and the Dutch Disease: Macroeconomic Management When Everybody Loves You." *World Development* 20, no. 11: 1587-97.

Appendix: The Simulation Model for Chile

Definitions

X_{nc}	= noncopper exports in nominal pesos
X_c	= copper exports in nominal pesos
GDP	= GDP in nominal pesos
M	= imports in nominal pesos
RGDP*	= real world imports from LDCs
P_c^*	= fixed dollar international price of copper
Dom. Cred.	= domestic credit
e	= real exchange rate
RGDP	= real GDP
USGDP	= US real GDP
X	= total exports
	$(X_{nc} + X_c)$
D6073	$\begin{cases}1 \text{ for } 1960\text{--}73 \\ 0 \text{ for } 1974\text{--}90\end{cases}$
G.EXP	= government expenditures
TOT	= terms of trade

Assumptions and Identities

Real GDP growth (from Central Bank of Chile)

1991	1992	1993	1994	1995
6.0	10.0	7.0	5.5	5.5

USGDP growth

1991	1992	1993	1994	1995
−0.2	2.0	3.0	3.0	3.0

TOT_t (World Bank projections, unified survey)

1991	1992	1993	1994	1995
112.5	106.9	96.0	98.0	100.0

$$\left(\frac{X_c}{\text{GDP}}\right)_t = \left(\frac{X_c}{\text{GDP}}\right)_{to} \cdot \frac{P_{c_t}^*}{P_{c_{to}}^*}, \text{ where } t_o = 1990, t = 1991, \ldots, 1995$$

1991	1992	1993	1994	1995
17.4	16.5	15.6	15.8	16.0

$$\left(\frac{\text{G.EXP}}{\text{GDP}}\right)_t = 21.5, \text{ historical average for } (1988\text{--}92), t = 1991, \ldots, 1995$$

$$\left(\frac{X}{GDP}\right)_t = \frac{X_{nc_t} + X_{c_t}}{GDP_t}$$

$$FLOW_t = \frac{M_t - X_t}{GDP_t}$$

$$OPEN_t = \frac{M_t + X_t}{GDP_t}$$

The Equilibrium RER

Noncopper export supply

$$\text{Log} \frac{X_{nc}}{GDP_t} = \underset{(14.4)}{1.30} + \underset{(29.4)}{0.62} \log \frac{X_{nc}}{GDP_{t-1}} - \underset{(-2.31)}{0.0001} \log USGDP_t$$
$$- \underset{(-4.37)}{0.89} \log RER_{t-1} - \underset{(-18.6)}{0.71} \ D6073$$

Demand for imports

$$\text{Log} \frac{M}{GDP_t} = \underset{(6.43)}{1.29} + \underset{(30.8)}{0.51} \log \frac{M}{GDP_{t-1}} + \underset{(1.43)}{0.34} \log GDP_{t-1}$$
$$- \underset{(-20.5)}{0.007} \log RER_{t-1} - \underset{(-28.7)}{0.295} \ D6073$$

The ERER (table 2)

$$\text{Log } e_t = 4.92 - 0.05 \text{ TREND } (1965 = 1) + 0.29 \log TOT_t$$
$$+ 1.87 \text{ FLOW}_t - 0.41 \log OPEN_t$$
$$+ 0.85 \log \left(\frac{G.EXP}{GDP}\right)_t$$

The variables and equations above generate the simulations for the ERER and the corresponding resource balance–GDP ratio.

The Actual RER Under a "No Policy Change" Scenario

$$MACRO_t = \Delta\log \left(\frac{\text{Dom. Cred.}}{GDP}\right)_t, \text{ where } t = 1991, \ldots, 1995.$$

$NOMDEV_t$ = sum of monthly devaluations from January to December 1991, t = 1991–95.

$\widehat{ERER}_t = \hat{e}$ from the previous simulation, $t = 1991\text{–}95$.

The RER (table 3)

$$\Delta\log e_t = 0.78\,(\log \widehat{ERER}_{t-1} - \log RER_{t-1})$$
$$+\; 0.32\,\Delta\log TOT_t + 1.59\,\Delta FLOW_t$$
$$-\; 0.45\,\Delta\log OPEN_t + 0.63\,\Delta\log \left(\frac{G.EXP}{GDP}\right)_t$$
$$+\; 0.04\,\Delta\log(\text{Dom. Cred.}/\text{real GDP})_t + 0.12\,NOMDEV_t$$
$$-\; 0.21\,NOMDEV_{t-1}$$

As before, the variables and equations above generate simulations of the RER and the corresponding resource balance–GDP ratio. The results are presented in table 6.

Table A1 Chile: basic data (millions of current pesos except where stated otherwise)

Year	GDP	Imports of goods and services	Exports of goods and services	Terms of trade (1980 = 100)	GDP deflator (1980 = 100)	CPI (1980 = 100)	Real exchange rate (1980 = 100)	Total government expenditures	Current government expenditures	Nominal exchange rate[a]	Domestic credit	Money (M1)	Quasi money (QM)
1965	18	2.4	2.5	152.9	0.00	0.01	294.3	5	4	0.00	4	1	1
1966	25	3.6	3.9	185.2	0.00	0.01	275.4	6	6	0.00	5	3	2
1967	33	4.5	4.9	176.4	0.00	0.01	261.7	8	7	0.01	1	3	2
1968	44	6.3	6.6	188.6	0.00	0.01	244.0	9	9	0.01	7	4	3
1969	65	9.8	11.4	222.8	0.00	0.02	234.1	14	14	0.01	9	6	5
1970	93	14.4	14.6	226.1	0.00	0.02	223.2	21	21	0.01	11	10	6
1971	124	14.8	13.4	172.3	0.00	0.03	242.7	34	34	0.02	17	21	10
1972	232	31	20	166.2	0.03	0.05	254.2	69	68	0.03	40	54	26
1973	1,150	180	160	187.2	0.14	0.23	398.2	487	484	0.36	101	229	217
1974	9,200	1,820	1,880	197.8	1.07	1.39	136.1	2,298	2,263	1.87	714	838	1,189
1975	35,450	9,730	9,040	118.5	4.74	6.6	103.7	7,449	7,361	8.50	4,008	2,995	4,516
1976	128,680	26,750	32,320	127.8	16.61	20.6	99.0	24,102	23,816	17.42	47,161	9,722	16,170
1977	287,770	64,520	59,340	114.4	33.80	39.6	106.4	57,025	55,970	27.96	129,200	34,200	27,600
1978	487,510	116,650	100,350	111.0	52.91	55.5	88.1	94,533	93,298	33.95	181,500	33,900	69,800
1979	772,200	201,610	179,740	118.5	77.41	74.0	87.4	151,242	143,420	39.00	294,000	55,100	124,600
1980	1,075,270	290,100	245,390	100.0	100.00	100.0	100.0	216,788	210,563	39.00	446,500	85,300	221,900
1981	1,273,120	340,620	209,020	84.3	112.21	119.7	118.1	292,545	288,685	39.00	610,300	81,900	32,990
1982	1,239,120	263,360	239,860	80.3	127.14	131.6	109.5	323,376	319,161	73.43	1,050,300	92,200	485,000
1983	1,557,710	332,090	374,470	87.5	160.98	167.5	87.7	400,246	387,257	87.53	1,279,100	112,200	589,500
1984	1,893,390	479,580	459,490	83.1	184.00	200.7	97.0	501,271	466,709	128.24	2,057,100	130,400	589,900
1985	2,576,640	678,120	749,210	77.2	244.28	262.3	70.4	782,302	650,398	183.86	3,062,900	148,400	912,500
1986	3,246,110	870,210	994,170	85.8	291.35	313.4	63.3	905,975	810,215	204.73	3,712,500	214,900	1,114,200
1987	4,159,760	1,223,730	1,394,260	59.4	353.12	375.7	60.2	1,087,479	964,083	238.14	4,454,200	229,200	1,564,500
1988	5,411,020	1,632,970	2,022,030	108.2	427.82	430.9	54.7	1,421,741	1,231,458	247.20	5,003,000	385,500	1,894,600
1989	6,778,400	2,320,100	2,566,000	110.8	487.31	503.7	52.8	1,461,135	1,326,168	297.37	5,573,700	441,600	2,548,900
1990	8,477,900	2,854,000	3,099,200	110.0	596.67	634.8	51.4	1,929,439	1,796,567	337.09	6,707,900	517,600	3,178,100

a. Pesos per US dollar.

Source: World Bank data base.

Table A2 Ghana: basic data (millions of current cedis except where stated otherwise)

Year	GDP at constant 1985 prices	Imports of goods and services	Exports of goods and services	Terms of trade (1980 = 100)	GDP deflator (1980 = 100)	CPI (1980 = 100)	Real exchange rate (1985 = 100)	Current government expenditures	Nominal exchange rate[a]	Domestic credit	Money (M1)	Quasi money (QM)
1965	293,200	392	251	181.4	4.0	2.7	72.8	212	0.71	348	240	60
1966	253,000	298	222	234.2	4.8	2.7	79.9	198	0.71	406	248	67
1967	250,667	315	274	278.0	4.8	2.7	60.4	225	0.87	481	241	78
1968	283,333	369	396	322.4	4.8	2.7	56.8	285	1.02	537	259	93
1969	285,571	428	447	411.3	5.6	3.6	59.2	285	1.02	577	290	99
1970	322,714	539	523	307.5	5.6	3.6	57.8	290	1.02	600	306	121
1971	312,625	536	443	192.8	6.5	3.6	57.6	324	1.04	736	321	154
1972	312,778	484	648	220.2	7.3	3.6	44.4	355	1.04	828	463	205
1973	389,111	635	820	283.9	7.3	4.5	50.8	382	1.33	843	564	230
1974	388,333	1,061	956	153.1	9.7	5.5	51.3	569	1.17	1,254	697	308
1975	330,188	974	1,023	110.7	12.9	7.3	58.9	689	1.15	1,598	1,009	377
1976	326,300	1,047	1,025	153.0	16.1	11.8	90.7	799	1.15	2,429	1,429	474
1977	328,324	1,289	1,171	247.0	27.4	24.5	177.2	1,409	1.15	3,848	2,393	651
1978	355,695	2,033	1,754	206.6	47.6	42.7	167.9	2,371	1.76	6,454	4,126	1,005
1979	348,420	3,150	3,169	161.2	65.3	66.4	144.7	2,903	2.75	7,406	4,680	1,262
1980	345,589	3,933	3,629	100.0	100.0	100.0	189.3	4,500	2.75	9,493	6,085	1,864
1981	340,498	3,966	3,454	67.7	171.8	216.4	432.3	6,384	2.75	15,438	9,413	2,616
1982	315,515	2,578	2,886	57.8	221.0	264.5	549.0	5,630	2.75	18,827	11,203	3,634
1983	317,872	11,022	10,225	75.0	466.9	590.0	388.8	10,787	8.83	32,429	16,717	4,086
1984	326,370	20,871	20,161	82.7	668.5	824.5	134.6	19,641	35.99	48,723	26,849	5,113
1985	343,048	39,800	33,185	76.5	806.5	909.1	100.1	32,241	54.37	77,823	38,310	8,410
1986	360,621	90,400	81,800	147.9	1,142.7	1,132.7	67.4	56,600	89.20	119,140	55,160	13,960
1987	348,104	174,700	157,800	122.1	1,591.1	1,583.6	49.3	74,700	153.73	205,380	84,170	21,800
1988	401,823	220,600	217,700	137.5	2,123.4	2,080.0	45.6	104,800	202.35	195,550	122,030	32,980
1989	419,822	n.a.	n.a.	94.5	n.a.	2,604.5	44.2	n.a.	270.00	242,990	186,390	53,360
1990	432,418	n.a.	n.a.	75.8	n.a.	3,574.5	44.0	n.a.	326.33	252,810	206,440	65,200

n.a. = not available.
a. Cedis per US dollar.

Source: World Bank data base.

129

Table A3 India: basic data (millions of current rupees except where stated otherwise)

Year	GDP	Imports of goods and services	Exports of goods and services	Terms of trade (1980 = 100)	GDP deflator (1980 = 100)	CPI (1980 = 100)	Real exchange rate (1980 = 100)	Total government expenditures	Current government expenditures	Nominal exchange rate[a]	Domestic credit	Money (M1)	Quasi money (QM)
1965	241,120	14,640	9,320	160.7	30.8	34.6	275.5	26,600	23,000	6.4	66,260	39,050	14,220
1966	276,620	21,150	13,250	168.2	35.0	38.4	239.6	30,400	25,000	7.5	74,750	43,010	16,060
1967	322,940	22,010	15,080	185.8	37.7	43.4	212.8	31,500	27,900	7.5	81,280	46,810	18,880
1968	332,790	18,970	15,970	174.8	37.8	44.7	218.8	30,400	30,500	7.5	87,970	51,030	20,810
1969	368,510	17,470	16,250	182.4	39.4	44.9	215.0	35,300	34,200	7.5	96,584	53,890	24,790
1970	402,630	18,160	16,390	201.3	40.7	47.2	218.2	39,300	38,000	7.5	106,978	60,378	28,937
1971	433,560	21,750	17,850	195.7	42.8	48.7	206.7	49,300	44,600	7.5	128,801	67,649	32,410
1972	478,650	20,490	21,490	229.9	47.8	51.8	197.0	55,200	47,500	7.6	148,512	76,477	40,660
1973	589,400	31,760	26,580	154.8	56.5	60.6	180.0	58,100	51,000	7.7	178,551	86,150	49,019
1974	696,280	47,790	36,860	118.3	66.7	77.9	149.6	77,000	60,800	8.1	205,381	101,040	60,475
1975	729,260	56,640	49,470	100.5	64.5	82.4	143.2	93,300	73,000	8.4	239,290	111,280	69,986
1976	801,480	56,140	61,260	126.0	68.9	76.1	119.5	104,100	81,100	9.0	277,813	122,343	84,394
1977	891,480	65,170	63,950	133.2	70.8	82.4	121.2	114,800	85,400	8.7	319,742	152,774	104,578
1978	1,041,900	74,230	71,150	169.1	77.6	84.5	118.9	133,500	97,200	8.2	374,884	178,499	128,173
1979	1,143,560	100,940	83,400	120.2	89.5	89.8	106.8	159,000	111,700	8.1	510,200	157,633	213,910
1980	1,360,130	135,960	90,290	100.0	100.0	100.0	100.0	180,300	130,800	7.9	623,600	176,857	260,480
1981	1,597,600	148,090	102,560	109.6	110.3	113.1	99.6	208,400	153,600	8.7	741,000	204,582	302,293
1982	1,781,320	157,360	115,630	109.9	118.5	122.0	101.1	244,200	182,700	9.5	864,200	232,469	362,860
1983	2,075,890	176,750	131,390	114.1	128.5	136.5	109.5	287,200	211,400	10.1	1,013,700	273,712	424,037
1984	2,313,870	194,840	158,460	120.6	138.1	147.9	107.9	351,300	243,500	11.4	1,211,800	308,553	507,026
1985	2,619,200	217,540	149,510	116.9	148.2	156.1	105.4	430,700	291,700	12.4	1,411,200	365,578	596,678
1986	2,919,760	223,590	165,430	127.3	158.1	156.7	110.2	518,100	346,300	12.6	1,667,600	412,414	712,302
1987	3,326,160	252,590	202,810	125.9	171.6	184.7	104.5	597,100	410,300	13.0	1,918,600	478,669	847,680
1988	3,949,920	319,690	259,830	134.9	185.8	202.0	103.6	700,600	472,000	13.9	2,300,400	543,174	999,606
1989	3,949,900	n.a.	n.a.	n.a.	n.a.	n.a.	n.a.	n.a.	n.a.	16.23	n.a.	n.a.	n.a.
1990	4,427,700	n.a.	n.a.	n.a.	n.a.	n.a.	n.a.	n.a.	n.a.	17.50	n.a.	n.a.	n.a.

n.a. = not available.
a. Rupees per US dollar.

Source: World Bank data base.

Table A4   Unit root tests for RER fundamentals

Variable	Chile ADF(0)[a]	Chile ADF(4)	India ADF(0)	India ADF(1)	Ghana ADF(0)	Ghana ADF(4)
log RER$_t$	−2.84	...	−0.67	...	−0.97	−2.00
Δlog RER$_t$	−5.14	...	−4.09	...	−2.70	...
log TOT	−1.48	...	−2.11	...	−1.22	...
Δlog TOT	−4.88	...	−4.18	...	−4.58	...
log OPEN	−2.32	...	−1.70	−2.83	−1.10	−1.83
Δlog OPEN	−3.08	...	−2.57	...	−3.00	...
log MGDP	−2.59	...	−2.31	...	−1.24	−1.70
Δlog MGDP	−4.70	...	−3.27	...	−3.23	...
FLOW	−2.74	...	−2.88	...	−1.34	...
Δlog FLOW	−6.19	...	−4.07	...	−4.15	...
log EXPGDP	−2.28	−2.56	−3.95	...	−3.55	−2.61
Δlog EXPGDP	−4.63	−4.38	−4.32	...	−5.61	...
log CUR	−2.57	−2.27	−3.23	...	−4.36	−1.58
Δlog CUR	−5.28	−4.38	−3.94	...	−5.36	...
MacKinnon critical values						
1%	−4.39	−4.47	−4.44	−4.44	−4.39	−4.47
5%	−3.61	−3.65	−3.63	−3.63	−3.61	−3.65
10%	−3.24	−3.26	−3.25	−3.25	−3.24	−3.26

ADF = augmented Dickey-Fuller statistic; MGDP = ratio of imports to GDP; EXPGDP = government expenditures as a share of GDP; CUR = current account; see table 4 for other definitions.

a. The ADF(K) test is based on the auxiliary regression: $\Delta X_t = \alpha_0 + \alpha_1 \text{TREND} + \alpha_2 X_{t-1} + \sum_{i=1}^{K} \beta_i \Delta X_{t-1}$, where k is given by the maximum lag for which the corresponding β_i is significant, and the ADF statistic is given by the t-statistic of the X_{t-1}'s coefficient.

Table A5   ARIMA models[a]

Chile

$(1 - 0.49L + 0.75L^2) \Delta \log \text{OPEN} = (1 - 0.52L^2)u_t$ $r^2 = 0.42$
$\quad(-2.79)\quad(4.86)\qquad\qquad\qquad(1.80)$ $DW = 1.71$

$(1 + 0.57L + 0.73L^2) \Delta \log \text{TOT} = (1 + 0.86L + 1.62L^2)u_t$ $r^2 = 0.52$
$\quad(3.48)\quad(5.25)\qquad\qquad\quad(3.76)\quad(6.08)$ $DW = 1.78$

$(1 - 0.68L) \Delta \log \text{G.EXP/GDP} = (1 + 1.05L)u_t$ $r^2 = 0.31$
$\quad(-3.41)\qquad\qquad\qquad\qquad(12.99)$ $DW = 1.60$

Ghana

$(1 - 0.58L) \Delta \text{FLOW}_t = (1 - 1.28L)u_t$ $r^2 = 0.33$
$\quad(10.9)\qquad\qquad(-3.23)$ $DW = 1.79$

$(1 + 0.39L - 0.20L^2) \Delta \log \text{TOT}_t = (1 - 1.44L)u_t$ $r^2 = 0.46$
$\quad(3.36)\ (-1.15)\qquad\qquad\quad(-6.87)$ $DW = 2.16$

a. The decomposition is based on the following steps. First, first differences of the logged variables are obtained. Second, the Box-Jenkins technique is used to identify and estimate an ARIMA model. Third, using the steady-state "gain function" approach (Cuddington and Winters 1987), a first-order difference equation in the permanent component of the series can be obtained as a linear function of the corresponding residuals. Finally, using the computational techniques suggested by Beveridge and Nelson (1981) and Cuddington and Winters (1987), the difference equation can be solved for the levels of the permanent components. The transitory component then obtains as the permanent minus the observed series.

5

The Natural Real Exchange Rate of the US Dollar and Determinants of Capital Flows

JEROME L. STEIN

A communiqué issued at the end of the Group of Seven meeting in March 1993 stated:

> We agreed that exchange rates should reflect economic fundamentals and that excess volatility is undesirable. We reviewed recent developments in the foreign exchange markets and affirmed our continued commitment to close cooperation in exchange markets. (*Wall Street Journal*, 30 April 1993, C-13)

There are several ambiguities in this statement. What are equilibrium exchange rates? What are the fundamentals? What is excess volatility? And what are the effects of different policies upon the exchange rates? These are perennial questions.

Approximately half a century ago, Ragnar Nurkse (1945) discussed the conditions of international monetary equilibrium. He stated that the International Monetary Fund is designed to provide for the orderly changes in exchange rates necessary to correct a "fundamental disequilibrium." For the IMF to do this, it is necessary to have some consensus view as to what constitute "equilibrium" or "disequilibrium" exchange

Jerome L. Stein is Eastman Professor of Political Economy at Brown University, Providence, Rhode Island. This chapter is dedicated to the memory of Victor Argy, who died in July 1993, while the final draft of this chapter was being written. The author is indebted to Polly Reynolds Allen, George H. Borts, John Devereux, Guay C. Lim, Paulo Onofri, Simon van Norden, and John Williamson for criticisms of an earlier draft. The current version embodies many of the suggestions of participants in seminars at the Institute for International Economics; the International Monetary Fund; the Université Aix-en-Provence–Marseille II; the Center for Economic Studies, University of Munich; the Institute for Advanced Studies, Vienna; the School of Business, Hebrew University, Jerusalem; and the University of Bologna and the Innocenzo Gasparini Institute for Economic Research (IGIER). I am indebted to Guay C. Lim of the University of Melbourne for table 7 and for econometric advice, which was always weighed carefully but not always followed.

rates. Nurkse's argument is timely for several reasons. First, the purchasing power parity (PPP) theory cannot provide a definition of the equilibrium rate and is incapable of precise interpretation. The only satisfactory way of defining the equilibrium rate of exchange is as that rate which keeps the balance of payments in equilibrium over a certain period. There is no presumption or theoretical justification for believing that an arbitrary PPP has any economic significance for balance of payments equilibrium. Second, the time horizon for balance of payments equilibrium should be one that evens out seasonal and cyclical influences. Third, we must exclude changes in reserves and short-term capital flows from the balance of payments—if we included changes in reserves, then the balance of payments would always balance, by definition. Short-term capital flows are the private-sector counterpart of changes in reserves and should simply be viewed as short-term loans rather than as responses to "fundamentals." Fourth, the balance of payments (exclusive of changes in reserves and short-term capital flows) can be kept equal to zero through macroeconomic policies and trade and capital flow restrictions. The example Nurkse cited was Great Britain in the years 1925–30. There was little change in the British gold reserves during that period, so in a literal sense it would seem that the pound was not overvalued. The British balance of payments was kept in equilibrium, however, only at the cost of depressed conditions at home relative to the rest of the world. Hence, the equilibrium exchange rate is ". . . one that maintains a country's external accounts in equilibrium without the need for wholesale unemployment at home" and is not maintained through controls on trade in goods and financial instruments. The concept of equilibrium exchange rates used in this paper will be consistent with Nurkse's.

Nurkse opposed free flotation of exchange rates because he felt that excess volatility, due to speculative capital flows, would result. This volatility would in turn induce constant shifts of domestic factors between tradable and nontradable goods industries, which could be disturbing and wasteful. Milton Friedman (1953, 158) disagreed and argued that:

> . . . advocacy of flexible exchange rates is *not* equivalent to advocacy of unstable exchange rates. The ultimate objective is a world in which exchange rates, while *free to vary,* are in fact highly stable. Instability of exchange rates is a symptom of instability in the underlying structure.

Almost fifty years after Nurkse wrote his essay, how much progress has been made toward resolving these issues? Edison and Pauls (1991) have written, "The general view of the economics profession is that we cannot explain exchange rate movements." Dornbusch (1987, 33ff.) says that ". . . theories across the board have failed to account for exchange rate behavior." As a response to these views, my colleagues and I have developed an approach called the natural real exchange rate (NATREX) model.[1] The aim of this paper is show to what extent the NATREX model can answer the following sets of questions, by focusing upon the real international value of the US dollar:

- To what extent has the real exchange rate been as stable as is justified by the "fundamentals," and to what extent are its variations noise? What *are* the fundamentals? What factors can explain the persistent and large deviations from purchasing power parity? Can we calculate whether a currency is over- or undervalued? If we can answer these questions, we can evaluate the performance of the free exchange rate regime.

- How do international financial markets affect the responses of the economy to internal and external disturbances? What are the determinants of capital mobility?

- There has been general concern about US current account deficits. What has produced the deficits? What policies could be adopted to reverse them? One theory claims that they have been the result of increases in the expected return on investment in the United States relative to other countries; another attributes the inflows that produced the deficits to the strong US fiscal policy stimulus and the declining private saving ratio. If the second theory is correct, are the government budget deficits sustainable?

How the NATREX Model Responds to These Questions

The Concept of the NATREX

This section begins by explaining, in a relatively intuitive and nontechnical manner, how the NATREX approach answers the questions just posed. Then the more technical structure of the model and its econometrics are presented. The NATREX is the *"natural real exchange rate,"* the rate that would prevail if speculative and cyclical factors could be removed while unemployment is at its natural rate. This is exactly what Nurkse had in mind in speaking of the "equilibrium exchange rate."

The nominal exchange rate N is the number of units of foreign currency purchased by a unit of domestic currency. The real exchange rate R is the amount of goods that one unit of local currency can purchase abroad relative to what it can purchase at home. (As thus defined, a rise in either

---

1. The NATREX theory has been applied to the United States, Australia, France, Germany, Latin America, Indonesia, Taiwan, and Japan. See Stein et al. (forthcoming).

the nominal or the real rate signifies an appreciation of the domestic currency). The relation between the real and nominal rates is $R = N/(p'/p) = Np/p'$, where p is the domestic and p' the foreign GDP deflator. The fundamentals are defined as the disturbances to productivity and social thrift at home and abroad, denoted by vector $Z(t)$, and are exogenous to the model. The specification of Z will vary by country.[2] For small countries the terms of trade are exogenous, but not for the United States. In some countries the world real rate of interest is exogenous. For the United States the world real rate of interest is endogenous. These fundamentals affect the real exchange rate $R(t)$, the real interest rate $r(t)$, the rate of capital formation dk/dt, and the rate of change of the foreign debt dF/dt (of equal magnitude but opposite sign to the current account CA), k = capital intensity = capital per unit of effective labor, F = foreign debt intensity = real debt per unit of effective labor.

The real exchange rate may be viewed as the sum of three elements in identity equation (1). The *medium-run equilibrium* conditions determining the NATREX are, first, that the basic balance of payments, or the balance in goods markets, is in equilibrium, and second, that there is portfolio balance between the holding of assets denominated in the home and in the foreign currency. The stocks of capital $k(t)$ and foreign debt $F(t)$ per unit of effective labor are given. The medium-run NATREX is $R[k(t), F(t); Z(t)]$. In the *longer run*, the disturbances $Z(t)$ affect the evolution of capital and foreign debt via the investment function and the current account. As the stocks of capital and foreign debt evolve, the medium-run equilibrium values of the real exchange rate and the real interest rate change. In the steady state, when capital and debt converge, the NATREX is $R^*[Z(t)]$. The interaction of the medium and the longer run is the contribution of the NATREX model. The NATREX itself is a moving equilibrium rate, because exogenous $Z(t)$ and endogenous capital $k(t)$ and debt $F(t)$ evolve over time:

$$R(t) = \{R(t) - R[k(t), F(t); Z(t)]\} + \{R[k(t), F(t); Z(t)] - R^*[Z(t)]\}$$
$$+ R^*[Z(t)] = Np/p'. \tag{1}$$

The actual real exchange rate often differs from the NATREX (the first term) as a result of speculative and cyclical factors, which are definitely not included in Z. For example, in 1993 the expectation of a recovery in the United States and of an easing of monetary policy in Germany, in view of that country's recession, affected the short-run nominal exchange rate and, given the slow change in relative prices, the real exchange rate as well. Short-run exchange rate variations are noise and

---

2. Stein et al. (forthcoming) consider different types of countries with different components of the fundamentals Z. The basic NATREX philosophy is the same for all, but the specific lines of causation and structural equations differ.

not reflections of rational expectations, for the following reason. The hypothesis of uncovered interest rate parity with rational expectations states that the mathematical expectation of the percentage change in the nominal exchange rate (over a one- or a three-month horizon) is equal to the appropriate current short-term interest rate differential. The hypothesis states that the points relating the mathematical expectation of the percentage change in the nominal exchange rate (over a one- or a three-month horizon) to the forward premium or discount lie along a 45–degree line. This is not the case. Figures 1 and 2, for Canada and Germany, illustrate this point. The regression coefficient is not significantly different from zero. It is well known that the current short-term nominal interest rate differential (equal to the forward premium or discount) conveys no information about subsequent exchange rate changes.[3] Studies by the Bank of Canada (Boothe et al. 1985) have shown that one cannot account for this failure by invoking an objective risk premium.

Although in the short run the exchange rate does not reflect the fundamentals, it does so in the longer run. We show that, as the time horizon lengthens, market pressures push the real exchange rate toward the NATREX, as they push the nominal exchange rate and relative prices to clear the goods markets and produce equilibrium in the basic balance of payments. The first term in equation (1), $\{R(t) - R[k(t), F(t); Z(t)]\}$, converges to zero. The fundamentals $Z(t)$, which change over time, determine the moving steady-state natural real exchange rate. Since $Z(t)$ evolves over time, the NATREX changes over time. It is not stationary.

The reason why the PPP hypothesis is often incorrect is that it fails to take into account the evolution of the fundamentals. The PPP hypothesis is that R is stationary,[4] so that variations in the nominal exchange rate are explained simply by changes in relative prices. The NATREX, generated by the fundamentals, is intended to replace the PPP theory. The PPP hypothesis arbitrarily assumes that the steady-state value $R^*[Z(t)]$ is constant and ignores the middle term in equation (1) concerning the evolution of capital and debt.

---

3. Almost everyone who has examined the data agrees that there is no informational content in the forward rate concerning subsequent exchange rate changes. The adjusted r^2 is close to zero. See Stein (1990, table 1; 1992). Some do not feel that the lack of relation indicates that short-run changes are noise, but instead claim that the fact that the means are the same is sufficient reason to accept rationality. We cannot accept this. Suppose that a watch is permanently stopped at 6 o'clock. It gives an unbiased estimate of the time, but how much would one be willing to pay for such a watch?

4. A variable is said to be stationary if its mean and variance are independent of time. In other words, variable $R(t)$ is stationary at constant value C if the mathematical expectation $E(R)$ converges to C as time increases. That is, lim $E[R(t)] \Rightarrow C$, as t increases.

Figure 1 Canada: relationship of spot and forward exchange rates, 1981–89[a]

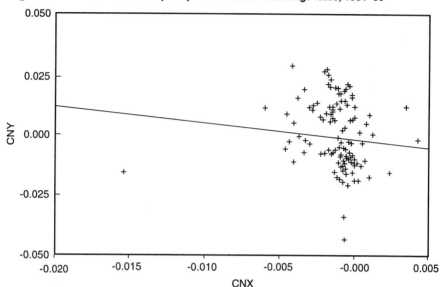

a. CNY = month-to-month percentage change in spot rate; CNX = premium on one-month-forward contract. Data are monthly and cover the period from May 1981 to September 1989.
Source: Stein (1990).

Figure 2 Germany: relationship of spot and forward exchange rates, 1981–89[a]

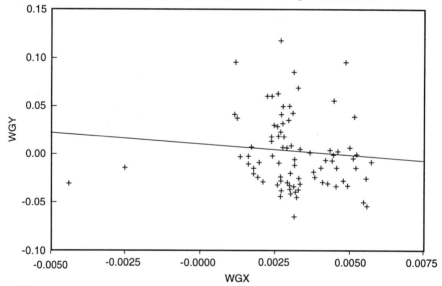

a. WGY = month-to-month percentage change in spot rate; WGX = premium on one-month-forward contract. Data are monthly and cover the period from May 1981 to September 1989.
Source: Stein (1990).

It is agreed that real exchange rates have not been stationary during the 20 years since rates were allowed to float.[5] Some authors take very long views and ask whether real exchange rates are stationary over a century or more. Corbae and Ouliaris (1991) test the stationarity hypothesis on the Australian real exchange rate for the period 1890–1984 and reject the stationarity hypothesis. Lothian and Taylor (1992) find that, for a period of almost two centuries, the real exchange rates of the pound sterling and the French franc are stationary. However, the convergence to stationarity is slow. They claim that the reason the real exchange rate is not found to be stationary over shorter periods, such as the post–World War II period or the last two decades, is that the unit root tests used to make the determination are low powered.[6]

What is the economic point of these stationarity tests? Suppose that over the horizon of a century or two the real exchange rate $R(t)$ is stationary at value $C(0)$. Does that mean that $C(0)$ is the equilibrium rate that should have been set at the Bretton Woods conference in 1946? Does it mean that the European Monetary System (EMS) should use $C(0)$ to set real exchange rates? Does it mean that the deviation $[R(t) - C(0)]$ measures market disequilibrium? Given that the convergence to stationarity is slow, what are the economic implications of the sustained deviations for the EMS? When there is a deviation, should or should not policy measures be undertaken to correct the situation? I think that this is a 1994 way of understanding Nurkse's objection to the use of PPP in determining equilibrium exchange rates.

The issue is not whether or not the real exchange rate is stationary over an arbitrary period, but whether it reflects the fundamentals Z. If by chance Z is stationary over an arbitrary period, our real exchange rate will tend to be stationary subject to qualifications below concerning the evolution of capital and debt. Then PPP will be valid for that period. If, as is the case, Z is not stationary, then neither will be the real exchange rate. Our model focuses upon the second and third terms in equation (1) and is an economic generalization of PPP. The NATREX is a moving-equilibrium PPP, based upon explicit fundamentals and endogenous changes in capital and debt. Our object is to explain why the equilibrium real exchange rate varies and how it responds to changes in the specific fundamentals. The PPP hypothesis ignores these questions.

---

5. See table 1 for tests of the stationarity of recent exchange rates.

6. Edison et al. (1994, 12), using the standard tests, found significant evidence for PPP at the 5 percent level in only 5 cases out of 26 country pairs they examined. Using a more powerful test, they found significant evidence for PPP at the 5 percent level in 5 out of the 26 cases examined. They conclude, "... even with appropriate critical values we find several instances of significant cointegrating vectors that reject symmetry and proportionality [crucial elements of PPP]. Unfortunately, there is no pattern in the coefficients of these cointegrating vectors, frustrating any attempt to provide an economic theory that might account for them" (p. 18). The NATREX model provides such a theory.

The NATREX model does not specify whether changes in the real exchange rate $R = Np/p'$ will be reflected in changes in the nominal exchange rate or in changes in relative prices. In point of fact, for the United States the variation is in the nominal exchange rate and not in relative prices.[7] We know that prices are less flexible than nominal exchange rates. This implies that the real exchange rate will converge faster to the NATREX under a regime of free rates than under fixed rates,[8] where the entire burden of adjustment is on relative prices, with adverse effects upon unemployment and inflation.

The NATREX Model: Theoretical and Empirical Results

This section describes and summarizes in an intuitive way some answers to the questions posed at the beginning of this paper. First, to what extent has the real exchange rate been as stable as is justified by the fundamentals, and what *are* the fundamentals? The fundamentals identified here, denoted by vector Z, are productivity and time preference at home and abroad. Productivity is measured by the growth rate of real GDP, and time preference by the ratio of social consumption to GNP. In the empirical analyses presented below, the fundamentals[9] are the moving average of the growth of real foreign GDP (MAFGROW), the moving average of the growth of real US GDP (MAGROWTH), and an index of the US social time preference,[10] which we shall refer to as the discount rate (DISRAT) and is equal to the ratio of consumption plus government purchases to GNP. (For the United States, government purchases are viewed as consumption.) We use a 12-quarter moving average of the growth of real GDP to abstract from the cyclical elements, which are excluded from our concept of the equilibrium exchange rate. Thus Z = (MAGROWTH, MAFGROW, DISRAT). The shorter run effects of *changes* in the fundamentals (dZ) are measured by the ephemeral (USFINT), which is the difference in real long-term rates of interest between the United States and the rest of the G-10 countries.

---

7. See figure 3, where the real and nominal rates practically coincide. This is not necessarily true for other countries.

8. This is seen in the cases of the Australian dollar—US dollar and French franc—deutsche mark exchange rates; see Stein et al. (1995).

9. We use the notation for Z contained in the regressions: see tables 8 through 11 below.

10. With a logarithmic utility function, the discount rate is equal to the ratio of optimal consumption to wealth. A rise in the discount rate (time preference) in the instantaneous logarithmic utility function raises the ratio of social consumption to wealth. See Merton (1990, 117). The discount rate adopted here is DISRAT = (social consumption)/GNP = (discount rate)(wealth/GNP).

Table 1 Tests of stationarity of basic variables

Variable	DF/ADF statistic[a]
I(1)[b]	
Nominal exchange rate (*C*, 1)	−1.795
Real exchange rate (*C*, 1)	−1.8
Current account—GNP ratio (*N*, 0)	0.3
Real long-term US interest rate (*C*, 1)	−1.4
Real long-term G-10 interest rate (*C*, 1)	−1.6
DISRAT = (*C* + *G*)/GNP (*C*, 1)	−2.4
Trade balance—GNP ratio (*C*, 1)	−1.6
Moving-average US real growth rate (*C*, 1)	−1.9
Moving-average G-10 real growth rate (*C*, 1)	−1.7
I(0)	
Differential between US and foreign real long-term interest rates (*N*, 1)	−1.8*
Investment income—GNP ratio (*C*, 1)	−2.8**
Percentage change in real exchange rate (*N*, 0)	−5.7**

* Significant at the 10 percent level, using MacKinnon critical values.
** Significant at the 5 percent level, using MacKinnon critical values.
a. The Dickey-Fuller (DF) statistic tests for stationarity of an autoregressive series AR(1), and the augmented DF statistic (ADF) refers to an AR($p > 1$) process. We test whether or not the constant *C* is significant and what order of lags (*j*) greater than unity is significant. We continue the UROOT tests until we have an equation where all of the regressors (exclusive of the first lag term) are significant. The notation (*C*,*j*) or (*N*,*j*) indicates whether the constant *C* is significant (or not *N*), and the *j* indicates the lags greater than one that are significant. The significance level depends upon whether or not there is a constant and the number of lags. The significance level for (*N*, 1) differs from that of (*C*, 1). If the ADF or DF statistic for a variable is significant, the variable is stationary, and we reject the hypothesis of a unit root. The sample period is the first quarter of 1973 through the fourth quarter of 1989.
b. Order of integration I(1) = nonstationary; I(0) = stationary.
Sources: Federal Reserve, Organization for Economic Cooperation and Development.

Table 1 indicates that the real exchange rate R and the fundamentals $Z(t)$ have not been stationary during the past 20 years.[11] Hence the PPP assumption of stationarity of the real exchange rate and of the fundamentals is not valid during the period of floating exchange rates. Moreover, it will be explained below why endogenous variables such as the current account–GNP ratio have not been stationary.

Second, two scenarios are described. In the first there is a change in social time preference, as measured by the social consumption ratio DISRAT = (*C* + *G*)/GNP. As noted above, no distinction is made between the private sector and the public sector; rather it is assumed that US government expenditures are consumption rather than investment.[12] For example, the Reagan tax cut, which increased private consumption but was not offset by a decline in government consumption,

11. The data come primarily from the Federal Reserve and are those used in the study by Hooper and Mann (1989). The real exchange rate of the dollar is vis-à-vis the G-10. The foreign growth rate refers to the G-18.

12. This assumption need not be true for other countries, nor even for the United States itself in all time periods.

represented an exogenous rise in time preference. This means that social (private plus public) saving declined.[13] In the second scenario, the growth rate of the US or the foreign economy increases as a result of a rise in investment. This may occur either because the Keynes-Tobin q-ratio has increased or because growth has increased as a result of greater immigration.[14]

Tables 2 and 3, respectively, describe the theoretical and empirical results. In table 2, column 1, the effects are shown of a rise in the time preference index which lowers the ratio of social saving to GNP. Column 2 of the table describes the effects of a rise in the growth rate resulting from a rise in investment. In both cases investment rises relative to saving. Since domestic social saving is inadequate to finance investment, this tends to increase the differential between domestic and foreign real rates of interest, which leads to a portfolio adjustment and a capital inflow. The capital inflow causes the currency to appreciate in real terms and leads to a current account deficit $CA = S - I$. Portfolio adjustment and capital inflows will tend to equalize real rates of interest. However, as long as investment less saving is not zero, the capital flow will continue even after real interest rates have been equalized.[15] The foreign debt rises as a result of the current account deficits. The evolution of the economy is different in the two cases. The longer run effects of changes in the fundamentals described in tables 2 and 3 refer to the movements of the real exchange rate and the ratio of the current account to GNP as capital and debt vary endogenously but have not as yet reached the steady state where the capital and debt intensities are constant.

The rise in DISRAT leads to a rise in foreign debt without a rise in capital intensity and capacity output. The rise in foreign debt reduces wealth, and the decline in wealth reduces consumption. As a result, social saving rises to equal investment, and the foreign debt stabilizes at a higher level. For example, if the decline in social saving were the result

---

13. Social saving is private saving $S' = $ GNP $- C - T$ (disposable income less consumption) plus government saving $S'' = (T - G)$; hence social saving $S = S' + S'' = $ GNP($C + G$), and DISRAT $= (C + G)/$GNP, where $C = $ consumption, $T = $ taxes, and $G = $ government purchases.

14. Investment per unit of effective labor $I = dk/dt + nk$, where k is capital per unit of effective labor and n is the growth rate of effective labor. A rise in the q-ratio raises dk/dt and raises investment. Given the q-ratio, which determines dk/dt, a rise in immigration raises n and raises investment. Growth is associated with either a rise in the q-ratio or a rise in n. To be sure, q will be affected by changes in n. Thus I depends upon q and n. Immigration is less important for the United States during the period considered than for countries such as Israel or even Germany.

15. See Niehans (1994) on why the convergence of real interest rates does not imply very much about capital mobility, which concerns the difference between saving and investment.

Table 2   Effects of a rise in time preference and a rise in investment and growth in the NATREX model

Rise in time preference DISRAT = (C + G)/GNP	Rise in investment GROWTH
Medium-run effects	
Rise in differential between domestic and foreign real long-term rate of interest; capital inflow; appreciation of the currency; current account deficits, rising debt.	
Longer run effects	
Higher debt, depreciated currency	Higher capital intensity and real GDP; current account surpluses; lower foreign debt appreciates currency; higher capital intensity tends to depreciate currency; ambiguous net effect.

Table 3   Summary of empirical results

Fundamental	Real exchange rate[a]	Current account/GNP
Z		
(C + G)/GNP	−	−
US growth	+	−
Foreign growth	−	+
dZ		
USFINT(−1)	+	n.s.

n.s. = not significant
a. A plus sign indicates an appreciation of the dollar, and a minus sign a depreciation, in response to an increase in the fundamental variable.

of a decline in government saving, the decline in wealth would raise private saving to offset the decline. This is not Ricardian equivalence but an equilibrating mechanism whereby the foreign debt converges to a sustainable level. The government budget deficit is sustainable, but the foreign debt stabilizes at a higher level.

The higher steady-state foreign debt, with no change in the profile of investment, implies higher interest payments on the debt. The real value of the currency will fall to produce a higher trade balance to finance the higher interest payments on the debt. The medium-run effect of a rise in DISRAT is an appreciation of the currency in real terms. The longer run effect is a depreciation of the currency in real terms below its initial level.

In the second case, where the growth rate increases as a result of a rise in investment, the *evolution* of the economy is quite different. The capital inflow equal to the current account deficit finances investment. As a result of the greater rate of investment, capital intensity rises and increases capacity output. The rise in capital gradually reduces the marginal product of capital and in turn the rate of investment. The rise in real GDP increases saving. The decline in investment and the rise in saving reduce the capital inflow and thus the current account deficit. Eventually, the rise in capacity output leads to a situation where saving exceeds investment, and there are capital outflows. The foreign debt declines and stabilizes at a lower level, and capital intensity converges to a higher level.

There are several different effects upon the real exchange rate. First, the lower debt (or possible conversion of the country from a debtor to a creditor) will reduce interest payments to foreigners and tend to cause the currency to appreciate in real terms. Second, the rise in capital per se tends to increase output relative to absorption and may have an adverse effect upon the country's terms of trade, or the rise in capital may increase wealth, which tends to increase imports. In either case, a rise in capital tends to lower the real value of the currency. The net effect upon the real exchange rate is ambiguous, the sum of these two opposing factors.

Empirically, the results in tables 8 to 11 below are summarized in table 3 for the United States and the G-10. The first column lists the fundamental variables: a rise in DISRAT = $(C + G)/GNP$, a rise in the US growth rate MAGROWTH, and a rise in the foreign growth rate MAFGROW. The second column refers to the change in the equilibrium real exchange rate R. The third column refers to the change in the equilibrium current account ratio to GNP. These are the moving-equilibrium effects along the growth trajectories as capital and debt vary endogenously.[16] The last row represents the medium-run effects of changes in the fundamentals, dZ, given capital and debt.

The medium-run effect of a rise in investment less social saving is to raise the real interest rate differential. This leads to portfolio adjustments and capital inflows, which eliminate the differential, although the capital inflow continues as long as $I - S$ is not zero. The medium-run effect dZ is therefore measured by USFINT(-1), where the "-1" denotes a one-quarter lag to avoid a simultaneous estimation problem. We show that real interest rates converge with a half-life of six quarters, so that the dZ effect is ephemeral. The *medium-run* effects (dZ) indicate that a rise in $I - S$, and thus in the real long-term interest rate differential, increases the real value of the dollar. The medium-run effect upon the current account is not significant.

The longer run effects of Z *along the trajectories* as the capital and debt intensities vary endogenously (but have not attained their steady-state values) are as follows. First, a rise in the index of time preference ($C + G$)/GNP = DISRAT leads to a depreciated dollar and a decrease in the current account. Second, foreign growth MAFGROW, stimulated by a rise in the foreign marginal product of capital, leads to a capital outflow

---

16. The later technical discussion of the econometric cointegration analysis and its relation to the theory will make these concepts more precise.

from the United States, a depreciation of the dollar, and an increase in the current account. US growth MAGROWTH, stimulated by a rise in the US marginal product of capital, leads to a capital inflow, a decrease in the current account, and an appreciated dollar.

The explanatory power of the NATREX model is summarized in figure 3 below for the real exchange rate and for the ratio of the current account to GNP. Three curves are plotted: the real value R of the dollar (denoted REXR), the NATREX implied by the model and the estimating equation,[17] and the nominal value N of the dollar (denoted NEXR). We conclude the following. First, REXR and NEXR track each other closely ($R = Np/p'$). This indicates that, for the United States vis-à-vis the other G-10 countries, relative prices are not able to explain much of the movement of the nominal exchange rate.[18] Second, the graph of the NATREX tracks the basic movement of the real exchange rate very well. This means that we are able to explain the movements in the real exchange rates by the fundamentals in the model. Third, there are significant brief deviations of REXR from the NATREX, due to speculative and cyclical factors. However, the actual R converges to the rate implied by the fundamentals. Thus there is *long-period rationality* in the foreign-exchange market, but not short-period rationality. This answers the first set of questions posed in the introduction.

The second set of questions concerns the extent of international capital mobility and the determinants of the current account. Figure 4 below shows that the NATREX model explains the evolution of the current account–GNP ratio on the basis of the fundamentals. In the figure, CAGNP is the ratio of the current account to GNP, and FCAGNP is the forecast of that ratio obtained from the NATREX model using the fundamentals Z. There is considerable international mobility of capital. The variation in the current account is sensitive to variations in investment and social saving, which depend upon the fundamentals in the NATREX model. An increase in US growth reduces (worsens) the US current account, an increase in foreign growth increases it, and an increase in DISRAT reduces it. A unit rise in DISRAT—for example, generated by a government budget deficit—will eventually raise the current account deficit ($-$CAGNP) by 0.5; the rest of the change produces a crowding out of private investment. The ratio of the current account to GNP is not stationary because investment less social saving relative to GNP is not stationary.

---

17. The derivation of the NATREX curve is based on the econometrics and is described below. It is a dynamic ex ante simulation of the longer run equation, based on table 9, where *previously predicted values* of the dependent variable are used as the lagged dependent variable.

18. This is why the monetary models of the nominal exchange rate have been so disappointing.

Figure 3 Actual real and nominal US dollar exchange rates and NATREX dynamic ex ante forecast, 1975–89

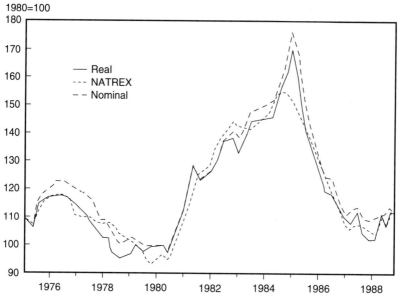

1980=100

Sources: Federal Reserve; Hooper and Mann (1989, figure 13).

Figure 4 Current account-GNP ratio and NATREX dynamic ex ante forecast, 1975–89

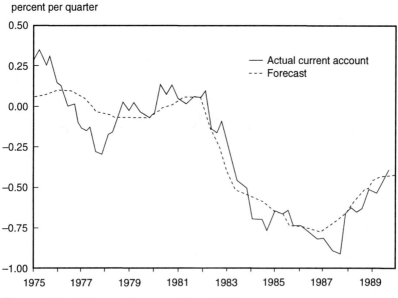

percent per quarter

Sources: Federal Reserve; Hooper and Mann (1989).

Table 4   Equations in the NATREX model for the United States and the other G-10 countries

(2) $y(k; u) = C(k, F, r; Z) + (dk/dt + nk) + B(R, k, F, k'; Z) = \text{GDP}$
(3) $y(k'; u') = C(k', F, r; Z) + (dk'/dt + nk') - B(R, k, F, k'; Z) = \text{GDP}'$
(4) $dk/dt = I(k, r; Z)$ $I_k < 0,$ $I_r < 0$
(5) $I = dk/dt + nk$
(6) $dF/dt = I - S - nF = -(CA + nF)$
(7) $S = y(k; Z) - rF - C(k, F, r; Z)$ $S_k > 0, S_F > 0$
(8) $d(r - r')/dt = -a(r - r')$

Note: y = GDP per effective worker; k = capital intensity; F = real foreign debt intensity (+) or net claims upon foreigners (−); r = real long-term interest rate; B = real trade balance per effective worker; CA = current account per effective worker; C = real social consumption per effective worker; rF = real interest payments (+) per effective worker; S = real saving per effective worker = GDP − rF − C; Z = vector of exogenous disturbances = (g, u, g, u', n), where g = parameter of time preference which raises the social consumption ratio; u = parameter of the productivity of capital which raises the q-ratio; n = growth of effective labor; a prime indicates the corresponding foreign variable. See text for equation (1) and subsequent equations.

The Theoretical Structure of the NATREX Model

Description of the Model

Equations (2) through (8) in table 4 describe the model. Our intertemporal optimization approach is more general and flexible than the conventional approach, which uses the maximum principle and an intertemporal budget constraint. The analysis here is based upon an intertemporal optimization with a robust feedback control to guarantee that the system will converge to the perfect-foresight steady state, which the agents know is unknowable at any time. We do not believe that a sovereign country has an intertemporal budget constraint, whereby the present value of the foreign debt is the same at the initial and terminal dates. The equilibrium debt is an endogenous variable. Countries are allowed to change their status from debtor to creditor and vice versa. The only requirement is that the foreign debt converge to a constant. Then the trade balance must be sufficiently large to pay the interest on the foreign debt. The following describes in nontechnical terms how our investment and saving functions are based upon rational optimization processes; the reader is referred to Infante and Stein (1973) for the derivations.

The model is characterized by endogenous stability without requiring perfect foresight. It is shown that the foreign debt is an endogenous variable whose steady-state value, like that of the capital stock, is determined by productivity and thrift at home and abroad. This approach is more general than the standard intertemporal optimization models, which require perfect foresight.

Equation (2) states that the goods market is in equilibrium at capacity output, and ignores the cyclical elements. Aggregate demand is equal to capacity output. The left-hand side of equation (2) is GDP per unit of effective labor $y(k; u)$, where k is capital intensity (capital per unit of effective labor) and u is a measure of productivity . The components of aggregate demand are consumption C, investment $I = dk/dt + nk$, and the trade balance B, to be discussed. The corresponding goods market balance for the rest of the world is given in equation (3). Foreign variables are denoted by primes.

Equations (4)and (5) are the investment equations. As a rule, economists have used the maximum principle of Pontryagin to derive optimal control laws. This is an open-loop type of optimization in that it yields an entire sequence of controls to be followed from initial conditions. The solution for the optimal control for the rate of change in capital intensity, or consumption function, is derived by knowing the steady-state value of capital intensity k^* where the marginal product of capital $y'(k^*; u)$ is equal to the sum of the discount and growth rates; the differential equations are solved backward from that value. Thereby a unique trajectory to the steady state is derived. There is saddle point instability: only if the economy travels along the stable arm will the system converge to the steady state. There must be perfect knowledge of the steady state and the production and utility functions to implement this procedure: *there is no room for error.* If the slightest error is made, the system will not converge to the unknown optimal steady state; instead the economy will follow an errant trajectory. Such a procedure is neither feasible nor sensible in economics, for two reasons. First, we do not have perfect knowledge of the production function $y(k; u)$, hence the steady-state value of k^* is unknowable. Hence the optimal control derivable from the maximum principle is not implementable. Second, the unknown optimal steady state may be changing over time in an unknown manner. For this reason, Infante and Stein used dynamic programming to derive a suboptimal feedback control (SOFC). This is a closed-loop control, where all that is necessary are *current measurements* of a variable, not perfect foresight. Using our equations, the SOFC will drive the economy to the unknown optimal steady state. *The trajectory of the SOFC is asymptotic to the unknown perfect-foresight trajectory, is implementable, and guarantees that the system will converge to the unknown and changing steady state.* This is not true for the optimal controls derived from the maximum principle.

Investment per unit of effective labor consists of two parts: the rate of change in capital intensity dk/dt, and nk, the investment per unit of effective labor required to keep capital intensity constant when effective labor is growing at rate n. The rate of change in capital intensity is derived from the dynamic programming SOFC. It states that the rate of change in capital intensity should be a positive function of the current

Keynes-Tobin q-ratio: the capital value of an asset relative to its supply price.[19] This is obtained, using current measurements, by capitalizing the *current observable* marginal product of capital $y'[k(t); u(t)]$ by the current world real rate of interest $r(t)$. This is equation (4), where the rate of change in capital intensity is negatively related to the current capital intensity $k(t)$ and to the current real rate of interest $r(t)$. The total investment per unit of effective labor (equation 5) is $dk/dt + nk$.

The social (public plus private) consumption function is a stabilizing function. It guarantees that the foreign debt will converge, without requiring perfect foresight. It states that consumption depends upon wealth or permanent income. Wealth is capital $k(t)$ less the real foreign debt $F(t)$, where a negative F represents claims on foreigners. The exogenous rate of time preference g = DISRAT is an element of vector Z. A rise in time preference raises social consumption $C = C(k, F; Z)$ for the given amount of wealth.

Social saving S per effective worker is GNP = GDP= $y(k; u)$, less interest payments to foreigners rF, where r is the real interest rate and F is the real foreign debt less social consumption $C(k, F; Z)$ per effective

---

19. The intertemporal optimization problem is to maximize the discounted utilities of per capita consumption $U(c)$ over an infinite (T approaches infinity) horizon. This is equation (A) subject to the constraint (equation B) that output per capita $f(k)$ equal investment $Dk + nk$ plus consumption c, where k is the capital per capita, n is the growth rate plus depreciation rate, δ is the discount rate, and W is "welfare":

$$\max W = \int_t^T U(c)e^{-\delta t}\, dt; \tag{A}$$

$$Dk = f(k) - nk - c. \tag{B}$$

The steady-state capital intensity k^* is such that:

$$f'(k^*) = n + \delta. \tag{C}$$

If there were perfect foresight, then the optimal rate of change of the capital intensity Dk would be given by equation (D):

$$Dk = -A(k^*)(k - k^*), \tag{D}$$

where $A(k^*) = (-\delta/2)\{[1 + 4U'(c^*)f''(k^*)/\delta^2 U''(c^*)]^{.5} - 1\}$

This is the stable arm of the trajectory. One must know exactly what are the values of k^* and c^* and $A(k^*)$ in order to use equation (D) for the optimal rate of change of the capital intensity. Since these cannot be known, Infante and Stein (1973) derived a suboptimal feedback control where one does not have to know the unknown and changing steady state, but we simply use current measurements of the marginal product of capital and its change. Our SOFC, given by equation (E), is easily implementable:

$$Dk = -A(k)[f'(k) - (n + \delta)]/[-f''(k)]. \tag{E}$$

A is evaluated using the current capital intensity k. The $f'(k)$ is the current marginal product of capital, and $f''(k)$ is the current change in the marginal product of capital. SOFC is asymptotic to the perfect-foresight control equation (D) and is guaranteed to drive the economy to the unknown k^*.

worker. To guarantee that the real foreign debt will converge when there are changes in time preference, we require that a rise in debt raise saving. That is, a rise in the foreign debt must lower social consumption by more than it lowers GNP. This is equation (7).

The rate of change of the foreign debt per effective worker dF/dt is investment (I) less saving (S) per unit of effective labor less nF. This is equation (6). Using equations (2) and (7), we may also state equation (6) as saying that the rate of change of the foreign debt intensity is the current account deficit per effective worker ($-CA$) less nF.

In the usual intertemporal optimization models (IOM) requiring perfect foresight there is an intertemporal budget constraint which states that the present value of the sum of future trade balance surpluses over an infinite horizon must be equal to the present level of foreign indebtedness. A country that begins period t with an initial foreign debt $F(t)$ must run future trade surpluses to completely service the debt. Our approach is more general. The object is to prevent the endogenous debt from exploding. The model implies (see the next section) that the dynamic system must lead to an endogenous steady-state value of the debt F^* such that the trade balance in the steady state B^* is equal to the interest payments rF^* on the debt.[20] The level of $F^*(Z)$ depends upon Z: productivity and thrift at home and abroad. A rise in time preference (an element of Z) will raise the steady-state value of $F^*(Z)$. Since the debt stabilizes at $F^*(Z)$, the present value of the debt at time T, as T goes to infinity, is $F^*(Z)/(1 + r)^T = 0$. Our model allows the steady-state debt $F^*(Z)$ to be determined by the fundamentals. A rise in time preference raises $F^*(Z)$. However, the steady-state trade balance B^* will equal the interest payments $rF^*(Z)$, and $F^*(Z)/(1 + r)^T$ goes to zero as t goes to infinity. Our intertemporal optimization is more general than the standard models.

The trade balance function B includes capacity and debt variables as well as the real exchange rate. To a large extent it is consistent with the estimates of Hooper (1989, table 3). The trade balance in equation (2) is the real value of exports X less the real value of imports M, where $B = X(R, k', F; Z) - M(R, k, F; Z)$. Exports are decreased and imports increased by an appreciation of the real exchange rate R, which is an

---

The term $[f'(k)(n + \delta)]$ is the current marginal product of capital $f'(k)$ less the sum of the discount rate and the growth rate. In the text, the real rate of interest r is used instead of $(n + \delta)$. Hence, we obtain equation (F) for the SOFC rate of change of the capital intensity:

$$Dk = I[f'(k) - r] = I(q - 1). \tag{F}$$

The Tobin q-ratio is $f'(k)/r$, so equation (E) and (F) state that Dk depends upon the current q-ratio.

20. The text implicitly assumes that $n = 0$. In fact, the steady-state condition that $dF/dt = 0$ means that the trade balance $B^* = (r^* - n)F^*(Z)$, where r^* is the real rate of interest in the steady state.

inverse measure of competitiveness. A rise in foreign wealth k' increases exports, and a rise in US wealth $(k - F)$ increases US imports.

Finally, equation (8) concerns portfolio balance or the relation between the US and the G-10 real rate of interest. Figure 5 plots US and G-10 real long-term interest rates. These data were used in the Federal Reserve study by Hooper and Mann. They measured real long-term bond yields by subtracting from the nominal US and G-10 long-term government bond yields a three-year centered moving average of CPI inflation rates ranging from six quarters in the past to six quarters in the future. They denote r = RLTUSQ as the real long-term US quarterly rate and r' = RLTFQ as the real long-term foreign quarterly rate. Let us denote the real long-term interest rate differential as USFINT = $r - r'$. The evidence concerning real interest rate convergence is for the period from the third quarter of 1973 to the first quarter of 1989.

We know that there will be portfolio substitution when the expected returns on domestic and comparable foreign assets differ, if there are no capital controls. The NATREX model focuses upon long-term investment and ignores short-term speculative capital flows. The difference $(r_{us} - r_f)$ between the returns on domestic and foreign currency–denominated long-term assets can be expressed as $(r_{us} - r_f) = i + E(D \log N) - i' = E[r + D(\log R) - r']$, where i and i' are the domestic and foreign long-term nominal interest rates, respectively, and N is the nominal value of the domestic currency. The real exchange rate $R = Np/p'$. Hence the difference $(r_{us} - r_f)$ can be expressed as the expectation of the US real long-term rate r plus $D(\log R) = DR$, the real rate of appreciation of the US dollar over the investment horizon less r'.

The anticipated real appreciation of the domestic currency over the investment horizon $E(D \log R)$ is its mathematical expectation, given all available information. This quantity is a function of the gap between the expected steady-state real exchange rate $R^*(Z)$ and the current rate $R(t)$. We require that investors use all relevant available information in making their decisions. From equation (9a) we know that the change in the real exchange rate DR is stationary at a value of zero:[21]

$$D(DR) = -0.197 - 0.69\, DR(-1) \quad \text{UROOT}(C,0) = -5.7.^{**} \qquad (9a)$$
$$(t =) \quad (-0.38)\,(-5.7)$$

MacKinnon 1% = -3.5

We may write the change in the real exchange rate as equation (9b), where $\epsilon(t)$ are the changes produced by the fundamentals in our model. We sum equation (9b) and obtain equation (9c) where τ goes from t to $t + h$:

---

21. The regression coefficient of $DR(-1)$ is significantly different from zero and hence DR is stationary. The constant is not significant; hence $E(DR)$ is equal to zero.

Figure 5 Long-term real interest rates in the United States and the other G-10 countries, 1975–89

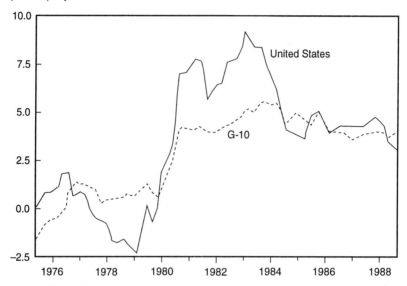

percent per year

Sources: Federal Reserve; Hooper and Mann (1989, figure 14).

$$DR = R(t + 1) - R(t) = \epsilon(t), \; E\epsilon = 0, \; \text{var } \epsilon > 0 \tag{9b}$$

$$R(t + h) = R(t) + \Sigma \, \epsilon(\tau). \tag{9c}$$

Moreover, we know that the level of real exchange rate $R(t)$ is not stationary because the fundamentals—time preference and growth—are not stationary. This means that the steady-state value of the real exchange rate $R^*[Z(t)]$ is changing over time in a way that becomes ever less predictable as the length of the horizon increases. The variance of $R(t + h)$, given $R(t)$, is positively related to the length h of the horizon. Therefore, in making long-term portfolio decisions, the expected change in the real exchange rate between the US dollar and the other G-10 currencies is assumed to be zero. Since $E(DR) = 0$, the real interest rates will tend to converge. This is what occurs.[22]

---

22. A further test of the convergence hypothesis is equation (9d). We perform a vector auto repression (VAR) on R and $(r - r)' = $ USFINT to determine, first, whether the interest rate differential is related to previous exchange rates, which would be the case if the expected change in the exchange rate were related to its previous history; second, what is the speed of convergence of the USFINT to a constant; and third, whether this constant is zero. Again the period is the third quarter of 1973 to the first quarter of 1989. It is clear that the lagged exchange rates are not significant and neither is the constant:

$$\text{USFINT} = 0.55 + 1.19 \, \text{USFINT}(-1) - 0.23 \, \text{USFINT}(-2) - 0.006 \, R(-1) + 0.002 \, R(-2). \tag{9d}$$
$$(t =) \quad (0.6) \quad (9.2). \quad\quad\quad (-1.5). \quad\quad\quad (-0.33). \quad\quad (0.11)$$

From these equations (and figure 5) we obtain several empirical results. First, the real long-term interest rates in the United States and the rest of the G-10 converge. Second, half of the initial deviation in $(r - r')$ from zero is eliminated in a year and a half. Third, there is no evidence that previous rates of change of the real exchange rate have any effect upon the process whereby real long-term interest rates converge. Fourth, there is no evidence of a risk premium between the US and the G-10 rate—the differential $(r - r')$ is independent of the net creditor or debtor position of the United States. Finally, during this period, the Granger causality ran from the US real long-term rate to that of the G-10 rather than the reverse. For these reasons we use equation (8) for the modeling: the real rates of interest converge to zero with a half-life, based upon equation (9d) in note 22, of six quarters.

We focus upon seven endogenous variables in the seven equations in table 4: capital intensity k, the real exchange rate R, real foreign debt intensity F, the domestic real rate of interest r, the foreign real rate of interest r', saving S, and investment I. (The rate of change of the foreign debt dF/dt is the current account deficit.) The exogenous parameters Z are productivity and time preference (or thrift) both at home and abroad. If we add a foreign capital formation equation $dk'/dt = I(k', r'; Z)$, then foreign capital is endogenous. For simplicity of exposition, however, we treat foreign capital as exogenous. Figure 6 shows the determination of the real exchange rate R and real interest rates r and r'; figure 7 describes the evolution of capital k and debt F.

Analytical Solution of the Model

The solution of the model proceeds in two steps. The medium run corresponds to the term $R[k(t), F(t); Z(t)]$, and the longer run system concerns the evolution of the endogenous capital and debt to produce the steady-state $R^*[Z(t)]$ in equation (1) above.

The Medium Run

The medium run is defined as the period in which capital stocks and foreign debt are taken as predetermined variables. The equations for equilibrium in the goods market, equations (2) and (3) for the United States and the G-10, respectively, can be written as equations (10) and (11), where we solve for the real exchange rate R. They are graphed in figure 6 as the IS curve for the United States and the IS' curve for the G-10. The real exchange rate is on the ordinate; the domestic (r) and foreign (r') real long-term interest rates are on the abscissa. The IS curve, describing goods market equilibrium, is negatively sloped in this space for the following reason. A rise in the US real rate of interest reduces

Figure 6 Determination of the real exchange rate and real interest rates[a]

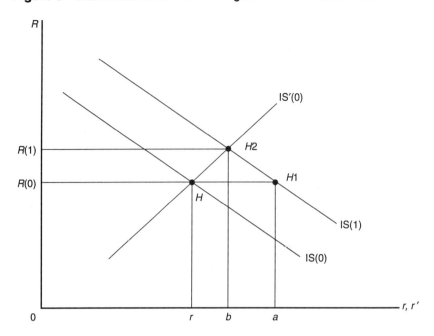

a. R = real exchange rate; r = real interest rate.

aggregate demand relative to capacity GDP. To equilibrate the goods market, the ratio $R = Np/p'$ of US to foreign prices must decline: the currency must depreciate in real terms. The decline in relative prices will increase US competitiveness and restore goods market equilibrium. No distinction is made in the NATREX model between changes in nominal exchange rates and in relative prices. In point of fact, the speeds of response differ, and the NATREX model provides a better explanation of a free-floating exchange rate regime than of a fixed rate regime. The foreign IS' curve is positively sloped in figure 6 because an appreciation of the US dollar against the G-10 currencies is a depreciation of the latter. Equation (8), repeated here, is the portfolio adjustment, describing the convergence of the real long-term interest rates r and r'.

Medium-run subsystem

$$d[r(t) - r'(t)]/dt = -a[r(t) - r'(t)] \quad \text{Interest rate convergence} \qquad (8)$$

$$R(t) = H[r(t), k(t), F(t); Z] \quad \text{IS curve} \qquad (10)$$

$$R(t) = h[r'(t), k'(t), F(t); Z'] \quad \text{IS' curve.} \qquad (11)$$

Figure 7 Trajectories of capital and debt to their steady-state values

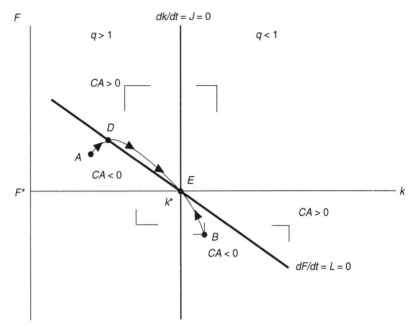

a. k = capital; F = debt. Asterisks denote steady-state values.

The dynamics of this system can be expressed as equations (8) and (12), and the medium-run equilibrium is given by equations (13) and (14) as described in figure 6.

$$dR/dt = b_1 dk/dt + b_2 dk'/dt - b_3 dF/dt + b_4(r - r'). \qquad (12)$$

Let the IS and IS' curves initially be IS(0) and IS'(0), respectively. The medium-run equilibrium is at point H where the real exchange rate is $R(0)$ [equation (13)] and real interest rates are equal [equation (14)].

$$R(t) = R[k(t), F(t); k'(t), Z] \qquad (13)$$

$$r(t) = r[k(t); k'(t), Z]. \qquad (14)$$

Suppose that there is either a decline in social saving or a rise in investment demand. The scenario in figure 6 corresponds to the medium-run scenario in table 2. The IS curve shifts to IS(1). To maintain goods market equilibrium when investment rises relative to saving, the real interest rate would rises. Given the real exchange rate $R(0)$, the domestic real interest rate will rise to 0a or point $H1$. The interest rate differential $H - H1$ will induce investors to purchase US and sell foreign long-term securities. The excess demand for goods in the United States and the redirection of portfolio investment to the United States will cause the US dollar to appreciate and lead to a convergence of real long-term interest rates.

If there were fixed exchange rates, the movement would first be from H to $H1$. Then, as prices rise gradually and portfolio balance occurs, the movement would be from $H1$ to $H2$. With free exchange rates, the real appreciation would be much more rapid. The movement would be closer to segment H–$H2$ as both the currency appreciates and real long-term interest rates converge. The *medium-run* movement of the exchange rate is described by the last term in equation (12). The medium-run equilibrium $H2$ is described by equation (13) for $R(t)$ and equation (14) for $r(t) = r'(t)$. The real rate of interest, given by equation (14), is independent of the foreign debt, because the debt merely reallocates wealth between the two countries and does not affect world saving. Points H and $H2$ do not remain fixed, because capital and debt change. These are the first three terms in equation (12).

The Longer Term Evolution of Capital and Debt

The trajectory of the real exchange rate to the longer run involves endogenous movements of capital and debt as described by equations (4) and (6) in table 4, and graphed as the phase diagram figure 7. This will correspond to the lower half of table 2 describing the scenarios. Substitute the real interest rate equation (14) into equation (4) for investment, equation (7) for saving, and equation (6) for the capital inflow to derive equation (15) for the rate of change in capital intensity dk/dt and equation (16) for the rate of change of the foreign debt (current account deficit, capital inflow).

The locus of points where $dk/dt = 0$ is graphed as the $J = 0$ curve in figure 7. This curve is independent of the foreign debt, because the foreign debt does not affect world saving and hence does not affect the world interest rate.[23] The rate of change in capital intensity will be zero at $k = k^*$, when the marginal product of capital is equal to the world rate of interest, equation (15a) which is the $J = 0$ curve. To the left of the curve, where $k < k^*$, the q-ratio exceeds unity and capital intensity rises; to the right, where $k > k^*$, the q-ratio is less than unity and capital intensity declines. The horizontal vectors describe the movement.

$$dk/dt = J(k; k', Z) \quad J_k < 0; \tag{15}$$

$$y'(k^*; u) = r(k^*, k'; Z) \text{ implies } J(k^*; k', Z) = 0. \tag{15a}$$

The rate of change of the foreign debt dF/dt is the capital inflow equal to investment less saving, as expressed in equation (16). This is the current

---

23. In figure 6 a rise in the foreign debt shifts both the IS and the IS' curve downward. That is, it lowers aggregate demand in the United States and raises it abroad. It depreciates the dollar but has no effect upon the real interest rate.

account deficit.[24] The equation for $dF/dt = 0$, equation (16a), is graphed as the $L = 0$ curve. It is the set of capital and debt where there is no capital flow: saving is equal to investment, and the current account (equal to saving less investment) is zero.

$$dF/dt = J - S = L(k, F; k', Z) \quad L_k < 0, L_F < 0 \tag{16}$$

$$L(k^\star, F^\star; k', Z) = 0 \text{ implies } S = J. \tag{16a}$$

The curve $L = 0$ is negatively sloped because a rise in capital raises saving relative to investment and reduces the debt.[25] Along $L = 0$, $S = I$ or $CA = 0$. A rise in debt raises saving less investment, because it reduces wealth and hence consumption, in the stable case that we consider. This means that above the $L = 0$ curve, saving exceeds investment, there are current account surpluses, and the debt declines toward $L = 0$. Below the curve, saving is less than investment, there are current account deficits, and the debt rises to the curve. The vertical vectors describe the movement.

Table 5 describes the theoretical effects of changes in the fundamentals Z upon the steady-state values of the capital $k^\star$ and debt $F^\star$ intensities. Solve the steady-state equations (15a) and (16a), where the asterisk denotes the steady-state value, for $dk^\star/dZ$ and $dF^\star/dZ$. These are described in the third and fourth columns in table 5. The signs of J_z and $L_z = J_z - S_z$ depend upon the fundamental that has changed, and are noted in the first two columns in table 5. For example, a rise in the parameter u of the marginal product of capital will raise both investment $J_z > 0$ and investment less saving $L_z > 0$. The steady-state capital intensity will rise ($dk^\star/dZ > 0$) and debt intensity will decline ($dF^\star/dZ < 0$).

The trajectories in figure 7 describe the movements to the steady state. Table 2 above described these scenarios, so we may be terse here. A rise in the US index of time preference $g = $ DISRAT corresponds to (i) a medium-run movement from H to $H1$ to $H2$ (or segment H–$H2$) in figure 6, and (ii) the subsequent movement of capital and debt along trajectory BE in figure 7. The initial effect is to raise the world rate of interest, raise the real value of the dollar, and produce current account deficits, which increase the debt. The steady-state debt rises ($dF^\star/dg > 0$), and capital declines ($dk^\star/dg < 0$) because of the rise in the world rate of interest, as the economy moves along trajectory BE in figure 7.

---

24. When $dF/dt = -(CA + nF) = 0$, then the current account deficit equals nF. To avoid cumbersome phrases in the description in the text, the $n = 0$ case is described.

25. It is also possible that a rise in capital lowers saving relative to investment and produces an upward-sloping $L = 0$ curve. As long as a rise in debt raises saving, and a rise in capital lowers investment, the system will be stable. We work with what we believe to be the relevant case, where a rise in capital raises $S - I$.

Table 5   Relation between disturbances to productivity and thrift in the United States and the G-10 and the steady-state comparative statics of the NATREX model

$$(17a)\ dk^*/dZ = J_Z/(-J_k);\ (-J_k) > 0$$

$$(17b)\ dF^*/dZ = [1/(-L_F)][L_kJ_Z/(-J_k) + L_Z];\ (-L_F) > 0$$

Disturbance	J_z	$L_z = (J - S)_z$	dk^*/dZ	dF^*/dZ
Rise in US mei[a] (u)	+	+	+	−
Rise in G-10 mei (u')	−	−	−	+
Rise in US time preference (g)	−	+	−	+
Rise in G-10 time preference (g')	−	−	−	−

a. Marginal efficiency of investment.

A rise in the US productivity of capital[26] u raises capital intensity ($dk^*/du > 0$) and lowers the steady-state debt ($dF^*/du < 0$), because the rise in capital raises the saving-investment differential. The initial effect is (i) above. The trajectory of capital and debt is ADE in figure 7. Initially, the rise in investment less saving leads to capital inflows. The current account, $S - I$, is in deficit. The debt rises along with capital along AD. As the capital is put into place, GDP rises and saving rises relative to investment even as capital continues to rise. Along trajectory DE, saving exceeds investment, there are current account surpluses, and the debt declines to F^*, which is below its initial level. This is the theoretical structure and analytical solution of the NATREX model.

Empirical Relations between Endogenous and Exogenous Variables

To answer the questions posed at the beginning of this paper, we must obtain quantitative estimates of the basic equations in the model. We proceed in several steps. No single econometric test by itself is free from problems. We adduce several different econometric equations that are directly related to the theory and obtain the same results each way. The "medium-run" system (figure 6) is examined first, and then the more fundamental longer run system (figure 7).

The Medium-Run System

First we examine equation (12), which determines the movement in the real exchange rate $R = Np/p'$, and which is graphically described in figure 6. The real exchange rate responds to the real long-term interest rate differential ($r - r'$), the gap between points H and $H1$, which is then

---

26. A rise in the foreign rate u' is treated symmetrically.

driven into equality at point H2. As the economy travels along the trajec- tories in figure 7, where capital and debt are evolving, point H2 in figure 6 changes. The growth of capital at home and abroad and the change in the foreign debt shift the IS and IS′ curves and change the locus of points H2. This is the substance of equation (12), which is associated with regression results reported in table 6.

In table 6 the dependent variable is the real exchange rate, and the parameters are the US growth rate, the foreign growth rate, the rate of change of the foreign debt, and the real long-term interest rate differen- tial. The NATREX model abstracts from cyclical elements. To filter these out, the growth of US capital is measured by dk/dt = MAGROWTH, a 12–quarter moving average of the growth of US real GNP; the growth of foreign capital is measured by $dk′/dt$ = MAFGROW, a 12–quarter mov- ing average of the growth of real GNP in the G-18 countries; the nega- tive of the growth of the real foreign debt = $(-dF/dt)$ is measured by MACAGNP, a 12–quarter moving average of the ratio of US current account to GNP. The real long-term interest rate differential $(r - r′)$ is measured by the lagged USFINT(-1).[27]

Table 6, which is one estimate of the medium-run NATREX, can be summarized as follows. First, the differential between US and foreign long-term real interest rates causes the dollar to appreciate. This is the movement from gap H–H1 to H2. The other variables concern the move- ment of point H2 as a result of the movement of capital and debt along the trajectories in figure 7. Second, US growth reflects a rightward shift of the IS curve in figure 6 and leads to a capital inflow, which causes the dollar to appreciate. Third, foreign growth reflects a rightward shift of the IS′ curve in figure 6 and leads to a capital outflow from the United States, which causes the dollar to depreciate. Fourth, the decline in the foreign debt (current account surplus) causes the dollar to appreciate. Fifth, the movement along trajectory DE in figure 7 is associated with an appreciation of the US dollar. Sixth, along trajectory AD, the effects of a rise in capital and in debt affect the real exchange rate in opposite direc- tions. Each of the first four of these effects is highly significant.

The joint hypothesis that the coefficients of MAGROWTH, MAFGROW, and MACAGNP were all zero was tested and rejected at the 1 percent level. Hence the use of these three basic economic vari- ables improves the explanatory power of the equation. The random walk hypothesis that the coefficient of the lagged dependent variable is unity is rejected: probability $[C(2) = 1] = 0.000$. The diagnostic statistics

27. The ratio of the current account to GNP was taken from data from the Organization for Economic Cooperation and Development, and the data for US and foreign (G-18) growth and real long-term interest rates are based on Federal Reserve (Hooper and Mann 1989) data supplied to the author.

Table 6 Evolution of the real exchange rate as a response to US and foreign real growth, current account, and real long-term interest rate differentials

$$R = C(1) + C(2)*R(-1) + C(3)*MAGROWTH + C(4)*MAFGROW + C(5)*MACAGNP + C(6)*USFINT(-1)$$

Variable	Coefficient	Standard error	t-Statistic	Significance level (2–tailed test)
Constant	41.2	6.82	6.04	0.00
REXR(−1)	0.677	0.055	12.4	0.00
MAGROWTH	1.67	0.62	2.68	0.01
MAFGROW	−2.64	0.94	−2.8	0.007
MACAGNP	4.38	2.0	2.2	0.03
USFINT(−1)	3.19	0.66	4.8	0.00

Note: Adjusted $r^2 = 0.96$; standard error of the regression = 3.9 (mean of the dependent variable = 118.6); F-statistic = 259.9 (probability of F-statistic = 0.00); probability [$C(3) = 0$, $C(4) = 0$, $C(5) = 0$] = 0.017; probability [$C(2) = 1$] = 0.000. Diagnostic statistics: serial correlation LM test, four lags, F-statistic probability = 0.17; ARCH test, four lags, F-statistic probability = 0.86; heteroskedasticity test, F-statistic probability = 0.2; Ramsey RESET F-statistic probability = 0.0.

on the residuals, which measure the error term, indicate that we can reject the hypothesis of autocorrelation and that of heteroskedasticity, but we cannot reject the hypothesis that there are omitted variables or simultaneous equation problems, or that there is correlation among the regressors. We discuss this issue in the next subsection.

The tracking of the equation in table 6 is very good. Figure 8 plots the actual real exchange rate REXR and the values predicted from a dynamic ex ante forecast FREXR. This forecast uses the previously forecasted value as the lagged value in the next observation; hence the good prediction is not due to the inclusion of a lagged dependent variable. The only large deviation, in 1984, is rectified early in 1985. The equation is structurally quite stable. The recursive residuals from the equation (not shown here) are almost always within the bands of plus or minus two standard errors.

The Trajectories of the Longer Run System

The crucial *endogenous* variables are X = (real exchange rate, foreign debt intensity, capital intensity). The medium-run system considered only the real exchange rate and used the evolution of capital and debt as regressors. The evolution of the debt, however, is an endogenous variable in the longer run system. We want to explain simultaneously the evolution of the real exchange rate and the current account, which was not done in table 6.

In this section we relate X to the longer run fundamentals. Theoretically the *exogenous* variables in vector Z are the fundamentals: pro-

Figure 8 Actual real US dollar exchange rate and dynamic ex ante forecast using a medium-run model, 1975–89

1980 = 100

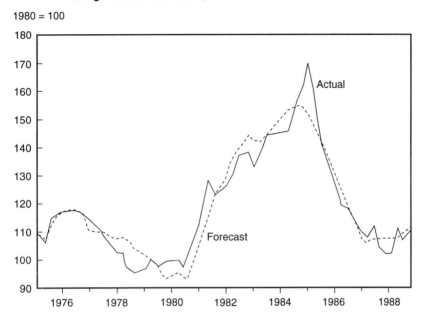

Sources: Federal Reserve; Hooper and Mann (1989, figure 13).

ductivity at home u and abroad u', and time preference at home g and abroad g'. Empirically we consider two measurable *endogenous* variables in vector X: the real exchange rate R = REXR and the ratio of the current account to GNP, denoted CAGNP. We have confidence in the measures of the real exchange rate and the flow variable, the current account. The real foreign debt intensity variable F in the model makes no distinction between equity and debt, or between direct and indirect investment. Hence instead of F we use dF/dt and measure $(-dF/dt)$ by the ratio of the current account to GNP. The cyclical elements will be in both the numerator and denominator, so that the ratio is less cyclical.

The empirical estimates of Z are closely related to the theoretical concepts in several respects. First, the US time preference or discount rate g = DISRAT is measured by the ratio of consumption plus government purchases to GNP. Again no distinction is made between private and government consumption, and it is assumed that government expenditures are primarily consumption rather than investment. To abstract from the cyclical elements,[28] social consumption $(C + G)$ is divided by GNP. Second, we do not have comparable data for the foreign country, that is, in the form of a weighted average (correspond-

---

28. A 12–quarter moving average of DISRAT was not a useful variable in the regressions.

ing to the weights in REXR) of the G-10 DISRAT. Hence we have an omitted variable g', which we know is an important determinant in the growth process.

Our focus in the empirical analysis is on the trajectories (e.g., *DE* or *BE* in figure 7) rather than upon comparative steady-state effects. The reason is that, to analyze comparative steady states involving capital and debt, we must have many observations along many steady states. The evolution of capital to the steady state takes a long time relative to our sample period of less than 20 years. No regression analysis is capable of estimating comparative steady-state effects under these conditions.[29]

Third, there is no way to measure the productivity variables (u, u') directly. However, given time preferences (g, g'), a rise in productivity stimulates capital formation and growth along trajectory *ADE* in figure 7. Given (u, u'), changes in time preference affect growth only insofar as they affect the world real rate of interest. This is trajectory *BE* in figure 7. Consequently, instead of the unobservable (u, u') they are proxied by the same growth variables, MAGROWTH and MAFGROW, as were used in table 6. Given DISRAT, the MAGROWTH variable should reflect the productivity variable u; and given the growth variables, DISRAT reflects time preference.

Fourth, the correlation matrix below (based on data from the first quarter of 1975 through the fourth quarter of 1989) indicates that the exogenous variables are not completely independent of each other:

	DISRAT	MAGROWTH	MAFGROW
DISRAT	1	−.166	−.237
MAGROWTH		1	.568
MAGROW			1

The US (MAGROWTH) and foreign (MAFGROW) growth rates are correlated. I conclude that there is a common shock that affects productivity in the United States and abroad, but the r^2 between them is only 32 percent. Therefore, both growth rates must be taken into consideration.

---

29. Formally, suppose that the dynamic system were $dx/dt + ax = aBZ$, in expectation. The expected steady state is $x^* = BZ$. The solution of the differential equation is $x(t) = BZ + [x(0) − BZ]e^{-at}$. Unless t is large, a regression of $x(t)$ on Z will not yield the slope B. This mathematical point explains the advice of Campbell and Perron (1991, 153), which is worth quoting: ''. . . for tests of the unit root hypothesis versus stationary alternatives the power depends very little on the number of observations per se but is influenced in an important way by the span of the data. . . . In most applications of interest, a data set containing fewer annual data over a long time period will lead to tests having higher power than if use was made of a data set containing more observations over a short time period.''

There is also a weak negative relation between DISRAT and the effects of the two growth rates. Presumably this results from a change in social saving that affects the world real rate of interest (a shift of the IS curve in figure 6 raises the world rate of interest from point H to point $H2$), which affects investment and growth.

Our exogenous variables are Z = (MAGROWTH, MAFGROW, DISRAT), we have an omitted variable (the weighted foreign DISRAT), and there is some correlation among the variables in Z. The object is to determine to what extent the NATREX model can explain the evolution of X = (real exchange rate, CAGNP), on the basis of the fundamentals. Then we can provide quantitative answers to the questions posed in the introduction. However, since we expect that there is more than one cointegrating equation, and since there is an omitted variable, no single econometric technique by itself will provide a satisfactory answer to these questions. Therefore, we use several techniques and obtain the same answers with each.

First, table 7 shows that there are two cointegrating vectors. This means that (as expected) there are two combinations of the variables (X, Z) which produce stationary residuals. Second, several different possible estimating equations are presented. Some are estimated by ordinary least squares (tables 9 and 11) and others by nonlinear least squares (tables 8 and 10). Third, the results of the different techniques are compared to show that the same results are obtained with each.

We exhibit several different estimating equations based upon the basic dynamic system equation (18) relating the endogenous to the exogenous variables. Variables X and Z are integrated of order I(1), as seen in table 1. Subtract $X(t - 1)$ from both sides and obtain equation (19). Variable e is an identically and independently distributed (iid) term with a zero expectation. As a first step, we shall use ordinary least squares to estimate equation (18) for endogenous variables X = (REXR, CAGNP).

$$X(t) = aX(t - 1) + bZ(t) + cZ(t - 1) + e \tag{18}$$

$$DX = X(t) - X(t - 1) = -(1 - a)X(t - 1) + bZ(t) + cZ(t - 1) + e. \tag{19}$$

The second step is a cointegration analysis. Suppose that the expectation of the change in the exogenous variable is zero when exogenous variable $Z(t)$ is equal to $Z(t - 1)$, that is, when $Z(t) = Z(t - 1)$, $E(DX) = 0$. Then the expected steady-state value of X is $X^* = BZ(t - 1)$ [equation (20)]. Hence the expected steady-state equation is equation (21). This "steady-state" $X^* = BZ$ is what we would like to capture as a cointegrating equation. Subtract equation (21) from both sides of equation (18) and derive equation (22). Subtract $X(t - 1)$ from both sides of equation (22) to derive equation (23):

Table 7   Results of Johansen maximum likelihood procedure (trended case), cointegration LR test based on trace of the stochastic matrix

Null	Alternative	Statistic	95% critical value	90% critical value
$r = 0$	$r \geq 1$	58.99	47.2	43.9
$r \leq 1$	$r \geq 2$	32.09	29.68	26.79
$r \leq 2$	$r \geq 3$	10.78	15.41	13.3
$r \leq 3$	$r = 4$	3.4	3.76	2.69

Note: There were 50 observations, maximum lag in VAR = 2. Variables included in the cointegrating vector were REXR, DISRAT, MAGROWTH, and MAFGROW; eigenvalues in descending order are .416, .347, .137, .066.

$$X^* = [(b + c)/(1 - a)] \, Z(t - 1) = BZ(t - 1) \tag{20}$$

$$X^* = aX^* + bZ(t - 1) + cZ(t - 1) + e \tag{21}$$

$$X(t) = BZ(t - 1) + a[X(t - 1) - BZ(t - 1)] + b[Z(t) - Z(t - 1)] + e \tag{22}$$

$$\begin{aligned} DX &= X(t) - X(t - 1) \\ &= -(1 - a)[X(t - 1) - BZ(t - 1)] + b[Z(t) - Z(t - 1)] + e. \end{aligned} \tag{23}$$

There are several components of the endogenous variable in equation (22). First is the value of B associated with the steady state in $X^* = BZ$. This is our sought-for cointegrating equation. Second, the error correction component is $a[X(t - 1) - BZ(t - 1)]$. The third part, $b[Z(t) - Z(t - 1)]$, is the reaction to changes in the fundamentals. The last two components are in equation (23) for DX.

The changes in the exogenous variables $DZ = [Z(t) - Z(t - 1)]$ in equations (22) and (23) should be D(DISRAT, MAGROWTH, MAFGROW). However, they do not show up very significantly in the estimation. We therefore use a market measure of DZ, which are the medium-run disturbances, as in table 6 above. In figure 6, changes in the fundamentals DZ shift the IS and IS′ curves and produce interest rate differentials $(r - r')$, such as $H - H1$, which lead to portfolio adjustments and capital flows which then produce a convergence. To avoid a simultaneous equation problem, we measure DZ by USFINT(-1), the real long-term interest differential lagged by one quarter. Both this measure of DZ and Z itself are significant in our estimating equations below.

Tables 9 and 11 use ordinary least squares to estimate equation (18). Tables 8 and 10 use nonlinear least squares in equation (22) to check the robustness of the results to the estimation method utilized. In equation (22) the nonlinear least squares technique estimates B, which is simultaneously in both the first and second terms, so the estimation is constrained by the requirement that the same B should be obtained.[30]

We obtain the same results whether we use ordinary or nonlinear least squares estimation. The results for the real exchange rate are presented in table 8 using the nonlinear method, and in table 9 using ordinary least squares. The results for the ratio of the current account to GNP are presented in table 10 using the former and in table 11 using the latter. The signs, quantitative estimates, and significance of the coefficients of Z are the same regardless of the estimation method used. The B = dR/dZ in the nonlinear least squares estimation corresponds to the longer run effects of Z. The ordinary least squares estimate in table 9 of the long-run effect of a change in $Z(i)$ upon the real exchange rate is $dR/dZ(i) = C(i)/[1 - C(2)] = 4C(i)$, where $C(i)$ is the regression coefficient of $Z(i)$ and $C(2) = 0.75$ is the coefficient of the lagged real exchange rate. For DISRAT we obtain, using ordinary least squares, −3.9, and using nonlinear least squares, −3.4; for MAFGROW we obtain, using ordinary least squares, −7.3, and using the nonlinear method, −8.1. The coefficients of MAGROWTH are positive but not significant.

Second, the residuals in the ordinary least squares equations are not serially correlated, are not heteroskedastic, and are stationary: the Dickey-Fuller statistic was −6.5.

Third, the model is quite stable over time as shown in figure 9, describing the recursive residuals[31] from equation (18a) table 9. The use

---

30. The Phillips-Loretan cointegration technique is not equation (22) but equation (22a), where the set $[X(t), Z(t)]$ are matched with no lags (Campbell and Perron 1991, 190):

$$X(t) = BZ(t) + a[X(t-1) - BZ(t-1)] + b[Z(t) - Z(t-1)] + e. \qquad (22a)$$

When equation (22) was used in table 8, significant and economically sensible results were obtained for vector B. When equation (22a) was used, however, the only significant result in vector B was the coefficient of DISRAT, which was not economically sensible, stating that a rise in the social consumption ratio appreciates the steady-state real value of the dollar. The rationale for cointegration tests is the avoidance of spurious correlation. Phillips showed (Campbell and Perron 1991, 176) that in the case of spurious correlation the following occur as the sample size increases: the Durbin-Watson statistic converges to zero; r^2 converges to a random variable; and the t-statistics of the coefficients diverge. We do not observe any of these warning signals.

31. Let the maintained model be $y = x\beta + u$, where $u \sim N(0, \sigma^2 I)$. The equation is estimated repeatedly using ever larger subsets of the sample data. In each period $(t - 1)$ a forecast is made of dependent variable $y(t)$ for the next period, using only the available information $x(t - 1)$ through period $(t - 1)$; that is, coefficient estimates $b(t - 1)$ are based upon the first $(t - 1)$ observations of (y, x). The one-step-ahead forecast error is $v(t) = y(t) - x'(t) b(t - 1)$. This process is continued until all of the sample points have been used. The recursive residual is $v(t)$ divided by the standard deviation of the forecast error. If the maintained model is valid, the recursive residuals will be independently and normally distributed with zero mean and constant variance σ^2.

Table 8 Nonlinear least squares estimates of determinants of the real exchange rate

REXR = [C(1) + C(2)*MAGROWTH(− 1) + C(3)*MAFGROW(− 1)
+ C(4)*DISRAT(− 1)] + C(5)*[REXR(− 1)
− C(2)*MAGROWTH(− 1) − C(3)*MAFGROW(− 1)
− C(4)*DISRAT(− 1)] + C(6)*USFINT(− 1) + e

Variable	Coefficient	Standard error	t-Statistic	Significance level (2–tailed test)
Constant	422.7	148	2.86	0.006
MAGROWTH	1.17	1.79	0.65	0.52
MAFGROW	−8.12	3.26	−2.49	0.016
DISRAT	−3.4	1.72	−1.99	0.05
C(5)	0.74	0.055	13.3	0.00
USFINT(−1)	2.5	0.62	4.05	0.00

Note: Adjusted r^2 = 0.96; Dickey-Fuller statistic for residual is UROOT(N,0) = −6.5. Sample period was the second quarter of 1975 through the fourth quarter of 1989; N = 59.

Table 9 Ordinary least squares estimates of determinants of the real exchange rate

REXR = C(1) + C(2)*REXR(− 1) + C(3)*MAGROWTH
+ C(4)*MAFGROW + C(5)*DISRAT + C(6)*USFINT(− 1) + e

Variable	Coefficient	Standard error	t-Statistic	Significance level (2–tailed test)
Constant	114.8	28.7	4.00	0.002
REXR(−1)	0.75	0.055	13.49	0.00
MAGROWTH	0.55	0.49	1.13	0.26
DISRAT	−0.98	0.365	−2.7	0.009
MAFGROW	−1.825	0.88	−2.1	0.04
USFINT(−1)	2.77	0.62	4.4	0.00

Note: Adjusted r^2 = 0.96; Durbin-Watson statistic = 1.76; LM test, four lags, probability = 0.25; ARCH test, four lags, probability = 0.98; heteroskedasticity test, probability = 0.26; augmented Dickey-Fuller statistic on residuals, UROOT(N,1) = −5.2; probability of null hypothesis [C(3) = 0, C(4) = 0, C(5) = 0] = 0.005. Sample period was the first quarter of 1975 through the fourth quarter of 1989; N = 60.

of recursive residuals generalizes the Chow test. If the maintained model is valid and not changing over time, the recursive residuals will lie about the zero point in figure 9 and within the bands representing plus or minus two standard errors. This is indeed the case. For these reasons, we can be confident that there is no spurious correlation underlying these empirical results.

The results of tables 8 through 11, which were summarized in table 3, are as follows. *US growth* appreciates the real exchange rate but not significantly. (However, in table 6, for the medium-run system, the appreciation was significant.) US growth significantly reduces the ratio of the US current account to GNP. This corresponds to the movement

Table 10 Nonlinear least squares estimation of the ratio of the current account to GNP

CAGNP = [C(1) + C(2)*MAGROWTH(− 1) + C(3)*MAFGROW(− 1)
+ C(4)*DISRAT(− 1)] + C(5)*[CAGNP(− 1)
− C(2)*MAGROWTH(− 1) − C(3)*MAFGROW(− 1)
− C(4)*DISRAT(− 1)] + C(6)*USFINT(− 1) + e

Variable	Coefficient	Standard error	t-Statistic	Significance level (2–tailed test)
Constant	9.4	3.7	2.5	0.01
MAGROWTH	−0.15	0.06	−2.5	0.015
MAFGROW	0.29	0.12	2.4	0.019
DISRAT	−0.12	0.04	−2.8	0.00
C(5)	0.84	0.06	13.2	0.00
USFINT(−1)	−0.0076	0.0097	−0.78	0.43

Note: Adjusted r^2 = 0.96; Dickey-Fuller statistic residuals = CAGNP−BZ gives UROOT(N,0) −2.2. Sample period was the second quarter of 1975 through the third quarter of 1989; N = 58. The dependent variable is measured as percent per quarter.

Table 11 Ordinary least squares estimate of the ratio of the current account to GNP

CAGNP = C(1) + C(2)*CAGNP(− 1) + C(3)*MAGROWTH
+ C(4)*MAFGROW + C(5)*DISRAT + e

Variable	Coefficient	Standard error	t-Statistic	Significance level (2–tailed test)
Constant	1.76	0.85	2.1	0.04
CAGNP(−1)	0.83	0.06	13.4	0.00
MAGROWTH	−0.034	0.016	−2.1	0.04
MAFGROW	0.06	0.019	3.24	0.002
DISRAT	−0.023	0.01	−2.25	0.029

Note: Based on equation (18) in the text. Adjusted r^2 = 0.95; Durbin-Watson statistic = 1.97; LM test, serial correlation, four lags, probability = 0.97; ARCH test, four lags, probability = 0.37; heteroskedasticity test, probability = 0.15; augmented Dickey-Fuller test residuals UROOT (N,1) −5.6; probability [C(3) + C(4) = 0] = 0.02; probability [C(3) = 0, C(4) = 0, C(5) = 0] = 0.005; Jarque-Bera normality test statistic = 2.86, probability = 0.24. Sample period was the first quarter of 1975 through the third quarter of 1989; N = 59. The CAGNP is measured as percent per quarter.

along trajectory *AD* in figure 7 above. *Foreign growth* depreciates the US dollar significantly, and it significantly increases the ratio of the US current account to GNP. This corresponds to the foreign country moving along its trajectory *AD* in figure 7. A rise in US time preference DISRAT significantly lowers the long-run value of the dollar and significantly reduces the current account. The DISRAT variable captures the movement along trajectory *BE* in figure 7. The *shorter run effect* of a rise in the differential between US and G-10 real long-term rates of interest appreciates the US dollar significantly but does not significantly affect the US current account.

Figure 9 Recursive residuals from the regression described in table 9

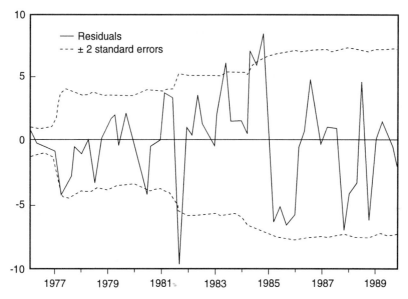

Sources: Federal Reserve; Hooper and Mann (1989).

The explanatory power of the NATREX, as the fundamental equilibrium exchange rate, is high. Figure 3 compares the actual real exchange rate REXR(t) with a dynamic ex ante simulation of the NATREX. The NATREX is derived by using the coefficients in table 9 and actual values of Z and dZ. However, instead of using the lagged dependent variable $R(t - 1)$, we use the *previously predicted value* $R'(t - 1)$ of the real exchange rate. The graph of the NATREX is $R'(t) = C(1) + C(2)*R'(t - 1) + \Sigma\ C(i)\ Z(i) + C(6)*USFINT(-1)$. It is seen that the real exchange rate converges to the NATREX, but there are some significant short-period deviations, resulting from nonfundamentals.[32] This deviation is the first term in equation (1). We attribute these deviations of the real exchange

32. John Williamson, commenting on an earlier draft of this paper, asked whether the model produced a large appreciation of the dollar's equilibrium exchange rate in the 1980s because of the high interest rates that were the complement of the fiscal policy of the period. His question concerns the interpretation of the dZ = USFINT(-1) effect in the equations. The USFINT effect may be given several interpretations. The first is that it is indeed our dZ or innovation effect of the fundamental variables, which reflect changes in investment less social saving at home and abroad, which includes the fiscal policy effects. This is our point of view. The second possible interpretation is that the USFINT also reflects shorter run nonfundamentals not contained in the NATREX model, such as monetary policy. Suppose that monetary policy were more restrictive in the United States, raising nominal long-term interest rates. This is not part of our fundamentals. Since prices are "sticky," the rise in nominal rates will be associated with a rise in the real long-term

rate from the "equilibrium exchange rate" to speculative factors, related to anticipated short-term nominal interest rates at home and abroad, and possibly to cyclical factors. The model is quite stable as shown in the recursive residuals in figure 9.

The real exchange rate and the rate of change of the foreign debt (the negative of the current account) are jointly determined in the model. Both are functions of the same fundamentals, as described in equations (18) and (22). Tables 10 (nonlinear least squares) and 11 (ordinary least squares) describe the results. The dependent variable is the ratio of the current account to GNP, denoted CAGNP, and the regressors are the same Z used to explain the real exchange rate. *We obtain the same results with ordinary as with nonlinear least squares.* The long run, measured by coefficient B in nonlinear least squares, refers to the movements along the trajectories in figure 7, not the steady state.[33]

The fundamentals significantly explain capital flows measured by the ratio of the current account[34] to GNP (to abstract from cyclical factors). Foreign growth significantly increases the current account, domestic growth decreases it, and a change in time preference toward current consumption (DISRAT) significantly decreases the current account. The growth variables reflect movements along trajectory *AD* in figure 7, where capital is rising and is partially financed by capital inflows, which raise the debt for a while. The time preference variable reflects movements along trajectory *BE* in figure 7 where capital intensity is declining but the debt is rising. The explanatory power of the fundamentals is high. Figure 4 is a dynamic ex ante simulation of the capital flow, based on table 11. The previously predicted values of the CAGNP are used as the lagged dependent variable. The fundamentals track the evolution of

---

interest rate differential. According to this interpretation, the explanatory power of the USFINT effect exaggerates the empirical explanatory power of the NATREX model per se, because it picks up shorter run effects of monetary policies. We do not believe that USFINT reflects monetary policy, because it is the real long-term interest rate differential, and monetary policy has a weak effect on real *long-term* interest rates.

33. In the steady state (denoted by an asterisk), debt intensity is unchanging. From equation (6), in the steady state $dF/dt = I - S - nF = -(CA^* + nF^*) = -(B^* - rF^* + nF^*) = 0$. This means that the steady-state trade balance $B^* = (r - n)F^*$ is equal to the product of $(r - n)$, the real rate of interest less the growth rate, times the steady-state value of the debt F^*. We know (table 5) that a rise in time preference raises the steady-state debt to a higher level F^*, which decreases consumption in a stabilizing manner. The higher steady-state debt means that the steady-state trade balance must rise to pay the higher interest payments, when the economy is in the efficient region where the interest rate exceeds the growth rate.

34. The current account is measured on a quarterly basis and GNP on an annual basis. Therefore, multiply each coefficient in tables 10 and 11 by four to obtain comparable annual figures.

the current account–GNP ratio very well. The recursive residuals (figure 10) indicate that the model is quite stable.

Conclusion and Policy Implications

The NATREX shares Nurkse's concept of an equilibrium exchange rate: the trajectory of the exchange rate that is consistent with external and internal balance, when speculative and cyclical factors are absent. The NATREX model focuses on the real and not the nominal exchange rate and answers the questions posed at the outset concerning the fundamental determinants of the real exchange rate. Equation (1) relates the nominal exchange rate $N(t)$ to the real exchange rate, the fundamentals, and relative prices. This analysis has both identified the fundamentals and shown that, over time but not in the very short run, the real exchange rate converges to its equilibrium as defined by the NATREX. *There is long-period, but not short-period, rationality.*

The real exchange rate $R = Np/p'$ is the ratio of relative prices at home and abroad in a common currency. This endogenous variable produces external equilibrium. We did not separate the roles of the nominal exchange rate N and relative prices p/p' because there is no consensus at present concerning the determinants of the rate of inflation in the medium run. The role of monetary aggregates as indicators or intermediate targets of the rate of inflation is the subject of controversy and inquiry.[35] For the United States and the rest of the G-10, the role of relative prices in the nominal exchange rate is quite small relative to the real exchange rate. This is seen in figure 3, where the real and nominal rates practically coincide. The reason why PPP theory is not valid is precisely that the fundamentals have been changing, and the evolution of the real exchange rate concerns the evolution of the second and third terms in equation (1) above.

The present study is also related to the work of Warwick McKibbin and Jeffrey Sachs and that of John Helliwell. They are concerned with capital flows and pose the following questions: What are the linkages between fiscal deficits and external deficits? Should trade deficits at home be interpreted as signs of US decline or unfair trade practices abroad, as the reflection of differential growth rates at home and abroad, or as the result of US macroeconomic policies? What would be the effects on the United States and the rest of the world of large cuts in the US budget deficit? Would its elimination be enough to eliminate US trade deficits? To answer these questions they developed a macro

---

35. See the March/April 1994 issue of *Federal Reserve Bank of St. Louis Review* concerning these issues. There has been great disillusionment about the use of monetary aggregates as indicators or intermediate targets for the rate of inflation. The conventional monetary models are disappointing in explaining relative rates of inflation.

Figure 10 Recursive residuals from the regression described in table 11

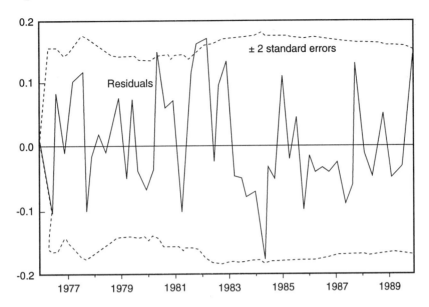

economic simulation of the world economy, founded on the theoretical work of Robert Mundell, J. Marcus Fleming, and Victor Argy, but which allows for dynamic effects. The full dynamic model is not solved analytically, and the model is not estimated by econometric techniques but is the result of a simulation.

Their conclusions are as follows.[36] First, in the longer run, US monetary policies have negligible effects on the trade balance. US trade deficits cannot be reduced by a depreciation of the US dollar caused by a US monetary expansion. The expansionary effects of the monetary policy offset the effects of the depreciation. Second, only fiscal policy changes can be relied upon to improve the trade balance. Third, even elimination of the US budget deficit would not entirely eliminate the US trade deficit. To accomplish that objective there must be an additional rise in the US private saving ratio. The results presented here are consistent with theirs, and we obtained the same quantitative estimates as did Helliwell.

Capital flows are defined as saving less investment, equal to the current account, and are not necessarily reflected by interest rate differentials.[37] Real long-term interest rates converge even though investment and saving are not equal. This is also seen in table 10 for the CAGNP, where the coefficient of USFINT(−1) is not significant. The NATREX

36. See McKibbin and Sachs (1991, tables 4–1 and 4–3, p. 98), and Helliwell (1991, 31, 33, 43–44).

37. See Niehans (1994) for an excellent discussion of this issue.

theory states that the fundamentals, productivity and thrift, determine the saving-investment differential and hence capital flows. The phase diagram in figure 7 indicates the trajectory of the current account as a response to the fundamentals.

There has been an active debate concerning the sensitivity of capital flows to disturbances of saving and investment.[38] On the basis of tables 10 and 11 we may answer the second and third sets of questions raised at the beginning of this paper, and explain why I believe there is a high degree of capital mobility. Our cointegrating equation for the CAGNP measured as percent per quarter is CAGNP = BZ. The Feldstein-Horioka view that there is no capital mobility means that $d(\text{CAGNP})/dZ = B = 0$—that is, disturbances to productivity and thrift in the longer run do not affect capital flows. This means that we should not find that the vector B of coefficients in tables 10 and 11 is significant. That is not the case. We find that each element in vector B is highly significant, both separately and jointly.[39] The high explanatory power of the results in tables 10 and 11 is summarized in figures 4, 10, and 11 and table 3.

The conclusions of McKibbin and Sachs and of Helliwell concern the relation between government expenditures and the current account (the third set of questions posed in the introduction). The social consumption or time preference DISRAT = $(C + G)/\text{GNP}$ is a highly significant variable in explaining the current account deficits. The recursive estimates of the coefficient of DISRAT in figure 11 are highly stable. In this measure, it does not matter whether government expenditures have increased or private consumption has increased (say, due to a tax cut). It is their sum that matters. The basic goods market balance [GNP = Y = $(C + G) + I + CA$] equation is given in equation (24a). The change in the current account resulting from a change in DISRAT = $(C + G)/Y$ is (24). The crowding-out effect is the final term in equation (24a):

$$1 = \text{DISRAT} + (I/Y) + \text{CAGNP} \tag{24}$$

$$d(\text{CAGNP})/d(\text{DISRAT}) = -1 - d(I/Y)/d(\text{DISRAT}). \tag{24a}$$

We do not ask what is the effect of Z upon the current account, given the real exchange rate. Our system jointly determines the real exchange rate and the current account deficit, so equation (18) is a reduced-form dynamic equation. Thus $B = dX/dZ$ is the total effect of a change in a fundamental upon an endogenous variable.

---

38. See the survey paper by Obstfeld (1993) and Polly Allen's discussion, and Niehans (1994).

39. The notes at the bottom of table 11 report test statistics. The probability that the coefficients of MAGROWTH, MAFGROW, and DISRAT are zero is 0.005. The residuals are normal (Jarque-Bera test statistic) and are not serially correlated, and there is no heteroskedasticity.

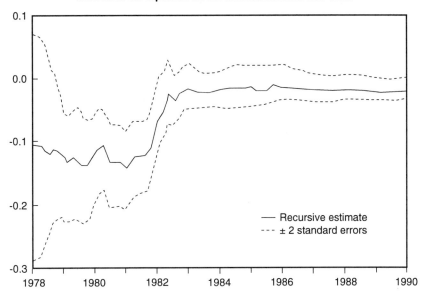

Table 10 gives the nonlinear least squares estimate of the effect of
DISRAT upon CAGNP as −0.12, or −0.48 on an annual basis. This is
the estimate of the movement along the trajectory. Table 11 gives the
corresponding longer run, ordinary least squares estimate[40] of the effect
of DISRAT upon CAGNP as $[-0.023/(1 - 0.83)]$, multiplied by four to
put it on an annual basis as −0.54. We obtain the same estimate (−0.5)
with both methods of estimation. The stability of the recursive estimate
of the coefficient of DISRAT as the sample size increases (figure 11)
indicates that no significant changes have occurred since 1982. Using the
value of −0.5 for $d(CAGNP)/d(DISRAT)$, we conclude that in the longer
run, along the trajectory BE in figure 7, half of the rise in social consumption is financed by capital inflows, which raise the foreign debt,
and half crowds out private investment. The crowding out occurs
because the decline in social saving shifts the IS curve to the right in
figure 6 and raises the world real rate of interest from H to $H1$. Alternatively, if the ratio of government expenditures to GNP declined by 1
percentage point with no change in private consumption, the current
account deficit as a percentage of GNP would decrease by 0.5. This is
exactly the same number obtained by Helliwell,[41] and is qualitatively

---

40. The lagged dependent variable must be taken into account, so we divide the value of
the regression coefficient of $Z(i)$ by $1 - 0.83$, where 0.83 is the coefficient of the lagged
dependent variable.

41. Helliwell (1991, 31) writes: ''Figure 1.2 brings together the effects of the fiscal and

consistent with the results of McKibbin and Sachs. The current account deficits in the 1980s cannot be explained without using the effects of DISRAT.

US growth generated by a rise in investment leads to capital inflows. Foreign growth generated by the rise in investment demand will lead to a capital outflow, a rise in the US current account, and a depreciation of the US dollar along the early part of the trajectory. From the viewpoint of the foreign country, this is a movement along trajectory *AD* in figure 7, where capital and debt are rising.

We have shown how the evolution of the real exchange rate and foreign debt are jointly determined, and that the fundamentals—productivity and thrift—generate significant capital mobility for the United States. Market-determined real exchange rates "make sense" as trends but not as short-run movements.

References

Allen, Polly Reynolds. 1993. Comments on a paper by Maurice Obstfeld presented at a conference on the International Monetary System, sponsored by the International Finance Section, Princeton University, Princeton, NJ.

Allen, Polly Reynolds, and Jerome L. Stein. 1990. "Capital Market Integration." *Journal of Banking and Finance* 14, no. 5 (November): 909–19.

Boothe, Paul, Kevin Clinton, Agathe Côté and David Longworth. 1985. *International Asset Substitutability: Theory and Evidence for Canada*. Ottawa: Bank of Canada.

Campbell, John Y., and Pierre Perron. 1991. "Pitfalls and Opportunities: What Macroeconomists Should Know About Unit Roots." In National Bureau of Economic Research, *Macroeconomics Annual 1991*. Cambridge, MA: MIT Press.

Corbae, Dean, and Sam Ouliaris. 1991. "A Test of Long-Run Purchasing Power Parity Allowing for Structural Breaks." *Economic Record* (March): 26–33.

Dornbusch, Rudiger. 1987. *Dollars, Debts and Deficits*. Cambridge, MA: MIT Press.

Edison, Hali, and Dianne Pauls. 1991. "Re-assessment of the Relationship between Real Exchange Rates and Real Interest Rates 1974–90." International Finance Discussion Paper No. 408. Washington: Board of Governors of the Federal Reserve System.

Edison, Hali J., Joseph E. Gagnon, and William R. Melick. 1994. "Understanding the Empirical Literature on Purchasing Power Parity." International Finance Discussion Paper No. 465. Washington: Board of Governors of the Federal Reserve System.

Friedman, Milton. 1953. "The Case for Flexible Exchange Rates." In Milton Friedman, *Essays in Positive Economics*. Chicago: University of Chicago Press.

Helliwell, John F. 1991. "The Fiscal Deficit and the External Deficit: Siblings but not Twins," In Rudolph G. Penner, ed., *The Great Fiscal Experiment*. Washington: Urban Institute.

Hooper, Peter. 1989. "Exchange Rates and the US External Adjustment in the Short and the Long Run." International Finance Discussion Paper No. 346. Washington: Board of Governors of the Federal Reserve System.

---

external deficits to show the extent to which the two deficits move together in response to an increase in government spending. . . . the ratio of the induced external deficit to the induced fiscal deficit . . . returns to . . . between .45 and .49 for the rest of the six year period. . . . the two deficits are closely related but [are] far from being twins."

Hooper, Peter, and Catherine L. Mann (1989). "The Emergence and Persistence of the U.S. External Imbalance, 1980–87." *Princeton Studies in International Finance*: 65.

Infante, Ettore, and Jerome L. Stein. 1973. "Optimal Growth with Robust Feedback Control." *Review of Economic Studies* 40, no. 1: 47–60.

Lothian, James R., and Mark P. Taylor. 1992. "Real Exchange Rate Behavior: The Recent Float from the Perspective of the Past Two Centuries." Working Paper. New York: Fordham University, Graduate School of Business.

McKibbin, Warwick, and Jeffrey Sachs. 1991. *Global Linkages*. Washington: Brookings Institution.

Merton, Robert C. 1990. *Continuous Time Finance*. Oxford: Basil Blackwell.

Niehans, Jurg. 1994. "Elusive Capital Flows: Recent Literature in Perspective." *Journal of International and Comparative Economics* 3: 21–44.

Nurkse, Ragnar. 1945. "Conditions of International Monetary Equilibrium." Essays in International Finance. Princeton, NJ: International Finance Section, Princeton University.

Obstfeld, Maurice. 1993. "International Capital Mobility in the 1990s." Paper presented at a conference on the International Monetary System sponsored by the International Finance Section, Princeton University, Princeton, NJ.

Stein, Jerome L. 1990. "The Real Exchange Rate," *Journal of Banking and Finance* 14, 5 (November) Special Issue: 1045–78.

Stein, Jerome L. 1992. "Fundamental Determinants of Exchange Rates." *Journal of International and Comparative Economics* 1, no. 2.

Stein, Jerome L., Polly Reynolds Allen, et al. Forthcoming. *Fundamental Determinants of Exchange Rates*. Oxford: Oxford University Press.

6

Estimates of FEERs

JOHN WILLIAMSON

The proposals for global macroeconomic management developed at the Institute for International Economics in the 1980s relied heavily on the use of exchange rate targets. Indeed, the target zone proposal as first presented (Bergsten and Williamson 1983; Williamson 1983) focused exclusively on exchange rate management. This original development of the target zone proposal was accompanied by an endeavor to calculate "fundamental equilibrium exchange rates" (FEERs) in the hope of fortifying the position that posing the right question could lead to answers that are sufficiently reliable to be useful even though they could not pretend to be precise.

The original version of this paper was written some seven years after those estimates were first published and five years after they were revised. During that period many competing estimates of equilibrium exchange rates were published: what was considered highly suspect in the heyday of benign neglect in 1983 became a minor growth industry as the trade imbalances produced by unmanaged floating became plain to see. It therefore seemed desirable to reexamine the concept of an equilibrium exchange rate developed in 1983, to recalculate the numbers implied, and to compare those numbers with the earlier estimates. Those tasks are attempted in this paper.

The original target zone proposal was subjected to strong academic criticism on the ground that a commitment to use monetary policy to manage the exchange rate might make matters worse rather than better by leading to the monetization of budget deficits (Dornbusch 1987). Furthermore, at the 1986 Tokyo economic summit the leaders of the Group of Seven major industrialized countries (the G-7) announced a decision to seek a set of "indicators" to ensure the mutual consistency of their macroeconomic policies; that decision implied a readiness to contemplate comprehensive policy coordination. These two developments stimulated Marcus Miller and me to design a "blueprint" that formalized explicitly the fiscal and global monetary rules that provide the natural complements to target zones (Williamson and Miller 1987). This proposal for comprehensive policy coordination still gives a key role, as one of two intermediate targets (along with an endogenous target for the growth of nominal domestic demand), to an exchange rate target.[1]

It makes sense to treat the exchange rate as an intermediate target only if one has a reasonably firm basis for identifying an appropriate concept of the equilibrium exchange rate and estimating its value. Many economists are still reluctant to accept that this is possible: the skepticism of Avinash Dixit ("I think we will never know what the right exchange rates are . . ."; Dixit 1990, 707) is typical. The only way of deciding whether the skeptics are right is to try to confound them, as is done in this paper.

A willingness to attempt to estimate equilibrium exchange rates has never implied a claim to omniscience. One reason for advocating that target zones should be wide has always been recognition of the difficulty of pinning down equilibrium levels of exchange rates precisely, especially after two decades of violent swings in market rates. But it would be nihilistic to argue that one should stabilize rates only after a pattern of rates has been demonstrated to be appropriate, for the probability is that rates will never stabilize long enough to permit a judgment that they are appropriate until policy aims at stabilizing them. If the G-7 had taken that attitude at the time of the Louvre Accord (February 1987), who knows how large the subsequent misalignments might have been?

---

1. The "blueprint" has in turn been criticized for supposedly "assigning" monetary policy to external balance and fiscal policy to internal balance (see Boughton 1989). This is not an accurate characterization of the blueprint, which in fact proposed a short-run assignment of monetary policy (specifically, of short-run interest differentials) to manage the exchange rate and fiscal policy to the rate of growth of nominal domestic demand. Those are *intermediate* targets, which would be *jointly* calibrated with the aim of achieving both external and internal balance in the medium term. Boughton was perfectly right to emphasize the need for fiscal policy to be consistent with the medium-run external balance target, as I recognized in Williamson (1991), but that does not dispose of the possible need for monetary policy to be varied in the short run with a view to exchange rate management—assuming one takes the view that markets need a little official help to prevent misalignments from emerging. Of course, one purpose of having wide bands around exchange rate targets is to allow monetary policy to be used for demand management most of the time, as first analyzed by McKinnon (1971). Recent reassessments of the effectiveness of exchange market intervention (Catte et al. forthcoming; Dominguez and Frankel 1993) reinforce the hope that monetary policy could be used principally for demand management.

The next section of this paper deals with concepts, notably the conceptual basis of the FEER and the contrasting concept of an equilibrium exchange rate based upon purchasing power parity (PPP). The study then proceeds to calculate a new set of FEERs on an ex ante basis (in contrast to the ex post basis used before); the calculations were, however, developed in 1990 and have not been updated since (for reasons explained in chapter 1). The calculation proceeds by first developing a set of current account targets for the G-7 and the rest of the world; then internal balance targets for the G-7 only are presented; finally, the simulations performed to calculate the FEER trajectories are described.

Concepts

The concept of the equilibrium exchange rate is an elusive one. Indeed, Joan Robinson (1947, 103) once wrote:

> It is now obvious that there is no one rate of exchange which is the equilibrium rate corresponding to a given state of world demands and techniques. In any given situation there is an equilibrium rate corresponding to each rate of interest and level of effective demand, and any rate of exchange, within very wide limits, can be turned into the equilibrium rate by altering the rate of interest appropriately. Moreover, any rate of exchange can be made compatible with any rate of interest provided that money wages can be sufficiently altered. The notion of the equilibrium exchange rate is a chimera. The rate of exchange, the rate of interest, the level of effective demand and the level of money wages react upon each other like the balls in Marshall's bowl, and no one is determined unless all the rest are given.

The term "fundamental" was prefixed to "equilibrium exchange rate" in my previous writings on the subject in order to hint at the approach to tying down the inherent ambiguity in the concept of the equilibrium exchange rate. "Fundamental" was and is intended to suggest an analogy to the concept of "fundamental disequilibrium" that provided the criterion for a parity change in the Bretton Woods system. Although that term was never formally defined, or at least not prior to a 1970 report of the executive directors of the International Monetary Fund (IMF 1970, chapter 5), the term acquired a reasonably clear meaning over the years: in particular, it implied an exchange rate that was inconsistent with medium-run macroeconomic balance. Conversely, therefore, the FEER is the exchange rate that *is* consistent with macroeconomic balance, meaning the simultaneous achievement of internal and external balance.

Internal balance implies acceptance of the historically determined wage rate and achievement of a level of effective demand such as to sustain the highest level of activity consistent with the control of inflation. Subject to some ambiguity in the concept of controlling inflation, which is further discussed below, it thus pins down two of the three elements of indeterminacy that concerned Joan Robinson (the levels of wages and of effective demand).[2]

Pinning down the third indeterminate element, the rate of interest, is more tricky. The traditional interpretation of external balance as overall balance (a capital flow that finances the current account imbalance with no change in reserves) does not suffice, because different interest rates are consistent with different capital flows and therefore with correspondingly different current accounts and hence exchange rates. One needs a criterion for picking out one of these pairs from the others.

My own approach to this problem has started by interpreting external balance in terms of a current account target rather than overall balance. A minimum criterion is to require that the current account outcome be sustainable.[3] This rules out the possibility of very large current account deficits financed by massive capital inflows attracted by exceptionally high interest rates: such a strategy may be feasible for a time if confidence exists, but sooner or later confidence will erode and the strategy will cease to be viable. Large current account surpluses may also not be viable, either because they imply a socially unacceptable postponement of consumption or because they provoke foreign pressures, although this is less clear-cut. But the fundamental point is that the criterion of sustainability is unlikely to be sufficient to pin down the current account target to a unique value. The problem of selecting a target current account surplus is discussed in detail shortly.

The Normative Element in a FEER

However that target is chosen, the definition of external balance contains a normative element. Indeed, the definition of internal balance may also be regarded as normative: although the value judgment incorporated in seeking as high a level of output as is consistent with the control of inflation may not appear controversial, the phrase "control of inflation" conceals a range of views as to how far and how fast inflation should be reduced. Since both internal and external balance involve normative elements, it follows that the FEER does as well: it is the equilibrium exchange rate (path) that would be consistent with ideal

---

2. Matters are slightly more complex if the highest level of activity consistent with the control of inflation is a positive function of the real wage—as is modeled in, for example, the GEM model used later in this paper—because then the real wage is increased by a real appreciation. This means that one has to solve simultaneously rather than sequentially for internal balance and the FEER.

3. Although steady-state paths are necessarily sustainable, sustainability is not restricted to steady-state outcomes. Any path that satisfies intertemporal budget constraints, and that can be followed indefinitely without surprises that would make agents wish that they had not acted as they did, is sustainable.

macroeconomic performance, and what is "ideal" is at least to some extent in the eye of the beholder.[4]

It has been argued that the adjective "equilibrium" should never have been employed to describe a normative construct such as the FEER (Bryant 1983, n. 8). It might indeed have made for greater exactitude if the FEER had been called an "optimal" or "appropriate" or "desirable" exchange rate (Bayoumi et al., chapter 2, use the last of these adjectives to describe their construct), thus directing attention explicitly to the normative criteria embodied in its definition. But, for better or worse, there is a long tradition of defining the constant level (or trend path) of the exchange rate consistent with a desired macroeconomic outcome as the equilibrium exchange rate: no great harm seems to be done by conforming to this tradition rather than battling for semantic purity.

The FEER as a Trajectory

The most familiar reason for expecting the equilibrium exchange rate to change over time is that inflation proceeds at different rates in different countries. *Ceteris paribus,* the currency of the faster inflating country will need to depreciate at a rate equal to the inflation differential in order to preserve equilibrium. (This is the core element of truth in the PPP doctrine.) Since, however, the FEER is defined as the *real* effective exchange rate consistent with macroeconomic balance, differential inflation does not cause the FEER to change: rather, maintaining the exchange rate at a constant FEER requires the nominal exchange rate to change at a rate equal to the inflation differential.

In addition, however, there are three well-established reasons for believing that in general the FEER will change over time. These reasons imply that the FEER has to be conceived as a trend path for the exchange rate rather than a constant level.

In the first place, when countries are growing at different rates, "productivity bias" will typically call for appreciation of the faster growing country's currency on the equilibrium trajectory. Balassa (1964) first noted the systematic tendency for productivity to grow more rapidly in sectors producing tradables than those producing nontradables, and for this differential to be greater in faster growing countries. Thus, if one measures inflation by a price index that encompasses both sectors, equal measured inflation would correspond to increasing competitiveness of the tradable sector in the faster growing country. To counter this and maintain competitiveness constant, the faster growing country

---

4. In practice, I suspect that Milton Friedman (1953, 6) was right in arguing that major differences in economic prescription typically stem from different visions of how the economy works rather than from different preferences, i.e., from positive rather than normative divergences.

needs a real appreciation of its currency, at least as measured by a broad price index.[5]

Second, a country in deficit will be accumulating net foreign liabilities. These have to be serviced. Hence, to maintain the current account balance constant, it will be necessary for the currency to depreciate in real terms in order to increase the trade balance to generate the interest payments on the increasing debt. Conversely, a country in continuing surplus needs a currency that is appreciating in real terms to support an increase in absorption relative to output.

Third, if the product of the income elasticity of import demand and the domestic growth rate exceeds the product of the income elasticity of export demand and the foreign growth rate, there will be a secular tendency for the current account to deteriorate (Johnson 1958; Houthakker and Magee 1969). This also will have to be offset by a continuing depreciation. Even if the products of elasticities and growth rates were equal, which Krugman (1989) argues is typically to be expected, a similar effect could arise if the initial levels of exports and imports were widely divergent (this is sometimes called the "gap factor").

For these three reasons, one must expect that the real exchange rate consistent with macroeconomic equilibrium will change gradually over time. In addition, unforeseeable events may lead to discontinuous changes in the FEER. Any "permanent" change in the terms of trade, such as an oil price shock, may cause a step change in the FEER. So can a change in a country's relations to the international capital market—for example, a loss of creditworthiness that compels elimination of a current account deficit, as happened to many middle-income debtor countries in Latin America and elsewhere during the 1980s.

Selecting a Current Account Target

As the preceding discussion indicates, the most controversial issue to arise at a conceptual level in defining the FEER involves the choice of targets for current account balances. It has been argued already that the chosen target for each country must be sustainable, but that this requirement will typically be insufficient to pin down the target to a unique value.

One simple rule of thumb that still seems to appeal in some quarters is for all countries to aim at a balanced current account. This is not a sensible objective. Countries can often expect to benefit by exporting or importing capital over a long period of years, when domestic savings are, respectively, greater or less than domestic investment opportunities

---

5. McKinnon (1984) urged use of a narrow price index confined to tradables, which requires less change. See Marston (1987) for quantitative estimates of the difference between alternative price indexes for measuring the US-Japan bilateral real exchange rate.

at the world interest rate. Assuming that countries are going to have balance of payments objectives at all (which would not be universally agreed), the aim should be to achieve that current account balance that transfers capital at a rate that is sustainable and desirable, and therefore consistent with macroeconomic equilibrium, rather than to eliminate all imbalances.

The problem is to identify the capital flow that should be regarded as consistent with equilibrium. One cannot simply assume that the actual capital flows over some short period of time were an equilibrium phenomenon to which the current account should adjust. In the first place, with a freely floating exchange rate, short-run causality largely runs in the opposite direction: whatever current account outcome results from past levels of income and competitiveness determines the need for finance (i.e., the net capital flow), and the exchange rate adjusts as needed to secure that flow. Alternatively, policy may alter interest rates with a view to influencing capital flows so as to avoid unacceptable exchange rate outcomes.

Second, even with a pegged or managed exchange rate, many capital flows are ephemeral, or may even be reversed rapidly. It is neither feasible nor desirable to try to adjust the current account in order to match short-run changes in capital flows: the social function of reserves is to provide a buffer stock that can adjust so as to avoid the need for transitory adjustment in the current account to match every variation in the capital account. Thus one needs some concept of the long-run or underlying capital flow in order to provide the target to which the current account should adjust.

Another old idea that has proved unhelpful is to identify an appropriate target by examining the balance of payments accounts and isolating some subset of the flows as long-term because they are invested in assets of a relatively long maturity.[6] One problem is that short-term speculative flows may well be placed in long-term assets (for example, when the objective is to speculate on a fall in long-term interest rates). Conversely, a buildup of working balances in short-term assets sometimes provides a rather stable inflow. The most guidance one may be able to get from the balance of payments accounts is by looking at the actual average flow over a lengthy period. But even then it is necessary to ask whether macroeconomic policy was being distorted in some way (e.g., through a restrictive monetary policy designed to attract a capital inflow, as happened in Britain in 1926–31, and again at various times in the postwar period) before accepting a realized flow as a target.

Recognition of the relevance of macroeconomic policy suggests a more promising approach. Instead of starting with the balance of payments

---

6. A new variant of this idea has been advanced by Yoshitomi (1990), who defines the "most basic" balance as the sum of the current account and direct investment.

accounts, one may examine the saving-investment balance. A familiar national income accounting identity states:

$$(X - M) = (S - I) - (G - T) \tag{1}$$

$$\frac{\text{Net investment in}}{\text{rest of world}} = \frac{\text{Net saving of}}{\text{private sector}} - \frac{\text{Public-sector}}{\text{deficit.}}$$

Hence, the underlying capital flow whose obverse provides an appropriate current account target is the difference between the net saving of the private sector and the public-sector deficit, both of which should for this purpose be cyclically adjusted to get their values at "internal balance."

Unfortunately even this approach contains a crucial ambiguity. In fact, two distinct principles may be proposed for identifying the public-sector deficit $(G - T)$ in equation (1). One of these poses the intertemporal optimization problem: given domestic saving behavior and investment opportunities, and the interest rates at which the country can lend to and borrow from the international capital market, what sequence of public-sector deficits and foreign borrowing would be expected to maximize intertemporal welfare? Clearly this optimization has to be conducted subject to the intertemporal budget constraint, which implies that a decision to borrow more now (and thus run bigger budget and current account deficits) means larger debt service payments (and thus higher taxes and a bigger trade surplus) in the future. In a world with "imperfect" capital markets, the optimization may also need to be conducted subject to a constraint that limits the maximum size of the debt to a level consistent with the maintenance of creditworthiness.

In conducting such an optimization, one implicitly optimizes both the course of budgetary policy, at least of the structural budget deficit or surplus, and of the current account. It can, however, be argued that the political process does not always deliver budgetary outcomes that are consistent with the maximization of intertemporal welfare. (This argument was popular with US economists during the Reagan-Regan years.) It would make little sense to target the exchange rate on achieving a current account outcome that was inconsistent with a country's fiscal policy. This line of reasoning suggests that the appropriate way of choosing the underlying capital flow is to identify the likely fiscal position, as well as the likely $(S - I)$ balance of the private sector, and then treat the current balance implied as the residual, which needs to be financed by the underlying capital flow. Naturally, since the intertemporal budget constraint still holds, a bigger fiscal—and thus current account—deficit in the short run still implies a bigger trade surplus and higher taxes to generate debt service at some date in the future.

This alternative approach would seem to have two advantages and one disadvantage:

- One advantage is that it is easier to predict the structural budget outcome for the next few years implied by the current stance of fiscal policy than it is to give a convincing answer to the question as to the *optimal* stance of fiscal policy.

- Another advantage is that the second approach avoids making what may be blatantly unrealistic assumptions about fiscal policy.

- On the other hand, this approach may involve calling an unsustainable trajectory the ''equilibrium trajectory,'' in circumstances in which fiscal policy and/or the current account are set on a path that does not appear to be sustainable in the medium term. This hardly seems a convincing choice of terminology or an adequate basis on which to estimate a normative construct.

FEERs are intended to be used as intermediate targets in securing the international coordination of economic policy. Sustainability would certainly seem to be an essential criterion of such targets. Subject to the constraint that they be sustainable, however, there is much to be said for leaving individual countries the maximum possible freedom to choose their own policies. In the present context, this suggests that it would be appropriate to start with the second concept discussed above, in which one takes existing fiscal policies in each country, and derive the implied set of current account balances when each country is also at internal balance.[7] One then needs to ask two questions of the implied set of current account balances:

- Are they individually sustainable? Or are the current account balances of some countries leading to a debt buildup that appears unsustainable in the medium term? An unsustainable debt buildup is one in which the ratio of debt to GNP or exports would not level out, or would level out only at such a high ratio as to jeopardize the maintenance of creditworthiness. (See Krugman 1985 or Marris 1985 for examples of the type of analysis required.)

---

7. From the standpoint of the governments engaged in the policy coordination process, this would translate into the procedure I described in my comment on a paper of James Boughton (Williamson 1991). Each participating country would be asked ''to identify the medium-run fiscal stance compatible with its current account target, a sustainable debt position, and a 'normal' real interest rate (say 3 percent). It would then identify a medium-run (say five-year) path for adjusting its fiscal deficit toward the target position. *Deviations* from that target path might then be allowed in the interest of stabilizing the growth of demand.'' The central point is that the country is expected to choose sustainable and consistent targets for the fiscal stance and the current account, but to seek to achieve those targets only gradually over a medium-run horizon.

- Are the sets of projected current account outcomes mutually consistent? That is, do they sum to a figure whose counterpart the rest of the world will be prepared to accept and able to finance? If not, then the set of plans must be judged collectively unsustainable.

If an individual country's current account trajectory is judged unsustainable, the solution is self-evident. The country needs to cut its planned fiscal deficit until the threat that an unsustainable foreign debt position will emerge has been eliminated.

Matters are more complicated if the problem is one of collective unsustainability, since then it is not self-evident which countries should be expected to modify their policies and how the needed changes should be divided up among them. One possibility would be to adopt the principle that policy should seek to promote investment rather than to thwart saving. This would imply that countries should seek to expand demand through the higher investment that would be induced by lower interest rates rather than through more expansionary fiscal policy. Current account deficits would rise in the countries with more interest-elastic investment schedules. (In principle saving might also be influenced by the lower interest rate, but empirical evidence suggests that saving is rather interest-inelastic.) However, even moderately reliable estimates of the relative interest elasticity of investment in different countries are presently lacking, which rules out this approach.

The natural alternative approach involves some concept of burden sharing. This could take the form of reducing the target surpluses of all countries equally, or of reducing all their target surpluses to a similar level. The first approach is unlikely to be feasible, for it would invite inflated statements of countries' objectives. Thus the only practical approach would seem to involve cutting back the claims of all surplus countries to an equal level (presumably in proportion to GNP), determined by the aggregate "available" deficit.

Hence the equilibrium exchange rate trajectory should be interpreted as that which would produce a current account (at internal balance) consistent with the expected saving-investment behavior of both private and public sectors, except when that behavior appears either individually unsustainable or collectively inconsistent. In the former case, the target current account balance would be that implied by the smallest fiscal adjustment needed to secure a sustainable outcome. In the latter case, the largest target surpluses would be reduced until the inconsistency is eliminated.

Ex Post versus Ex Ante

It is possible to seek to calculate FEERs on either an ex post or an ex ante basis. An ex post approach involves seeking to estimate the set of real effective exchange rates that would have been needed to achieve simultaneous internal and external balance in each country during some past period. Those estimates can then be updated in the light of subsequent cumulative inflation differentials, productivity bias, and any real shocks that are judged relevant. This is the approach I previously adopted for calculating the equilibrium exchange rates of the G-5 currencies (Williamson 1983).

An ex ante approach seeks to estimate the set of real effective exchange rates (or paths) needed to achieve simultaneous internal and external balance by some date in the medium-run future, and to maintain balance thereafter. I have already implemented this approach in estimating a FEER for the Canadian dollar (see the appendix to Wonnacott 1987). It requires three types of inputs:

■ current account targets (i.e., an interpretation of ''external balance'')

■ estimates of ''internal balance''

■ a multicountry macroeconometric model linking income, real exchange rates, and current account outcomes, in order to calculate the exchange rates that would be needed in order to achieve simultaneous internal and external balance.

This is the approach pursued below.

Macroeconomic Balance versus PPP

The main competitor to the FEER in offering a conceptual basis for estimating equilibrium exchange rates has been purchasing power parity (PPP). The appeal to PPP can mean several different things.

The weakest PPP condition requires that the equilibrium level of the exchange rate vary, *ceteris paribus,* in order to offset differential inflation. This is entirely unobjectionable: indeed, it is embodied in the concept of the FEER developed above. Note, however, that the actual level of the equilibrium exchange rate will change at the inflation differential only in the absence of productivity bias and the other real shocks discussed earlier.

A stronger use of PPP involves the identification of some initial period when the economy was judged to be in equilibrium. The current equilibrium exchange rate will be the rate that prevailed in that base period, adjusted by the cumulative inflation differential since that time. This procedure has two snags. The first is that it is rarely possible to identify a satisfactory base period when the economy was in equilibrium in all relevant respects for a sufficiently lengthy period of time to give some assurance that the actual exchange rate was the equilibrium exchange rate. The second is that it assumes away productivity bias and other real shocks that may have changed the equilibrium real exchange rate since the base date.

Both these two "relative PPP criteria" use PPP only to calculate *changes* in the equilibrium exchange rate over time. The traditional "absolute PPP criterion" claims that the equilibrium exchange rate can be identified solely on the basis of price data, as the exchange rate that equalizes purchasing power in two countries. (The PPP exchange rate is £1 = $1.50 if £1 will buy the same bundle of goods in Britain that $1.50 buys in the United States.) This PPP concept is highly apt for certain purposes, notably for that of comparing living standards in different countries: it is regrettable that the primitive and frequently misleading procedure of making such comparisons on the basis of market exchange rates is still so often employed instead. But it is equally regrettable that the absolute PPP criterion should still be urged for the purpose of identifying the exchange rate that is consistent with macroeconomic balance, in view of the massive empirical evidence that the relative price structure consistent with macroeconomic balance depends on the characteristics of the economy, including the level of development and the trade balance it needs to generate.[8]

McKinnon and Ohno (1986) proposed a modified PPP criterion. This envisages searching for the exchange rate at which a country neither imports nor exports inflation, as indicated by the realized rate of inflation. McKinnon and Ohno give the impression that they regard this as simply a novel practical method of seeking the traditional absolute PPP level, but in fact it is unlikely to yield similar results. Indeed, it seems most unlikely to yield an unambiguous criterion at all.

The reason is that an economy can learn to accommodate itself to any of quite a wide range of real exchange rates, each of which is (at internal balance) associated with a particular current account balance. Once it has learned to accommodate a particular level, any *change* from that rate will tend to generate inflationary (or disinflationary) pressures. For example, the high dollar of the mid-1980s forced Europe and Japan to learn to live with undervalued currencies; eventually both succeeded in mastering inflation despite the exchange rate, as labor became reconciled to lower real wages. When the dollar depreciated after 1985 this had the effect of exerting disinflationary pressures in Europe and Japan long before the dollar had fallen far enough to restore macroeconomic balance, which led McKinnon to complain that the dollar had become undervalued. But eventually Europe and Japan adjusted to the possi-

---

8. See the studies of the UN–World Bank–University of Pennsylvania International Comparisons Project headed by Irving Kravis, and in particular Kravis and Lipsey (1978). Other articles in the same symposium are also relevant, as well as Isard (1977) and other chapters in this volume, notably chapter 7.

bility of higher real wages, at which point the McKinnon-Ohno criterion would indicate a different equilibrium exchange rate, involving a lower value for the dollar. (In fact, the Japanese complained of imported inflation when the yen depreciated to a rate still far stronger than the McKinnon-Ohno estimate of PPP.)

Presumably everyone agrees that the fundamental criterion for choosing a target exchange rate should be its consistency with macroeconomic balance. The first element of macroeconomic balance is "internal balance," the requirement that output Y should be equal to a level Y^* consistent with noninflationary full employment. Standard theory says that Y depends positively on absorption (i.e., consumption plus investment) A and on the real exchange rate r, as follows:[9]

$$Y = Y(A, r), Y_1 > 0, Y_2 > 0. \qquad (2)$$

Standard theory also says that the current account balance B depends negatively on absorption (since higher absorption implies higher imports) and positively on the real exchange rate (which increases net exports once the J-curve—the phenomenon whereby the trade balance at first worsens following a depreciation—has worked itself out):

$$B = B(A, r), B_1 < 0, B_2 > 0. \qquad (3)$$

The locus YY of points for which Y as given by equation (2) is equal to its target level Y^* is shown by the downward-sloping line in figure 1. A lower (less competitive) real exchange rate reduces net exports and has to be offset by higher absorption to keep output constant. Similarly, the locus BB of points for which the second element of macroeconomic balance—external balance—is satisfied, where B as given by equation (3) is equal to the target value B^*, is shown by the upward-sloping line in figure 1: the larger net exports resulting from real depreciation have to be offset by higher absorption to keep the current balance constant. Full macroeconomic balance therefore requires a specific level of absorption A^* and a specific level of the real exchange rate r^*.

There is no particular reason why r^* need be equal to one—that is, why PPP need hold. Indeed, suppose that it did hold in some initial situation. Suppose that the country is a net oil importer and that a (permanent) rise in the price of oil on the world market then occurs. This would shift the locus BB leftward but would leave YY unaffected. The new equilibrium involves a higher real exchange rate (i.e., a devaluation) as well as a lower level of absorption (to make room for the increase in real net exports needed to reequilibrate the current account).

---

9. The real exchange rate is defined here so that an increase implies a real depreciation of the domestic currency.

Figure 1   Internal and external balance

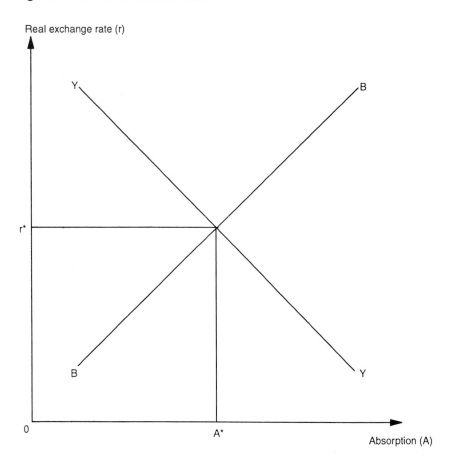

PPP would no longer hold. This proves, on the basis of a very general model, that PPP is in general inconsistent with macroeconomic balance.

The equilibrium exchange rate depends not just on the terms of trade, but also on the size of the current account target and on the full-employment target, which influences the position of the YY curve. It might still be true that in practice PPP would give a good empirical approximation of the equilibrium exchange rate. This would be true if trade elasticities were extremely high, so that the BB curve (and perhaps the YY curve too) was very flat. But in fact the empirical evidence is pretty clear that price elasticities of demand for manufactured goods in international trade,[10] although high enough to satisfy the famous

_____

10. This is not true of homogeneous primary products—what in a previous incarnation McKinnon (1979) called "tradables II"; these he sharply distinguished from "tradables I,"

Marshall-Lerner condition, are not particularly high. Accordingly one must reject the PPP criterion not just as a conceptually incorrect basis on which to estimate the equilibrium exchange rate, but also as not even providing a useful empirical first approximation.

The implications are important. Many long-run foreign-exchange forecasts made in 1990 envisaged a strong future *appreciation* of the dollar against the yen and the deutsche mark.[11] Since most models of the US balance of payments were then forecasting an *increasing* US current account deficit at then-current real exchange rates, such forecasts must have been based on PPP (which did indeed show that goods in general were cheaper in the United States than in Japan or Germany). The erroneous belief that the dollar was likely to appreciate strongly in the medium term sent wrong signals to businesses that had to make the investment decisions that determined whether or not the US payments deficit would increase or shrink. Not only did those businessmen who looked at the forecasts get an unduly pessimistic view of the likely attractiveness of the United States as a manufacturing base, but the expectation of a strong *future* dollar held up the current value of the dollar and thus curbed investment spending by those businessmen who base their decisions on current exchange rates. Moreover, these silly forecasts helped the yen to again become seriously overvalued in 1991–92, driving the Japanese current account surplus back up and setting the stage for a destructively rapid yen appreciation in 1993–94.

Another context in which PPP comparisons had a pernicious effect in perverting public debate concerns the exchange rate at which sterling joined the ERM. The purchasing power parity criterion implied an equilibrium rate around DM3.41 = £1 in the second half of 1989 (Goldman Sachs estimates quoted in *The Economist*, 7 October 1989, p. 102). The fact that such a rate would be inconsistent with a satisfactory macroeconomic equilibrium did not prevent widespread advocacy of the "hard currency option," which contributed to the pound joining the ERM at a rate well above its FEER.[12]

PPP comparisons are indispensable for comparing living standards, but they are the wrong basis on which to calculate equilibrium exchange rates. They are wrong conceptually, and they provide seriously misleading advice. For that purpose they should be abandoned, once and for all.

---

which are the differentiated products that dominate trade in manufactures whose producers "face a downward sloping demand curve from foreign and domestic buyers" (McKinnon 1979, 74). He subsequently seems to have assumed away the existence of tradables I.

11. See *The Currency Forecaster's Digest*. The February 1990 issue reported consensus forecasts of ¥187 and DM2.51 to the dollar in 1993. [That was written in March 1990. Rates as of the end of 1993 were ¥112 and DM1.74.]

12. This paragraph is unaltered from that written in late 1990.

Current Account Targets

The basic principles for choosing current account targets suggested above may be summarized as follows. First, examine past imbalances and their relationship to savings availability and investment levels to see whether they appear to reflect rational economic behavior as opposed to misguided government policies. Second, examine whether any imbalances that appear rational are also likely to be sustainable. If not, reduce the target below the past outcome to the point needed to ensure sustainability. Third, check that the resulting pattern of outcomes is internationally consistent. If it is not, modify the targets of all countries whose targets are particularly high (or low, as the case may be) until consistency is achieved.

The first step in implementing such a program is to take stock of such guidance as economic theory offers on when ''rational economic behavior'' suggests that domestic saving should be supplemented by foreign borrowing (or partially directed into foreign lending). The standard microeconomic rule is, of course, to borrow from (lend to) the rest of the world when domestic saving falls short of (exceeds) those investment opportunities that have a positive present value evaluated at the world interest rate. Since such information is not readily available, however, it is in practice necessary to resort to approximate approaches.[13] Two of these can be found in the literature: the debt cycle (or ''stages'' theory) and an application of the life-cycle hypothesis that attributes saving variations to demographic structure.

Investment Needs: The Debt Cycle

The debt-cycle theory of the balance of payments posits basically that the propensity to save is relatively constant over time, whereas medium-run current account outcomes evolve in a systematic way in response to capital accumulation. When a poor country is first integrated into the world economy, it has a low capital-labor ratio and hence a high marginal return on capital at the level of investment that can be financed by the limited flow of domestic saving. Hence the country borrows from abroad. Over time the country builds up both its capital stock and its international debt. The higher level of capital increases output, a part of which is diverted into servicing the external debt. In due course debt service comes to exceed the capital inflow, and the resource transfer becomes negative: this is the second stage of the debt cycle. An unthrifty country may settle down into a steady state in this stage.

---

13. The ''necessity'' of such resort is challenged by those with sufficient faith that free markets would produce optimal macroeconomic outcomes if governments would eschew attempts at macroeconomic management. Those who accept this view will obviously be opposed to the type of enterprise being pursued in this paper.

The third stage arises if and when the country generates domestic saving larger than its domestic investment requirements, and exports the excess saving abroad. This increases the negative resource transfer, but the benefit is that external debt gradually decreases.

The fourth stage of the debt cycle comes about if the country remains a capital exporter long enough to repay its (net) external debt and become a creditor. Initially the resource transfer remains negative, since its capital outflow exceeds its interest receipts, which become positive once the country becomes a net creditor.

As the buildup of external assets continues, a time will come when debt service exceeds the capital outflow and the country moves to stage 5. This is the position of a "mature creditor," which enjoys a positive resource transfer as it plows back a part of its foreign investment income into new investment and uses the remainder to increase its consumption.

The sixth and "final" stage of the debt cycle arises if and when a mature creditor starts to live off its (foreign) capital, consuming not merely its interest income but importing capital as well. This is a pathological case which is (ceteris paribus) precluded by the customary canons of rational behavior. One expects instead that a thrifty country will settle down into a steady state in stage 5, where its current account surplus is equal to a part of its interest income just large enough to support a rate of foreign asset accumulation equal to the growth rate of the domestic economy.

The bottom line of the debt-cycle theory is that one expects to find rich countries with a high capital stock per head exporting capital and poor countries with little capital per head importing it. (But note that there is no necessary presumption that the rich countries will export real resources and that the poor countries will have a positive resource transfer; on the contrary, such a situation is inherently transitory.)

Two qualifications of this theory seem to command general assent. One is that the countries in the best position to supplement domestic saving profitably by foreign borrowing are not the poorest ones, but those that have already made substantial investments in infrastructure and especially human capital and now need to complement those basic investments by investing in activities with more easily appropriable returns. These are typically middle-income countries. The other is that many resource-exploiting activities are highly capital-intensive, so that countries like Australia and Canada that rely heavily on exploiting natural resources may remain capital importers long after their level of per capita income might have led one to expect them to start exporting capital.

Savings Variations: The Impact of Demographic Factors

The life-cycle hypothesis, which provides the basis for an alternative (or additional) theory of the determinants of medium-run current account imbalances, started out by hypothesizing that individuals seek to maximize lifetime utility, and to that end tend to save during their earning years so as to shift consumption to their retirement years, when income typically falls off. In a current version of the theory, the lifetime is divided into four phases. The first phase, that of childhood, precedes entry into the labor force at age 15 to 20 and is characterized by an absence of both income and saving. The second phase, of young adulthood, is marked by high earnings but also by high expenditures on forming a household and raising children. At age 40 to 45 (or somewhat later in countries where college education is financed by parents rather than taxes), responsibilities of childrearing ease as the children go off to college or to work, and a period of 10 to 20 years of high savings in anticipation of retirement commences. Once retirement starts, earnings fall off much more than expenditures and saving tends to turn negative.

To the extent that most individuals follow such a saving pattern in the attempt to maximize lifetime utility, the demographic structure of a society will be an important determinant of its saving rate. Specifically, societies with a large proportion of the population in the high-saving, preretirement phase will tend to have a high overall saving rate, while societies with a large proportion already retired will tend to have a low saving rate. Investment needs will also be influenced by demographic factors, since rapid population growth—and especially a rapid increase in the number of young households—will tend to increase the need for investment.

Given the sharp fall in the birthrate experienced by most industrial countries at some time in the postwar period, these demographic factors are quite important. Table 1 shows estimates of the impact of future demographic changes on total saving rates and current account balances for three major economies, from an impressive study by Masson and Tryon (1990), supplemented by some additional figures for Japan from the work of Noguchi (1989). The figures of Masson and Tryon compare the projected future outcome with those of a simulation that assumed the demographic structure to remain frozen at that of 1995. Similarly, Noguchi's estimates related the impact of demographic changes to a base position of 1985; the first column shows his estimate of the resulting change over the decade 1985–95, and the remaining columns show the impact of the additional demographic changes expected thereafter.

The estimates in table 1 reveal very different patterns in the United States, on the one hand, and Germany and (especially) Japan, on the other. In the United States the baby boom generation has not yet started to enter the high-saving phase of the life cycle, and the labor force is continuing to grow, fed by substantial net immigration. As the proportion of the labor force in the preretirement years grows up to the year 2015, saving will mount, and a large part of the increased saving will flow into a stronger current account. In Germany, in contrast, the dominant factor will be the increasing weight of the elderly, and hence the

Table 1 United States, Japan, and Germany: estimated macroeconomic impact of demographic changes after 1995 (deviations from baseline in percentages of GNP)

	1995	2000	2005	2015	2025
United States					
Saving[a]	n.a.	1.1	3.1	3.7	1.4
Current account balance	n.a.	1.1	2.5	3.0	2.7
Japan					
Saving[a]	n.a.	−1.2	−3.3	−6.3	−8.2
Current account balance	n.a.	−2.5	−3.8	−4.5	−4.0
Saving	−1.9[b]	−1.3	−2.0	−5.3	−6.1
S − I	−1.0[b]	1.6	2.3	1.5	−3.8
Germany					
Saving[a]	n.a.	−1.2	−1.7	−2.8	−2.9
Current account balance	n.a.	−0.5	−1.8	−2.5	−0.9

n.a. = not applicable (since 1995 is base date).

a. Sum of change in general government financial balance and private saving.
b. Comparison with 1985.

Sources: Masson and Tryon (1990, table 8); second two rows on Japan are from Noguchi (1989, table 4).

saving rate and the current account balance will tend to decline.[14] The same effect is even more powerful in Japan, where the birthrate fell abruptly in the late 1950s. Note, however, that whereas both sources broadly agree on the impact of demographic changes on saving, Noguchi suggests that for the next 20 years or so this will be more than offset by declining investment needs, implying that demographic factors may not after all reduce the Japanese current account surplus until the 2020s. However, Masson and Tryon also investigate the impact on investment, and even though this turns negative after 2005—and the fall in investment exceeds the decline in savings after 2015—they conclude that the Japanese current account will weaken progressively. Moreover, Noguchi's analysis assumes a fixed capital-labor ratio, whereas one might expect that ratio to rise if investment needs were tending to decline more than saving.

Signing the G-7 Targets

Having examined the guidance that theory can provide, we turn to an examination of data. Table 2 presents data on average current account imbalances in the G-7 countries for 1986–88, and table 3 gives data on saving and investment for 1986–87, those being the most recent periods for which data were available when this study was undertaken in 1990.

14. This was written when German unification was still no more than a hypothetical possibility, and thus took no account of the massive investment that has been directed to the new *Länder*.

Table 2   Selected balance of payments data for the G-7 countries, 1986–88 averages

	United States	Japan	Germany	France	United Kingdom	Italy	Canada
Current account balance							
Billions of US dollars	−135.9	84.1	44.7	−1.9	−10.7	−1.4	−7.7
Percentages of GDP	−3.0	3.6	4.2	−0.2	−1.3	−0.1	−1.8
Net long-term capital inflow (billions of US dollars)	46.5	−127.7	−21.1	−1.7	−16.0	2.4	9.2

Source: International Monetary Fund, *International Financial Statistics*, January 1990.

Table 3 Saving and investment in the G-7 countries, 1986–87 averages[a] (percentages of GDP)

	United States	Japan	Germany	France	United Kingdom	Italy[b]	Canada
Net saving							
Household	4.1	10.8	7.7	5.5	2.9	n.a.	6.4
Corporate	2.1	2.3	2.3	2.6	4.4	n.a.	3.9
Government	–3.8	5.0	1.5	–1.0	–1.2	–6.8	–3.5
Total	2.5	18.2	11.4	7.1	5.1	10.0	6.8
Net investment							
Household	2.7	3.2	0.0[c]	3.3	1.9	n.a.	3.2
Corporate	1.9	6.6	5.4	2.1	2.2	n.a.	6.9
Government	0.3	4.3	1.7	1.3	1.2	3.6	1.5
Total	5.0	14.2	7.0	6.7	5.5	8.9	11.6
Current account	–3.2	4.0	4.3	–0.1	–0.5	–0.1	–1.9
Statistical discrepancy	–0.1	0.4	0.0	0.0	–1.0	0.0	0.0
Memorandum: gross saving	14.9	32.2	23.7	19.7	17.8	21.5	18.4

a. Components may not sum to totals because of rounding.
b. Data are for 1986 only.
c. By convention.

Source: Organization for Economic Cooperation and Development, *OECD National Accounts*, 1989.

The data reveal the three Anglo-Saxon countries in current account deficit, Japan and Germany in surplus, and France and Italy in approximate balance. To what extent can the theories discussed above justify this pattern?

The deficit of the *United States* appears pathological from the standpoint of the debt-cycle theory, since the United States probably still has the highest overall capital-labor ratio in the world. However, the life-cycle approach provides a very different perspective. Among the G-7 countries, only Canada and the United States are expected to have labor forces growing at 1 percent per year or more in 1991–96 (as against 0.6 percent or less in the others), implying relatively high investment needs. At the same time, saving is low in part for demographic reasons, and the projections shown in table 1 indicate that future changes in the demographic profile can be expected to eliminate the current account deficit in due course (by 2000, or earlier if these demographic forces are already operating in the period 1990–95).

However, table 3 also reveals that the low US saving rate is not explained entirely by low private saving, but that government dissaving (the budget deficit) was at that time the second-largest among the G-7 and a major explanation of the low overall saving rate. Budget deficits are more convincingly explained by political cowardice than by intertemporal optimization. There is more hope in 1994 that the US budget deficit will decline in the coming years than there was during the years of tax fetishism when this study was first done, and there is certainly wide agreement that such a reduction is desirable. The stylized fact to have emerged from the econometric modeling of recent years is that about half of the counterpart to a lower budget deficit is to be found in a lower current account deficit (Helliwell 1989),[15] so that the figures in table 3 suggest that elimination of the budget deficit would reduce the US current account deficit to 1.3 percent of GNP.

Canada is a country that has traditionally satisfied a part of its heavy investment needs (caused by the capital intensity of operations to exploit its natural resources) by importing capital; as a result it has a high ratio of "debt" (more accurately, of its net international investment position) to exports or GNP. It ran current account surpluses for several years in the first half of the 1980s, but the traditional deficit reemerged in 1985 as the economy recovered from recession. Since Canada is also projected to have a growing labor force over the next decade, a continuing current account deficit seems appropriate.

---

15. This assumes that the exchange rate is free to adjust: specifically, that the dollar can depreciate in real terms when the budget deficit falls and interest rates decline as a consequence. The exercise undertaken in this study can be thought of as identifying the level to which the dollar would need to fall.

In 1990 it might also have been argued that *Britain* should target a current account deficit, on the basis that the supply-side obstacles to growth formerly presented by recalcitrant unions and apathetic management had been broken, and that the economy needed a higher sustained rate of investment over the next few years in order to catch up with its European neighbors. Offsetting this argument, however, is the fact that, even at current low oil prices, Britain is receiving an important source of transitory income from its North Sea oil fields. When the oil price was high, prior to 1986, I argued that Britain should be saving half the oil revenues and investing them primarily abroad through the medium of a current account surplus. I would not argue that on the basis of recent oil prices, but to go to the other extreme and argue for targeting a current account *deficit* would seem justified only if investment were actually higher than in the European neighbors with whom Britain ought to be catching up. Even after the investment boom of 1988, which is not reflected in the data in table 3, that was not the case. Hence I posit the appropriate target for Britain as current account balance.

Japan has a very high saving rate and large long-term capital exports. It still has heavy unmet investment needs in urban infrastructure (Balassa and Noland 1988), which suggests that the scale of past current account surpluses was excessive. Nevertheless, demographic factors do make Japan a natural candidate to run current account surpluses now and at least over the next few years (although the sources cited in table 1 differ as to when demographic developments may be expected to eliminate the surplus). With a bulge of Japanese workers in their high-saving preretirement years and an expectation that their saving will collapse or even turn negative as these workers start to retire, it makes good economic sense for Japan to build up part of its investments in the form of foreign assets. (Some Japanese also express a precautionary desire for a trillion-dollar foreign nestegg to finance the reconstruction of Tokyo should the inevitable future earthquake prove particularly severe.)

Germany is the other G-7 country with a particularly high saving rate. Prior to union with the former East Germany, the Federal Republic had few obvious unmet investment needs, and accordingly Germany was a natural candidate to be a surplus country. Since all the models that were used in this study still reflected the old West German economy rather than a united Germany, it is appropriate at this stage to treat Germany as targeting a surplus.

Both *France* and *Italy* have been quite close to current account balance in recent years. Both have small long-term capital flows, fairly typical overall rates of saving and investment (Italy's massive budget deficit being offset by high private saving), and no conspicuous demographic abnormalities. A balanced current account seems an appropriate target for both countries.

Sustainability

Having decided that it is appropriate for the United States and Canada to accept deficits, for Japan and Germany to target surpluses, and for the remaining three G-7 countries to seek current account balance, we must next ask how large the imbalances could be without threatening to become unsustainable. Sustainability provides a constraint on deficit rather than surplus countries.

Consider first the United States. The preceding analysis suggested that, *ceteris paribus*, achievement of a balanced budget might be expected to reduce the current account deficit to some 1.3 percent of GNP by 1995. A steady-state deficit of this size would imply that the "debt"-GNP ratio (again, "debt" here is broadly defined as the overall international investment position) would settle down at a little under 20 percent, assuming 7 percent per year growth in nominal income.[16] This is well below the 40 percent ratio that a common rule of thumb treats as a danger point.[17] However, the United States is still a relatively closed economy: using the 8.8 percent export-GNP ratio of 1988, the debt-export ratio would stabilize at 211 percent, marginally above the other traditional rule of thumb for a safe level of external debt (a rule of thumb that found some empirical support in Underwood 1990), which suggests a 200 percent ceiling to the debt-export ratio.

Admittedly one can question the relevance of the debt-export ratio as a creditworthiness indicator for a country like the United States that borrows in its own currency. On the other hand, one can also argue that a country that borrows in its own currency has less scope to run up foreign debts before creditors start to fear the debt buildup, precisely because it is easier to get away with inflating debt away than with repudiating it. Moreover, after the evidence from Latin America of the devastating effect that a debt crisis can have on economic growth, it seems only sensible to ensure that the debt ratios stabilize well short of critical levels. A deficit of 1 percent of GNP, which would imply a steady-state debt-GNP ratio of 14 percent and a debt-export ratio of 162 percent, satisfies that criterion, while a deficit of 1.3 percent would be somewhat marginal. Thus the current account target that will be adopted for the United States is a deficit equal to at most 1 percent of GNP.

The other G-7 country that should run a current account deficit, according to the earlier argument, is Canada. The sustainability con-

---

16. Let D be foreign debt and Y nominal income. When $\hat{Y}/Y = \hat{D}/D = 0.07$ and $\hat{D}/Y = 0.013$, $D/Y = (\hat{D}/Y)/(\hat{Y}/Y) = 0.012/0.07 = 0.186$.

17. Admittedly that rule of thumb was based on gross debt rather than the net international investment position, but for most of the relevant countries the two items that differentiate the two measures, namely, gross foreign assets and the direct investment position, tend to offset each other and are both small relative to gross debt.

straints are much less strict in Canada, primarily because of its greater openness (a 27 percent export-GNP ratio in 1988, rather than about 9 percent as in the United States), and secondarily because of its faster expected growth rate of nominal income (due to faster real supply-side growth). A deficit of 2 percent of GDP would lead the debt-GNP ratio asymptotically (down) to around 25 percent and the debt-export ratio (down) to around 92 percent, well below the levels the traditional rules of thumb assert to be safe, which are in fact close to the current levels. However, it is not clear that Canadians would be happy to target such a large deficit. A target deficit of 1.5 percent of GNP has therefore been adopted. Canadians might like to note that the concept of the current account used by the Canadian authorities excludes retained earnings, which are typically slightly over 1 percent of GDP according to estimates made by the Treasury office of the US embassy in Ottawa. Thus the target deficit assigned to Canada implies a deficit of under 0.5 percent of GNP on the Canadian concept.

International Consistency

While the criterion of sustainability suggests a basis for limiting the current account deficits that countries should target, it does not impose any similar limits on surplus countries. Switzerland has been running surpluses of several percent of GNP for over a decade, and there is no obvious reason why this should not continue for several more decades (as, indeed, it did in Britain prior to World War I). When I discussed Swiss balance of payments policy with several Swiss officials in 1986, they were incredulous at the suggestion that they might have a target for the current account balance. They were happy with the 5 percent of GNP that then seemed in prospect but asserted that they would not wish to alter policy if some lower figure were to materialize. They saw absolutely no need to formulate a target for the current account.

This attitude is understandable from the standpoint of an individual small country. Where a surplus is the result of a restrictive demand policy or forced saving, rather than a result of private-sector choices, one can argue that it is against the interests of the country. But in cases in which the private sector is content to save and invest abroad so that a current account surplus neither brings monetary expansion nor involves real wage repression and fiscal restraint, a large surplus may well be indefinitely sustainable.

The argument for disciplining surplus countries rests on quite different grounds. It is based on the recognition that the international system will not function properly unless the targets pursued by different countries are mutually consistent. If the sum of targeted surpluses exceeds the sum of targeted deficits, there is a danger that monetary policies will be too loose or that trade restrictions will be intensified. It was precisely to avoid such dangers that, during the planning for the postwar years, Keynes was anxious to incorporate pressures on surplus countries to participate in the adjustment process (that desire resulted in the never-used scarce currency clause in the IMF Articles of Agreement).

The idea that some countries should be encouraged to reduce their current account surpluses and to save less is regarded in some quarters as rather shocking. In a capital-short world, how can it be right to discourage saving? The answer is that first provided by Keynes (who did actually make a number of important contributions to economics that deserve to endure): increased saving is a social virtue only when it is translated into increased investment, and not when it decreases output. If countries that could make productive use of increased saving from abroad have their deficits constrained by creditworthiness considerations, attempts by other countries to run surpluses collectively greater than those deficits will result in lower global output and not higher global investment.

Hence the logic of first estimating the magnitude of the deficits that can safely be financed by those areas that seem to be logical candidates to import capital. Since the G-7 is not a closed system, it is insufficient to do that for the G-7 countries alone. Table 4 shows a disaggregation of the rest of the world into a further seven regions.

The first of these regions consists of three small European surplus countries: Belgium, the Netherlands, and Switzerland. This seems a natural surplus area, with no major unsatisfied investment needs and with high saving rates appropriate to their demographic structure.

The second region consists of the remaining small OECD countries. Most of these have been in heavy deficit for some years, although the scale of the deficits relative to GDP has been falling. A further decline would seem both probable and desirable; a reasonable target might be a deficit of the same percentage of GDP as that assigned to Canada.

The third region consists of the major oil-exporting countries (the IMF's "fuel exporters," excluding Ecuador, Mexico, Nigeria, and Venezuela, which are included among the countries with recent debt-servicing difficulties). This region had returned to current account balance prior to the Gulf crisis, after the massive imbalances due to oil price changes over the preceding 15 years. It moved into modest surplus in 1990 as a result of higher oil prices but was expected to go into deficit for several years because of the need for reconstruction following the Gulf War. In the longer term, however, current account balance seems a reasonable projection as long as oil prices remain between $16 and $20 per barrel.

The fourth region consists of Korea and Taiwan, which both ran massive current account surpluses in recent years. Bela Balassa and I argued elsewhere (Balassa and Williamson 1987) that this was an irrational policy, since the marginal rate of return on domestic investment would exceed that on foreign assets, and Maxwell Fry (1989) has found

Table 4 Current account balances and targets for 14 countries and regions

Country or region	Current account			As a percentage of GNP		GNP (billions of current dollars)	
	Billions of current dollars						
	Actual 1989 outcome (1)	Base case 1995 target (2)	Alternative 1995 target (3)	1989 = (1)/(6) (4)	1995 = (2)/(7) (5)	1989 (6)	1995 (7)
United States	−106	−79	0	−2.0	−1.0	5,230	7,850
Japan	57	69	23	2.0	1.5	2,825	4,600
Germany	53	28	9	4.3	1.5	1,230	1,835
France	−3	0	0	−0.3	0.0	970	1,465
United Kingdom	−34	0	0	−4.4	0.0	780	1,170
Italy	−11	0	0	−1.3	0.0	825	1,415
Canada	−17	−11	−11	−3.6	−1.5	470	740
Total G-7	−61	7	21			12,330	19,075
Belgium, Netherlands, and Switzerland	15	13	4	2.5	1.5	590	880
Small OECD countries	−36	−32	−32	−2.6	−1.5	1,380	2,105
Total OECD	−82	−12	−7			14,300	22,060
Fuel exporters[a]	0	0	0	0.0	0.0		
Korea and Taiwan	16	8	3	5.2	1.5	307	555
Highly indebted countries (15)	−11	−23	−23	−1.2	−1.5	940	1,520
Other developing countries	−19	−34	−34	−1.4	−1.5	1,340	2,295
Total developing countries	−14	−49	−54				
CMEA	2	−32	−32	0.1	−1.0	2,240	3,210
Former statistical discrepancy	−94	−94	−94				

CMEA = Council for Mutual Economic Assistance (the former socialist countries of Central and Eastern Europe).

a. Excluding Ecuador, Mexico, Nigeria, and Venezuela (which are included in the highly indebted countries).

Sources: International Monetary Fund, *World Economic Outlook* and *International Financial Statistics; OECD Economic Outlook;* Central Bank of China (Taiwan), *Financial Statistics; World Bank Atlas;* Economic Commission for Latin America and the Caribbean, *Preliminary Overview of the Economy of Latin America and the Caribbean;* United Nations, *Monthly Bulletin of Statistics; Amex Bank Review,* April 1990; and projections described in the text.

that empirical evidence supports our conjecture. Although both countries have sought to reduce their current account surpluses from the absurdly inflated levels of 1987, and Korea went into modest deficit in 1990, Taiwan at least is reluctant to target a return to balance, let alone deficit. I assume, with some reluctance, that they should be assigned surplus targets of the same percentage of GDP as the other surplus countries.

The next two groups of countries, those with recent debt-servicing difficulties and all other developing countries, are both groups that would be expected to import capital according to the debt-cycle theory. However, the ability of both regions, especially the highly indebted countries, to run current account deficits was still severely constrained by their creditworthiness in 1990. I argued at that time that some easing of the negative transfer was to be hoped for as the Brady Plan came into play and the debt crisis eased, but that a current account deficit of around 1.5 percent of GDP was the most that seemed realistic for the highly indebted countries. A similar target was assigned to the remaining developing countries. With the benefit of hindsight those projections look pessimistic.

The final region consists of the countries that were members of the Council for Mutual Economic Assistance (CMEA) in 1990. These had been close to balance in the period prior to this analysis being undertaken. I assumed that the reforms that had just been launched in those countries would be sufficiently successful at integrating them into the global economy by 1995 as to permit them by then to be able to finance substantial current account deficits and make profitable use of the resulting resources. The projection assumed that they would be able to borrow at a rate of 1.0 percent of GNP.

Table 4 shows estimates of current account outcomes in 1990, and also of the suggested targets for 1995. GNP projections[18] were combined with the assumptions about target current account deficits as percentages of GNP laid out above. They yield a gross total of 1995 target deficits of $211 billion. On past experience, however, a large part of this will find its counterpart in the world current account deficit, the statistical discrepancy, rather than in surpluses in other countries. I projected the statistical discrepancy to remain at the same $94 billion in 1995 as the IMF was then estimating it had been in 1989. (This proved far too optimistic: IMF estimates published in 1993 indicate that the discrepancy was $105 billion in 1989 and will be $156 billion in 1994.) That then left $117 billion to be distributed among the surplus areas—Japan, Germany, Benelux and Switzerland, and Korea and Taiwan.

---

18. Estimates of 1990 GNP were constructed by updating the estimates of 1988 GNP in the 1989 *World Bank Atlas*. GNP estimates for 1995 were constructed by assuming annual dollar inflation of 4.2 percent and making conventional assumptions regarding real growth.

Surpluses have been distributed pro rata to projected 1995 GNPs: it transpires that the consistent surplus is 1.5 percent of GNP. A range of 1 to 2 percent of GNP seems a reasonable estimate of the sort of medium-run imbalances that countries can prudently aim to run when there is a serious case for importing or exporting capital.

On 11 June 1990, an advisory panel to the Japanese Ministry of Finance recommended that Japan aim to maintain a current account surplus. This recommendation was attacked on publication by unnamed US officials. The above analysis suggests that these attacks were misplaced. Japan's 1990 surplus ($36 billion) was only 1.2 percent of GNP, actually a little below the level that, it has just been argued, would be consistent with a satisfactory outcome for the United States. It would have been helpful if Japan had avoided the large rebound of its surplus that occurred in 1992–93 following the real depreciation of the yen, but the US policy of trying to browbeat Japan into rhetorical support for total elimination of its surplus while shying away from action to help keep the yen at a sensible level was about as stupid as it is possible to conceive.

Since establishment of current balance targets is by far the most speculative part of the process of calculating FEERs, it is important to test the sensitivity of the results to alternative specifications of the external targets. The third column of table 4 shows one alternative set of targets for current account balances. The essential difference is that this column ignores the demographic argument for the United States to remain a capital importer into the mid-1990s, and adopts instead the proposal of Bergsten (1988) for the United States to restore current account balance promptly.[19] Other deficit and balance targets are left unchanged, so that the entire counterpart to elimination of the US deficit is found in much smaller surpluses on the part of the surplus countries.

Internal Balance

The second requirement of a FEER is that the current account target should be achieved when the domestic economy is at "internal balance," meaning the highest level of activity consistent with the continued control of inflation. The calculation of FEERs thus requires estimates of the extent to which the various economies involved are operating below potential or, conversely, are overheating. Similarly, estimates of the growth of productive potential are needed to know how fast output must grow to maintain internal balance once this has been achieved.

---

19. Even more extreme proposals have sometimes been expressed: for example, in 1987 the Joint Economic Committee of the US Congress urged restoration of a surplus. But since its report betrayed no recognition that every billion-dollar increase in the current account surplus would require roughly a $2 billion decrease in the budget deficit, it can perhaps be discounted.

Table 5 Estimates of potential growth rates of the G-7 countries
(percentages per year)

Country	IMF estimate	OECD estimate	Adopted figure
United States	2.6	2.7	2.7
Japan	4.25	4.0	4.1
Germany	2.9	2.3	2.6
France	3.0	2.5	2.8
United Kingdom	2.5	2.9	2.7
Italy	3.0	3.0	3.0
Canada	3.4	3.5	3.5

Sources: Updates made in early 1990 of estimates in IMF (1988, annex), Adams and Coe (1990), and Torres and Martin (1989, table 6).

Both the IMF and the OECD produce estimates of potential output and its rate of growth. Table 5 shows what were in early 1990 the most recent estimates of both organizations for the rates of growth of productive potential of the G-7 countries, which were in most cases reassuringly similar (the average difference was 0.28 percent, and the maximum difference—for Germany—was 0.6 percent). The assumptions adopted in this study are the midpoints between the two sets of estimates, as shown in the third column.

The output gaps estimated by the two organizations also appear to have been reassuringly similar in the past (Torres and Martin 1989, chart 2). The most recent assessment of the size of output gaps at the time the simulations were performed was that in the May 1990 issue of the IMF's *World Economic Outlook* (pp. 8–9), which made the following comments:

> In several major industrial countries, unemployment rates remained remarkably stable in 1989 at levels that are broadly consistent with current estimates of the natural rate of unemployment: in the United States, the unemployment rate has remained at 5¼ percent of the labor force; in Japan, at 2¼ percent; in Germany, at 7 percent; and in Canada, at 7½ percent. In several other countries, including France, Italy, and Spain, unemployment rates, although declining, remained at historically high levels. In the United Kingdom, the unemployment rate continued to decline throughout 1989, from 7 percent in January to 5¾ percent in December, a level that appears to have contributed to inflationary pressures. In all the major industrial countries unemployment rates edged lower in the first quarter of 1990.

Simon Wren-Lewis, who contributed one of the simulation studies to the project, argued that British GDP was about 4 percent above trend in the second quarter of 1989. Given the slowdown in growth in the second half of 1989, this might have left it about 3 percent above trend at the end of the year. I assumed somewhat arbitrarily that the French and Italian GDPs were both 3 percent below trend at that time, to reflect the IMF's comment that their unemployment rates remained at historically high levels. Other countries were assumed to be at their NAIRUs (nonaccelerating-inflation rates of unemployment).

The "blueprint" of Williamson and Miller (1987, appendix A) suggests that countries should aim to eliminate 2 percentage points of GNP of an output gap each year until internal balance is achieved. Applying that rule, the desirable growth rate for Britain would be 0.7 percent in 1990 (2.7 minus 2.0) and 1.7 percent in 1991 (to eliminate the remainder of the gap), and thereafter would be 2.7 percent (the growth rate of potential output). Similarly, France and Italy would need to grow above trend for two years. The growth rates shown in the final three columns of table 6 are the base case target growth rates that were used in the study.

Once again, it is important to get a sense of the impact that variations in these targets would have on the FEERs. The variant (shown as a memorandum item in table 6) assumes that there was excess demand equal to 1 percent of GDP in the United States at the start of 1990 and therefore that the desirable growth rate was 1 percent lower than the growth of capacity in 1990.

The Simulations

Six multicountry macroeconometric models were used to identify the real effective exchange rate trajectories that would simultaneously achieve external and internal balance in the sense described in the preceding sections. Listed alphabetically by their acronyms, the models are the following.

EAG. The External Adjustment with Growth model was developed at the Institute for International Economics by William R. Cline for his study on the impact of elimination of the US current account deficit on the rest of the world (Cline 1989). This is not a full macroeconomic model but is limited to the foreign sector, generating estimates of the components (and totals) of the current account balances of 17 regions implied by assumptions about output and competitiveness (real exchange rates). While a model of this character is unable to answer a full range of questions, it is well suited to generate estimates of FEERs.

GEM. The Global Econometric Model was developed for international forecasts and simulations at the National Institute of Economic and Social Research (NIESR) in London. The full model, which contains over 600 variables and equations, is described in detail in NIESR (1990); a summary description is provided in Currie and Wren-Lewis (1990). The model used to produce the simulations reported below is a stripped-down version called steady-state GEM, produced by omitting the short-run dynamics from the full GEM model. Steady-state GEM is described in Barrell and Wren-Lewis (1989).

Table 6   Output gaps and target growth rates of the G-7 countries, 1990–95

Country	Output gap at start of 1990[a] (percentages of GDP)	Target growth rate of GDP (percent per year)		
		1990	1991	1992–95
United States	0.0	2.7	2.7	2.7
Japan	0.0	4.1	4.1	4.1
Germany	0.0	2.6	2.6	2.6
France	3.0	4.8	3.8	2.8
United Kingdom	−3.0	0.7	1.7	2.7
Italy	3.0	5.0	4.0	3.0
Canada	0.0	3.5	3.5	3.5
Memorandum: variant for United States	−1.0	1.7	2.7	2.7

a. A negative figure indicates current output above trend.

Source: Based on International Monetary Fund, *World Economic Outlook*, May 1990, pp. 8–9 as explained in text.

Interlink.   The global macroeconometric model of the OECD, called Interlink, is described in Richardson (1988). Updated simulation studies of the model are described in Richardson (1990).

Intermod.   Intermod is a global macroeconometric model, designed for policy simulation rather than forecasting, that was developed at the Canadian Ministry of Finance as a variant of the Multimod model of the IMF. (Multimod is used to construct medium-run scenarios for the *World Economic Outlook*.) It is described in Meredith (1989).

Mimosa.   The Multinational Integrated Model for Simulation and Analysis is a global macroeconometric model developed at two French research institutes, the Centre d'Etudes Prospectives et d'Informations Internationales (CEPII) and the Observatoire Français des Conjonctures Economiques. It is reported in MIMOSA Modelling Group (1990).

MSG.   MSG2, the current version of the McKibbin-Sachs global macroeconomic model, is described in McKibbin and Sachs (1989). Its tracking performance through the 1980s is examined in McKibbin (1989).

Some of the principal features of these models are described and compared in appendix 1.

Each of the groups responsible for the models sought a simulation that would achieve the target paths for internal and external balance (as specified in tables 4 and 6, respectively), given their own assumptions about a baseline (meaning what would happen if no policy changes were made). These results, which were based on data available up to May 1990, are presented, discussed, and compared in appendix 2.

Table 7   Estimates of base case FEERs[a] (percentage changes from fourth quarter of 1989)

Model	US dollar	Japanese yen	Deutsche mark	French franc	Pound sterling	Italian lira	Canadian dollar
EAG	−14	27	33	−11	−18	−15	−30
GEM	−9	15	18	−8	−10	−12	−6
Interlink	0	11	17	−9	0	−14	−8
Intermod	−7	−1	11	−2	−2	1	−5
Mimosa	−20	32	19	2	−23	31	n.a.
MSG	−8	10	7	n.a.	n.a.	n.a.	n.a.

n.a. = not available.

a. A negative number signifies that the currency was overvalued.

Source: Appendix 2.

Table 7, which summarizes the results, shows for each model the deviations of actual effective exchange rates from the estimated FEERs in the last quarter of 1989. For example, the EAG model estimated that the dollar's FEER was 14 percent below its actual value (meaning the dollar was 14 percent overvalued), and that the yen's FEER was 27 percent above its actual value.

As one has to expect, there is a fair amount of variation among the estimates. The range between the highest and the lowest estimate is 13 percentage points for the franc, 20 percentage points for the US dollar, 23 percentage points for the pound, 25 percentage points for the yen and the Canadian dollar, 26 percentage points for the deutsche mark, and a staggering 46 percentage points for the lira. As noted above, one reason for having a wide target zone is to accommodate the considerable range of uncertainty that will inevitably surround estimates of FEERs made after a period when exchange rates have varied greatly. Even so, the range is wide.

One source of variation in FEER estimates is the assumptions about target values for external and internal balance. Tables 8 and 9 show how the estimates in table 7 would change if the targets were altered to the two alternative cases chosen. According to the EAG model, the bottom line is that elimination of the US current account deficit (the alternative case for external balance, shown in table 8) would require an extra effective dollar depreciation of about 7 percent, which would come entirely through additional appreciation of the yen and the deutsche mark. One percent slower US growth in 1990 (the alternative case for internal balance, shown in table 9 for the only two models that produced results for this case) would reduce the needed dollar depreciation by only 2 percent according to both models.

Table 10 shows estimates of the trend changes in FEERs[20] according to the only two models that succeeded in generating such estimates. The

---

20. As explained above, these trend changes reflect productivity bias, foreign asset accumulation, and the Houthakker-Magee effect.

Table 8 Estimates of FEERS with alternative target of United States in current account balance (percentage changes from fourth quarter of 1989)

Model	US dollar	Japanese yen	Deutsche mark	French franc	Pound sterling	Italian lira	Canadian dollar
EAG	−21	40	40	−13	−19	−17	−32
GEM	−17	30	24	−8	−10	−12	−6
Intermod	−13	1	16	3	−2	2	−7
Mimosa	−26	55	23	2	−23	29	n.a.
MSG	−12	27	11	n.a.	n.a.	n.a.	n.a.

n.a. = not available.

Source: Appendix 2.

Table 9 Estimates of FEERs with alternative target of 1 percent less US growth (percentage changes from fourth quarter of 1989)

Model	US dollar	Japanese yen	Deutsche mark	French franc	Pound sterling	Italian lira	Canadian dollar
EAG	−12	26	32	−11	−18	−15	−30
GEM	−7	15	18	−9	−10	−12	−7

Source: Appendix 2.

differences between the models are much more dramatic than the differences given by the models as to the implications of changing the objectives. This suggests that this should be a priority area for further research.

While steady-state GEM and EAG both allow GDP and the real exchange rate to be changed exogenously, the other four models used in the study required changes in fiscal and monetary policy in order to induce the changes in output and current accounts that would get the economy to macroeconomic equilibrium. Hence they yielded estimates of the changes in budget balances required. Table 11 shows these estimates: according to Interlink, for example, the United States would have required a fiscal contraction of a mere 0.8 percent of GDP, but Germany would have needed a massive fiscal expansion of 5 percent of GDP (a figure that seemed social-science fiction when the simulations were run, but that has since been surpassed as a result of German reunification). Once again, there is an uncomfortable range of cross-model variation.

A range of estimates such as that in table 7 can be reduced to a single central estimate of a FEER in two different ways. One possibility is to average the different figures, perhaps employing weights that reflect in some rough way one's confidence in the different models. The alternative is to select one of the models and discard the others.

Table 10 Estimates of trend changes in FEERs[a] (percent per year)

Model	US dollar	Japanese yen	Deutsche mark	French franc	Pound sterling	Italian lira	Canadian dollar
Base case							
EAG	0.0	0.8	1.0	-0.5	-0.3	0.2	-0.7
GEM	-1.1	2.8	1.1	-1.4	-2.3	-1.6	-1.9
United States in current balance							
EAG	0.3	0.3	0.8	-0.4	-0.3	0.3	-0.6
GEM	-0.8	2.8	1.0	-1.4	-2.3	-1.6	-1.9
Less US growth in 1990							
EAG	0.0	0.8	1.0	-0.5	-0.3	0.2	-0.7
GEM	-1.1	2.8	0.9	-1.3	-2.4	-1.4	-1.8

a. Positive numbers denote appreciations.

Source: Appendix 2.

Table 11 Estimated changes in fiscal balances necessary to accompany FEERs (percentages of potential or baseline GDP)

Model	United States	Japan	Germany	France	United Kingdom	Italy	Canada
Base case							
Interlink	-0.8	1.0	5.0	0.9	-1.2	0.6	0.2
Intermod	-1.8	0.6	2.4	-0.8	-2.7	-2.0	-2.9
Mimosa	-1.7	-0.1	0.8	-0.9	-0.7	-2.2	n.a.
MSG[a]	-3.0	0.0	2.5	n.a.	n.a.	n.a.	n.a.
Alternative current account targets							
Intermod	-4.2	0.6	2.4	-2.0	-3.8	-3.1	-3.6
Mimosa	-2.7	1.2	1.6	-0.9	-1.0	-1.6	n.a.
MSG[a]	-6.0	0.5	1.8	n.a.	n.a.	n.a.	n.a.

n.a. = not available.

a. Change in 1995 budget deficit as percentage of baseline GDP.

Source: Appendix 2.

The latter course seems the more attractive. There is a danger that averaging the results of different models could lead to a set of figures that would be dismissed as illogical by all reasonable models. Perhaps more important, choosing an average would make it difficult to calculate variants on the initial figures or to update the estimates.

Selecting one of the models does not mean that it was a waste of time to calculate (or examine) the others. The results of the discarded models still perform two vital functions. One is to help select the model that will be chosen to generate the FEER estimates: clearly one wants these to be central. The other function is to give some idea of the sensitivity of the estimates to the choice of a model (or, strictly speaking, to a model-cum-baseline, since differences in baselines influence the estimates as well as differences in the models per se).

Three criteria would seem to be relevant in selecting one of the models in preference to the others. The first is that just indicated: that it should give results that are typical of the group of models as a whole. Another criterion is that the model be a priori well suited to the estimation of FEERs. A third criterion is that it should be easy to compute variations in FEERs to reflect changing conditions or outlooks.

Table 12 addresses the first of these criteria. It shows the rank order of the estimates in table 7. For example, Mimosa has the smallest (algebraic) estimate of the dollar's FEER relative to its average value in the fourth quarter of 1989, EAG the second-smallest, GEM the third-smallest, and so on. A model that yields typical results should be rank-ordered third or fourth for the first three currencies, third for the next three (where there are only five sets of results), and second or third for the Canadian dollar (where only four models gave results). The final column sums the number of times that each model is ranked as typical. One model clearly stands out on this criterion: GEM is classified as typical for every one of the seven currencies; its nearest competitor is Interlink, which qualified in three of the seven cases. The remaining four models had only one central value among them.

The second criterion suggested above is that the model should be well suited a priori to the task of estimating misalignments. I would argue that GEM is also well qualified on this score. It is the only working model with a regularly updated baseline that has been specifically modified for the purpose of estimating misalignments (by the construction of steady-state GEM). Its advantages are demonstrated by the fact that only it and EAG were able to generate estimates for the alternative internal balance case and for the trend changes in FEERs. With large dynamic models like Interlink, Intermod, and MSG, one is never quite sure that the results are reflecting what one is seeking, rather than a quirk of the sophisticated dynamic structure that is irrelevant to the question in hand about (quasi) steady states. Moreover, GEM is the only model that does not require forward projections

Table 12 Rank-order of estimates in table 7

Model	US dollar	Japanese yen	Deutsche mark	French franc	Pound sterling	Italian lira	Canadian dollar	Frequency of central rank-order
EAG	2	5	6	1	2	1	1	0
GEM	3	4	4	3	3	3	3	7
Interlink	6	3	3	2	5	2	2	3
Intermod	5	1	2	4	4	4	4	0
Mimosa	1	6	5	5	1	5	n.a.	0
MSG	4	2	1	n.a.	n.a.	n.a.	n.a.	1

n.a. = not available.

Source: Table 7.

Table 13 Final estimates of FEERs (percentage excess of first-quarter 1990 FEER over actual rate in fourth quarter of 1989)

	US dollar	Japanese yen	Deutsche mark	French franc	Pound sterling	Italian lira	Canadian dollar
Base case							
FEER	−11	13	15	−2	−11	−6	−7
Real appreciation against US dollar		25	28	10	0	5	4
Trend in FEER	−1.1	2.6	1.0	−1.2	−2.1	−1.4	−1.8
Real trend against US dollar		3.7	2.1	−0.1	−0.9	−0.3	−0.7
Alternative external target: US current account balance							
FEER	−22	22	20	−1	−11	−6	−7
Real appreciation against US dollar		49	46	21	10	15	14
Trend in FEER	−0.7	2.6	0.9	−1.2	−2.1	−1.4	−1.7
Real trend against US dollar		3.3	1.6	−0.5	−1.4	−0.7	−1.0
Alternative internal target: 1 percent less US growth							
FEER	−8	12	15	−3	−11	−7	−8
Real appreciation against US dollar		21	24	4	−3	1	0
Trend in FEER	−1.1	2.6	0.9	−1.2	−2.1	−1.4	−1.7
Real trend against US dollar		3.7	2.0	−0.1	−0.9	−0.3	−0.7
Memorandum:							
Percentage appreciation of FEER if target current account increases by 1 percent of GNP	11	10	6	6	3	6	3

Source: Simulations run by Simon Wren-Lewis on steady-state GEM.

Table 14 Comparison of actual effective and US dollar exchange rates with FEERs for the G-7 currencies, 1981–90

	US dollar	Japanese yen	Deutsche mark	French franc	Pound sterling	Italian lira	Canadian dollar
Effective exchange rates (1985 = 100)[a]							
Actual							
1981 Q1	74	116	100	104	119	90	93
1983 Q1	86	100	103	105	96	104	108
1984 Q4	100	93	99	98	97	98	106
1985 Q1	107	91	97	98	94	100	104
1985 Q3	98	92	99	101	107	95	100
1987 Q1	72	123	116	102	94	102	94
1987 Q4	67	126	116	101	103	103	96
1989 Q4	70	120	115	93	106	106	113
1990 Q1	68	112	118	94	108	108	111
Estimated FEERs[b]							
1983 Q1	74	110	108	107	88	n.a.	n.a.
1984 Q4	73	104	114	107	90	n.a.	n.a.
1990 Q1	62	136	132	91	94	100	105

US dollar exchange rate[c]

Actual

1981 Q1	206	2.09	4.86	2.31	1,001	1.19
1983 Q1	236	2.41	6.89	1.53	1,399	1.23
1984 Q4	246	3.05	9.36	1.22	1,891	1.32
1985 Q1	258	3.26	9.96	1.12	2,021	1.35
1985 Q3	239	2.85	8.69	1.38	1,896	1.36
1987 Q1	153	1.84	6.13	1.54	1,306	1.34
1987 Q4	136	1.71	5.75	1.75	1,249	1.31
1989 Q4	143	1.81	6.17	1.59	1,336	1.17
1990 Q1	148	1.69	5.74	1.66	1,255	1.18

Equilibrium dollar rate[b]

1983 Q1	205	1.98	5.79	1.64	n.a.	n.a.
1984 Q4	198	2.04	6.51	1.52	n.a.	n.a.
1990 Q1	114	1.41	5.61	1.59	1,272	1.13

n.a. = not available; Q = quarter.

a. Taken from line *reu* in *International Financial Statistics*.

b. Assuming domestic prices remain constant.

c. Taken from line *rf* (*rh* for pound sterling) in *International Financial Statistics*. Data are expressed as currency units per dollar, except for the pound.

Sources: International Monetary Fund, *International Financial Statistics*, various years; Williamson (1985, tables 11 and 13); and table 13 above.

to establish some form of baseline, but works entirely off historical data.

GEM also qualifies admirably according to the third criterion. EAG is its only competitor in terms of the ease of calculating new FEER estimates using varying or updated assumptions.

Hence all three criteria suggest the adoption of GEM's estimates of FEERs. GEM's estimates were therefore updated by one quarter, to yield the results shown in table 13. These were in turn translated into figures for the effective exchange rate on one of the IMF's measures, to permit comparison with the historical data[21] and my own earlier estimates of FEERs, as shown in the top panel of table 14.

The bottom half of table 14 translates the effective rates into the set of implied bilateral exchange rates.[22] The final line of that table can be compared with the historical rate for the first quarter of 1990 (shown three lines above) to see how large the bilateral misalignments were at that time. According to the estimates, both the yen and the deutsche mark were undervalued in terms of the dollar at that time, while the three other European currencies were near equilibrium against the dollar (but therefore overvalued against the mark).

My earlier estimates of FEERs led in some cases to figures that were noticeably different from the 1990 estimates. The question arises: To what extent is it possible to explain these differences by the sort of shocks that the theory says can change FEERs (which are not supposed to be natural constants as the relative version of PPP asserts, let alone natural constants always equal to unity as the absolute version of PPP claims), or do these differences imply that at least one set of the numbers must be drastically wrong?

Table 15 assembles evidence relevant to this question. The first column shows the percentage difference between the new estimate of the FEER and the most recent previous estimate, for the fourth quarter of

---

21. Actual exchange rates are shown for the quarters to which my previous FEER estimates applied and for certain key dates in recent international monetary history: the first quarter of 1981 (when the Reagan administration took office), the first quarter of 1985 (when the dollar overvaluation peaked), the third quarter of 1985 (the Plaza Agreement), the first quarter of 1987 (the Louvre Accord, when the G-7 attempted to stabilize the dollar), and the fourth quarter of 1987 (when the dollar hit its lowest level of the 1980s, prior to the 1988 New Year bear squeeze).

22. These nominal bilateral rates are calculated on the assumption that internal price levels would not change as exchange rates were altered to achieve the FEERs. This contradicts the customary view that a part of any nominal exchange rate change is neutralized by induced inflation in the devaluing country and disinflation in the revaluing country. The reason for not allowing for this effect in the figures presented is that estimates of its importance vary drastically, with some of the models denying its importance altogether or even reversing the sign.

Table 15   Factors explaining changes in FEERs between fourth quarter of 1984 and first quarter of 1990 (percentage changes)

Country	Actual difference	Trend factors	Oil price change	Current balance targets	Total	Unexplained residual
			Explained by:			
United States	−15	−6	−2	+6	−2	−13
Japan	+32	+14	+14	+7	+35	−3
Germany	+16	+5	+2	+4	+11	+5
France	−15	−6	+2	−9	−13	−2
United Kingdom	+4	−11	−12	+10	−13	+17

a. A negative number indicates a fall in the equilibrium value of the currency.

Sources: Tables 10 and 13 above, and calculations described in the text.

1984. It can be seen that, except for the pound, the new FEER estimates differ sharply from those made previously.

Theory identifies five factors that could have changed FEERs between the last quarter of 1984 and the first quarter of 1990. These are:

■ differential income elasticities interacting with different growth rates (the Houthakker-Magee effect)

■ productivity bias

■ asset accumulation

■ the oil price decline

■ changes in current balance targets.

The first three of these factors should be captured by the estimates of trend changes in FEERs shown in table 10 and the third row in table 13. Using the latter, one would have expected the dollar's FEER to depreciate by 6 percent over five and a quarter years, the yen's FEER to appreciate by 14 percent, and so on, as shown in the second column of table 15.

The average oil price declined by $12.8 per barrel, from $29.1 per barrel in 1982–85 to $16.3 per barrel in 1986–89. Such a "permanent" change in the oil price has strong effects on the relative payments positions of different industrial countries, and therefore on their FEERs, as calculated by McGuirk (1983). Her table 12 showed estimates of the changes in real effective exchange rates that would have been necessary to offset the impact of the increase in the real price of oil between 1972 and 1980. I estimate the $12.8 per barrel decline in the "permanent" oil price in early 1986 as some 52 percent of the real rise between 1972 and

1980. The third column of table 15 therefore shows (the negative of) 52 percent of the estimates shown in McGuirk (1983, table 12, column 6).

FEER estimates can also be altered by changes in the current account targets assigned to the various countries. The United States was assigned a target deficit of $12 billion, or 0.4 percent of GNP, in my earlier study; that figure has been increased to 1 percent in the present study (table 4). GEM implies that an increased current deficit of 0.6 percent of GNP is consistent with a 6 percent real effective appreciation of the dollar (memorandum item of table 13), so that is the figure inserted in the fourth column of table 15. Japan and Germany were given target current account surpluses of 2.2 percent of GNP in the earlier study, as against 1.5 percent in the present one: the lower surplus of 0.7 percent of GNP is (according to GEM) equivalent to appreciations of the yen and the mark of 7 percent and 4 percent, respectively. France was given a target deficit of 1.5 percent of GNP in the earlier study and balance in the present one, implying a real depreciation of 9 percent. Finally, Britain was assigned a target surplus of 3.2 percent of GNP in 1984—half of the annual transitory oil income, which amounted to some 6.4 percent of GNP in the early 1980s (Atkinson et al. 1983)—and has a target of balance in the present study, implying a real appreciation of 10 percent.

The fifth column in table 15 sums the estimates made for the impact of trend factors, the oil price decline, and changes in current account targets. The final column then subtracts the fifth column from the first to find how much of the actual change in the FEER estimate can be explained by the factors the theory accepts to be relevant. It can be seen that the large changes in the estimated FEERs of the yen, the deutsche mark, and the French franc are pretty much what the theory should have led one to expect. On the other hand, very little of the substantial depreciation of the dollar's FEER is explained. Worse still, the theory would have led one to anticipate a sizable depreciation of the sterling's FEER, in contrast to the modest appreciation of the actual estimate. Even if one halved the allowance for the oil price change, on the reasoning that the importance of oil to the British economy has fallen greatly since the time to which the McGuirk estimates relate, the difference would remain uncomfortably large.

The bottom portion of table 14 also reveals that the estimated equilibrium bilateral nominal exchange rates changed dramatically between the end of 1984 and the beginning of 1990. The largest of these changes, which also happens to be the one that is easiest to analyze in the manner done above for the FEERs, is the massive 42 percent appreciation of the yen in terms of the dollar; this is displayed in the first row of table 16.

In addition to the five factors discussed above, changes in the equilibrium nominal exchange rate depend on the inflation differential. The US wholesale price index (WPI) increased by 9.1 percent over the period, as against an increase of 3.6 percent in Japan. The differ-

Table 16   Factors explaining rise of equilibrium value of Japanese yen versus US dollar

Item	Percentage
Actual appreciation of estimated equilibrium	42
Inflation differential (WPI)	5
Houthakker-Magee effect	0
Productivity bias	12
Asset accumulation	6
Oil price decline	13
Changes in current balance targets	2
Total	38
Unexplained residual	4

WPI = wholesale price index.

Sources: International Monetary Fund, *International Financial Statistics*, various issues; Marston (1987); McGuirk (1983, table 12); table 13 of this paper; and calculations described in the text.

ential of approximately 5 percent is recorded in the second row of table 16.

The third row of that table records that nothing has been imputed to the Houthakker-Magee effect. This reflects the recent argument of Paul Krugman (1989) that the product of income elasticities and growth rates is typically uniform, because growth primarily takes the form of increasing the range of differentiated products, so that faster growth tends both to increase exports and to have an import-decreasing effect (as well as the standard effect of sucking in more imports), that jointly leave the balance of payments unaffected.

The fourth row utilizes an impressive study by Richard Marston (1987). This study compared the rate of appreciation needed in terms of different price indexes in order to offset productivity bias and leave US-Japanese competitiveness unchanged. Marston calculated that, over the 10 years 1973–83, a real appreciation of the yen by 35.7 percent in terms of the consumer price index (CPI) would have been required to keep competitiveness constant. Since in fact the yen depreciated in terms of the CPI by 9.0 percent, while it appreciated in terms of the WPI by 4.4 percent, one may estimate (as a first approximation) that the needed yen appreciation in terms of the WPI would have been 22 percent. If that rate of 2.2 percent per year was maintained in the 1980s, the appreciation required to offset productivity bias over 1984–90 was 12 percent, as shown in the third row of table 16.

Between the end of 1984 and the end of 1989 the net international investment position of the United States fell by $668 billion, while that of Japan rose by $219 billion. If the real rate of return on those assets is 4 percent per year, the United States would need to earn an additional $27 billion (0.5 percent of GNP) per year, and Japan would need to earn $9 billion per year less (0.3 percent of GNP), in order to restore balance.

Using the rules of thumb in the memorandum item of table 13, this would require a 6 percent effective depreciation of the dollar and a 3 percent effective appreciation of the yen. If the cross rates among all other currencies are held constant, GEM estimates that this would require a 6 percent real bilateral appreciation of the yen against the dollar, as shown in the fifth row of table 16.

Table 15 included estimates of the changes in dollar and yen effective rates needed to neutralize the oil price decline. GEM estimates that accomplishing those changes, with other cross rates unchanged, would have required a real bilateral yen appreciation of 13 percent, as shown in the sixth row of table 16.

Similarly, achieving the effective changes indicated in table 15 to accommodate changed current balance targets would have required a bilateral yen appreciation of 2 percent.

Summing those six effects, one finds that it is possible to explain a nominal appreciation of the equilibrium value of the yen against the dollar of 38 percent since the end of 1984--very close to the 42 percent change in my actual estimates. Devotees of PPP should note that not much more than one-eighth of this appreciation is explained by relative inflation.

Nevertheless, not all the evidence is as reassuring to the case for exchange rate targeting as that in table 16. It remains true that table 7 shows wide variations between comparable estimates produced by different models, while table 15 shows an uncomfortably large unexplained residual for two of the five currencies. The strongest conclusion that seems justified is that present modeling techniques may be just about adequate to support the estimation of FEERs. There remains an obvious need to improve the state of the art.

Appendix 1: The Models Used

As stated in the text, six global macroeconometric models were employed in performing the simulations that underlie the FEERs:

- EAG (External Adjustment with Growth), developed by William R. Cline at the Institute for International Economics

- Steady-state GEM, a version of the Global Econometric Model maintained at the National Institute of Economic and Social Research in London that suppresses the short-term dynamics of the larger model to focus on long-run issues

- Interlink, the global macroeconometric model of the OECD

- Intermod, a global macroeconometric model developed at the Canadian Department of Finance by modifying the IMF's Multimod model

- Mimosa (Multinational Integrated Model for Simulation and Analysis), developed in Paris by the Centre d'Etudes Prospectives et d'Informations Internationales (CEPII) and the Observatoire Français des Conjonctures Economiques

- MSG2, the McKibbin-Sachs Global model.

This appendix starts by comparing certain features of those models and proceeds to describe how the first round of simulations (those reported in appendix 2) were performed.

The single common feature of all of these models is that they embody a set of equations specifying countries' current account flows as a function of expenditure (and/or income) levels and relative prices, with the latter dependent on nominal exchange rates and domestic price levels. All the models except EAG also model the dependence of expenditure, income, and exchange rates, and the evolution of domestic prices, on monetary and fiscal policy, although much of this detail is suppressed in the steady-state version of GEM.

The models differ in the following important respects.

Coverage

EAG identifies 17 regions: each of the G-7 countries, the other industrial countries together as a single region, each of three major Latin American countries, the rest of Latin America together, Taiwan, the three other East Asian newly industrializing countries (NICs) together, the oil exporters, Africa, and the rest of the world. GEM identifies 13 regions: each of the G-7 countries and, in much less detail, the Netherlands, Belgium, the rest of OECD Europe, OPEC, the developing countries, and the former centrally planned economies. Interlink has 29 regions: each of the OECD countries (with Belgium and Luxembourg treated together), plus OPEC, the East Asian NICs, other developing countries in Asia, Africa, and Latin America, and the former Soviet bloc. Intermod has 10 regions: each of the members of the G-7 plus the small industrial countries, the high-income oil exporters, and the other developing countries. Mimosa has 15 regions: each of the G-7 except Canada, the rest of the European Community, the rest of Western Europe, Canada together with Australia and New Zealand, the East Asian NICs, other Asian countries, the Middle East and North Africa, sub-Saharan Africa, Latin America, and the Soviet Union (as it then was) and Eastern Europe. The MSG model has only seven regions: the United States, Japan, Germany, the rest of the participants in the ERM (at the time the model was constructed), the rest of the OECD (which includes two of the G-7 countries, namely, Canada and Britain), the non-oil-exporting developing countries, and the oil-exporting countries. All the models except Mimosa and MSG are in principle capable of generating estimates of FEERs for all the G-7 currencies; Mimosa omits only the Canadian dollar, but MSG is limited to the dollar, the deutsche mark, and the yen.

Commodity Disaggregation

EAG has no commodity disaggregation except for a partial breakout of oil trade (accomplished by treating the oil exporters as a group and treating the oil-exporting sectors of Britain and Mexico as separate "countries"). GEM does not model bilateral flows, but it recognizes that the current account balance of each individual country or region will depend upon real commodity prices (including the oil price), as well as interest rates and the stocks of external assets and liabilities. Interlink disaggregates into food, raw materials, energy, manufactures, and services. Intermod and MSG disaggregate into manufactures, oil, and commodities, with each region producing a differentiated manufactured product but oil and commodities being homogeneous. Mimosa identifies agriculture and food, energy, raw materials, manufactures, nonfactor services, and factor services.

Stock-Flow Relations

All the models cumulate current account imbalances to track the development of net external asset positions, and then project net factor service payments by applying assumed or projected interest costs to those positions. Several of the models, such as Intermod and MSG, also cumulate investment into capital stocks and fiscal deficits into national debts. Mimosa uses a "putty-clay" specification of the capital stock. (That is, capital is assumed to be malleable like putty when an investment is made, permitting the choice of capital intensity to respond to relative prices; but once an investment is made, the capital intensity cannot be altered.)

Expectations

EAG, steady-state GEM, Interlink, and Mimosa do not embody forward-looking expectational hypotheses. Intermod is available in versions incorporating either rational or adaptive expectations; the rational expectations version was chosen for the simulations, primarily because it converges much faster (although the lags are nonetheless long). MSG incorporates rational expectations in the financial markets, with international as well as intertemporal arbitrage. It has a mixture of forward-looking (rational) and liquidity-constrained behavior determining spending decisions.

Baseline Solution

A typical forecasting model is used to construct a baseline forecast given assumptions about the future development of both exogenous and policy variables. Some of these assumptions are explicit and obvious, for example, about the future world price of oil. In the set of simulations undertaken in 1990, which are reported in appendix 2, the modelers were asked to assume that the oil price would remain at $18 per barrel in terms of end-1989 prices. Other assumptions are "technical," meaning that they do not represent what is expected to happen but rather provide a baseline on "uncontroversial" assumptions, against which users can explore the implications of making their own forecasts. A typical example is the assumption of unchanged real exchange rates. Unfortunately, many of the assumptions that go into the construction of a baseline forecast are much less obvious than the examples just cited, but collectively they may have a substantial impact on the forecast.

Matters are more difficult still (from the standpoint of estimating FEERs in the way attempted in the first round) with a model exclusively designed for simulation, such as Intermod, since the model is designed only to give the *changes* in policies needed to induce specified *changes* in outcomes, as compared with a largely arbitrary baseline. This means that it is necessary to construct a base case set of projections that can then be compared with the desired outcomes; Intermod is then used to find the policy changes needed to achieve those target outcomes.

EAG does not have a well-defined baseline since it is not used for regular forecasting, but any specified level of exchange rates (together with assumptions about future growth rates) can be fed into the model in order to explore the implications of different exchange rate levels. The model implicitly assumes that exchange rate changes are accompanied by variations in internal demand that just neutralize the impact on growth of changes in the exchange rate.

Steady-state GEM does not require a future baseline, since it is designed to calculate the set of exchange rates that would achieve the targets now had they prevailed sufficiently long in the past. "Sufficiently long" means the length of the longest lag from the exchange rate to trade flows.

Interlink employed the early-1990 baseline forecast of the OECD, details of which are confidential.

Intermod was used in conjunction with a base case projection constructed ad hoc on the basis of what seemed to be implied by the May 1990 issue of the IMF's *World Economic Outlook*, which uses the technical assumption of no future changes in real exchange rates.

Mimosa is used for forecasting as well as simulation, and the modeling team employed their baseline forecast at the time the simulations were undertaken (June 1990).

For MSG a baseline was constructed by assuming that fiscal deficits remained at the same percentages of GNP as in 1989, and assuming fixed rates of money growth equal to 1990 rates of inflation.

Simulation Procedures

The six models used distinctly different procedures in the simulations undertaken in 1990.

In the case of *EAG*, assumptions were specified about domestic growth rates and the path of real exchange rates, and the model yielded trajectories for the current account. Those were then compared with the desired current account targets. It was found that several groups of non-G-7 countries developed implausibly large current account imbalances, so ad hoc modifications were made in order to bring these countries close to their targets in a way that could be expected to be neutral among the G-7 currencies, whose mutual exchange rates provide the focus of the study.[23] The initial real exchange rate trajectories were then modified in a manner calculated to bring the current balance trajectories closer to their targets. This iterative procedure was terminated when the current balance trajectories were deemed acceptably close to the targets in 1995 and reasonably close to trend in subsequent years.

Steady-state GEM uses a combination of parameters from steady-state versions of GEM's equations plus constants and trends estimated independently over 1970–88 in order to generate estimates of what each country's current account balance would be if all the independent variables were at their trend values, given exchange rates at their actual values. The procedure for solving the model for the FEER is as follows. One first estimates the trend current account as the actual current account adjusted for three main factors:

- deviations of world activity and commodity prices from trend

- deviations of domestic activity from its (steady inflation) equilibrium level

- additional deviations of trade flows from trend, for example as a result of lags.

---

23. Three specific changes were made. First, Cline's "original" (though constrained) estimates of income elasticities were used in place of his "compromise" estimates (an average of the original and uniform elasticities), to avoid Korea and Taiwan developing improbably large deficits over extended time horizons. Second, the oil exporters' propensity to spend on imports was modified so as to generate the target current account balance (without this modification OPEC would have become a large deficit region). Third, an ad hoc modification of the income elasticities was made to the Brazilian equation, to avoid Brazil becoming a massive surplus country. None of these modifications impinge directly on the core part of the model that generates the results of key interest in this study, namely, the relations among the G-7.

One compares the trend current account with the target and then uses steady-state GEM to calculate the exchange rate changes that would be needed to achieve the target. Unlike the other models, this approach tells one directly the present value of the FEER; that is, the exchange rate that, had it prevailed for a long enough period, would now reconcile internal and external balance.

Since steady-state GEM includes trend factors, nonunitary income elasticities, and asset accumulation, the (real effective) exchange rate that equates the trend current account to the target will in general change over time. FEERs were therefore calculated for 1995 as well as 1990. The difference provided the estimate of the rate of appreciation or depreciation of the FEER.

Interlink is used for both forecasting and simulation. The simulations sought to achieve specified outcomes for output and the current account in 1994, the last year for which the medium-run baseline had been established. This baseline was calculated prior to any allowances for German unification.

The simulations exogenized exchange rates, nominal interest rates, producer prices, and nominal wage rates. This was done because the object of the exercise was restricted to establishing the set of exchange rates that would be consistent with achieving the objectives for internal and external balance. Interlink has a strong tendency to return real exchange rates to their baseline levels via changes in domestic infla-tion, so that without the inflation equations turned off it is difficult to achieve large changes in real exchange rates that are sustained into the medium term. Similarly, it is unlikely that monetary policy would have had a sufficiently powerful influence on exchange rates in the model to enable it to achieve the exchange rate targets. Moreover, fiscal policies were adjusted without constraints (such as those suggested in William-son and Miller 1987) designed to rule out imprudently large budget deficits.

Questions can be asked about the legitimacy of this procedure. Why should one be interested in establishing intermediate targets with desir-able properties if there are no mechanisms able to achieve those targets, or if the instrument changes needed to reach the intermediate targets would be so extreme as to create problems greater than the benefits of reaching the intermediate target? A possible answer is that the parts of the model linking the intermediate targets to outcomes for GNP and the balance of payments (the equation blocks covering aggregate demand and supply and trade flows) are more robust than those linking fiscal and monetary instruments to the intermediate targets. For example, the lack of a satisfactory equation describing exchange rate determination precludes the possibility of identifying the monetary policy needed to achieve a desired exchange rate objective, but that does not make it pointless to ask what exchange rate would be consistent with medium-run targets for output and the current account. It simply means that one cannot be confident that adequate policies to achieve the exchange rate target could be found. Some of us would argue that a commitment to target zones for exchange rates centered on the estimated FEERs would change the forces that determine exchange rates and thus render redundant the (poor) equations linking monetary policy to exchange rates, which is to say that one could hope to harness the Lucas critique.

That is not to deny that serious problems might arise in achieving the intermediate targets. Clearly it is important at some stage to inquire into this issue. If such problems occur, one would wish to know the reasons, and it is conceivable that those reasons would lead one to modify the intermediate targets or to delay the attempt to reach them. The claim made here is simply that those checks can usefully be delayed to a subsequent stage. The aim is to make progress on one problem at a time. The one tackled here is the identification of an intermediate target for the (real effective) exchange rate. For this purpose, fiscal impulses and exchange rates were varied in order to seek a simulation that would achieve the targets for external and internal balance.

Intermod is a simulation model rather than a forecasting model. It provides estimates of the *changes* in exchange rates that would be needed to achieve a specified set of *changes* in current account balances. Hence to construct estimates of the exchange rate trajectories that would achieve target current account outcomes one needs also a set of projections, for example of what would happen in the absence of policy change. A set of projections using the standard technical assumption of no future changes in real exchange rates was constructed for this purpose. These projections were compared with the targets for internal and external balance, and then simulations were run on Intermod to find what shocks to fiscal and monetary policy would be needed to achieve the desired changes in current account balances without unduly disturbing internal balance. The changes in exchange rates on the trajectories that achieved the desired changes in current accounts were then superimposed on the base case trajectories to generate the estimates of FEERs.

A notable feature of Intermod is its strong self-stabilizing properties. Variations in the inflation rate tend to push output toward its supply-side capacity.[24] Model-consistent expectations also help to ensure

---

24. This is assumed to grow at the same rate of 2.5 percent per year in all countries. Equal steady-state growth rates is a standard conclusion of neoclassical growth theory; however, the convergence time has usually been regarded as a century or more, so that the assumption of equal growth rates in the short run is questionable (even neglecting endogenous growth theories). On the other hand, the assumption is a purely technical one, used to generate baseline data. It has (almost) nothing to do with the model's properties, which are affected only to the extent that nonlinearities in the model cause the shock-minus-control results to vary as a function of levels of the baseline data.

speedy convergence. Moreover, it is assumed that each country has a target ratio of (public) debt to GNP, and the model includes a fiscal feedback rule that "adjusts the average tax rate in response to both changes in the debt-GNP ratio and the gap between the actual debt-GNP ratio and its target level" (Meredith 1989, 12). This rule is intended to preclude simulations that promise good results in finite time by pursuing policies that threaten to violate the government's intertemporal budget constraint in the long run.

One consequence of the fiscal feedback rule is to make it impossible to achieve the prolonged changes in fiscal positions that are needed to adjust the current account. This feedback rule was therefore suppressed. (Permanent) variations in government expenditure were then used to try to achieve the desired current balance positions. Although this raises a question as to whether the model's long-term solvency constraints were satisfied, the solution did not exhibit symptoms that suggested that ill-defined terminal conditions were causing problems. On the contrary, the deviations of exchange rates from their baseline paths showed a rather surprising tendency to die away over time.

Intermod cannot be used to estimate trend changes in exchange rates.

Mimosa treats fiscal policies and exchange rates, as well as the world level of interest rates, as policy variables that can be altered directly in order to achieve the targets for internal and external balance. Like most of the other modeling groups, the modelers chose first to calculate a set of multipliers giving the change in each of the various 1995 targets produced by each of the instruments. They used those multipliers in order to estimate an appropriate combination of instruments, and iterated until they achieved a satisfactory outcome. Exchange rate changes were assumed to take place in one jump in 1990, while fiscal expansion involved an annual increase in public spending. The abruptness of the assumed exchange rate changes precluded achieving the growth profile laid out in table 6, so the modelers aimed at achieving the same cumulative growth over the period 1990–95. (They argued that it was more important to ensure that the J-curve had been played through by 1995 than to achieve the ideal growth path.)

MSG does not settle down to a steady state with a constant real exchange rate over any relevant time horizon (i.e., not within 90 years), although major fluctuations generally subside within 5 to 10 years. The reason for the long delay is that the model gives an important role to asset stocks, and it takes a long time for these to stabilize. If the current account reaches the level specified as "external balance" in 1995, stock positions will in general be changing, and with them expenditure patterns and real exchange rates.

The model pins down terminal conditions by assuming that any change in the budget deficit as a result of discretionary fiscal policy is accompanied by a permanent future tax change just big enough to cover the interest cost of servicing the increased debt. This allows for meaningful changes in short-run fiscal policy while avoiding the possibility of unsustainable debt accumulation in the long run.

Five simulations were run. The first assumed that fiscal deficits as a ratio to GDP remain unchanged at their 1989 levels, and assumed a fixed money growth rate equal to the 1990 rate of inflation. This provided a base case. The next two simulations used an iterative procedure to find a path for fiscal policy that would hit a specified set of current account targets, with the first of these two simulations using the same fixed monetary growth rule as in the base case and the second using optimal control to select a money growth path to target output at the baseline level. The next two simulations repeated those procedures, this time aiming for an alternative set of current account targets.

It can be seen that the solution methods have some rather striking differences across models, and doubtless this is also true of the baselines used by the various models. This heterogeneity should diminish the danger of getting similar but incorrect results by chance, at the cost of increasing the expectation that the results may differ significantly.

Appendix 2: Results of the Simulations

The simulations reported in this appendix were performed in the spring of 1990. Simulations on EAG and Intermod were performed at the Institute for International Economics by Su Zhou, and I visited the OECD to supervise the simulation on Interlink. The other models were simulated by the modeling groups themselves.

The targets specified for external and internal balance were those laid out in tables 4 and 6 of the text.

The principal results of the simulations on the EAG model are displayed in table A1. In order to achieve current account balances close to the targets specified in column 2 of table 4 by 1995 (without strong changes in subsequent years) while following the growth path stipulated in table 6, the model implied that it would be necessary for the dollar to depreciate in real effective terms by 14 percent (relative to the last quarter of 1989), for the yen to appreciate by 27 percent, and so on. The second row shows the implied need for bilateral (real) changes against the US dollar: the yen, for example, would have needed to appreciate by 43 percent, from its actual value in late 1989 of ¥143 to the dollar to ¥100 to the dollar. This assumed that Japanese (and US) prices would have remained unchanged: to the extent that the Japanese price level fell and the US price level rose in response to the yen's appreciation, the yen would have needed to appreciate even more in nominal terms. The third row shows the trend changes in FEERs (the annual appreciation in terms of the real effective exchange rate) needed to main-

Table A1 Estimates of FEERs in the EAG simulations[a]

	US dollar	Japanese yen	Deutsche mark	French franc	Pound sterling	Italian lira	Canadian dollar
Base case							
FEER	−14	27	33	−11	−18	−15	−30
Implied real appreciation against US dollar	0	43	42	5	−2	0	−18
Trend real appreciation of FEER	0	0.8	1.0	−0.5	−0.3	0.2	−0.7
Trend real appreciation against US dollar	0	0.8	0.9	−0.5	−0.1	0.3	−0.5
Alternative current account targets							
FEER	−21	40	40	−13	−19	−17	−32
Implied real appreciation against US dollar	0	62	55	10	3	6	−16
Trend real appreciation of FEER	0.3	0.3	0.8	−0.4	−0.3	0.3	−0.6
Trend real appreciation against US dollar	0	0.1	0.3	−0.7	−0.4	0	−0.7
Less US growth in 1990							
FEER	−12	26	32	−11	−18	−15	−30
Implied real appreciation against US dollar	0	40	39	3	−3	−2	−19
Trend real appreciation of FEER	0	0.8	1.0	−0.5	−0.3	0.2	−0.7
Trend real appreciation against US dollar	0	0.8	0.9	−0.5	−0.1	0.3	−0.5

a. Figures in the first two lines in each panel show necessary percentage changes from actual exchange rates in the fourth quarter of 1989. Figures in the second two lines in each panel are in percentages per year: negative numbers indicate depreciation of the equilibrium value of the currency.

Source: Simulations undertaken by Su Zhou on the EAG model.

tain the current account in balance in the mid-1990s, and the final row shows the implied changes in real bilateral rates against the dollar.

The other two panels of table A1 display similar results for the variant cases. The first of these assumed that the US current account should be in balance by 1995, and the second that the United States economy had 1 percent excess demand at the start of 1990.

Table A2 displays the current account outcomes of the EAG simulations. The EAG model generates a much smaller statistical discrepancy than that customarily observed and embodied in the targets specified in table 4: the counterpart was allowed to fall in the rest-of-the-world part of the model.

Table A3 displays results from the *GEM* model in a similar form, except that implied bilateral rates against the dollar were not calculated. The quite different method of solving the model to calculate FEERs implies that there are no simulation outcomes to compare with the targets.

Table A4 shows the estimates of FEERs made on the *Interlink* model. Interlink is not suited to estimating trend changes in exchange rates, and only the base case was calculated in this instance. The memorandum item shows the size of the fiscal stimulus that the model estimates would be needed in order to achieve the FEERs and associated current account targets while retaining internal balance. Table A5 shows the (1994) deviations from the baseline for both GDP and the current account outcome that the simulations were aimed at achieving, and compares them with the changes that were in fact reached in the final simulation.

The results of the simulations on the *Intermod* model are presented in table A6. The first row displays how real effective exchange rates would need to have changed relative to their levels in the fourth quarter of 1989 in order to reach the estimated FEERs in the base case. The most striking feature of the results is the estimate that the yen was near equilibrium in late 1989. Another interesting feature of Intermod's results (not shown in the table) is that the *nominal* exchange rate changes that the model estimates to be needed to reach equilibrium are often *smaller* than the corresponding real changes, in contrast to the standard presumption that in part any nominal exchange rate change is dissipated in changes in inflation. The explanation is that in this model exchange rates are changed as a result of changes in fiscal policy, which has an offsetting effect on inflation; for example, a country that needs to improve its current balance deflates, which reduces the pressure of demand and thus prices, as well as weakening the exchange rate, which does indeed tend to increase prices as expected. No changes in monetary policy were introduced with the aim of offsetting the impact of fiscal policy on domestic demand, because monetary policy is rather ineffective for that purpose according to the model.

The results of pursuing the alternative set of current account targets, in which the United States would achieve a zero current balance, are

Table A2 Current account balances in the EAG simulations (billions of US dollars)

	Base case			US in current account balance			Less US growth		
	1994	1995	1995 target	1994	1995	1995 target	1994	1995	1995 target
United States	-75	-77	-79	-1	2	0	-74	-76	-79
Japan	65	70	69	23	25	23	64	70	69
Germany	27	29	28	9	10	9	26	28	28
France	-2	-1	0	1	2	0	-1	1	0
United Kingdom	1	1	0	1	2	0	0	0	0
Italy	-1	0	0	2	3	0	-1	0	0
Canada	-10	-12	-11	-11	-12	-11	-10	-12	-11
Other industrial countries	-17	-18	-19	-26	-27	-28	-17	-18	-19
OPEC	-2	-2	0	-2	-2	0	-2	-2	0
East Asian NICs	9	10	8	3	3	3	9	10	8
Rest of world	-11	-11	-74	-6	-4	-74	-13	-14	-74
Statistical discrepancy	-16	-11	-78	-8	2	-78	-19	-13	-78

Source: Simulations undertaken by Su Zhou on the EAG model.

Table A3 Estimates of FEERs from the GEM simulations[a]

	US dollar	Japanese yen	Deutsche mark	French franc	Pound sterling	Italian lira	Canadian dollar
Base case							
FEER	−9	15	18	−8	−10	−12	−6
Trend real appreciation of FEER	−1.1	2.8	1.1	−1.4	−2.3	−1.6	−1.9
Alternative current account targets							
FEER	−17	30	24	−8	−10	−12	−6
Trend real appreciation of FEER	−0.8	2.8	1.0	−1.4	−2.3	−1.6	−1.9
Less US growth in 1990							
FEER	−7	15	18	−9	−10	−12	−7
Trend real appreciation of FEER	−1.1	2.8	0.9	−1.3	−2.4	−1.4	−1.8

a. Figures in the first line of each panel show necessary percentage changes from actual exchange rates in the fourth quarter of 1989. Figures in the second line of each panel are in percentages per year: negative numbers indicate depreciations of the equilibrium real value of the currency.

Source: Simulations undertaken by Simon Wren-Lewis and Ray Barrell.

Table A4   Estimates of FEERs from the Interlink simulations[a]

	US dollar	Japanese yen	Deutsche mark	French franc	Pound sterling	Italian lira	Canadian dollar
FEER	0	11	17	–9	0	–14	–8
Implied real appreciation against US dollar	0	11	15	–7	1	–12	–7
Memorandum: fiscal stimulus needed to achieve targets (percentage of potential GDP)	–0.8	1.0	5.0	0.9	–1.2	0.6	0.2

a. Figures are necessary percentage changes from actual exchange rates in the fourth quarter of 1989. Only the base case was simulated.

Source: Simulations undertaken by Paul O'Brien and John Williamson on the Interlink model.

Table A5   Targets and simulated changes in the Interlink model

	United States	Japan	Germany	France	United Kingdom	Italy	Canada
Target change in 1994 GDP (percentages of potential)	0	0	0	2.5	0	3.0	4.0
Simulated change in 1994 GDP (percentages of potential)	0.06	−0.14	0.37	2.99	−0.01	3.12	3.24
Target change in current balance (billions of dollars)	50	−23	−78	4	20	19	10
Actual change in current balance (billions of dollars)							
1993	47	−11	−57	4	16	19	8
1994	58	−11	−79	5	19	23	10

Source: Simulations undertaken by Paul O'Brien and John Williamson on the Interlink model.

Table A6 Estimates of FEERs from the Intermod simulations[a]

	US dollar	Japanese yen	Deutsche mark	French franc	Pound sterling	Italian lira	Canadian dollar
FEERs							
Base case	−7	−1	11	−2	−2	1	−5
Alternative current account targets	−13	1	16	3	−2	2	−7
Memorandum: fiscal stimulus needed to achieve targets (percentages of baseline GDP)							
Base case	−1.8	0.6	2.4	−0.8	−2.7	−2.0	−2.9
Alternative current account targets	−4.2	0.6	2.4	−2.0	−3.8	−3.1	−3.6

a. Figures are necessary percentage changes from the fourth quarter of 1989.

Source: Simulations undertaken by Su Zhou on the Intermod model.

Table A7 Estimates of FEERS from the Mimosa model

	US dollar	Japanese yen	Deutsche mark	French franc	Pound sterling	Italian lira
Base case[a]						
FEER	-20	32	19	2	-23	31
Implied real appreciation against US dollar	0	59	78	52	12	106
Implied nominal appreciation against US dollar	0	87	100	66	-7	125
Alternative current account targets[a]						
FEER	-26	55	23	2	-23	29
Implied real appreciation against US dollar	0	92	95	62	18	118
Implied nominal appreciation against US dollar	0	113	112	71	-4	133
Memorandum: fiscal stimulus needed to achieve targets (percentages of baseline GDP)						
Base case	-1.7	-0.1	0.8	-0.9	-0.7	2.2
Alternative current account targets	-2.7	1.2	1.6	-0.9	-1.0	-1.6

a. Figures are necessary percentage changes from actual exchange rates in the fourth quarter of 1989.

Source: Simulations undertaken by Jean-Pierre Chauffour on the Interlink model.

Table A8 Estimates of FEERs from the MSG model

	US dollar		Japanese yen		Deutsche mark		Rest of EMS		Rest of OECD	
	Nominal	Real	Nominal	Real	Nominal	Real	Nominal	Real	Nominal	Real
Base case[a]										
Fixed money growth	−7	−7	13	12	14	12	−6	−5	1	0
Optimized money growth	−8	−8	10	10	6	7	1	1	−1	−1
Alternative current account targets[a]										
Fixed money growth	−10	−10	29	27	14	13	−6	−5	−1	−1
Optimized money growth	−9	−9	23	24	7	8	−2	−2	−1	−2
Memorandum: fiscal stimulus needed to achieve targets (percentages of baseline GDP)										
Base case	−3.0		0.0		2.5		0.0		−3.0	
Alternative current account targets	−6.0		0.5		1.8		−2.0		−4.7	

a. Figures are necessary percentage changes from actual exchange rates in the fourth quarter of 1989.

Source: Simulations undertaken by Warwick McKibbin on the MSG model.

shown in the second row of table A6. The exchange rate changes estimated to be needed remain comparatively modest.

The memorandum items again show the size of the fiscal stimulus associated with achievement of the FEERs.

The results of the *Mimosa* simulations are presented in table A7. These show the change in the real effective exchange rate needed to reach the estimated FEER, and the implied bilateral real and nominal appreciations vis-à-vis the dollar, for all currencies except the Canadian dollar. It will be seen that Mimosa, unlike Intermod, generally produces the conventional result that nominal exchange rate changes are larger than the real changes. It can also be seen that Mimosa finds the Italian lira to be the most undervalued of the five nondollar currencies on a bilateral basis. The memorandum item again shows the fiscal prerequisites for reaching the FEERs.

The results of the *MSG* simulations are summarized in table A8. These results differ from those generated by the other models in two respects. First, only three of the G-7 countries are modeled separately: hence estimates of equilibrium exchange rates are generated only for the yen and the mark. Second, simulations were performed on the basis of two alternative assumptions about monetary policy: a constant rate of growth of the money supply (equal to the 1990 inflation rate), and a monetary policy that chose monetary growth optimally to maintain output on the "internal balance" path. In most cases the differences between these two alternative specifications of monetary policy are small.

The table shows changes in both nominal and real exchange rates against the dollar. The differences are small and show no systematic tendency for one to be greater than the other. As in earlier tables, the memorandum item shows the fiscal preconditions for achieving the FEERs.

References

Adams, Charles, and David Coe. 1990."A Systems Approach to Estimating the Natural Rate of Unemployment and Potential Output of the US." *IMF Staff Papers* 37, no. 2 (June): 232–93.

Atkinson, F. J., Brooks, S. J., and S. G. F. Hall. 1983. "The Economic Effects of North Sea Oil." *National Institute Economic Review* 104 (May).

Balassa, Bela. 1964. "The Purchasing Power Parity Doctrine: A Reappraisal." *Journal of Political Economy* 72, no. 6 (December): 584–96.

Balassa, Bela, and John Williamson. 1987. "Adjusting to Success: Balance of Payments Policy in the East Asian NICs." POLICY ANALYSES IN INTERNATIONAL ECONOMICS 17. Washington: Institute for International Economics.

Balassa, Bela, and Marcus Noland. 1988. *Japan in the World Economy*. Washington: Institute for International Economics.

Barrell, Ray, and Simon Wren-Lewis. 1989. "Fundamental Equilibrium Exchange Rates for the G7." CEPR Discussion Paper No. 323. London: Centre for Economic Policy Research.

Bergsten, C. Fred. 1988. *America in the World Economy: A Strategy for the 1990s*. Washington: Institute for International Economics.

Bergsten, C. Fred, and John Williamson. 1983. "Exchange Rates and Trade Policy." In William R. Cline, ed., *Trade Policy in the 1980s*. Washington: Institute for International Economics.

Boughton, James M. 1989. "Policy Assignment Strategies with Somewhat Flexible Exchange Rates." In B. Eichengreen, M. Miller, and R. Portes, eds., *Blueprints for Exchange Rate Management*. London: Centre for Economic Policy Research.

Bryant, Ralph. 1983. "Alternative Futures for the International Monetary Fund," chapter 2. Washington: Brookings Institution (unpublished).

Catte, Pietro, Giampaolo Galli, and Salvatore Rebecchini. Forthcoming. "Concerted Interventions and the Dollar: An Analysis of Daily Data." In P. B. Kenen, F. Saccomanni, and F. Papadia, eds., *The International Monetary System*. Cambridge: Cambridge University Press.

Cline, William R. 1989. *United States External Adjustment and the World Economy*. Washington: Institute for International Economics.

Currie, David, and Simon Wren-Lewis. 1990. "Evaluating the Extended Target Zone Proposal for the G3." *Economic Journal* 100, no. 399 (March): 105–23.

Dixit, Avinash. 1990. Review of Paul Krugman's "Exchange-Rate Instability." *Journal of Economic Literature* 28, no. 2 (June): 705–7.

Dominguez, Kathryn M., and Jeffrey A. Frankel. 1993. *Does Foreign Exchange Intervention Work?* Washington: Institute for International Economics.

Dornbusch, Rudiger. 1987. "Exchange Rate Economics: 1986." *Economic Journal* 97, no. 385 (March): 1–18.

Friedman, Milton. 1953. *Essays in Positive Economics*. Chicago: University of Chicago Press.

Fry, Maxwell J. 1988. "Should Taiwan Reduce Its Current Account Surplus?" University of Birmingham (mimeographed).

Helliwell, John. 1989. "Fiscal Policy and the External Deficit: Siblings, But Not Twins." In R. G. Penner, ed., *The Great Fiscal Experiment*. Washington: Urban Institute.

Houthakker, Hendrik S., and Stephen P. Magee. 1969. "Income and Price Elasticities in World Trade." *Review of Economics and Statistics* 51, no. 2 (May): 111–25.

International Monetary Fund. 1970. *The Role of Exchange Rates in the Adjustment of International Payments: A Report by the Executive Directors*. Washington: International Monetary Fund.

International Monetary Fund. 1988. *World Economic Outlook* (October).

Isard, Peter. 1977. "How Far Can We Push the Law of One Price?" *American Economic Review* 67, no. 5 (December): 942–48.

Johnson, Harry G. 1956. "Increasing Productivity, Income-Price Trends, and the Trade Balance." *Economic Journal* 64 (September): 462–85.

Kravis, Irving B., and Robert E. Lipsey. 1978. "Price Behavior in the Light of Balance of Payments Theory." *Journal of International Economics* 8, no. 2 (May): 193–246.

Krugman, Paul R. 1985. "Is the Strong Dollar Sustainable?" In *The US Dollar: Prospects and Policy Options*. Kansas City: Federal Reserve Bank of Kansas City.

Krugman, Paul R. 1989. "Differences in Income Elasticities and Trends in Real Exchange Rates." *European Economic Review* 33, no. 5 (May): 1031–54.

Marris, Stephen. 1985. *Deficits and the Dollar: The World Economy at Risk*. POLICY ANALYSES IN INTERNATIONAL ECONOMICS 14. Washington: Institute for International Economics.

Marston, Richard C. 1987. "Real Exchange Rates and Productivity Growth in the United States and Japan." In S. W. Arndt and J. D. Richardson, eds., *Real-Financial Linkages Among Open Economies*. Cambridge, MA: MIT Press.

Masson, Paul R., and Ralph W. Tryon. 1990. "Macroeconomic Effects of Projected Population Aging in Industrial Countries." IMF Working Paper 90/5. Washington: International Monetary Fund.

McGuirk, Anne K. 1983. "Oil Price Changes and Real Exchange Rate Movements Among Industrial Countries." *IMF Staff Papers* (December).

McKibbin, Warwick J. 1989. "The World Economy from 1979 to 1988: Results from the MSG2 Model." Brookings Discussion Papers in International Economics No. 72. Washington: Brookings Institution.

McKibbin, Warwick J., and Jeffrey D. Sachs. 1989. *The McKibbin-Sachs Global Model.* Brookings Discussion Papers in International Economics No. 78. Washington: Brookings Institution.

McKinnon, Ronald I. 1971. *Monetary Theory and Controlled Flexibility in the Foreign Exchanges.* Princeton Essays in International Finance No. 84. Princeton, NJ: Princeton University.

McKinnon, Ronald I. 1979. *Money in International Exchange: The Convertible Currency System.* New York: Oxford University Press.

McKinnon, Ronald I. 1984. "An International Standard for Monetary Stabilization." POLICY ANALYSES IN INTERNATIONAL ECONOMICS 8. Washington: Institute for International Economics.

McKinnon, Ronald I., and Kenichi Ohno. 1986. "Getting the Exchange Rate Right: Insular versus Open Economies." Economics Dept., Stanford University (mimeographed, December).

Meredith, Guy. 1989. *Intermod 2.0: Model Specification and Simulation Properties.* Canadian Department of Finance Working Papers No. 89-7. Ottawa: Department of Finance.

MIMOSA Modeling Group. 1990. *MIMOSA: A Model of the World Economy.* Working Paper No. 90-02. Paris: Centre d'Etudes Prospectives et d'Informations Internationales and Observatoire Français des Conjonctures Economiques.

National Institute of Economic and Social Research. 1990. *GEM Model Manual.* London: National Institute of Economic and Social Research.

Noguchi, Yukio. 1989. "Japan's Fiscal Policy and External Balance." Hitotsubashi University, Tokyo (mimeographed).

Richardson, Pete. 1988. *The Structure and Simulation Properties of OECD's Interlink Model.* OECD Economic Studies No. 10. Paris: Organization for Economic Cooperation and Development.

Richardson, Pete. 1990. "Simulating the OECD Interlink Model under Alternative Monetary Policy Rules." Paper presented to the Brookings Conference on the Empirical Evaluation of Alternative Policy Regimes (8–9 March).

Robinson, Joan. 1947. "The Foreign Exchanges." In Joan Robinson, *Essays in the Theory of Employment.* Oxford: Basil Blackwell. Reprinted in *Readings in the Theory of International Trade.* London: Allen and Unwin, 1950.

Torres, Raymond, and John P. Martin. 1989. *Potential Output in the Seven Major OECD Countries.* OECD Department of Economics and Statistics Working Paper No. 66. Paris: Organization for Economic Cooperation and Development (May).

Underwood, John. 1990. "On the Sustainability of External Debt." Paper presented to the Workshop on Net External Asset Positions at the Kiel Institute for World Economics (5–6 March).

Williamson, John. 1983. "The Exchange Rate System." POLICY ANALYSES IN INTERNATIONAL ECONOMICS 5 (rev. ed., 1985). Washington: Institute for International Economics.

Williamson, John. 1991. "Comments on J. Boughton, 'The Role of Policy Assignment and Cooperation in Intermediate Exchange Rate Regimes.' " In Hans J. Blommestein, ed., *International Economic Policy Coordination and Reality.* Amsterdam: North-Holland.

Williamson, John, and Marcus H. Miller. 1987. "Targets and Indicators: A Blueprint for the International Coordination of Economic Policy." POLICY ANALYSES IN INTERNATIONAL ECONOMICS 22. Washington: Institute for International Economics.

Wonnacott, Paul. 1987. ''The United States and Canada: The Quest for Free Trade.'' POLICY ANALYSES IN INTERNATIONAL ECONOMICS 16. Washington: Institute for International Economics.

Yoshitomi, Masaru. 1990. ''Why Is the Yen So Weak?'' Paper presented at the US-Japan Financial Core Group meeting at the Institute for International Economics (23–24 July).

7

An Assessment of the Evidence on Purchasing Power Parity

JANICE BOUCHER BREUER

Gustav Cassel's (1922) idea that the nominal exchange rate should reflect the purchasing power of one currency against another remains, 70 years later, an enduring precept of international economics.[1] It has provided and continues to provide a well of intellectual scrutiny for academics and a basis for decisions by government agencies and businesses alike. Cassel proposed that a purchasing power exchange rate (let us define it as k) exists and is measurable by the reciprocal of one country's price level, $1/P$, against another's, $1/P^*$. The terms $1/P$ and $1/P^*$ are the domestic country's and the foreign country's "internal" purchasing power, respectively. They measure the units of goods that could be purchased with one unit of each currency. Cassel wrote further that the purchasing power rate is the rate toward which the nominal exchange rate s, defined as units of domestic currency per unit of foreign currency, would tend, in the absence of trade imbalances, speculation, central bank intervention, and other impediments to trade. In other words, purchasing power parity would prevail. Formally,

Janice Boucher Breuer is associate professor of economics at the University of South Carolina, Columbia, SC. She thanks Stanley Black, Peter Clark, Hali Edison, Steven Husted, Maurice Obstfeld, Myles Wallace, John Williamson, and Mark Wohar for their comments.

1. In fact, some historians have noted that the concept of purchasing power parity has been around for three or more centuries. See Officer (1976) and references cited therein. However, Officer emphasizes that Cassel was the first to operationalize purchasing power parity and empirically test it.

$$s = (1/P^*)/(1/P) = P/P^* = k. \qquad (1)$$

Let $(s \cdot P^*)/P$ define the real exchange rate r. When absolute purchasing power parity holds, $r = 1$. The more relaxed relative version of equation (1), which accommodates the use of price indices, permits r to be some constant scalar θ.

Aspects of Purchasing Power Parity Studies

Were Cassel alive today he would no doubt be surprised at the research agenda, not to mention the debate, spawned by his idea. There has been no dearth of academic studies of purchasing power parity. A word search of the Economic Literature Database shows 80 entries with ''purchasing power parity'' in the title published between 1974 and 1992. These entries do not include unpublished manuscripts and essays in multiauthor volumes. Table 1 provides a sampling of studies of purchasing power parity and lists some of their salient features. These studies feature different sample periods, different currencies, different specifications, and different estimation methods.

Sample periods commonly investigated are the 1920s (a period of hyperinflation in Germany) and the era of flexible exchange rates that began in 1973. Occasionally studies are undertaken of the Bretton Woods fixed exchange rate era or the earlier period of the gold standard. Some studies span various regimes.

The currencies investigated also differ, although the majority of studies focus on bilateral rates of the industrialized countries against the US dollar. Sometimes these studies include tests of bilateral rates of one currency other than the US dollar against another by computing the cross rates from the data set, whereas others explicitly select a bilateral rate against a currency other than the US dollar for the base. More recently, purchasing power parity has been tested for developing countries.

The specifications used to test purchasing power parity also differ, according to whether the trivariate relationship between the exchange rate, the domestic price series, and the foreign price series; the bivariate relationship between the exchange rate and the domestic-foreign price ratio; or the univariate real exchange rate is being examined. The trivariate relationship is the most general. It imposes neither symmetry (price coefficients of the same magnitude but opposite sign) nor proportionality (price coefficients restricted to be [1, −1]). The bivariate specification implicitly imposes symmetry, and the univariate specification imposes symmetry and proportionality.

The specifications may also differ according to whether the exchange rate or the price series is the dependent variable. They may further differ according to the price series used; whether the wholesale or the consumer price index is the more appropriate has not been settled, and therefore many studies offer results based on both series.

Finally, various methods have been used to test purchasing power parity, especially since the mid-1980s. Recent studies use Dickey-Fuller and augmented Dickey-Fuller tests of the real exchange rate; Perron-type tests of the real exchange rate where allowance for a one-time structural break is incorporated; variance ratio tests; the Engle-Granger two-step method; error correction models; the maximum likelihood estimation procedure offered by Johansen and Juselius (1990); and, most recently, fractional integration methods.

Tests of Purchasing Power Parity: Then and Now

Equation (2) presents the regression specification typically used to test purchasing power parity. The exchange rate s and the domestic and foreign price series p and p^* are expressed in logarithms:

$$s_t = \alpha + \beta(p_t - p_t^*) + u_t, \tag{2}$$

where α and β are estimated regression coefficients, t denotes time, and u is an error term.

Prior to the mid-1980s, tests of purchasing power parity centered on coefficient restrictions. Absolute purchasing power parity would be confirmed if $\alpha = 0$ and $\beta = 1$. Less strict versions permit α to be nonzero, since transportation and transactions costs as well as differing goods and weights thereof in the price indexes of the domestic and the foreign country may create measurement error not construed to be a violation of purchasing power parity. Purchasing power parity was also frequently tested using a first-differenced specification of equation (2). Frenkel's (1978, 1981) work confirming purchasing power parity using data from the hyperinflation of the 1920s is perhaps the best known. Officer's (1976) survey and Isard's (1976) study rejecting the law of one price are other familiar works.

Before the mid-1980s, the methods used to test purchasing power parity were ordinary and generalized least squares. Since the mid-1980s, advances in econometrics for nonstationary time series[2] modeled in a bivariate or multivariate framework have revealed the pitfalls of conducting classical inference using an equation like equation (2) when the data are nonstationary but cointegrated (see Engle and Granger 1987

---

2. Nonstationary time series have a mean and a covariance that are not independent of time. Much of the econometric literature cited in this study addresses time series that have a trend in the mean, or a unit root. Such series are "integrated of order 1" and referred to as I(1) series. First differences of such series are stationary processes.

Table 1 Characteristics of studies of purchasing power parity

Characteristic	Abuaf and Jorion	Adler and Lehmann	Ardeni and Lubian	Cheung and Lai (1993a)
Period studied				
Fixed parities		X		
Flexible exchange rates	X	X		X
1920s			X	
Pre–World War II	X	X		
Specifications				
$[s, p, p^*]$			X	X
$[s, (p - p^*)]$ or $[p, s \cdot p^*]$				
$[s - p + p^*]$	X	X		
Price index used				
Consumer price index	X	X	?	X
Wholesale price index		X	?	X
Methods used				
OLS or GLS				
Engle-Granger Dickey-Fuller[a]			X	
Error correction model				
Johansen and Juselius				X
Dickey-Fuller[a]	X	X[b]		
One-time break				
Variance ratio				
Fractional integration				
Results				
Symmetry and proportionality?	imposed	imposed	found in 7 of 10 cases	rejected in most cases
Stationary relationship between e, p, and p*?	Yes	No	No	Yes, more often for most general specification

Characteristic	Cheung and Lai (1993b)	Choudry et al.	Corbae and Ouliaris	Davuytan and Pippenger
Period studied				
Fixed parities	X			
Flexible exchange rates	X	X[c]	X	X
1920s				X
Pre–World War II	X			
Specifications				
$[s, p, p^*]$				X[d]
$[s, (p - p^*)]$ or $[p, s \cdot p^*]$	X	X	X	
$[s - p + p^*]$		X		X
Price index used				
Consumer price index	X	X	X	X
Wholesale price index		X		
Methods used				
OLS or GLS				X
Engle-Granger Dickey-Fuller[a]		X		
Error correction model			X	
Johansen and Juselius				
Dickey-Fuller[a]		X		
One-time break				
Variance ratio				
Fractional integration	X			
Results				
Symmetry and proportionality?	symmetry imposed	imposed	imposed	symmetry imposed
Stationary relationship between e, p, and p^*?	Yes, but not for subsamples	Yes, except when sample includes announcement to intervene	No	Yes

(table continues next page)

Table 1 Characteristics of studies of purchasing power parity (continued)

Characteristic	Diebold et al.	Edison and Klovland	Flynn and Boucher	Frenkel
Period studied				
Fixed parities		X	X	
Flexible exchange rates			X	X
1920s		X		X
Pre–World War II	X[e]			
Specifications				
$[s, p, p^*]$				
$[s, (p - p^*)]$ or $[p, s \cdot p^*]$		X	X	X
$[s - p + p^*]$	X		X	
Price index used				
Consumer price index	X	X[f]	X	X
Wholesale price index	X		X	X
Methods used				
OLS or GLS		X		X[d]
Engle-Granger Dickey-Fuller[a]		X	X	
Error correction model		X		
Johansen and Juselius				
Dickey-Fuller[a]			X	
One-time break			X	
Variance ratio				
Fractional integration	X			
Results				
Symmetry and proportionality?	imposed	symmetry imposed; proportionality rejected except in cases where structural factors included	imposed	symmetry imposed
Stationary relationship between e, p, and p^*?	Yes	Yes	No	Yes, but only for 1920s

Characteristic	Glen	Grilli and Kaminsky	Kim	Kugler and Lenz
Period studied				
Fixed parities		X	X	
Flexible exchange rates	X	X	X	X
1920s				
Pre–World War II	X	X	X	
Specifications				
$[s, p, p^*]$				X
$[s, (p - p^*)]$ or $[p, s \cdot p^*]$			X	
$[s - p + p^*]$	X	X	X	
Price index used				
Consumer price index	X		X	X
Wholesale price index	X	X	X	
Methods used				
OLS or GLS				
Engle-Granger Dickey-Fuller[a]			X	
Error correction model			X	
Johansen and Juselius				X
Dickey-Fuller[a]		X	X	
One-time break				
Variance ratio	X	X		
Fractional integration				
Results				
Symmetry and proportionality?	imposed	imposed	imposed	found for 6 of 15 cases
Stationary relationship between e, p, and p^*?	Yes	Yes, but not always for post–World War II period	Yes, in most cases, but not in the flexible rate period	Yes, in 10 of 15 cases for DM-base currencies

(table continues next page)

Table 1 Characteristics of studies of purchasing power parity (continued)

Characteristic	Liu	McNown and Wallace	Patel
Period studied			
Fixed parities			
Flexible exchange rates	X	X	X
1920s			
Pre–World War II			
Specifications			
$[s, p, p^*]$	X		X
$[s, (p - p^*)]$ or $[p, s \cdot p^*]$		X	
$[s - p + p^*]$		X	
Price index used			
Consumer price index	X	X	
Wholesale price index	X	X	X
Methods used			
OLS or GLS			
Engle-Granger Dickey-Fuller[a]	X	X	X[g]
Error correction model		X	
Johansen and Juselius	X		
Dickey-Fuller[a]		X	
One-time break			
Variance ratio			
Fractional integration			
Results			
Symmetry and proportionality?	found in fewer than half the cases	symmetry imposed; proportionality found in 3 of 4 cases	not tested
Stationary relationship between e, p, and p^*?	Yes, in 6 of 9 cases in Latin America	Yes, for high inflation economies with WPI	No, except for 3 of 15 currencies

Characteristic	Perron and Vogelsang	Pippenger	Taylor and McMahon
Period studied			
Fixed parities			
Flexible exchange rates		X	
1920s			X
Pre–World War II	X		
Specifications			
[s, p, p*]		X	
[s, (p − p*)] or [p, s · p*]		X	X
[s − p + p*]	X		X
Price index used			
Consumer price index	X		
Wholesale price index		X	X
Methods used			
OLS or GLS			
Engle-Granger Dickey-Fuller[a]		X	X
Error correction model			X
Johansen and Juselius			
Dickey-Fuller[a]		X	X
One-time break	X		
Variance ratio			
Fractional integration			
Results			
Symmetry and proportionality?	imposed	not tested	not tested
Stationary relationship between e, p, and p*?	Yes, with allowance for level shift in mean	Yes, for 7 of 9 Swiss franc-based currencies	Yes, in most cases except for pound sterling

OLS = ordinary least-squares; GLS = generalized least-squares
a. And augmented Dickey-Fuller.
b. F-tests for autocorrelation in the real exchange rate were used.
c. The flexible period is October 1950 to May 1960 for the Canadian dollar.
d. Absolute and relative purchasing power parity are tested.
e. The period under study is that of the gold standard.
f. GNP price deflator.
g. The Stock and Watson (1989) method for common trends was also used.

and Stock and Watson 1988). Briefly, classical hypothesis testing of equation (2) is inappropriate when the regressors are nonstationary because their variances do not converge to a constant. Reported standard errors will thus be underestimated. However, pure first-differencing of the data may also be inappropriate if the error term in equation (2) is not itself a unit root series.

The more recent methods of testing for purchasing power parity generally contrive a looser version of equation (2). Tests of coefficient restrictions may be absent; instead the emphasis is on whether the level of the exchange rate and domestic and foreign price series trend together, or are cointegrated. Cointegration is tested by examining whether deviations from the relationship between the exchange rate and price series tend to return to some fixed mean (i.e., are stationary) or whether they wander aimlessly about with no fixed mean (i.e., are nonstationary or contain a unit root). A finding in favor of cointegration leads to the conclusion that "long-run" purchasing power parity prevails. "Long-run" purchasing power parity means, in the cointegration context, that the exchange rate and the domestic and foreign price series bear a stable relationship over time. This concept of purchasing power parity does not require the real exchange rate to be constant; it admits fluctuations in the real exchange rate about a constant. Furthermore, no restrictions are placed on α or β.

Other, more recent tests of purchasing power parity address the stochastic behavior of the real exchange rate. These tests are in fact restricted versions of the cointegration tests. They implicitly constrain β in equation (2) to equal one, so that the behavior of the real exchange rate rather than an exchange rate–price relationship is studied. Like the cointegration tests, these tests are based on advances in the statistical theory of unit root processes. The tests seek to determine whether the real exchange rate behaves as a unit root series. Evidence of unit root behavior in the real exchange rate emerges if the real exchange rate appears to wander aimlessly (i.e., is nonstationary) with no obvious mean. If this is the case, purchasing power parity is rejected, since at a minimum it requires the real exchange rate to fluctuate about some constant. Evidence against unit root behavior emerges when the real exchange rate appears to fluctuate about a fixed mean (constant) with a tendency to return to it (i.e., is stationary). In this case, long-run purchasing power parity is confirmed.

Parts A and B of figure 1 illustrate an exchange rate–price relationship that would statistically confirm long-run purchasing power parity. The figures depict an exchange rate and a relative price series that are cointegrated. Although departures from the theorized relationship occur, they do not appear to wander further and further away over time. Parts C and D of the figure, by way of contrast, depict an exchange rate and a relative price series that would likely not be cointegrated. Long-run

Figure 1 Cointegration and noncointegration

$$s_t = \alpha + \beta(p_t - p_t^*) + u_t$$

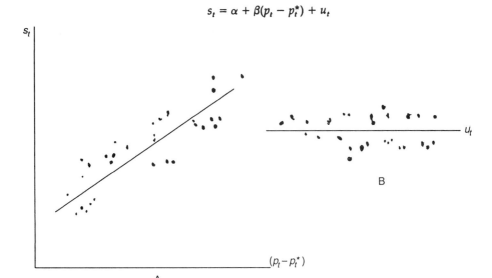

Cointegrated series: long-run purchasing power parity confirmed

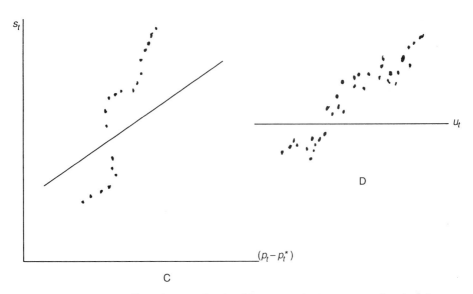

Noncointegrated series: long-run purchasing power parity rejected

purchasing power parity would be rejected. The figure shows the departures from the theorized relationship to be getting ever larger over time, with no tendency to return to it. Graphs similar to those in parts B and D could be drawn for the real exchange rate with similar conclusions.

The following section offers a discussion of recent econometric techniques and their application to purchasing power parity. The table summarizes works from the 1980s and 1990s, but section four ("Results of Recent Studies of Purchasing Power Parity") is a review of work done from 1990 on. Readers familiar with the econometrics of cointegration and unit root tests and with many of the recent studies may wish to skip the next two sections.

Recent Methods for Testing Purchasing Power Parity

Cointegration

Engle and Granger (1987) define a set of nonstationary series, integrated of the same order, to be cointegrated when some linear combination of them produces a series that is stationary. Less technically, if a set of nonstationary series share common trends so that the trends cancel out when linearly combined, they are cointegrated.

Consider the matrix $X_t = [x_{1t}, x_{2t}, \ldots, x_{pt}]$, which includes a total of p dependent and independent variables, each of which is nonstationary. If the linear combination, $u_t = AX_t$, is stationary with matrix A of nonzero rank less than p, then the column vectors of X_t are cointegrated. That is, if $u_t = \rho u_{t-1} + \epsilon_t$, where $|\rho| < 1.0$ so that u_t is stationary, the series are cointegrated. On the other hand, if $\rho = 1.0$ so that u_t is nonstationary, the series are *not* cointegrated. Notice that cointegration does not preclude serial correlation of u_t.

The rank of the matrix A reveals the number of cointegrating relationships. If the rank of $A = p$, then each series is individually stationary so that cointegration is not an issue; on the other hand, if the rank of $A = 0$, the series are not cointegrated. When the rank of $A < p$, the series are cointegrated where the rank determines the number of cointegrating relationships. For example, if rank of $A = p - 1$, the vectors of X_t are pairwise cointegrated. That is, any pair of series will form a cointegrating relationship. If the rank of $A = 1$, each vector of X_t must be present before a jointly stationary relationship emerges.

The Engle-Granger and Error Correction Tests for Cointegration

Engle-Granger tests of cointegration can be performed in several ways. The Engle-Granger two-step test is the original test for cointegration.

The test applies either the standard or the augmented Dickey-Fuller test for a unit root to the residual from the first-stage "cointegrating regression" of the levels of the variables. For purchasing power parity studies where $X_t = [s_t, p_t, p_t^*]$ and each series is nonstationary, the cointegrating regression, using the logarithms of the exchange rate and domestic and foreign price series, is:

$$s_t = \alpha + \beta_1 p_t + \beta_2 p_t^* + u_t. \tag{3}$$

Depending on the specification used, β_1 may or may not be set equal to $-\beta_2$. Additionally, $\beta_1 = -\beta_2$ may be set equal to 1.[3] The restrictions amount to imposing symmetry and proportionality on the coefficient values. Cheung and Lai (1993a) point out that the imposition of symmetry and proportionality may affect conclusions about cointegration. They favor the least restrictive version for testing long-run purchasing power parity. However, as equation (1) shows, the traditional interpretation of purchasing power parity requires symmetry and proportionality.

The augmented Dickey-Fuller test for cointegration is:

$$\Delta u_t = \theta u_{t-1} + \Sigma_i \eta_i \Delta u_{t-1-i} + \epsilon_t. \tag{4}$$

The Dickey-Fuller test does not include lags of Δu_t. These tests examine whether $\theta = 0$, which is equivalent to testing for a unit root in u_t (i.e., $\rho = 1$).[4] If the hypothesis that $\theta = 0$ cannot be rejected, the exchange rate and the domestic and foreign price series are *not* cointegrated. The existence of a long-run relationship would be rejected. Engle and Yoo (1987) provide the critical values. Some studies report the closely related Phillips-Perron Z statistics, which take account of possible autocorrelation and heteroskedasticity.

An alternative test for cointegration can be performed using an error correction model. The error correction representation theorem (Granger 1983) states that for cointegrated series there exists an error correction representation:

$$\lambda(1-L)X_t = \phi u_{t-1} + \epsilon_t, \tag{5}$$

where $(1 - L)$ is the difference operator, λ contains the coefficients of the dependent and explanatory variables; $\phi \neq 0$, and u_{t-1} is the "equilib-

---

3. The cointegrating regression cannot be used to draw inferences about β_1 and β_2, since p and p^* are nonstationary, so their standard errors will not be asymptotically convergent; however, the parameter estimates of equation (3) will be superconsistent (Stock 1987) if u_t is stationary.

4. The test specification is equivalent to $u_t = \rho u_{t-1} + \Sigma_i \eta_i \Delta u_{t-1-i} + \epsilon_t$ since $\theta = 1 - \rho$.

rium error'' or ''error correction mechanism.'' The error correction representation of equation (3) is[5]:

$$\Delta s_t = \gamma + \lambda_1 \Delta p_t + \lambda_2 \Delta p_t^* + \phi u_{t-1} + v_t. \tag{6}$$

The error correction model may include lagged differences of s_t, p_t, and p_t^* to correct for any serial correlation in the error term v_t. Cointegration demands that the coefficient on u_{t-1} be nonzero. An inability to reject $\phi = 0$ means that the exchange rate and the domestic and foreign price series are not cointegrated. Kremers et al. (1992) recommend this test because of the implicit common factor restriction in the Dickey-Fuller and augmented Dickey-Fuller tests.

In the error correction representation, the adjustment of the levels of the exchange rate and domestic and foreign prices to their long-run equilibrium relationship is captured in u_{t-1}. The short-run dynamics are captured by the deviations of the variables (Δ) from their means. Since the error correction model comprises stationary variables, classical inference can be conducted.

The error correction model also shows that pure first-differencing of equation (2) would be potentially misspecified since it would omit the error correction term u_{t-1}. On the other hand, if u_t is a unit root series, then $[s_t, p_t, p_t^*]$ are not cointegrated, and pure first-differencing of all variables, including u_t, is appropriate.[6] In this case a first-differenced specification may be correct from a statistical perspective; however, purchasing power parity at a minimum obligates $[s_t, p_t, p_t^*]$ to share an underlying trend. Without cointegration, it may seem senseless to test for an alternative conception of purchasing power parity.

A drawback of the Engle-Granger method is that it does not estimate the number of cointegrating relationships among the p variables (of which there are three in this case). It has been applied primarily for bivariate systems. Another drawback is the inability to test inferences about the estimates of $\mathbf{A}$. Finally, the test also imposes an implicit normalization, since the researcher must choose which variable will be dependent.

The Johansen-Juselius Test for Cointegration

The Johansen (1988) and Johansen-Juselius (1990) method is a maximum likelihood procedure that uses canonical correlations to extract inferences about the number of cointegrating relationships. An inability to

---

5. In some studies, $X_t = [s_t, (p_t - p_t^*)]$, so the error correction representation would enter the price variable in relative format.

6. To see this, let $u_t = u_{t-1} + v_t$. Substitute for u_{t-1} using equation (3), lagged, and rearrange to get $\Delta s_t = \beta_1 \Delta p_t + \beta_2 \Delta p_t^* + v_t$. The result contains no error correction term.

reject the null hypothesis of zero cointegrating vectors means the absence of cointegration. The procedure also permits hypothesis testing of the parameters of **A**. It also avoids arbitrary normalizations. The method has been gaining popularity, although its use is somewhat limited since many standard statistical packages do not carry the method as an option.

The Johansen-Juselius method is used more frequently in multivariate settings. However, the results are often sensitive to the number of lags used in the estimation. Typically, researchers will perform the estimation trying different lag lengths to ensure that the results are robust. Also, the method often produces parameter estimates of **A** that are quite large and may seem at odds with a priori hypotheses. A detailed discussion is beyond the scope of this paper. The reader is referred to the references cited above.

Dickey-Fuller and Augmented Dickey-Fuller Tests for Stationarity of the Real Exchange Rate

The Dickey-Fuller (1979) and augmented Dickey-Fuller (1981) tests for a unit root, discussed above, can be adapted to test for nonstationarity in the real exchange rate r_t, defined as $(s_t - p_t + p_t^*)$. The real exchange rate is equivalent to the residual u_t in equation (3) when the restrictions $\alpha = 0$ and $\beta_1 = -\beta_2 = 1$ are imposed. As with the tests for cointegration between s_t, p_t, and p_t^*, some tests report Phillips-Perron Z statistics since they are more robust to autocorrelation and heteroskedasticity.

The test specification is:

$$\Delta r_t = \alpha + \delta t + \theta r_{t-1} + \Sigma_i \eta_i \Delta r_{t-1-i} + v_t, \tag{7}$$

where t is a time trend. Lags of Δr_t may be necessary to ensure that v_t is white noise. The null hypothesis is that $\theta = 0$, which implies that the real exchange rate contains a unit root.

At issue in these tests is whether the real exchange rate is a random walk (unit root series) or is stationary.[7] If the null hypothesis of $\theta = 0$ cannot be rejected, the real exchange rate is considered a random walk. Critical values from Fuller (1976, table 8.5.2) must be used. Random walk behavior means that the real exchange rate is the outcome of a sequence of real shocks, each of which permanently alters the level of the real exchange rate. That is, there is no tendency for the real exchange rate to return, however slowly, to its mean or trend. Consequently, purchasing power parity cannot hold. On the other hand, rejecting ran-

---

7. Cumby and Obstfeld (1984) offer perhaps the earliest attempt at discerning whether the real exchange rate is nonstationary. They apply the Ljung and Box Q-test at up to 12 lags to monthly series of the real exchange rate. They find evidence of nonstationarity.

dom walk behavior means neither that the real exchange rate is a fixed constant nor that deviations about the constant are independent and identically distributed, but only that it is a stationary stochastic process with some degree of reversion to a mean value.

Perron-Type Tests

Perron (1989) criticizes unit root tests on the grounds that a series that is stationary about a trend with a one-time structural break mimics the behavior of a unit root series. Thus, the power of unit root tests to distinguish between alternative hypotheses may be low. Perron's work was meant to be applied to pure economic time series such as the real exchange rate or GNP, but his point also applies to "generated" series such as the cointegrating regression residual u_t (although modification of critical values would be necessary).

Perron recommended detrending a series with allowance for a level shift and/or change in trend. The researcher may impose the date for the breakpoint based on a priori information, or may estimate the breakpoint as in Perron and Vogelsang (1992). Dummy variables are introduced to the Dickey-Fuller or augmented Dickey-Fuller test to capture these changes.

Zivot and Andrews (1992) and Christiano (1992) have since argued that the critical values offered in Perron are too low because the researcher preselects the date at which the structural break may have occurred. They suggest that the data be allowed to pick the structural breakpoint. Their method requires recursive estimation. Breakpoints ranging from $[2, \ldots, T - 1]$ are tested. The natural breakpoint is the one that maximizes (in absolute value) the test statistic on which unit root behavior is assessed. In theory, the estimated date for the break would match the researcher's a priori hypothesis about the date for the structural break. The value of the "maximum" test statistic is compared with the critical values provided in Zivot and Andrews (1992). If the test statistic exceeds (in absolute terms) the critical value, then it is concluded that the real exchange rate is not a unit root but rather stationary about a trend with a one-time break.

Variance Ratio Tests

Variance ratio tests provide another test for long-run purchasing power parity. Cochrane (1988) first introduced variance ratio tests for GNP. Variance ratio tests complement unit root tests as another way of detecting random walk behavior. They exploit the fact that the variance of the first difference of a unit root series grows proportionally with the time separating two observations. For example, $\mathrm{var}(y_{t+1} - y_t) = \sigma^2$ whereas $\mathrm{var}(y_{t+k} - y_t) = k \cdot \sigma^2$. Thus, for a unit root series, $\mathrm{var}(y_{t+k} - y_t)/k \cdot$

$\text{var}(y_{t+1} - y_t) = 1$ for any $k = 1, \ldots, T$.[8] On the other hand, for a stationary white noise series or one with negative autocorrelation, the ratio approaches zero as k approaches infinity. A stationary series with positive serial correlation will have a variance ratio greater than one. Thus, the behavior of the variance ratio reveals information about the stochastic behavior of a series. Like the Dickey-Fuller and augmented Dickey-Fuller tests and the Perron-type tests, the variance ratio tests are typically conducted for the real exchange rate.

Fractional Cointegration Tests

Fractional cointegration tests of purchasing power parity apply fractional integration analysis to the cointegrating regression residual (or equilibrium error) between the exchange rate and the domestic and foreign price series. Fractional integration tests entertain a broader range of alternative hypotheses to the unit root hypothesis. The alternative hypotheses admit integration of order less than one but greater than or equal to zero. A series that is integrated of order d where $0 < d < 1$ is fractionally integrated. Consequently, fractionally integrated series exhibit reversion to a mean, but at a much slower rate than a stationary series. Moreover, the covariance may or may not be stationary depending on the magnitude of d. Fractional cointegration also provides information about the percentage of a permanent or real shock that is responsible for keeping the series away from its mean after x months.

Cheung and Lai (1993b) find that the tests tend to have more power than augmented Dickey-Fuller tests in detecting mean reversion, particularly for $0.35 < d < 0.65$. Fractional integration methods rely on spectral analysis and have not yet been widely employed. Furthermore, the proper error correction representation has yet to be developed.

Results of Recent Studies of Purchasing Power Parity

This section reviews studies of purchasing power parity published in the 1990s that use any one or more of the estimation techniques discussed in the preceding section. The studies also vary in the currencies they examine and the time periods they consider. The studies selected for this review are those that, in at least one instance, find cointegration between the exchange rate and the domestic and foreign price series or stationarity of the real exchange rate, with the conclusion that long-run purchasing power parity holds. These studies thus offer evidence that

---

8. The variance ratio estimator is biased in small samples. Cochrane (1988) provides the correction.

may be regarded as a contradiction to the premise of the authors in this volume, namely, that the real exchange rate may change over time so that purchasing power parity does not hold.

The emphasis in this section on studies that find evidence of long-run purchasing power parity is not meant to validate the results; in fact, the next section will offer an assessment of the newer methods and the findings obtained through their use. It is worth mentioning that the evidence reviewed below for or against cointegration between the exchange rate and the domestic and foreign price series or stationarity of the real exchange rate is only a part of a body of research investigating purchasing power parity with the use of newer econometric techniques. Indeed, many newer studies find to the contrary, and others produce mixed results, depending on the currency studied, the time period considered, the test specification used, or the estimation method invoked.[9] A judicious review would likely conclude that no consensus has yet emerged.

Reader Beware

The studies of purchasing power parity discussed below offer a subtle but important change in interpretation from earlier studies that tested levels and first-differenced formulations of purchasing power parity by testing coefficient restrictions. In earlier work, satisfaction of coefficient restrictions played a central role in evaluating purchasing power parity. Also, the earlier studies explicitly tested whether the real exchange rate was a constant.

As already mentioned, many of the recent studies of purchasing power parity focus on the stochastic behavior of the regression error in equation (3) without requiring that coefficient restrictions be satisfied. That is, in equation (3), α may be nonzero and β_1 and β_2 may be different from $[1, -1]$. Absent the coefficient restrictions, the traditional conception of purchasing power parity set out in equation (1) is not really being tested. (Edison et al. 1994 also make this point.) For example, if cointegration is determined between the exchange rate and the domestic and foreign price series, yet the coefficient restrictions on the βs are not obeyed, then the exchange rate's value is not fully accounted for by the purchasing power of the domestic and foreign currencies. Recent studies that test for the stationarity of the real exchange rate impose the coefficient restrictions but do not test whether the real exchange rate is a constant through all time; rather they test whether there is reversion back to a fixed value.

---

9. Numerous studies that have tested purchasing power parity using cointegration methods failed to detect cointegration. See table 1 in this paper and Edison et al. (1994), Fisher and Park (1991), Mark (1990), Baillie and Selover (1987), and Edison (1985).

The review below considers the work of Abuaf and Jorion (1990), Cheung and Lai (1993a, b), Glen (1992), Grilli and Kaminsky (1991), Kim (1990), Kugler and Lenz (1993), Liu (1993), Perron and Vogelsang (1992), and Pippenger (1993). A critical evaluation of the studies is then presented and a possible reconciliation offered.

Abuaf and Jorion (1990)

Abuaf and Jorion (1990) apply Dickey-Fuller and augmented Dickey-Fuller tests in a seemingly unrelated regression framework. Their data span two periods: 1973–87 and 1900–72. The real exchange rate is constructed using the consumer price index. Currencies of 10 industrialized countries are studied. The US dollar is the base currency. Their results using the data spanning 1900–72 reject the random walk. For the 1973–87 data set, random walk behavior is rejected when the critical values are adjusted for a nonzero constant. Their evidence suggests that the real exchange rate tends to revert to a mean value.

Cheung and Lai (1993a)

Cheung and Lai (1993a) use the Johansen-Juselius method for the trivariate system $[s_t, p_t, p_t^*]$. The method imposes neither the symmetry nor the proportionality restriction discussed above. Cheung and Lai do, however, test the restrictions. For the sake of comparison, Cheung and Lai redo the estimation for the bivariate system $[s_t, (p_t - p_t^*)]$. They also perform augmented Dickey-Fuller tests for a unit root in the real exchange rate. A comparison of the methods illustrates the dramatic change in results when the symmetry and/or the proportionality restriction is imposed. Their data cover 1974–89 and five industrialized-country currencies, with the US dollar as the base currency. They report results for both the consumer price index and the wholesale price index.

Cheung and Lai report evidence of cointegration for all five currencies. They reject the hypothesis of zero cointegrating vectors. In some cases they reject the hypothesis of one cointegrating vector in favor of two, meaning that the exchange rate and the domestic and foreign price series are pairwise cointegrated. The coefficient estimates of β_1 and β_2—see equation (3)—vary from a low of 1.035 to 25.422 when the consumer price index is used, and from 0.35 to 11.414 when the wholesale price index is used. In all cases, except for the dollar-pound rate using the wholesale price index, proportionality is rejected. In four out of five cases symmetry is rejected when the consumer price index is used and in three out of five cases when the wholesale price index is used.

Edison et al. (1994) show that the critical values used to test the symmetry and proportionality restrictions may be too low and thereby lead to too-frequent rejection of the restrictions. They find several cases contrary to those reported by Cheung and Lai; however, their data set extends to 1992 whereas that of Cheung and Lai does not. On the other hand, Edison et al. also show that the critical values used by Cheung and Lai may be too low and lead to more frequent rejection of "no cointegration," and thus in favor of long-run purchasing power parity.

Cheung and Lai compare these results with results using bivariate and univariate specifications. For the univariate real exchange rate, which imposes the symmetry and proportionality restrictions, they find that unit root behavior cannot be rejected for the real exchange rate, regardless of the price index used. Their results sharply contrast with those obtained when the restrictions are relaxed. Results from the bivariate specifications are more similar to those from the trivariate specification.

Cheung and Lai (1993b)

Cheung and Lai (1993b) apply fractional integration methods to the cointegrating regression residual from a bivariate specification with the domestic price series as the dependent variable. Their data are annual and span 1914–89. Subperiods are also investigated. The authors study five industrialized-country currencies, with the US dollar as the base. The price series used is the consumer price index. Cheung and Lai determine that the cointegrating regression residual over the full sample is fractionally integrated such that reversion to a mean exists and "no cointegration" is rejected. Their results support cointegration for the full sample. For the subsamples, long-run purchasing power parity is rejected since order 1 integration (unit root behavior) could not be rejected.

Glen (1992)

Glen (1992) employs variance ratio tests to study long-run purchasing power parity. He uses monthly data for the post–Bretton Woods era and annual data spanning 1900–87. He compares the results for the real exchange rate computed with the consumer price index and with the wholesale price index. Nine exchange rates of industrialized countries against the dollar are examined, as well as two cross rates. For the flexible-rate era, Glen finds that as the time separating observations increases from 2 to 32 months, more rejections of random walk behavior are compiled so that, at longer horizons, reversion to the mean prevails. The Canadian dollar is the only currency for which random walk behavior is not rejected. The variance ratio statistics indicate mean reversion albeit with strong positive serial correlation.[10]

10. Huizanga (1987) reaches similar conclusions for a much shorter time span. He per-

Grilli and Kaminsky (1991)

Grilli and Kaminsky (1991) study the real dollar-pound exchange rate computed from the wholesale price index. Their data are annual and span 1885–1986. Their sample spans various exchange rate regimes: the gold standard, fixed rates, flexible rates, and the interwar period. They report Phillips-Perron Z statistics over the full sample and over nine subsamples. They also report variance ratio test statistics.

Grilli and Kaminsky reject random walk behavior of the real exchange rate for the full sample but not for the subsamples using the Z statistics. Thus, stationarity of the real exchange rate is supported over a century. Frankel (1986) reaches similar conclusions for the dollar-pound exchange rate using a long span of data. Variance ratio tests suggest similar conclusions. However, using the variance ratio tests, the authors find that the real exchange rate is a random walk for the post–World War II subperiods, except where the time separating observations is 48 months or less. The result seems counterintuitive, since we might expect reversion to a mean to be more easily detected over longer horizons. The results are also opposite to Glen's findings about the length of time separating observations.

Kim (1990)

Kim (1990) compares several different tests for long-run purchasing power parity. Using the Phillips-Perron Z statistics, he tests for a unit root in the real exchange rates of five currencies of industrialized countries. He also uses the Engle-Granger test for a unit root in the cointegrating regression residual from a bivariate specification. Finally, he estimates an error correction model and tests for the significance of the equilibrium error term as a way of detecting long-run purchasing power parity. He compares results for the consumer price index with those from the wholesale price index. His data roughly cover 1900–87. He also examines subperiods.

Kim finds the real exchange rate to be stationary when the wholesale price index is used for all five currencies. However, when the consumer price index is used instead, only the French franc–dollar rate is stationary. Thus, cointegration is detected more frequently when the wholesale price index is used at least with the univariate specification. The Engle-Granger method for the bivariate specification is also used. In four of five cases cointegration is confirmed using the wholesale price index.

---

forms the equivalent of variance ratio tests by applying spectral analysis to real exchange rates using monthly data from 1974 to 1986. Plots of the variance ratios suggest strong reversion to the mean at horizons of four years or longer. However, statistical tests do not reject unit root behavior. Huizanga argues that the large standard deviations make detection of a unit root debatable. He concludes in favor of reversion to a mean.

Results from the error correction model find the same thing. The Engle-Granger method detects cointegration in only two of five cases when the consumer price index is used.

Kim's findings suggest, at least for a bivariate specification, that the wholesale price index is a better guide to the long-run purchasing power exchange rate.

Kugler and Lenz (1993)

Kugler and Lenz (1993) use the Johansen-Juselius method for determining whether long-run purchasing power parity holds for bilateral exchange rates between the deutsche mark and the currencies of 15 industrialized countries. Kugler and Lenz test for the number of cointegrating vectors in a trivariate specification of purchasing power parity and also test the symmetry and proportionality restrictions. They also show that the results are sensitive to the lag length selected for the estimation. Their study covers 1973–90; the consumer price index is used.

Kugler and Lenz find cointegration for 10 currencies regardless of the lag length selected. For six of the currencies, the symmetry and proportionality restrictions are not rejected. These results contrast with the findings of Cheung and Lai (1993a), although the exchange rates Cheung and Lai studied were bilateral dollar rates and the sample period differed by one year. For the remaining five currencies, mixed results were obtained depending on the lag length used in the estimation. Kugler and Lenz conclude that long-run purchasing power parity prevails against the deutsche mark for a number of currencies, not all of which participate in the European Monetary System.

Liu (1993)

Liu (1993) studies long-run purchasing power parity for nine Latin American countries using quarterly data spanning the period from the late 1940s to 1989. He presents results for the consumer and wholesale price indexes and for various lag lengths used in the augmented Dickey-Fuller and Phillips-Perron test statistics applied to the cointegrating regression residual. A trivariate specification is used where the domestic price series is regressed on the exchange rate and the foreign price series. The specification is appropriate for Latin American countries, which typically retain some control over the nominal exchange rate. The Johansen-Juselius method is also used to test for cointegration. Four lags are specified.

For the wholesale price index, evidence of cointegration is found for two of the six currencies for which wholesale price data were available.

For the consumer price index, results for four of the nine currencies provide evidence of cointegration. Occasionally, conclusions from the augmented Dickey-Fuller and Z statistics contradict each other. Results from the Johansen method, which does not rely on any normalization, indicate cointegration for all cases regardless of the price index; the null hypothesis of zero cointegrating vectors is rejected using the trace test. However, Kim's results from the maximum eigenvalue test, which compares the null of r cointegrating vectors against $r + 1$ and so on, provide contradictory conclusions of no cointegration except for Venezuela.

Perron and Vogelsang (1992)

Perron and Vogelsang (1992) investigate whether the real exchange rate is stationary about a trend, with a shift in level (change in intercept or mean) occurring at an unknown date. They examine the real exchange rate for the pound sterling and the Finnish markka against the US dollar. They compare results from the consumer price index with those from a GNP deflator. Their data are annual and span more than a century. They estimate a shift in level to occur in 1937 for the Finnish data and in 1943 for the British data when an instantaneous change in the mean is modeled. When the change is modeled to be gradual, the break for the Finnish data occurs in 1945 and for the British data in 1944. In each case Perron and Vogelsang reject the random walk hypothesis in favor of a real exchange rate that is stationary about a one-time change in the real exchange rate's mean. Oddly, they conclude that long-run purchasing power parity has been maintained despite the contradiction posed by the finding that the real exchange rate changed.

Pippenger (1993)

Pippenger (1993) examines the exchange rates of nine currencies of industrialized countries against the Swiss franc. The wholesale price index is used to compute the real exchange rate. His data cover 1973–88. He rejects random walk behavior of the real exchange rate for four of the nine currencies (using a 5 percent marginal significance level). Thus, his results favor long-run purchasing power parity for a select set of countries. A test of the cointegrating regression residual from a bivariate specification, although more general, yields identical conclusions. When a trivariate specification is tested, cointegration is detected for seven of the nine currencies. Like Cheung and Lai, Pippenger finds more evidence in favor of cointegration when the most general specification is used.

Long-Run Purchasing Power Parity as the Equilibrium Exchange Rate: An Assessment

A discernible pattern emerges from the more recent studies. Cointegration between the exchange rate and domestic and foreign price series and stationarity of the real exchange rate are more apt to be confirmed for studies that meet two of four conditions: When the span of data is long enough to capture a statistical equilibrium relationship, typically 70 or more years; when the trivariate specification that does not impose symmetry and proportionality is used; when bilateral exchange rates other than against the US dollar are used; and when the countries studied experienced rapid periods of inflation or deflation. Rejections of purchasing power parity occur most frequently for the flexible exchange rate era. But do findings of cointegration constrain the real rate to be fixed, and do they establish the "equilibrium" nominal and real rates?

An Evaluation of and Answers from the Extant Literature

A review of the extant literature (excluding the essays covered in this volume) points to a "yes" answer, but only by presumption. Most studies of purchasing power parity begin with the assumption that the purchasing power rate k is a constant, defined as the long-run equilibrium rate. Some studies prefer to couch purchasing power parity in terms of the real exchange rate and assume that it is a constant, defined as the long-run equilibrium real rate. However, since more recent studies emphasize purchasing power parity as a long-run concept, the real exchange rate need only be stationary rather than fixed. Stationarity compels the real exchange rate to return to its mean in the long run. The mean is considered the long-run equilibrium rate, which is fixed.[11] Lengthy and sizable departures from it may arise. Thus, the model of long-run purchasing power parity admits changes in the real exchange rate but not in its mean.

The studies that confirm a stationary relationship between the exchange rate and domestic and foreign price series (i.e., cointegration) where symmetry and proportionality have not been imposed, as they are in the studies of real exchange rate stationarity, are not truly testing long-run purchasing power parity. The cointegrating regression residual has been referred to as the real exchange rate in these studies. But without the coefficient restrictions implied by purchasing power parity being imposed, it is hard to interpret the significance of the finding of cointegration.

Additionally, the parlance of cointegration uses the term "equilibrium" to refer to any user-defined model. A finding of cointegration between x, y, and z is interpreted to mean that the series obey an equilibrium relationship, however defined and regardless of whether x, y, and z reflect equilibrium in their own markets. For example, if I test for cointegration between the deutsche mark–dollar exchange rate and US and German incomes and discover they are indeed cointegrated, what

---

11. Perron and Vogelsang (1992) is an exception.

should I say about the finding? In the parlance of cointegration, I would say that the deutsche mark and US and German incomes obey a long-run equilibrium relationship. But that does not imply that the equilibrium exchange rate is defined by it. Cointegration defines an equilibrium on statistical grounds; economic structure should be relied upon for economic interpretation. This simple example illustrates how the terminology used to describe cointegration can be misleading and warns against singular interpretations.

Interpretation of a finding of cointegration between the exchange rate and domestic and foreign price series as an equilibrium may be further obscured by omitted stationary variables. A finding of cointegration between $[s_t, p_t, p_t^*]$ does not rule out a relationship with another stationary set of variables, such as oil prices, fiscal policies, or deviations from full employment, in addition to or exclusive of the domestic and foreign price series. Cointegration tests are not specifically designed to address this possibility.

Furthermore, the studies discussed above, in addition to those listed in table 1, define the purchasing power rate by the ratio of the foreign to the domestic price series, using the actual price series without regard to whether the price series in each country reflects a desired equilibrium. For example, numerous studies (e.g., Taylor and McMahon 1988, Frenkel 1981) confirm purchasing power parity during the period of hyperinflation in Germany during the 1920s, although few would claim that the nominal and real exchange rates were the outcome of an underlying macroeconomic equilibrium.

Even if there was macroeconomic equilibrium, the *observed* or *actual* exchange rate may deviate from the *desired* or *sustainable* or *fundamental* equilibrium level.[12] Indeed, the monetary model of exchange rate determination takes purchasing power parity as a building block. Relative purchasing power is determined by relative money supplies and demands at home and abroad. The model, however, does not make the distinction between whether purchasing power defined by the money market represents a "desired" as distinct from "actual" equilibrium. In general, the literature on purchasing power parity does not address the distinction between actual and desired—a point articulated by Bayoumi et al. in this volume. Consequently, purchasing power parity has remained as the ready-made yardstick for assessing the "equilibrium" exchange rate. Its simplicity may be both its appeal and its shortcoming.

The list of explanations that have been offered for rejection of purchasing power parity is also telling, if only because none of the explanations challenge the validity of the purchasing power rate as a measure of the long-run equilibrium rate. Rejections of purchasing power parity have

---

12. The terms "desired," "sustainable," and "fundamental" are used interchangeably here.

been attributed to transportation costs, measurement error, price stickiness, simultaneous equations bias, and, more recently, imposition of stringent coefficient restrictions and a span of history too short to capture long-run equilibrating forces. These explanations tacitly adhere to the belief that purchasing power parity would be upheld "if only. . . ."

A Cursory Review of Alternatives

The papers in this volume, in contrast, assume that the actual exchange rate (real or nominal) is not necessarily a desired or a sustainable equilibrium outcome—a position against which a good bit of debate may arise. To draw a parallel, one need only consider the debate regarding the stochastic behavior of output and whether its actual path is a desired path.

The papers in this volume forgo the notion that domestic relative to foreign purchasing powers establish the long-run equilibrium nominal rate and force the real exchange rate to be stationary, let alone a constant, strictly equal to one. The models instead include factors additional to purchasing powers in calculating the desired or fundamental equilibrium nominal exchange rate. The real exchange rate also responds to these factors. The models characterize an equilibrium where internal and external balance obtain and are sustainable. They are necessarily intertemporal. Calculation of the desired equilibrium exchange rate not only requires assessing what factors affect the exchange rate but also extracting their desired equilibrium values. Reaching agreement on the desired equilibrium values complicates the task.[13] The models may or may not be equivalent to structural exchange rate models. (See the papers by Edwards and Elbadawi, in chapters 3 and 4.) Structural models seek to explain actual exchange rate movements, not equilibrium paths, although their foundations are closely related to the models developed in this volume.

The models also challenge the fixity of the real exchange rate—a corollary of Cassel's idea about the *nominal* value of a currency that is much more difficult to embrace, and the ramifications of which have largely gone unchallenged. The models in this volume assume that the real exchange rate need not be constant. The time path of the equilibrium real exchange rate may change if the equilibrium of the underlying fundamentals that determine it changes. In fact, Stein (chapter 5) argues that the real exchange rate inherits the properties of the underlying fundamentals: if they are stationary, so will be the real exchange rate; if they are not, neither will be the exchange rate. The papers by Edwards and Elbadawi, by construction, do not necessarily contradict purchasing

---

13. The paper by Bayoumi et al. demonstrates the range of desired equilibrium real exchange rates produced with various plausible desired fundamental values.

power parity. They define the real exchange rate as the nominal rate multiplied by the ratio of importable (or traded) to nontraded goods prices. Structural changes could, in consequence, change the real exchange rate without contradicting purchasing power parity.

A Reconciliation

The Casselian purchasing power parity model of the equilibrium real rate as a fixed constant, equal to one or some constant scalar, can be reconciled with the newer interpretation of real exchange rate stationarity and with the alternative models offered in this volume that permit fluctuations in the equilibrium real exchange rate, if one treats the latter two as models of episodic equilibrium departures from a fixed, "ultra-long-run" real exchange rate.[14] Suppose 14 historical episodes each spanning five years are identified in the latter models across which the equilibrium real exchange rate changes. Fourteen episodes of five years each add up to 70 years, the time period identified in many studies over which real exchange rate stationarity is confirmed. During each five-year episode the real exchange rate may fluctuate about its intra-episodic mean. Nonstationarity within some of the episodes need not be ruled out. If the mean of the equilibrium real exchange rate across the episodes turns out to equal one (or some constant scalar), with the condition that the episodes evolve about the mean in a stationary fashion when the 70–year time frame is considered, then purchasing power parity and episodic changes in the equilibrium exchange rate may be construed as consistent. That is, despite structural changes through time, the tendency may be to revert to the purchasing power rate in the ultra-long run.

The reconciliation implies that the ultra-long-run real exchange rate is that which emerges after the effects of all real shocks either have been negated or have dissipated. A sequence of real shocks that, *ceteris paribus*, would permanently alter the real exchange rate may *jointly over time* have no discernible impact on the real exchange rate—that is, they negate each other. For example, one real shock may today push the real exchange rate away from its purchasing power level, with its effect permanent until another real shock returns the real exchange rate back to its purchasing power level. The simplicity of the story, however, belies the statistical sophistication needed to discern the mix of shocks that over time produce the purchasing power outcome.

The interpretation of the ultra-long run as one over which all real shocks have jointly negated each other presents a twist on the older

---

14. The term was suggested by John Williamson. The newer interpretations of purchasing power parity that rely on cointegration tests that do not impose symmetry and proportionality will not be addressed, since they present a clear departure from traditional purchasing power parity.

view, which recognizes that purchasing power parity is about nominal relationships, which are more likely to prevail in the absence of *permanent* changes in real factors. However, the older view also affords a reconciliation between the newer interpretations of purchasing power parity and the Casselian construct. In the older view, purchasing power parity would be observed in the long run if each and every real shock were temporary. Temporary behavior requires only that the effects of the shock completely vanish over some time horizon; no conditions are placed on the pace of dissipation. Thus, the newer interpretations of purchasing power parity that require real exchange rate stationarity can be said to fit the Casselian interpretation. As well, the models introduced in this volume produce real exchange rate fluctuations that may be enduring.

In either case, purchasing power parity offers an ultra-long-run view of the equilibrium real exchange rate, whereas the alternatives presented in this volume present a medium- to long-run view. In fact, the distinction between ultra-long run and long run is not inane. Fractional cointegration models of the real exchange rate capture the distinction precisely (see Dueker 1993). Fractional cointegration admits that the real exchange rate reverts to a mean, but very gradually, so that purchasing power parity may be violated over the long run but not in the ultra-long run. Fractional cointegration recognizes that the size and mix of nominal and real factors influence the evolution of the real exchange rate over time.

Conclusion

Cassel's concept of purchasing power parity has, for the past 70 years, influenced thinking about what constitutes the equilibrium value of a currency. His idea has also spawned an academic industry to test it empirically. The academic profligacy directed at purchasing power parity may not be surprising when several factors are considered: the broad availability of exchange rate and price data and their relative ease of acquisition; distinct historical episodes that provide a nice laboratory for comparative exercises; and, perhaps most significant, the concept's intuitive appeal juxtaposed against what had been an increasingly frequent rejection of it, at least through the late 1980s.

As econometric practices have advanced, confirmations of a stationary relationship between the exchange rate and the domestic and foreign price series have become increasingly frequent and have been regarded as confirmations of long-run purchasing power parity. But the latest findings do not necessarily bear witness to the suitability of relative internal purchasing powers as the best measure of the equilibrium value of the nominal exchange rate or to the fixity of the real exchange rate. The newer interpretations of purchasing power parity represent weakenings of traditional or Casselian purchasing power parity. The weakenings have largely gone unacknowledged in the more recent studies (Edison et al. 1994 is an exception). Many of the more recent studies that claim to have supported long-run purchasing power parity have instead found support for a much weaker version of it. Unfortunately, the results have been interpreted to overturn the earlier (pre-late 1980s) consensus, based on estimation using ordinary and generalized least-squares techniques, rejecting Casselian purchasing power parity.

The first weakening was the distinction made between the short and the long run, where only the long run served as the basis for rejecting or confirming purchasing power parity. The distinction is not damaging; it has long been recognized that the influence of monetary versus real factors played a role in the purchasing power parity relationship. The short and the long run were distinguished by the interplay and eventual impact of monetary and real factors. The newer literature on purchasing power parity offers a statistical construct for making the distinction. Thus, the distinction between the short and the long run was made well prior to the newer literature on purchasing power parity, where the long run is defined in statistical terms.

A second and related point is that newer interpretations began to require stationarity of the real exchange rate, rather than fixity as required by traditional purchasing power parity. In this light, the real exchange rate fluctuates and may exhibit large and sustained deviations from its estimated mean as long as the deviations revert to the mean. The estimated mean is regarded as a purchasing power value, although the estimates may be far from the mean of unity required under absolute purchasing power parity. The weakening also implies that the effects of all shocks to the purchasing power parity relationship are either temporary or have, over time, negated each other so as to maintain purchasing power parity. Whereas the newer studies of purchasing power parity define "temporary" to be anything less than the "long run," I prefer "ultra-long run" since it conveys a time horizon over which the purchasing power rate is achieved. In the ultra-long run the real exchange rate may be thought of as fixed—all temporary fluctuations have subsided, and all permanent shocks have collectively offset each other. In the long run, fluctuations in the real exchange rate are permitted to be temporary but sizable and long-lasting, or to be permanent.

Third, most recently the coefficient restrictions implicit in the original conception of purchasing power parity have been disregarded. An absence of symmetry and proportionality as required under the traditional interpretation of purchasing power parity means that domestic relative to foreign prices do not fully account for the level of the nominal exchange rate, even in the long and the ultra-long run. This represents a fundamental change in the traditional meaning of purchasing power parity. Studies that use cointegration methods are most subject to this reinterpretation.

The weakenings make the newer interpretations of purchasing power parity a departure from the traditional construct. At the same time, the traditional construct of purchasing power parity at best presents a paradigm for a desired equilibrium exchange rate, but only in the ultra-long run, when the effects of real shocks have vanished. But does a finding that purchasing power parity holds in the ultra-long run necessarily confer upon purchasing power parity a pivotal role in guiding exchange rate policy? To be sure, the distinction between the long run and the ultra-long run is important in the policy realm. Pursuit of an equilibrium real exchange rate that emerges only in the ultra-long run may be misguided if there are important real factors that are driving the equilibrium real exchange rate away from its purchasing power rate for lengthy periods of time in the interim. Economic costs may be introduced that could be avoided with a better measure of the medium- to long-run equilibrium exchange rate. Such an equilibrium rate need not be a fixed target but rather one that moves in response to changes in desired internal and external conditions over the medium to long run.

The essays in this volume have made a persuasive argument against purchasing power parity's suitability as a guide to the long-run equilibrium exchange rate. They have developed exchange rate models predicated on desired equilibrium conditions using the concept of internal and external balance. The models permit changes in the desired equilibrium real exchange rate and thus depart from purchasing power parity's fixity of the equilibrium real exchange rate. However, the two conceptions of the equilibrium real exchange rate may be reconciled by considering purchasing power parity as an ultra-long run constraint in which the effects of real shocks have disappeared and by considering the exchange rate models developed in this volume as representations of the long run in which real shocks play a role.

What remain unclear at this stage are the objectives for computing a desired long-run equilibrium rate. Is it that a system of rates fixed at their desired long-run equilibria will ensure, through precommitment to the rate, desired internal and external outcomes? Or is it that policy should be designed to create the internal and external conditions under which the desired equilibrium rate naturally emerges? Suffice it to say that, much like the debate among economists regarding the stochastic behavior of output and what the appropriate policy prescription should be, a debate about the exchange rate models offered in this volume is likely to emerge.

References

Abuaf, Niso, and Philippe Jorion. 1990. "Purchasing Power Parity in the Long Run." *Journal of Finance* 45 (March): 157–74.

Adler, Michael, and Bruce Lehmann. 1983. "Deviations from Purchasing Power Parity in the Long Run." *Journal of Finance* 38 (December): 1471–87.

Ardeni, Pier G., and Diego Lubian. 1989. "Purchasing Power Parity during the 1920s." *Economic Letters* 30: 257–62.

Baillie, Richard T., and David Selover. 1987. "Cointegration and Models of Exchange Rate Determination." *International Journal of Forecasting* 3: 43–51.

Cassel, Gustav. 1922. *Money and Foreign Exchange After 1914*. London.

Cheung, Yin-Wong, and Kon S. Lai. 1993a. "Long-Run Purchasing Power Parity during the Recent Float." *Journal of International Economics* 34: 181–92.

Cheung, Yin-Wong, and Kon S. Lai. 1993b. "A Fractional Cointegration Analysis of Purchasing Power Parity." *Journal of Business and Economic Statistics* 11 (January): 103–12.

Choudry, Taufiq, Robert McNown, and Myles Wallace. 1991. "Purchasing Power Parity and the Canadian Float in the 1950s." *Review of Economics and Statistics* 73 (August): 558–63.

Christiano, Lawrence J. 1992. "Searching for a Break in GNP." *Journal of Business and Economic Statistics* 10 (July): 237–50.

Cochrane, John. 1988. "How Big Is the Random Walk in GNP?" *Journal of Political Economy* 96 (October): 893–920.

Corbae, Dean, and Sam Ouliaris. 1988. "Cointegration and Tests of Purchasing Power Parity." *Review of Economics and Statistics* 70 (August): 508–11.

Cumby, Robert E., and Maurice Obstfeld. 1984. "International Interest Rate and Price Level Linkages under Flexible Exchange Rates: A Review of Recent Evidence." In John F. O. Bilson and Richard C. Marston, eds., *Exchange Rate Theory and Practice*, 121–51. Chicago: University of Chicago Press.

Davuytan, Nurham, and John Pippenger. 1985. "Purchasing Power Parity Did Not Collapse during the 1970s." *American Economic Review* 75 (December): 1151–58.

Dickey, David, and Wayne Fuller. 1979. "Distribution of the Estimators for Autoregressive Time Series with a Unit Root." *Journal of the American Statistical Association* 74 (June): 427–31.

Dickey, David, and Wayne Fuller. 1981. "Likelihood Ratio Statistics for Autoregressive Time Series with a Unit Root." *Econometrica* 49 (July): 1057–72.

Diebold, Francis X., Steven Husted, and Mark Rush. 1991. "Real Exchange Rates under the Gold Standard." *Journal of Political Economy* 99: 1252–71.

Dueker, Michael J. 1993. "Hypothesis Testing with Near-Unit Roots: The Case of Long-Run Purchasing Power Parity." *Federal Reserve Bank of St. Louis Review* 75 (July-August): 37–48.

Edison, Hali. 1985. "Purchasing Power Parity: A Quantitative Reassessment of the 1920s Experience." *Journal of International Money and Finance* 5 (September): 361–72.

Edison, Hali, Joseph E. Gagnon, and William R. Melick. 1994. "Understanding the Empirical Literature on Purchasing Power Parity: The Post Bretton Woods Era." International Finance Discussion Paper No. 465. Washington: Board of Governors (April).

Edison, Hali, and Jan Tore Klovland. 1987. "A Quantitative Reassessment of the Purchasing Power Parity Hypothesis: Evidence from Norway and the United Kingdom." *Journal of Applied Econometrics* 2: 309–33.

Engle, Robert F., and C. W. J. Granger. 1987. "Cointegration and Error Correction: Representation, Estimation, and Testing." *Econometrica* 55 (March): 251–76.

Engle, Robert, and Sam Yoo. 1987. "Forecasting and Testing in Cointegrated Systems." *Journal of Econometrics* 35 (May): 143–59.

Fisher, Eric O., and Joon Y. Park. 1991. "Testing Purchasing Power Parity under the Null Hypothesis of Cointegration." *Economic Journal* 101 (November): 1476–84.

Flynn, N. Alston, and Janice L. Boucher. 1993. "Tests of Long Run Purchasing Power Parity using Alternative Methodologies." *Journal of Macroeconomics* 15 (Winter): 109–22.

Frankel, Jeffrey. 1986. "International Capital Mobility and Crowding Out in the US Economy: Imperfect Integration of Financial Markets or of Goods Markets." In R. W. Hafer, *How Open Is the US Economy?* Lexington, MA:

Frenkel, Jacob A. 1978. "Purchasing Power Parity: Doctrinal Perspective and Evidence from the 1920s." *Journal of International Economics* 8: 169–91.

Frenkel, Jacob A. 1981. "The Collapse of Purchasing Power Parities During the 1970's." *European Economic Review* 16: 145–65.

Fuller, Wayne. 1976. *Introduction to Statistical Time Series.* New York: John Wiley and Sons.

Glen, Jack D. 1992. "Real Exchange Rates in the Short, Medium, and Long Run." *Journal of International Economics* 33: 147–66.

Granger, C. W. J. 1983. "Cointegrated Variables and Error-Correcting Models." UCSD Discussion Paper No. 83–13. San Diego: University of California, San Diego.

Grilli, Vittorio, and Graciela Kaminsky. 1991. "Nominal Exchange Rate Regimes and the Real Exchange Rate: Evidence from the United States and Great Britain, 1885–1986." *Journal of Monetary Economics* 27 (April): 191–212.

Huizanga, John. 1987. "An Empirical Investigation of the Long-Run Behavior of Real Exchange Rates." *Carnegie-Rochester Conference Series on Public Policy* 27: 149–214.

Isard, Peter. 1977. "How Far Can We Push the Law of One Price?" *American Economic Review* 67: 942–48.

Johansen, Soren. 1988. "Statistical Analysis of Cointegration Vectors." *Journal of Economic Dynamics and Control* 12: 231–54.

Johansen, Soren, and Katarina Juselius. 1990. "Maximum Likelihood Estimation and Inference on Cointegration—With Application to the Demand for Money." *Oxford Bulletin of Economics and Statistics* 52 (May): 169–210.

Kim, Yoonbai. 1990. "Purchasing Power Parity in the Long Run: A Cointegration Approach." *Journal of Money, Credit, and Banking* 22 (November): 491–503.

Kremers, Jeroen J. M., Neil R. Ericsson, and Juan J. Dolado. 1992. "The Power of Cointegration Tests." *Oxford Bulletin of Economics and Statistics* 54: 325–48.

Kugler, Peter, and Carlos Lenz. 1993. "Multivariate Cointegration Analysis and the Long Run Validity of PPP." *Review of Economics and Statistics* 75: 180–84.

Liu, Peter C. 1993. "Purchasing Power Parity in Latin America: A Cointegration Analysis." *Weltwirtschaftliches Archiv:* 662–80.

Mark, Nelson. 1990. "Real and Nominal Exchange Rates in the Long Run: An Empirical Investigation." *Journal of International Economics* 28: 115–36.

McNown, Robert, and Myles S. Wallace. 1989. "National Price Levels, Purchasing Power Parity, and Cointegration: A Test of Four High Inflation Economies." *Journal of International Money and Finance* 8 (December): 533–46.

Officer, Lawrence. 1976. "The PPP Theory of Exchange Rates: A Review Article." *IMF Staff Papers* 23: 1–60.

Patel, Jayendu. 1990. "Purchasing Power Parity as a Long Run Relation." *Journal of Applied Econometrics* 5: 367–79.

Perron, Pierre. 1989. "The Great Crash, the Oil Price Shock, and the Unit Root Hypothesis." *Econometrica* 57 (November): 1361–1401.

Perron, Pierre, and Timothy J. Vogelsang. 1992. "Nonstationarity and Level Shifts with an Application to Purchasing Power Parity." *Journal of Business and Economic Statistics* 10 (July): 301–20.

Pippenger, Michael K. 1993. "Cointegration Tests of Purchasing Power Parity: The Case of Swiss Exchange Rates." *Journal of International Money and Finance* 12: 46–61.

Stock, James H. 1987. "Asymptotic Properties of Least Squares Estimators of Cointegrating Vectors." *Econometrica* 55: 1035–56.

Stock, James H., and Mark W. Watson. 1988. "Variable Trends in Economic Time Series." *Journal of Economic Perspectives* 3 (Summer): 147–65.

Taylor, Mark, and Patrick C. McMahon. 1988. "Long Run Purchasing Power Parity in the 1920s." *European Economic Review* 32 (January): 179–97.

Zivot, Eric, and Donald W. K. Andrews. 1992. "Further Evidence on the Great Crash, the Oil-Price Shock, and the Unit Root Hypothesis." *Journal of Business and Economic Statistics* 10 (July): 251–70.

8

On the Concept and Usefulness of the Equilibrium Rate of Exchange

STANLEY W. BLACK

In a world where exchange rates can fluctuate by 2 percent per day and 20 percent per year, economists are asked to evaluate the causes and consequences of such fluctuations. If we are to go beyond the Panglossian response that ''the market knows best,'' we need some concept of an *equilibrium* rate of exchange as a standard against which to measure actual exchange rate changes. Gustav Cassel (1922) pointed out what the Bullionists knew, namely, that exchange rates must fluctuate to offset changes in relative inflation rates of different currencies. But this notion of purchasing power parity (PPP) only accounts for the *monetary* part of the fluctuations of exchange rates, which may also vary because of *real* factors, such as changes in the terms of trade, business cycles, or changes in the level of capital flows. Nurkse (1945) defined the equilibrium rate of exchange such that the balance of payments must be in equilibrium without artificial restrictions on trade flows at full employment.

Nurkse's concept finds its quantitative expression in the papers by Williamson and by Bayoumi et al. in this volume. Stein's paper in this volume offers a neoclassical version of the equilibrium rate of exchange, since he assumes that output is at full employment and makes no adjustment for a target current account balance. Edwards and Elbadawi, in their papers, focus on the equilibrium real exchange rate for less developed countries in a model that is concerned not with the employment gap but rather with relative inflation rates, transitory capital flows, and

Stanley W. Black is Georges Lurcy Professor of Economics at the University of North Carolina, Chapel Hill.

the terms of trade. Finally, Breuer examines recent studies of PPP, to determine what they imply about the variability of the equilibrium real exchange rate.

Fundamental Equilibrium versus Market Equilibrium

The fundamental equilibrium exchange rate (FEER), as defined by John Williamson (1983, 14), is "that [real exchange rate] which is expected to generate a current account surplus or deficit equal to the underlying capital flow over the cycle, given that the country is pursuing 'internal balance' as best it can and not restricting trade for balance of payments reasons." This definition requires both an empirical model relating the current account to the exchange rate and the output level as well as normative judgments on the "underlying capital flow" and the policy mix leading to "internal balance." As Williamson notes, the FEER can be calculated either on an ex ante basis, anticipating a path to future external and internal balance, or ex post, as the exchange rate that would have been consistent with external and internal balance in the past.

Williamson's FEER may be distinguished from a model-based current equilibrium exchange rate associated with *existing* levels of output and capital flows and from the observed market rate, which is affected by speculation, central bank intervention, and other factors left out of the models. The purpose of calculating the FEER is to establish a benchmark against which to measure *misalignments* in market exchange rates. By definition of the FEER, these misalignments must be due to temporary factors such as deviations from internal balance, trade restrictions, abnormal capital flows, divergent fiscal-monetary policy mixes, speculation, or central bank intervention. Awareness of such misalignments then signals the need for policy changes to correct them. Both the misalignments and the associated disturbances are regarded as harmful and to be avoided, if possible.

Reasons for avoiding misalignments include the associated undesirable fluctuations in absorption, the costs of adjusting to widely fluctuating exchange rates, unemployment associated with major adjustments, erosion of manufacturing capacity during misalignments, ratchet effects on inflation during depreciations, and protectionism generated in response to trade deficits. Thus both the causes and the effects of misalignments are deleterious, providing ample reasons for engaging in the somewhat hazardous effort of making the calculations.

However, there remain serious questions about the methods and purposes of these efforts. Since normative choices *must* be made in measuring the FEER, there are bound to be disagreements about the results.

The potentially controversial choices that have to be made include the model to be used, the policy mix used to achieve internal balance, the timing of the implementation of that policy, and the target for the current account balance. Even if there is agreement on the choice of model and the target level of capital flows, different combinations of fiscal and monetary policy can be used to achieve internal balance. Williamson solves this problem by choosing the sustainable level of capital flows independently of the monetary-fiscal mix.

Alternative Concepts of the Equilibrium Exchange Rate

The "Fundamental Equilibrium Exchange Rate" (FEER)

Williamson's FEER measures the real exchange rate as the ratio of the price of foreign to that of domestic goods, or ep'/p, where the prime denotes the foreign country, on the implicit assumptions that exports and imports are priced in the seller's currency and that those prices are relatively sticky as compared with exchange rates. By adjusting output for internal balance, the FEER also assumes a Keynesian less-than-full-employment situation. In Williamson's notation, where A is absorption, B is the balance on current account, Y is GDP, and $r = ep'/p$,

$$B = B(A, r), \quad B_1 < 0, B_2 > 0$$
$$Y = Y(A, r), \quad Y_1 > 0, Y_2 > 0.$$

Thus, if $B \neq B^*$ and/or $Y \neq Y^*$ (where an asterisk denotes the target level of the variable), adjustments in both expenditure policy A and the real exchange rate r are required to achieve internal and external balance. These equations take the familiar form of a Keynesian structural model of an open economy, along the lines of J. Marcus Fleming and Robert Mundell. In practice Williamson uses alternative structural models to make the calculations. The paper in this volume by the International Monetary Fund (IMF) team (Bayoumi et al.) uses an identical framework for their definition of the "desired" equilibrium exchange rate, or DEER, which is then calculated either by comparative static methods or with an explicit model.

Hysteresis Effects

Bayoumi et al. argue that an initial disequilibrium in the current account will lead to the accumulation of additional external debt (or assets) during the adjustment period, requiring an *additional* change in the exchange rate to offset the required interest payments (or receipts) on this debt. Note that if the initial exchange rate and its future path are consistent with rational expectations, they will already incorporate an allowance for this effect. The model-based calculations of Bayoumi et al. are supposed to be consistent with rational expectations. Thus no additional hysteresis effect is allowed for.

The "Natural Real Exchange Rate" (NATREX)

Jerome Stein's NATREX model defines the real exchange rate inversely, as the ratio of the prices of domestic to foreign goods, $R = Np/p'$, where the nominal price of the domestic currency in terms of foreign currency $N = 1/e$, so that $R = p/ep'$ (again the prime denotes the foreign country). The current real exchange rate is then decomposed into medium-run and long-run components, which I shall denote as R_n and R^*, in Stein's equation:

$$R = (R - R_n) + (R_n - R^*) + R^*. \tag{1}$$

R_n is what Stein calls the "natural" real exchange rate (NATREX).

Besides this purely notational difference, Stein, by focusing on what he calls the medium run, adjusts for cyclical factors by using moving averages for the explanatory variables. This procedure puts $Y \equiv Y^*$, and macroeconomic policy is therefore exogenous to the model. However, absorption still depends on the real interest rate (r in Stein's notation), $A = A(Y^*, r)$, $1 > A_1 > 0$, $A_2 < 0$, while the current account $B = B(Y^*, R)$, $B_1 < 0$, $B_2 < 0$, with R the real exchange rate defined as above. Therefore, in equilibrium, from Stein's equation:

$$B(Y^*, R) = Y^* - A(Y^*, r), \tag{2}$$

omitting the stock of foreign assets F for simplicity. Similarly for the foreign country,

$$B'(Y'^*, R) = Y'^* - A'(Y'^*, r'). \tag{3}$$

The difference between Stein's and Williamson's equilibrium real exchange rates can be seen in figure 1. Assume that current macroeconomic equilibrium is at Y_0, B_0, with the real exchange rate R_0. Williamson adjusts output to full employment Y^*, which moves the current account balance to C and requires an adjustment in R and in absorption to move to the target point D. Stein's estimation procedure gives him the implied current balance $Y^* - A(Y^*, r)$, which corresponds to point E, requiring a *different* real exchange rate, the NATREX, which is unrelated to any target level of B. If in fact his moving-average Y^* is close to actual Y, the NATREX

Figure 1   FEER and NATREX

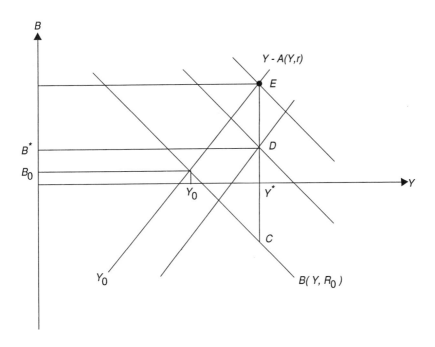

will not be far from the actual real exchange rate. For each level of the real interest rate r, Stein has a different implied current balance and therefore a different level of R, giving the IS curve of his figure 6.

Since medium-run equilibrium requires equality of real interest rates, the solution for R_n and r can be represented in Stein's figure 6 by the intersection of the two curves, which he calls IS and IS'. The NATREX is the level of the real exchange rate that equates both implied current balances $Y^* - A$ to B *and* $Y'^* - A'$ to B'. Note that there is no requirement that $B = -B'$ or that either be equal to some normative target level. The single-equation, reduced-form version of the NATREX, estimated in Stein's table 6 and shown in his figure 3, is based on changes in this equilibrium, as given in his equation (12). The "natural" real rate R_n allows $r \neq r'$ and net foreign asset stocks to be changing at whatever rate is given by the *existing* current account. The long-run equilibrium real rate R^* occurs at an equilibrium real rate of interest $r = r'$ with asset stocks in equilibrium ($B = -B' = 0$) for given values of the exogenous variables Z.

From this discussion it appears that Stein's concept of the NATREX R_n is some distance from Williamson's FEER. Like the FEER, it depends on the model chosen. But while it does not *appear* to require the normative choice of a particular definition of full-employment output Y^* and a target current account B^*, or a means to reach Y^*, in practice even stronger assumptions are required. For example, the assumption that a 12–quarter moving average of *actual* output growth is an adequate proxy for Y^* means that a moving average of actual unemployment is accepted as equilibrium unemployment. Similarly, the acceptance of the implied full-employment current balance as an equilibrium concept means that actual capital inflows are accepted as the basis for the equilibrium exchange rate. Stein finds evidence that the real interest rate differential is mean-reverting—see his equation (9a)—and uses this to argue that real interest differentials will be eliminated over time.

These factors make the NATREX appear to be much closer to Williamson's concept of the current equilibrium exchange rate than to the FEER or to Nurkse's "external accounts in equilibrium without the need for wholesale unemployment at home." This is borne out by Stein's figure 3, which shows the NATREX to have risen 63 percent from 1980 to 1985 while the actual real dollar exchange rate rose 70 percent. In contrast, Williamson's US dollar FEER moved about 6 percent over the same period.

Some additional questions may be raised about Stein's model. From his table 4, the seven *endogenous* variables are the real exchange rate R, capital intensity k, foreign debt F, domestic and foreign real interest rates r and r', and domestic saving and investment S and I. *Exogenous* variables include the "discount rate" $g = (C + G)/Y$, which represents absorption (less investment) relative to GNP, and the "productivity of capital" u, which is equal to a moving average of the rate of growth of output.

When it comes, however, to estimating the model in table 6 and figure 3, the NATREX is related only to changes in capital intensity k and k', foreign debt F, and the interest differential $r - r'$. The endogenous capital intensity is itself not measured; instead it is set equal to the exogenous "productivity of capital," which is measured by the moving-average rate of growth of output. Changes in foreign debt are measured by a moving average of the current account. No effort is made to adjust this to allow for possibly transitory capital flows. The entire expansion in the US current account deficit during the 1980s is thus accepted as "normal."

Finally, the evolution of the real exchange rate and the current account in tables 8 to 11 of Stein's paper is taken to depend on the "exogenous" variable DISRAT or g, which is consumption plus government spending relative to GNP. In fact DISRAT is clearly a cyclical variable, as implied by the permanent income hypothesis and shown by plotting it against any cyclical variable. The correlation coefficient between DISRAT and the unemployment rate is 0.66 over the period 1959–88, using quarterly data. This makes its use as an exogenous variable in tables 8 through 11 suspect.

The "Equilibrium Real Exchange Rate" (ERER)

The papers by Sebastian Edwards and Ibrahim Elbadawi apply to the problems of developing countries a somewhat different concept of the equilibrium exchange rate, which Williamson refers to as the "Chicago" definition. I prefer to consider it the "small country" or "dependent economy" model, since it arises from the well-known Salter-Swan (Salter 1959, Swan 1960) nontraded goods model for a country that is too small to affect its own terms of trade. In this model the observed real exchange rate RER, defined as the ratio of the price of traded goods to nontraded goods P_t/P_n, depends both on exogenous variables such as the terms of trade or the level of tariffs, and on policy factors such as the excess supply of domestic credit. The equilibrium real exchange rate ERER is defined as the level of the RER that is the equilibrium response to the exogenous factors when the policy variables follow sustainable paths. In most cases these papers calculate ex post ERERs that would have produced equilibrium in the past, although Elbadawi calculates an ex ante or forward-looking ERER for Chile.

Edwards's version of the model uses a simple process of lagged adjustment to equilibrium augmented by disequilibrium factors, whereas Elbadawi uses cointegration techniques to identify the equilibrium relationship and an error correction framework to estimate the adjustment process. The formulation of both papers begins from a structural model and solves for a reduced-form equilibrium relationship, which is then subjected to a process of adjustment, much as in Stein's model.

The structural model takes the "fundamentals" for the real exchange rate to be absorption relative to output, the terms of trade, trade taxes, and government spending (on nontraded goods) relative to GDP. Absorption relative to GDP, which is just one minus the ratio of the current account to GDP, is assumed to depend on sustainable capital flows and the exchange rate. Thus, as with Williamson, the current account target depends on sustainable rather than actual capital flows.

The fundamental assumptions of the dependent-economy model as used by Edwards and Elbadawi are that domestic prices are flexible and that exports and imports are homogeneous products whose prices are set in world markets. In the small countries they deal with, the macroeconomic problems include high inflation, dual exchange markets, and shocks to the terms of trade. In contrast, the FEER models used by Williamson and the IMF team deal with large countries that export and import differentiated products whose prices are sticky, and whose macroeconomic problems include fiscal deficits, unemployment, inflation, and oil price shocks. Thus the models seem appropriately differentiated for different types of economies.

Alternative Calculations

The range of variability of FEERs that can be obtained from different calculation techniques provides some kind of bound on the range of uncertainty on the resulting numbers, assuming that there is agreement on the *targets*. For example, Williamson's table 7, comparing the results of different models, shows that they yield estimates of FEERs for the same country that diverge as much as 13 percent for the French franc, 20 percent for the US dollar, 25 percent for the yen and the deutsche mark, and 46 percent for the Italian lira! As Williamson notes, the last figure is uncomfortably large, perhaps because one or two of the models that produced figures for him tend to yield extreme results. The choice of the median model results gives some reassurance but reinforces awareness of the uncertainty involved in the calculations.

Bayoumi et al. offer a different perspective on the effects of alternative calculations. First, they examine the robustness of comparative static calculations to alternative internal and external targets and find them much more sensitive to the latter than to the former. Alternative elasticities make some differences, as do alternative assumed lags in adjustment. Next, they use a model to achieve the same targets as in the comparative static case, alternatively by shifting currency preferences (equivalent to a change in exchange rate) and by changing fiscal policy. As might be expected, these have different implications for interest rates in deficit and surplus countries. In deficit countries, currency shifts crowd out investment while fiscal contraction to improve the current account crowds it in. These alternative techniques for achieving external balance therefore yield different calculations of the desired exchange rate change. The investment-friendly fiscal approach cuts domestic absorption sharply at first, but then, as investment and output rise over time, it leads to a smaller fall in absorption and a *larger* required exchange rate change to achieve the same external objective! This difference in the FEER according to whether monetary or fiscal methods are used to reach it reveals another fundamental uncertainty in the concept, which Williamson had thought to avoid by focusing on the current account rather than the overall balance as a target.

The Target Zone Approach

Beyond the methodological questions are the objectives for which the FEERs are to be used. As designed by John Williamson (1983), the "target zone" approach to international macroeconomic policy coordination can be thought of as a way to put teeth into the "surveillance" of the appropriateness of flexible exchange rates envisaged by the Second Amendment to the Charter of the International Monetary Fund. During the 1980s divergent fiscal policies in the United States, Germany, and Japan led to significant exchange rate misalignments and current account imbalances, as internal objectives predominated in the largest industrial countries. The costs of these misalignments were to be found in associated costs of adjustment, unemployment, ratchet effects on inflation, undesirable fluctuations in consumption, and misguided trade policies adopted to protect domestic industries faced with overvalued currencies. The inability of the IMF to influence the domestic policies leading to misalignments was to be overcome by using target zones to indicate the need for policy changes.

It used to be generally accepted that one country's *domestic* policies were beyond questioning by others. Meetings of international bodies such as the Group of Seven (G-7), the Organization for Economic Cooperation and Development (OECD), or the IMF did not address domestic policies unless they had important spillovers onto other countries. In contrast, exchange rate policies and other policies directed at explicitly international variables have always been considered proper topics for international consultation and debate. But since exchange rates may be misaligned either because of failure to achieve internal balance *or* because of choice of an unsustainable monetary-fiscal mix, the adoption of target zones based on the FEER presents an opening to discuss domestic policy variables that would otherwise be off limits. Is this approach likely to be successful?

To make the issue concrete, suppose that FEER targets had been adopted during the early 1980s. The preferred method of reducing the US current account deficit at the time would presumably have included fiscal tightening. But as demonstrated by Bayoumi et al., an alternative policy mix to achieve the same current account could have involved monetary ease. In other words, it's not enough simply to give governments a target exchange rate and expect them to use the analyst's preferred monetary-fiscal mix to get there. Governments have a way of sticking to their domestic policy choices regardless of external objectives. Williamson and Miller (1987) recognized this problem in their "blueprint" proposal for coordinated macroeconomic and exchange rate policy, discussed below, and proposed the use of fiscal policy to achieve internal balance consistent with external balance.

The question is whether targets for exchange rates can be an effective "discipline" to influence domestic macroeconomic policy to remain consistent with the external target. The evidence from the Bretton Woods era shows that they can, except with respect to large, reserve currency countries like the United States (Michaely 1970). Floating exchange rates led to deemphasis rather than complete abandonment of external objectives (Black 1978). The target zone approach by choosing a pattern of exchange rates would reemphasize a *consistent* set of external objectives for different countries. Obtaining agreement on such a set of objectives at an international level would be difficult but has occurred at least twice in recent memory, at the Smithsonian in 1971 and the Louvre in 1987. Williamson offers his own set of consistent objectives in his paper providing 1990 estimates of FEERS.

But what about the use of target zones *without* commitments by governments to use monetary and fiscal policies to achieve the targets? The Louvre Accord of February 1987, where agreement was reached on a set of target zones without agreed monetary and fiscal policies, created serious strains within a year because of divergent monetary policy objectives in the United States, Germany, and Japan. The example suggests that noncredible commitments can paradoxically worsen policy outcomes by encouraging the pursuit of inconsistent objectives.

Alternative Uses of FEERs

FEERs as an Antidote to PPP

At a minimum, FEERs attempt to give some indication of changes in equilibrium real exchange rates. In itself, this is a useful antidote to the common practice of assuming that equilibrium real exchange rates never change. The doctrine of purchasing power parity has within it the valid core of truth that changes in price levels due to purely monetary factors should not lead to changes in real exchange rates, since they should be offset by changes in nominal exchange rates. However, in popular discussion this is often transmuted into the notion that PPP provides *the* equilibrium rate, which is equivalent to assuming the equilibrium real rate is constant!

Breuer's paper shows that recent econometric tests that focus on *long-run* PPP have weakened the concept. Long-run PPP tests for an eventual return to an equilibrium level that may or may not be constant. This potentially allows for wide fluctuations of real exchange rates. The strongest support provided for PPP merely suggests that real exchange rates follow a stationary stochastic process, which again allows for wide fluctuations. The one paper cited by Breuer as explicitly testing for constancy of the real exchange rate, by Perron and Vogelsang, rejects that hypothesis.

As may be seen from the significant fluctuations in ERERs calculated by Edwards and Elbadawi, movements in the real exchange rate are particularly important for relatively small countries whose terms of trade and sustainable capital inflows may change significantly from time to time. Such fluctuations appear to be milder for the large industrialized countries with relatively low inflation differentials analyzed by Williamson and Bayoumi et al.

Use of FEERs to Correct for the Effect of Transitory Capital Flows

For both industrialized and less developed countries, transitory capital movements, whether generated by monetary or fiscal policy or by market forces, frequently shock the balance of payments and the exchange rate. To the extent that these may be nonsustainable or temporary in nature, the implied exchange rate movements will likewise involve temporary departures from equilibrium levels. The identification of temporary exchange rate movements is a key use of the equilibrium exchange rate concept, since it can help avoid overreaction to such changes by either the private or the public sector.

Use of FEERs to Explain Factors Underlying Exchange Rate Changes

The ability of models to forecast exchange rates on a systematic basis has been tested and found wanting. One of their remaining uses consists in explaining changes in exchange rates ex post. Changes in FEERs as examined in Williamson's tables 15 and 16 are an effective demonstration of this use of the equilibrium concept, at least for the deutsche mark, the yen, and the French franc.

FEERs as a Weapon to Influence Policy

In cases where temporary capital flows have been caused by nonsustainable monetary or fiscal policies, deviations from the FEER constitute a "warning signal"—something like the "divergence indicator"in the European Monetary System (EMS)—that would suggest a change in the underlying policy. It therefore provides those who disagree with or suffer negative consequences from that policy, whether domestic or foreign, with a weapon to brandish in policy discussions. Naturally this is an unwelcome prospect for those in charge of policy. The associated current account targets may also have the unintended consequence of leading policymakers to adopt palliatives that treat the symptom rather than the disease. Williamson argues that current account targets can reassure labor that jobs will not be exported through current account deficits. Experience suggests that workers are more likely to trust to protectionism than to exchange rate changes. If the current account target is thought of merely as an intermediate step to obtaining the equilibrium exchange rate, it is less likely to be adopted as a target in its own right and therefore less likely to cause mischief.

This is not just a hypothetical issue. A notable example occurred during 1985, when the combination of expansionary fiscal policy and tight monetary policy during the US recovery pushed the dollar to its post–1973 peak and the US current account to a large deficit. The response of labor and the Congress was to call for protection against "unfair" trade practices. While it is true that Treasury Secretary James A. Baker III then renewed the practice of intervention in the foreign exchange market to push the dollar down, he did this as an alternative to adopting any fundamental shift in the monetary-fiscal policy mix. At the time, US fiscal policy was set in concrete; monetary and exchange rate policy had to adapt. Under such conditions the current account was slow to adjust, although adjust it did, as shown in Cline (1992).

Use of FEERs in IMF Surveillance

With the loosening of the external constraint provided by the Second Amendment to the IMF Charter, countries have been free to adopt exchange rate policies of their choosing, subject only to "surveillance" by the IMF. The objective according to Article IV of the Charter is to help "assure orderly exchange arrangements and promote a stable exchange rate system." The IMF's Principles of Exchange Rate Surveillance define "disorderly" exchange rates as involving protracted large-scale intervention, extensive official borrowing, or the application of balance of payments restrictions or monetary or fiscal policies that provide abnormal incentives to capital flows. Surveillance is carried out both through annual bilateral consultations under Article IV and through multilateral discussions in the context of the semi-annual *World Economic Outlook*. During the 1980s this process took on a somewhat haggard look, as the United States' monetary and fiscal policies, adopted for "domestic" reasons, also provided abnormal incentives to capital flows. More recently, it became obvious to many that German unification called for a realignment of currencies within the EMS. Yet in neither case was the IMF successful in affecting the situation. The availability of FEER calculations could be an important component of a more effective IMF surveillance process.

Macroeconomic Policy Coordination

The Williamson-Miller "blueprint" for international macroeconomic policy coordination gave a key role to FEERs: to help achieve a consistent set of balance of payments targets complementing targets for internal balance. From a different point of view, the "blueprint" proposed fiscal policy rules for internal balance to complement the FEERs, which had earlier been proposed by Williamson (1983) to provide guidance for target zones for exchange rates. Target zones were designed to avoid the development of excessive current account imbalances through exchange rate misalignments.

An extended period of academic and policy focus on the benefits of international economic policy coordination during the 1980s has given way to a regression toward domestic policy objectives in the United States, Europe, and Japan, due not only to recessions in economic activity striking each in succession, but also to political changes that emphasize domestic problems. In this environment, current account imbalances are likely to reflect behavioral and policy responses to divergent domestic economic conditions, such as the deflation of the "bubble" economy in Japan, the reunification of Germany, and economic recovery ahead of the rest of the world in the United States. Policymakers are tempted to export deflation or adopt "managed trade." Under these conditions, could explicit economic policy coordination based on rules such as those contained in the blueprint be effective?

Certainly, increased use of fiscal policy in each of the three countries mentioned would be more appropriate than reliance on trade policy or monetary policy alone. The blueprint points them in the right direction. Japan's recession and current account surplus imply a need for fiscal stimulus, while the US position is approximately a mirror image. The yen has already appreciated sharply in the last few years, promising further adjustment ahead. Germany, in contrast, is recovering from recession combined with a current account deficit brought on by reunification and the associated inflationary wage shock. Returning to high employment is likely to require real depreciation of the mark in order to permit German industry to regain competitiveness in world export markets.

The papers in this volume go a long way to clarifying alternative concepts of the equilibrium exchange rate and in showing how to measure them. Despite the uncertainties of measurement and the conceptual problems that remain, their usefulness in helping economists evaluate past movements of actual exchange rates and likely or appropriate prospective future changes will be ample repayment for the efforts that go into their calculation.

References

Black, Stanley. 1978. "Policy Responses to Major Disturbances of the 1970's and Their Transmission through International Goods and Capital Markets." *Weltwirtschaftliches Archiv* 114: 614–41.

Cassel, Gustav. 1922. *Money and Foreign Exchange After 1914*. London.

Cline, William R. 1992. "US External Adjustment: Progress, Prognosis, and Interpretation." In C. Fred Bergsten, ed., *International Adjustment and Financing: The Lessons of 1985–1991*. Washington: Institute for International Economics.

Michaely, Michael. 1970. *The Responsiveness of Demand Policies to Balance of Payments: Postwar Patterns*. New York: National Bureau of Economic Research.

Nurkse, Ragnar. 1945. "Conditions of International Monetary Equilibrium." Princeton Essays in International Finance No. 4. Princeton, NJ: Princeton University Press.

Salter, W. E. G. 1959. "Internal and External Balance: The Role of Price and Expenditure Effects." *Economic Record* 35: 226–38.

Swan, Trevor. 1960. "Economic Control in a Dependent Economy." *Economic Record* 36: 51–66.

Williamson, John. 1983. "The Exchange Rate System." POLICY ANALYSES IN INTERNATIONAL ECONOMICS 5, rev. ed. 1985. Washington: Institute for International Economics.

Williamson, John, and Marcus H. Miller. 1987. "Targets and Indicators: A Blueprint for the International Coordination of Economic Policy." POLICY ANALYSES IN INTERNATIONAL ECONOMICS 22. Washington: Institute for International Economics.

Index

Díaz-Alejandro, Carlos F., 93
Dickey-Fuller statistics, 80, 82, 104, 257, 259–60, 263, 266
Diebold, Francis X., 250
Discount rate. *See* Social time preference
Dixit, Avinash, 178
Dollar, Canadian
  calculated DEERs for, 31, 46, 55
  FEERs estimates for, 209, 215, 231, 234–35, 237
  in PPP studies, 264
Dollar, US
  in Bretton Woods system, 27
  calculated DEERs for, 28, 30–34, 46, 50, 53
  factors explaining rise of yen against, 221–22
  FEERs estimates for, 7, 209, 230–35, 237–39
  PPP studies of, 263–65
Domestic credit, in ERER model, 71–75, 84, 86–87, 101–02
Dominguez, Kathryn M., 14
Dornbusch, Rudiger, 13, 95, 134
Dual nominal exchange rate systems, 63

East Asia, policy use of equilibrium exchange rates in, 17
EAG. *See* External Adjustment with Growth (EAG) model,
The Economist, 13
Edison, Hali, 134, 139, 250, 264
Edwards, Sebastian, 2, 10, 13–15, 94, 109, 270, 279, 284
Elasticities
  absorption and, 26
  of current account, 21, 25
  of demand for tradables with respect to price, 190
  in EAG model, 226
  of import demand with respect to income, 182
  of investment with respect to interest rate, 186
  in Multimod, 26
  sensitivity of DEERs estimates to changes in, 33–34, 56
Elbadawi, Ibrahim A., 2, 10, 13, 14, 270, 279, 284
Engle, Robert F., 96, 256
Engle-Granger method, 256, 258, 265
Equilibrium, definition of, 13
Equilibrium exchange rates. *See also* Desired equilibrium exchange rate (DEER); Equilibrium real exchange rate (ERER); Fundamental equilibrium exchange rate (FEER); NATREX
  "Chicago" or "dependent economy" model of, 285
  cointegration tests of, 10
  definition, 134
  for developing countries, 9–11
  impact of interest rate changes on, 12

inadequacy of PPP as measure of 2, 19, 76, 94, 134, 137
markets' lack of views on, 2
policy importance of, 16–17, 290
policy use in East Asia of, 17
fiscal policy and, 11
"underlying balance" approach to, 20
Equilibrium real exchange rate (ERER)
  calculated indexes for, 111–16
  for Chile, 112
  definition of, 94, 100, 285
  ex ante versus ex post approach to, 96
  for Ghana, 115
  for India, 116
  limitations of, 10–11
  similarity to FEER of, 10
Equilibrium real exchange rate (ERER), model of
  absorption in, 96, 99
  basic, 96–98
  capital flows in, 70, 106
  domestic credit in, 71–75, 84, 86–87, 101–02
  economic growth and fiscal policy in, 84
  forward-looking, 98–102
  fundamentals in, 83–84, 86, 94
  government expenditure in, 70, 96–98, 107
  interest rates in, 99
  nontraded goods in, 97
  openness of economy in, 98–99, 106
  private-sector expenditure in, 97
  productivity growth in, 98, 107
  terms of trade in, 69–70, 98, 105, 182
  tariffs in, 68–69
Error correction methods, 101–02, 108–11, 109, 164, 257–58, 265
European Monetary System, 19, 139
Exchange Rate Mechanism, 6, 7, 16, 191
Exchange rate system
  Bretton Woods, 27
  differing role of FEERs according to, 16
  dual nominal, 63
  target zone-based, 9, 16, 177, 228, 286, 290
Expectations, modeling of, 99, 151, 224, 282
External Adjustment with Growth (EAG) model
  commodity disaggregation in, 224
  construction of baseline in, 225
  country and regional coverage in, 223
  current account estimates from, 233
  description of, 207
  elasticities in, 226
  FEERs estimates from, 209, 230–32
  procedures for simulations in, 226
External balance, 13, 22, 36, 94, 180, 189–90, 286, *See also* Current account; Trade balance
External debt. *See* Foreign debt; Net international investment position

Feldstein, Martin, 11
Fiscal policy. *See also* Government expenditure

in "blueprint" for international coordination
of economic policy, 287, 290
in ERER model, 84
in Germany, 210
impact on equilibrium exchange rate of
changes in, 11, 25, 47–49
impact on trade balance of, 171
implications of FEERs for, 212
in Interlink model, 210, 227
in Intermod model, 232
in Japan, 291
in selection of current account targets, 184
sustainability of US, 11, 198
Flynn, N. Alston, 250
Foreign capital formation, in NATREX model,
153
Foreign debt. *See also* Net international
investment position
impact of social time preference changes on,
142
in NATREX model, 142, 147, 150–51, 156–58
relation to current account of, 156–57
Former socialist countries, current account
targets for, 204
Forward exchange rates, 137–38
Fractional cointegration models, 261, 264, 272
France, current account targets for, 199, 236
Frankel, Jeffrey A., 14, 265
French franc
calculated DEERs for, 31–34, 52
FEERs estimates for 209, 231, 234–35, 238
PPP studies of, 265
Frenkel, Jacob A., 20, 247, 250
Friedman, Milton, 134, 181
Fundamental equilibrium exchange rate
(FEER). *See also* Equilibrium exchange rates
definition of, 179, 280
deutsche mark—dollar, 6
difference between NATREX and, 282–83
ex ante versus ex post approach to, 5, 186–87,
280
impact of change in debt service or terms of
trade on, 182
impact of loss of creditworthiness on, 182
impact of oil price changes on, 219
normative element in, 180–81
potential policy influence of, 289–90
potential use in IMF surveillance of, 286, 290
role in intermediate exchange rate systems
of, 16
similarity to ERER of, 10
as trajectory, 181–82
use in correcting for transitory capital flows
of, 288
use in explaining exchange rate changes of,
289
Fundamental equilibrium exchange rates
(FEERs), estimates of
assumptions implicit in calculation of, 281
base case, 209

in "blueprint" for international coordination
of economic policy, 16
differences between 1984 and 1990, 215
from EAG model, 231
final revised, 216
for G-7 currencies, 6–7, 209, 215, 230–32, 234–
35, 237–40
interest rates and, 180
from Interlink model, 235
from Intermod model, 237
from Mimosa model, 238
from MSG model, 239
policy implications of, 7, 212
sensitivity to changes in current account
targets of, 205
from steady-state GEM, 234
translation into bilateral exchange rates of,
215, 220
trend changes in, 211, 219
with United States in current account
balance, 210
variation within, 209, 286
versus actual exchange rates, 217, 218
Fundamentals
decomposition into permanent and
transitory, 111, 132
definition of, 136
differences in specification of, 13
distinguished from monetary variables, 67,
74
in ERER model, 83–84, 86, 94
in NATREX model, 140–41, 157–58, 160–63
stationarity of, 139, 141

Gap factor, 182
GEM. *See* Steady-state GEM
Germany. *See also* Deutsche mark
current account targets for, 199, 236
demographics and saving in, 194, 195
effects of reunification on, 291
fiscal policy in, 7, 210
Ghana
actual exchange rates in, 104, 105, 114
capital flows in, 106
cointegrating regression for, 108
droughts in, 114
ERER indexes for, 112, 113–15
exchange rate misalignment in, 115, 119
government expenditure in, 107
inflation in, 102–03, 114, 121
macroeconomic and exchange rate policy in,
102, 110, 113–15
terms of trade in, 104, 106, 113
Glen, Jack D., 251, 264
Global Econometric Model. *See* Steady-state
GEM
Goldstein, M., 20
Government expenditure. *See also* Fiscal policy
in Chile, Ghana, and India, 107
composition of, 12–13, 107

in ERER model, 96–98
as fundamental, 13
impact on real exchange rate of, 70, 89, 107, 110
in NATREX model, 140
proxies for, 84
in real exchange rate dynamics equation, 88
Granger, C. W. J., 96, 153, 256
Great Britain. *See also* Pound sterling
current account targets for, 199, 236
interwar balance of payments policy in, 134
Grilli, Vittorio, 251, 265
Group of Seven (G-7) countries. *See also names of countries*
calculated DEERs for, 28, 30–34, 50, 52
capital flows in, 196
current accounts and trade balances of, 26, 30, 43, 196, 233, 236
FEERs estimates for, 6–7, 209, 215, 230–32, 234–35, 237–40
output gaps in, 26, 30, 208
potential and target growth rates in, 206, 208, 236
real exchange rates in, 29, 146, 161, 217–18
saving and investment in, 197
Growth, economic
in ERER model, 84
in NATREX model, 140, 143–45, 166–67
as proxy for productivity growth, 84
Growth rates, potential and target, in G-7 countries, 206, 208, 236

Helleiner, G., 116
Helliwell, John F., 170, 172, 173
Houthakker-Magee effect, 182, 221
Huizanga, John, 264
Hysteresis, 22, 34–39, 281

"Immaculate transfer", 7
India
actual exchange rates in, 106–07, 116
capital flows in, 107
cointegrating regression for, 108
droughts in, 111
ERER indexes for, 112, 115–16
exchange rate misalignment in, 117, 120
government expenditure in, 107
inflation in, 102–03, 114, 121
macroeconomic and exchange rate policy in, 102, 110, 121
terms of trade in, 106
Infante, Ettore, 148
Inflation
in Ghana and India, 102–03, 114, 121
in Intermod model, 228, 232
internal balance and, 180
in McKinnon-Ohno modified PPP, 188
nominal exchange rates and, 12, 181
Interest rate differentials, 140, 144, 151, 153, 168–69, 284

Interest rates
in DEERs calculations, 27
elasticity of investment with respect to, 186
in ERER model, 99
in FEERs calculations, 180
as fundamental, 14, 136
impact of change in currency preferences on, 44
long-term, in United States and other G-10 countries, 152
in NATREX model, 12, 14, 140, 144, 159, 167, 171, 284
role in determining equilibrium exchange rates of, 12
Interlink
commodity disaggregation in, 224
construction of baseline in, 225
country and regional coverage in, 223
description of, 208
estimates of needed fiscal policy changes from, 210
FEERs estimates from, 232, 235
fiscal policy in, 227
procedures for simulations in, 227–28
targets and simulated changes in, 236
Intermod
commodity disaggregation in, 224
construction of baseline in, 225
country and regional coverage in, 223
description of, 208
FEERs estimates from, 232, 237
fiscal feedback rule in, 229
fiscal policy in, 227
inflation in, 228, 232,
modeling of expectations in, 224
procedures for simulations in, 228–29
self-stabilizing properties of, 228
stock-flow relations in, 224
Internal balance, 23, 94, 179–80, 189–90, 205–07
International Monetary Fund, 8, 133, 286, 290
International policy coordination, use of equilibrium exchange rates in, 16–17, 178, 290, *See also* "Blueprint" for international coordination of economic policy; Target zones
Intertemporal budget constraint, 70, 150, 184, 229
Intertemporal optimization, 147, 149, 150, 184
Investment. *See also* Capital flows; Saving and investment
crowding out of, 11, 145, 173
effect of exchange rate stability on, 94
in G-7 countries, 197
interest rate elasticity of, 186
in NATREX model, 142–44, 148–51
as proxy for productivity growth, 98
Isard, Peter, 247
Italy, current account targets for, 199, 236 *See also* Lira, Italian

country and regional coverage in, 223
description of, 207
FEERs estimates from, 232, 234
procedures for simulations in, 226–27
Stein, Jerome, 11–15, 270, 279, 282
Sterling. *See* Pound sterling
Suboptimal feedback control, 149
Surplus countries, current account targets for,
201–02
Sustainability
of current account, 23, 180, 185–86, 200–01
of fundamentals in ERER model, 100
of US fiscal policy, 11
Swiss franc, PPP tests of, 267
Switzerland, 201, 202
Symansky, Steve, 8
Symmetry constraint, 3, 246, 257, 273

Taiwan, current account targets, 201, 202
Target zones, 9, 16, 177, 228, 286, 290
Tariffs
as fundamental, 13
impact of change on equilibrium exchange
rate of, 68–69, 83
proxies for, 84, 99
Taylor, Mark, 8, 38, 253
Technological progress, 83, 84, 88, 98, *See also*
Productivity change and producitivity bias
Terms of trade
in Chile, Ghana, and India, 103, 104, 106,
113
effect of change on actual real exchange rate
of, 88, 110
effect of change on equilibrium exchange rate
of, 69–70, 98, 105, 182
as fundamental, 13, 136
in real exchange rate dynamics equation, 86
Thrift. *See* Saving; Social time preference
Time preference. *See* Social time preference
Tokyo economic summit, 177

Trade balance
as alternative external target, 32
DEERs calculated using, 32, 51, 53
of G-7 countries, 26, 30, 43
impact of fiscal policy on, 171
in NATREX model, 150
Trade policy. *See* Tariffs
Tryon, Ralph W., 194–95

Uncovered interest rate parity, 137
"Underlying balance" approach to equilibrium
exchange rate, 20
United States. *See also* Dollar, US
current account targets for, 198, 200, 210, 236
demographics and saving in, 194, 195
fiscal position of, 11, 210
indebtedness ratios of, 200
net international investment position of, 221

Variance ratio tests, 260–61, 264, 265
Vogelsang, Timothy J., 253, 267

Wallace, Myles S., 252
Wealth, in NATREX model, 149
Williamson, John, 1, 7, 20, 23, 96, 177, 201–02,
207, 279–80, 286–87, 290
Wren-Lewis, Simon, 21, 24, 206

Yen
appreciation required to offset productivity
bias, 221
calculated DEERs for, 31–34, 50
erroneous PPP forecasts for, 191
explanations of nominal appreciation against
dollar of, 221–22
FEERs estimates for, 6–7, 209, 215, 230—32,
234—35, 237—39
Yoshitomi, Masaru, 183

Zivot, Eric, 260

Other Publications from the
Institute for International Economics

POLICY ANALYSES IN INTERNATIONAL ECONOMICS Series

BOOKS

Currencies and Politics in the United States, Germany, and Japan
C. Randall Henning/*September 1994*
ISBN paper 0-88132-127-3   432 pp..

Estimating Equilibrium Exchange Rates
John Williamson, editor/*September 1994*
ISBN paper 0-88132-076-5   320 pp.

SPECIAL REPORTS

FORTHCOMING

Reciprocity and Retaliation in US Trade Policy
Thomas O. Bayard and Kimberly Ann Elliott

The Globalization of Industry and National Governments
C. Fred Bergsten and Edward M. Graham

The Political Economy of Korea–United States Cooperation
C. Fred Bergsten and Il SaKong, editors

International Debt Reexamined
William R. Cline

Trade, Jobs, and Income Distribution
William R. Cline

Overseeing Global Capital Markets
Morris Goldstein and Peter Garber

Foreign Direct Investment in the United States, Third Edition
Edward M. Graham and Paul R. Krugman

Global Competition Policy
Edward M. Graham and J. David Richardson

Toward a Pacific Economic Community?
Gary Clyde Hufbauer and Jeffrey J. Schott

Managing the World Economy: Fifty Years After Bretton Woods
Peter B. Kenen, editor

Measuring the Costs of Protection in Japan
Yoko Sazanami, Shujiro Urata, and Hiroki Kawai

The Uruguay Round: An Assessment
Jeffrey J. Schott

The Case for Trade: A Modern Reconsideration
J. David Richardson

The Future of the World Trading System
John Whalley, in collaboration with Colleen Hamilton

For orders outside the US and Canada please contact:

Longman Group UK Ltd.
PO Box 88
Harlow, Essex CM 19 5SR
UK

Telephone Orders: 0279 623923
Fax: 0279 414130
Telex: 81259

Canadian customers can order from the Institute or from either:

RENOUF BOOKSTORE
1294 Algoma Road
Ottawa, Ontario K1B 3W8
Telephone: (613) 741-4333
Fax: (613) 741-5439

LA LIBERTÉ
3020 chemin Sainte-Foy
Quebec G1X 3V6
Telephone: (418) 658-3763
Fax: (800) 567-5449